1399

**Books are to be returned on or before
the last date below.**

Serbi

THE BRADT TRAV

PUBLISHER'S FOREWORD
Hilary Bradt

The first Bradt travel guide was written in 1974 by George and Hilary Bradt on a river barge floating down a tributary of the Amazon. In the 1980s and '90s the focus shifted away from hiking to broader-based guides to new destinations – usually the first to be published on these places. In the 21st century Bradt continues to publish these ground-breaking guides, along with others to established holiday destinations, incorporating in-depth information on culture and natural history alongside the nuts and bolts of where to stay and what to see.

Bradt authors support responsible travel, with advice not only on minimum impact but also on how to give something back through local charities. Thus a true synergy is achieved between the traveller and local communities.

*

In the last decade Serbia's reputation has shifted from association with Europe's last war to being the latest tourist hot spot. Belgrade's nightlife attracts an increasing number of young people, but I first became enthused when a birding friend turned up with a Serbian birdwatchers' T-shirt, and regaled me with descriptions of the untouched countryside and helpful people. Laurence Mitchell has more than done the country justice. His detailed descriptions of hotels and restaurants, and his ability to 'paint the picture', ensures that travellers who venture to this new destination will not be disappointed.

Hilary Bradt

Hilary Bradt

19 High Street, Chalfont St Peter, Bucks SL9 9QE, England
Tel: 01753 893444; fax: 01753 892333
Email: info@bradtguides.com
www.bradtguides.com

Serbia

THE BRADT TRAVEL GUIDE

Laurence Mitchell

Bradt Travel Guides Ltd, UK
The Globe Pequot Press Inc, USA

First published March 2005

Bradt Travel Guides Ltd
19 High Street, Chalfont St Peter, Bucks SL9 9QE, England
Published in the USA by The Globe Pequot Press Inc,
246 Goose Lane, PO Box 480, Guilford, Connecticut 06437-0480

British Library Cataloguing in Publication Data
A catalogue record for this book is available from the British Library

ISBN-10: 1 84162 118 8
ISBN-13: 978 1 84162 118 0

Photographs
Front cover Dragan Bosnic/NTOS archive
Text Laurence Mitchell (LM), Lukács Sándor / NPG Egretta (LS)

Illustrations Carole Vincer
Maps Matt Honour

Typeset from the author's disc by Wakewing
Printed and bound in Italy by Legoprint SpA, Trento

Author

Laurence Mitchell graduated from the University of East Anglia with a degree in environmental science, since which his career path has followed an interesting, if occasionally shaky, trajectory. At various times he has taught English in rural Sudan, surveyed historic farm buildings in Norfolk, and pushed a broom in a psychiatric hospital and a pen in a local government office. He retrained as a geography teacher in the late 1980s and worked at this for a dozen or so years before finally giving it up for the uncertain rewards of travel writing and photography.

His first experience of Serbia was in the 1970s, hitch-hiking through what was then Yugoslavia on his way to Greece; he did the same again four years later en route to India. He eventually returned in 2003 for the first of three lengthy visits during which he compiled the material for this, his first guidebook.

FEEDBACK REQUEST

At Bradt Travel Guides, we're well aware that a guidebook starts to go out of date on the day it is published – and that you, our readers, are out there in the field doing research of your own. You'll find out before us when a fine new family-run hotel opens or a favourite restaurant changes hands and goes down hill. Why not tell us about your experiences so that we can ensure forthcoming editions are as accurate as possible? We'll be sure to reply personally. You can write to us at Bradt Travel Guides, 19 High St, Chalfont St Peter, Bucks SL9 9QE or send us an email to info@bradtguides.com.

Contents

LIST OF MAPS

Acknowledgements

I would like to offer my heartfelt thanks to all those who helped me shape this book. Firstly, the team at Bradt who gave me the opportunity in the first place; who offered encouragement and patiently answered my novice queries: Tricia Hayne, Adrian Phillips and Selena Dickson. I would like to thank Peter and Diana Beckley of the Norfolk and Norwich Novi Sad Association who pointed me in the right direction early on, particularly in Vojvodina, and Sandie Reed in Scotland who cheerfully gave me lots of useful background information, especially on traditional music and dance in Serbia. I am also indebted to Ivo Miesen in the Netherlands, who supplied helpful advice on cycling in the country, and Ben Haines in London who allowed me to make use of his collated notes on Belgrade. In preparing the final text I would like to thank Dragan Simić for his comments on the wildlife section and for sharing his encyclopaedic knowledge of Serbian birdlife.

In Belgrade, I must thank: Milica Čubrilo and Zorica Jovanov at the Tourist Office of Serbia for their assistance and support; Sanja Gosnjak and David Webb at the British embassy; Branko Rabotić of Belgrade Sightseeing for his interest in the guide, and Vlade Pandžić aka 'Smehuljko' – TV clown, composer and thinker – at the Fresco Gallery, whose stage name describes him perfectly. I am particularly grateful to Branislav Bajagić who gave up his time to show me the delights of rural central Serbia and introduced me to the joys of domestically produced *šljivovica* – *Živeli*!

In Novi Sad, I am indebted for the help I received from Gordana Stojaković, Tatjana Vanić and Ivan Ivanović at the Tourist Information Centre. I would also like to thank Dr Miroslava Filipović of Alma Mons development agency; the staff of the Vojvodina Museum, particularly Dragan Vujkavić; Nemed who guided me through the underground galleries of the Petrovaradin Fortress, and Biljana Marčeta, director of Magelan Corporation.

Further afield, my thanks go to Ivana Nikolić and her father for showing me around Kladovo, to artist Zuzana Holúbeková for filling me in on the naïve art tradition of Kovačica, to photographer Samir Delić for helping me out of a tight spot in Sjenica, and to Jasmina Davidović of the Srem Museum in Sremska Mitrovica.

In Niš, the cycling gastronomes Miša and Saša Kolić offered friendship, hospitality and invaluable local advice, as did Nebojša Krstić of the Niš Tourist Organisation. A little further south, Slavica Jovanović and her mother enthusiastically demonstrated Pirot's *ćilim* weaving tradition for me.

I am also grateful to the many taxi drivers, waiters and hotel reception staff I came across during the course of my travels in Serbia who willingly shared their opinions and gave me precious insight into their country. I am also indebted to the helpful and courteous staff at many of Serbia's smaller regional tourist offices.

Most of all I would like to thank my wife, Jackie, who provided love, support and understanding throughout and who uncomplainingly kept home fires burning with the expert skill of one who possesses a Brownie firelighter's badge.

Introduction

Serbia suffers from an image problem. Mention the name to many and they will inevitably come up with some sort of negative connection: Slobodan Milošević, war crimes, bad deeds in Bosnia, mafia-style gun-running. Then they may go on to declare that they are not entirely sure where Serbia is – or exactly what it is. Is it a country? Something to do with Yugoslavia?

This is not entirely their fault: in the early 1990s, when the Balkans were permanently in the news with the bloody break-up of the former Yugoslavia, it was easy to get the impression that Serbia was at the heart of all the problems there, and that, somehow, the country had only itself to blame. Five years later, with the NATO bombing campaign over Kosovo, it was back in the news again, once more coming across in the media as an intransigent maverick state that was getting all it deserved. This was only part of the picture of course, and Serbs suffered in those conflicts just as much as Bosnians, Croats and Kosovar Albanians did. This is not to deny any sins of the past but merely to acknowledge that it would be a gross mistake to simply equate the activities of Milošević and his warlords with those of the Serbian people as a whole. People do not always get the leaders they deserve.

In communist times, Serbia was firmly at the centre of Tito's unified Yugoslav Republic but since the painful break-up of the federation, it has been a nation forced to reinvent itself. With a culture that goes back to a golden age that existed well before the 500-year-long Ottoman conquest, this has not been as difficult as it may sound. Serbian culture is drawn from the totality of its history: Westward-looking but with echoes of an Ottoman past.

The long period of Turkish rule has left its mark on the food, the music and the language of the region, as have influences from Austria and Hungary to the north. While a Habsburg city like Novi Sad, a place resolutely part of the central European milieu, lies just an hour's drive north of Belgrade, travelling to the south of the country brings the visitor to very different towns like Novi Pazar, where the Turkish influence is still strong and the skyline bristles with minarets.

Tourism and Serbia never were natural bedfellows. Even in the days when the former Yugoslavia received millions of visitors annually, few ventured away from the Dalmatian coast to see what Serbia had to offer. The general perception was that Serbia and Belgrade, the capital, were vaguely unpleasant places where all of the factories were. This is far from the truth. Belgrade itself, the largest city in the Balkans, may not be the most elegant of capitals, but it has a vitality undiminished by years of power cuts, sanctions and international isolation. The weekend does not hold much meaning here, as many of Belgrade's citizens treat every night pretty much the same and stay out until the early hours, whatever day of the week it is. Belgrade seems such a dynamic, sophisticated place these days that it is hard to believe that only a few years ago it was suffering sanctions and having bombs rained down on it. Perhaps resilience is a national characteristic? Today it is a vibrant, welcoming city where tradition and modernity comfortably co-exist; where gypsy music merges with pop and hip-hop in its pavement cafés. The days of shortages are now long gone and the only thing Belgrade currently lacks is tourists.

As well as a dynamic capital with museums, galleries and a nightlife equal to anything in the region, there are smaller country towns worth visiting, and medieval churches and monasteries tucked away in a timeless, bucolic landscape. Neither is Belgrade the last word in urban sophistication – smaller university cities like Novi Sad and Niš have their own individual appeal.

In a landscape punctuated by river valleys, gorges and rolling hills, nature lovers are well catered for. National parks such as Tara in the west, and Đerdap Gorge in the east, are ideally situated for outdoor activities such as hiking, cycling and birdwatching, while Zlatibor and the southern mountain resort of Kopaonik offer winter skiing.

Perhaps the greatest attraction of all, considering the years of being manipulated by their own leaders, sanctioned by the UN and bombed by NATO, is the welcome Serbs extend to foreign visitors. Tourists are still a rarity and it would appear that few Serbs bear a grudge for their country's past pariah status.

Given time, Serbia can – *will* – turn its negative image around. Mention Serbia to someone who has just returned from time in the country and they will come up with a different list of associations from those in the first paragraph: delicious food, beautiful countryside, friendly people, low prices, good music, safe travel and excellent nightlife.

It seems astonishing that writing this at the beginning of the 21st century, at a time when information overload is the usual peril for anyone trying to buy a guidebook for almost anywhere in the world, that Serbia is virtually ignored. Up until now, it has been easier to research a trip to an obscure South Sea island than it has to find up-to-date information on a country that lies so close to home. Hopefully, I have rectified this situation to some extent with the publication of this guide. Serbia should get the recognition – and visitors – it deserves. Please visit Serbia, you know it makes sense.

Part One

General Information

SERBIA AT A GLANCE

Location In the central part of the Balkan Peninsula of southeast Europe, with Hungary to the north, Romania to the northeast, Bulgaria to the southeast, Albania and Macedonia to the south, Bosnia-Herzegovina to the west, and Croatia to the northwest.

Status Republic currently in a loose union with Montenegro; the province of Kosovo and Metohija in the south is currently under UN administration.

Size 88,361km² including the autonomous territories of Kosovo and Metohija (10,887km²) in the southwest and Vojvodina (21,506km²) in the north.

Climate A temperate, continental climate, with warm summers up to 30°C and snowy winters down to −5°C in mountain areas.

Longest river The Danube (588km), flowing west to east through Serbia.

Highest peak Ðeravica (2,656m)

Population Around 10 million including Kosovo-Metohija (2002 estimate), of whom approximately 66% are Serbs and 17% Albanians, with Hungarians, Romanians, Croatians, Bulgarians, Roma and Vlachs among a total of 37 minority groups.

Government Parliamentary democracy

Capital Belgrade (population approximately 1.6 million)

Major cities and towns Novi Sad (300,000), Niš (250,000), Kragujevac (177,000), Leskovac (156,000), Subotica (150,000)

Language The official language is Serbian, which is written in both the Cyrillic and Latin alphabets.

Religion The main religion is Eastern Orthodox with minorities of Islam and Catholic and Protestant Christian.

Weights and measures Metric system

Time GMT+1

Currency Serbian dinar (1 dinar = 100 para)

International telephone code +381

Electricity 220 volts AC, 50 Hz. Round, two-pin sockets

Public holidays January 1–2 (New Year), January 7–8 (Orthodox Christmas), February 15 (Statehood Day), May 1–2 (Labour days), Orthodox Easter is variable.

Flag Red, white and blue horizontal stripes

Background Information

GEOGRAPHY AND CLIMATE
Geography

With a surface area of 88,361km², Serbia is roughly the same size as Portugal or Austria, although Americans might prefer to compare it to the states of Maine or Kentucky. Serbia, together with Montenegro, occupies a mere 2.1% of the European land mass. This makes it a relatively small country, only about one-third of the size of the former Yugoslavia. It does, however, hold a central position in eastern Europe: excluding Montenegro, with which it remains in a loose federation, and Kosovo, technically an autonomous province of Serbia despite temporary UN stewardship, Serbia has a 2,397km border with a total of seven independent countries.

Almost one-fifth of the population live in the capital, Belgrade. Throughout most of the rest of the country, Serbia's population is distributed fairly evenly with an average population density of 111 people per km². There is a higher density in the mostly ethnic Albanian province of Kosovo and Metohija in the far south (180 people per km²).

Serbia lies at the crossroads of Europe, both politically and geographically, and its river valleys provide the fastest link for international roads and railway connections between western and central Europe, on one side, and Asia Minor and the Middle East on the other. These roads follow the course of the river Morava, which splits near to the city of Niš leaving the southern Morava to lead the way to Thessaloniki, and the valley of the Nišava to lead east to Sofia and Istanbul.

Serbia's rivers belong to three separate drainage systems: those of the Adriatic, the Black Sea and the Aegean. Three of the country's rivers are navigable but by far the most important is the Danube, which passes for 588km across Serbia as part of its 2,857km, eight-country journey to its mouth at the Black Sea. At Belgrade, the Danube, which enters Vojvodina from Hungary in the north and defines the border with Croatia as far south as Bačka Palanka, is joined by its major tributary, the river Sava, while just north of the capital in Vojvodina, the river Tisa flows into the Danube on the stretch between Belgrade and Novi Sad. Most of southern Serbia is drained by another Danube offshoot, the Morava River, which flows north to meet the Danube near Smederevo east of Belgrade.

The northern province of Vojvodina, north of the river Danube, is mostly flat arable land, with the exception of the 80km-long, forest-covered Fruška Gora range that hugs the south bank of the Danube, just to the south of Novi Sad. The highest point here is Crveni Cot, which rises to 539m. The flat lands that make up most of northern Serbia belong to the Pannonian Plain and its rim: Macva, the Sava valley, the Morava valley, Stig and the Negotin marshes. Another feature of this region is large expanses of remnant sand dunes, most notably the Deliblato sands, which stretch in a crescent northeast to southeast in the southern part of the Banat close to Belgrade.

South of the river Danube, the east of the country has limestone ranges and basins, with older mountains and hills further south near the Bulgarian border. To the southwest, beyond the rolling hills of the Šumadija ('forested area') of central Serbia, lies the Sandžak, a transition zone both culturally and topographically, which forms the border region with Bosnia-Herzegovina and Montenegro. South of here, the landscape becomes increasingly mountainous as it approaches the Kosovo frontier.

The southern two-thirds of Serbia are ringed by mountains: the Dinaric Alps to the west, the Šar and Prokletije ranges to the south in Kosovo, and the Stara Planina to the east. Generally, the highest relief is in the intermontane Kosovo region. Of the 15 mountains that reach over 2,000m, the highest peak is Đeravica (2,656m) in Kosovo's Prokletije range, close to the borders of Albania and Montenegro. In Serbia proper, the highest peak is Pančićev Vrh (2,017m) in the Mt Kopaonik National Park on the Serbia–Kosovo border.

Much of Serbia's intensive agriculture takes place in the flat and fertile Pannonian Plain, formerly an inland sea, which covers a vast tract of Vojvodina. Other regions in which large-scale, mechanised agriculture takes place include parts of Kosovo and Metohija, and the Kruševac and Leskovac districts. In areas like the Šumadija, southwest of Belgrade, fruit production and viniculture replace pure arable farming, while forestry, cattle- and sheep-farming take place in the more rugged, mountainous regions of Zlatibor, Rudnik, Stara Planina, Kopaonik and Šar. Overall, 55% of Serbia is arable land and 27% forest.

Climate

The climate is moderate continental, with four distinct seasons. The average air temperature in Belgrade is 11.9°C. Autumn is longer than spring, often with extended periods of warm, sunny, anticyclonic weather called 'old wives summer'; in contrast, spring is often short and rainy. Winter is not especially harsh by eastern European standards, with only an average of 21 days annually below 0°C. The average temperature in January is 0.4°C making it the coldest month of the year. Summers generally begin abruptly, with July and August being the hottest months overall, having average temperatures of 21.7°C and 21.3°C respectively. A characteristic wind of the region, known as the *košava*, sometimes blows from the southeast in autumn and winter bringing fair and dry weather. Usually this occurs when there is high pressure to the northeast over Ukraine in combination with low pressure over the Adriatic. Belgrade has an average of 139 days of precipitation per annum (including 27 days of snow), which is most intense in the months of May and June and at its least in February. The country as a whole receives an average precipitation of between 600mm and 800mm annually in the plains – about the same as that of southeast England – and between 800mm and 1200mm in highland regions.

NATURAL HISTORY AND CONSERVATION

With a wide range of habitats, Serbia offers more ecological diversity than other similar-sized countries in the region like Hungary or Bulgaria. For such a small country, there is an unusually large number of species, some of which are endemic to Serbia. Broadly speaking, Serbia has six main habitat-zones that can be categorised as: high montane rocky areas; coniferous forests; sub-Mediterranean and southern European forest (mainly deciduous); upland Mediterranean vegetation; and steppe/wooded steppe.

Serbia has a rich and varied fauna, with nearly 80% of European bird species being recorded in the country as either breeding or on migration; it is also home to 66% of Europe's mammals, butterflies and insects and 50% of its freshwater fish. Over 90 species of mammals are present, with several mammals that are scarce elsewhere in Europe finding a haven here. There are at least 110 species of freshwater fish, with 14 sub-species that are found only in the region; seven fish species are listed on

Europe's Red List. Compared with Britain, which has only 12 different species of reptile and amphibian, Serbia has 70 species of reptile alone, a much greater number than in either Romania or Bulgaria.

Together with Montenegro, Serbia is home to 4,300 species of plant, 2% of the world's total number (while only having 0.035% of total global land mass), and of these 400 are endemic to the region. These include rare endemic trees such as the pines *munika* and *molika*, and the distinctive *omorika* that was discovered only 100 years ago by the Serbian botanist Josif Pančić. Many of the plants that grow wild in Serbia are valued for their medicinal properties and are still widely used by some rural communities. Of its plant communities, 9% are found only in the Balkans and 2% solely in Serbia itself.

With plentiful forest to provide ideal habitat, countless species of fungi are found in Serbia, including over 100 species mentioned in the European Red List. Species such as the Royal cep (*Boletus regius*), considered as one of the most threatened in the world, has much of its distribution within Serbia's borders. Rarities aside, Serbia is actually the world's greatest exporter of edible cep species, and mushroom picking is an important source of income for many rural families. Serbia's forests also provide a rich habitat for other species of fungi that have been identified as having important medicinal properties in the treatment of cancer, one example being *Ganoderma applanatum*. There is currently great concern that the ecological damage caused by the hostilities of 1999 has yet to reveal the true scale of the damage done to Serbia's fungi, as highly toxic substances inevitably permeate any fungi population. What seems certain is that the economic hardships suffered by the economy will necessitate more clear-cutting of Serbia's forests in the future, thus removing valuable natural habitat.

Birds

In total, 380 different species of birds have been recorded, a large number of which pass through on passage to their breeding grounds in northern Europe. Some 250 species find suitable habitat for breeding in the country, while some species migrate from the north to winter in Serbia.

The Pannonian Plain of Vojvodina offers wetland areas that are attractive to many species of birds. Among these, Zasavica, Kovilijski Rit, Obedska and Čarska Bara all provide valuable habitat. In the Stari Begej-Čarska Bara Ramsar site alone, with a range of habitats that include pools, fishponds, meadows and willow forests, over 260 species have been recorded up to now. These include pygmy cormorant (*Phalacrocorax pygmeus*), bittern (*Botaurus stellaris*), little bittern (*Ixobrychus minutus*), night heron (*Nycticorax nycticorax*), squacco heron (*Ardeola ralloides*), great white egret (*Egretta alba*), purple heron (*Ardea purpurea*), spoonbill (*Platalea leucorodia*), ferruginous duck (*Aythya nyroca*), white-tailed eagle (*Haliaeetus albicilla*), bee-eater (*Merops apiaster*), common redstart (*Phoenicurus phoenicurus*), Savi's warbler (*Locustella luscinioides*) and lesser grey shrike (*Lanius minor*). Also in Vojvodina, the two largest heronries in Serbia are to be found at Dubovac and Bečej, while spectacular seasonal crane (*Grus grus*) migration can be observed at Slano Kopovo Lake.

Away from the wetlands, the Deliblato Sands (*Deliblatska Peščara*) zone to the northeast of Belgrade, which supports spacious steppe woodland, scrub, conifer plantations and arable land, provides a further specialised habitat, with notable steppe birds such as saker and red-footed falcons (*Falco cherrug* and *Falco vespertinus*), corncrake (*Crex crex*), bee-eater (*Merops apiaster*), roller (*Coracius garrulus*), nightjar (*Caprimulgus europaeus*), wryneck (*Jynx torquilla*), grey-headed woodpecker (*Picus canus*), woodlark (*Lullula arborea*), skylark (*Alauda arvensis*), sand martin (*Riparia riparia*), whinchat (*Saxicola rubetra*) barred warbler (*Sylvia nisoria*), lesser grey shrike (*Lanius minor*), red-backed shrike (*Lanius collurio*) and the rare raptor, imperial eagle (*Aquila heliaca*).

A diverse and interesting selection of birds is also found to the south of Belgrade, where the landscape transforms into more mountainous terrain. Birds of prey, in particular, are well represented. In the southwest, the Uvac and Mileševka Griffon Vulture reserve is noteworthy as one of the best places in the Central Balkans for watching raptors. The national parks such as Kopaonik in the south, Tara in the west and Đerdap (Iron Gates) in the east, close to the Romanian border, are equally rewarding, as are some of the gorges like Ovčar-Kablar, Zlot, Sićevo and Jerma. Raptors of particular interest in these mountainous areas include Levant sparrowhawk (*Accipter brevipes*), long-legged buzzard (*Buteo rufinus*), Egyptian vulture (*Neophron percnopterus*) and griffon vulture (*Gyps fulvus*), while smaller birds of note include: red-rumped swallow (*Hirundo daurica*), wallcreeper (*Tichodroma muraria*), rock thrush (*Monticola saxatilis*), shore lark (*Eremophila alpestris*), sombre tit (*Parus lugubris*), lesser grey shrike (*Lanius minor*), woodchat shrike (*Lanius senator*), red-backed shrike (*Lanius collurio*), cirl bunting (*Emberiza cirlus*), rock bunting (*Emberiza cia*), black-headed bunting (*Emberiza melanocephala*), Ortolan bunting (*Emberiza hortulana*), barred warbler (*Sylvia nisoria*), subalpine warbler (*Sylvia cantillans*), Bonelli's warbler (*Phylloscopus bonelli*), nutcracker (*Nucifraga caryocatactes*), alpine chough (*Pyrrhocorax graculus*), pallid swift (*Apus pallidus*), Spanish sparrow (*Passer hispaniolensis*) and rock sparrow (*Petronia petronia*).

Additional information on the relative abundance of breeding birds in Serbia may be found at www.fatbirder.com/links_geo/europe/serbia/html.

Conservation

A large number of the species found in Serbia are protected by European and international law, or are included in the Red List of endangered species. Serbian law itself protects a total of 380 plants, 490 animals and 100 types of fungus.

National parks

There are five national parks throughout the country, all in upland areas (Tara, Fruška Gora, Đerdap, Kopaonik and Šara), which provide some degree of protection, together with three wetland regions that are protected by the International Ramsar Convention (Ludoš Lake, Obedska bara and Stari Begej-Carska bara). Until recently, Serbia suffered little from internal pollution problems but it is widely claimed that the NATO hostilities of 1999 brought widespread ecological damage that has spread beyond its borders (see box, *The Danube River* in *Along the Danube* chapter) and which may end up having global repercussions.

The **Tara National Park** covers about 20,000ha at an altitude of between 250m and 1,500m. It is located in a bend of the Drina River in a mountainous region of western Serbia that includes the Tara and Zvijezda ranges, and was given national park status in 1981. This national park consists of a group of mountain peaks and deep gorges, the most striking being the Drina Gorge. Karst caves and pits are also a feature of the landscape. Three-quarters of the park is covered by forest, mostly coniferous, and Tara is home to a rare endemic species of tree, the Pančić spruce, which is under state protection, and an endemic insect, the Pančić locust. The mountain slopes are host to more than 100 bird species including golden eagle (*Aquila chrysaetos*), peregrine falcon (*Falco peregrinus*) and griffon vulture (*Gyps fulvus*), as well as 24 species of mammal, 17 of which are protected. Rarities such as brown bear, chamois, wildcat and otter are all present.

The **Fruška Gora National Park** in Vojvodina covers over 10,000ha of low hills that stretch east to west above the flat, low Pannonian Plain. Meadows, orchards, grain fields and vineyards cover the lower slopes while, above 300m, dense deciduous forests dominate, with maple and white oaks in addition to the greatest concentration of lime (linden) trees in Europe. More than 1,400 species of flora are found within the park boundaries, including over two dozen species of orchid and many hundred species of medicinal herbs. Two hundred species of bird are found in the area, with elusive rarities like imperial eagle (*Aquila heliaca*) among a variety of raptors; woodpeckers too, are well-represented. Other fauna includes rare mammals like wildcat, badger, pine marten, lynx, wild boar and mouflon, as well as several species of bat.

The **Đerdap (Iron Gates) National Park** lies in eastern Serbia, on the border with Romania, covering some 63,680ha. The natural phenomenon that the park is centred upon is the Đerdap Gorge, the longest and deepest gorge in Europe. The gorge, better known as the Iron Gates, which stretches for a distance of around 100km, is actually comprised of a whole series of gorges: Golubačka Klisura, Gospoď in Vir, Kazanska Klisura and Sipska Klisura. The terrain and the favourable climate here have made this an important area for tertiary flora and fauna. As well as being rich and diverse, the Đerdap flora is notable for its distinct relict character, with species that include: bear-hazel bush, small nettle, walnut, lilac, silver linden and Montpellier maple. The fauna has relict qualities too, and includes brown bear, lynx, wolf and jackal. Golden eagle (*Aquila chrysaetos*), black stork (*Ciconia nigra*) and eagle owl (*Bubo bubo*) are among the many bird species present.

The **Kopaonik National Park** in south-central Serbia consists of nearly 12,000ha in the high plateau area of the mountainous area delimited by the valleys of the Ibar, Jošanica, Toplica and Brzeća rivers. Away from the more disturbed environs of the ski resort, this park is one of the most important centres of biodiversity in the whole of the Balkans, with 91 endemic and 82 sub-endemic species to its credit. Of a total of 1,500 species of flora, three endemic species are worth mentioning – Kopaonik houseleek, Kopaonik violet and Pančić cuckoo flower – while noteworthy among the avifauna are golden eagle and crossbill. The rare viviparous lizard also thrives on the mountain's higher slopes.

In Kosovo, along the border with Macedonia, the **Šara** (Šara Planina) **National Park** encompasses 39,000ha of high alpine landscape of bare rock, forest and glacial lakes. About 2,000 species of plant are present, 20 of which are endemic to the region, and among these are Natalia's ramonda, Balkan pine and Macedonian oak. Šara Planina is one of the richest zones for butterflies in Europe, with 147 species present, and has around 200 bird species including golden eagle, griffon vulture and capercaillie (*Tetrao urogallus*). Mammals found in the park include wildcat, lynx, brown bear and chamois, together with endemic relict species of rodents like Dinaric vole.

The **Uvac and Mileševka Griffon Vulture Sanctuary**, 255km southwest of Belgrade in the Zlatibor region is, as its name implies, a refuge for the now-endangered griffon vulture (*Gyps fulvus*). The sanctuary offers an opportunity to observe griffon vultures sitting on their nests and roost ledges before they launch themselves into the morning thermals. Other bird species of note here include goosander (*Mergus merganser*), short-toed eagle (*Circaetus gallicus*), lesser-spotted eagle (*Aquila pomarina*), golden eagle (*Aquila chrysaetos*), peregrine falcon (*Falco peregrinus*), hobby (*Falco subbuteo*), rock partridge (*Alectoris graeca*), corncrake (*Crex crex*), Scops owl (*Otus scops*), eagle owl (*Bubo bubo*), green woodpecker (*Picus viridis*), woodlark (*Lullula arborea*), rock thrush (*Monticola saxatilis*), nutcracker (*Nucifraga caryocatactes*) and rock bunting (*Emberiza cia*).

Of the three wetland areas designated for protection by the International Ramsar Convention, that of **Stari Begej–Čarska Bara** stands out in particular. This 1,767ha reserve is situated southwest of Zrenjanin, in the middle of the Banat region, between the Tisa and Begej rivers. It is actually a complex of various wetland ecosystems –

lakes, swamps, meadows and willow and white poplar forest – that is mostly used for recreational purposes like sports fishing. With 250 recorded species (140 breeding, the rest migrants) the reserve is of special importance to birds, although its value as a habitat for wetland flora and a wide variety of fish species – carp, pike and perch – should not be overlooked.

Lake Ludaš (*Ludaško Jezero*) lies further north, 12km east of the town of Subotica and near the Hungarian border. This 593ha reserve is one of the few remaining natural lakes of the Pannonian Plain and is important for its breeding birds, which include black-necked grebe (*Podiceps nigricollis*), purple heron (*Ardea purpurea*), squacco heron (*Ardeola ralloides*) and little bittern (*Ixybrychus minutus*) among others. It is also an important feeding station for migratory birds on passage.

Obedska Bara, the third of the Ramsar Convention sites lies 50km west of Belgrade. The site is important for threatened breeding bird species including little egret (*Egretta garzetta*), night heron (*Nycticorax nycticorax*), little bittern (*Ixobrychus minutes*) and bittern (*Botaurus stellaris*), black stork (*Ciconia nigra*) and white stork (*Ciconia ciconia*), spoonbill (*Platalea leucorodia*), white-tailed eagle (*Haliaeetus albicilla*), lesser-spotted eagle (*Aquila pomarina*) and imperial eagle (*Aquila heliaca*), little crake (*Porzana parva*) and spotted crake (*Porzana porzana*), and middle-spotted woodpecker (*Dendrocopos medius*). The site also includes rare insects, fish, reptiles, amphibians and mammals, as well as rare and relict water lilies.

Zasavica, another protected reserve near Sremska Mitrovica, is also very important for its 200 plant species and 120 bird species, 80 of which breed in the area.

Ecological damage

Despite the valuable conservation work carried out in the above locations, the lack of chemicals used in farming practices and a generally good environmental record for much of Serbia's industry, there is much concern in some quarters about the amount of ecological damage wrought by the NATO air raids of 1999. In particular, the Serbian Institute for Nature Protection points at the way NATO attacked non-military targets such as industrial complexes, refineries and nuclear research centres during the hostilities. It demonstrates how rivers, the Danube in particular, were heavily polluted due to leakages from stricken industrial complexes along its banks and gives evidence of how some national parks became targets themselves, how depleted uranium was widely used in warheads, and how so-called 'smart' bombs were often far from clever. Most alarmingly, the Institute also suggests that NATO (with the implication that it really means the USA) purposefully utilised new weapons like graphite bombs for the first time during these hostilities, using Serbia as a sort of practice run for, as yet, untested devices. Naturally, these are controversial and emotive issues, and accusations that foreign visitors should be, at the very least, fully aware of. More information on this topic is available at www.ecology.co.yu/ecology.

HISTORY
Early settlement

The first evidence of settlement in the area that is now Serbia comes from Lepenski Vir on the Danube, close to the Romanian border. This site, only recently discovered in 1985, is the oldest-known Neolithic site in Europe and dates from around the 7th millennium BC. From what remains, it appears to have been a reasonably developed civilisation, and strange life-size stone sculptures have been found here that appear to represent fish-headed men. No doubt these early settlers took advantage of the river's plentiful fish supply and so the figures may represent some form of fish divinity totem, although nothing else resembling these sculptures has been found elsewhere in the Balkans or Danube delta.

The region entered the Iron Age when Illyrian tribes from the west colonised the Balkan Peninsula during the 6th century, together with Thracian settlers who came from the east. These groups were followed shortly, in the 4th century BC, by Celts from the north. The Illyrians were skilled manufacturers of iron implements and weapons, and held some degree of trade with the Greek city states further south. The arrival of the Romans resulted in their being subdued by the greater number and superior military power of the new invaders. The Romans, with their well-trained and disciplined troops, continued to expand their empire deeper into the Balkans, incorporating the Illyrians into their army as they marched inexorably on. Finally in AD9, under the rule of Emperor Tiberius, the Roman Empire formally annexed all of the Illyrian territories.

The Romans made their mark on the region in typical fashion, building roads and constructing garrisons for their troops. They conquered the Celtic fortress at Singidinum, which had been built on a hill overlooking the confluence of the Sava and Danube rivers, a settlement that, after many more invasions, would go on to become Serbia's capital, Belgrade. Similarly, they developed the fortress at Taurunum nearby at modern-day Zemun and built a bridge over the Sava to connect the two. Singidunum became an important crossroads for the empire, linking the Roman provinces of Moesia, Dacia, Pannonia and Dalmatia, while a military road – a *Via Militaris* – passed through from west to east, from Sirmium (now Sremska Mitrovica) through Singidunum to Viminacium (Kostulac) and on to Byzantium.

Three centuries later, with the emergence of a rival empire to the east, the Roman Emperor Diocletian was forced to divide the territory into two halves, so that in AD395, the eastern half – that which roughly corresponds to modern-day Serbia, Montenegro, Macedonia, Bulgaria and Greece – found themselves under the influence of Byzantium. Singidunum had now become a border town on the edge of the eastern empire, an unfortunate location in geopolitical terms that would have some bearing on its later misfortunes. This division into two opposing empires created a political and cultural fault line whose effect is still felt today as one of the crucial factors in Balkan discord: in the west, corresponding to present-day Croatia and Bosnia-Herzegovina, they looked to Rome, so the inhabitants of this region became Roman Catholic by and large and made use of a Latin alphabet; to the east of the line the focus of power was Constantinople – present-day Istanbul – which resulted in the population of this region becoming Orthodox Christian and learning to use a Cyrillic script.

The arrival of the Serbs

As the Roman Empire finally disintegrated in the 5th century AD, Barbarian raiders started to appear – Huns, Goths and Avars from the central Asian steppe. It was also about this time that the Slavs started to arrive. Their first appearances in the region were as raiders, but by the beginning of the 7th century they were starting to settle in considerable numbers. The first Slavs had been undifferentiated in terms of the ethnic divisions of today, but by the time they started to colonise the Balkans they could be recognised as two distinct groups according to the route of their migration into the region. The Slavs who would later become the Croats, that occupied the western territories, migrated from lands they had established in southern Poland, while the other group, the *proto*-Serbs, made their home in the lands that lay to the south of the Danube, having moved from an area that is now the Czech Republic where they had been briefly settled. These two tribes already had, and would continue to have, closely entwined histories; quarrelsome cousins who then, as now, spoke an almost identical language. It was these Slavic tribes, together with the Romanised pastoralists, the Vlachs (see box, *The Vlachs* in the *People* section of this chapter) that displaced or absorbed the Illyrians, Greeks, Thracians, Romans and

Dacians living in the western Balkan region at the time. Just a small coastal enclave of Illyrian language and culture managed to survive the influx intact. This enclave would later delineate the boundaries of what is now Albania.

The first Serbian kingdom

As the Croatian tribes settled the territories of the Adriatic littoral, a region they still populate today, the Serbs occupied an area they termed Raška, which is now known by its Turkish name of Sandžak. This territory gave the Serbs the name of 'Rascians', by which they were known for several centuries. Raška was not the whole extent of their settlement, and other lands settled by Serbs at this time included tracts of present-day Montenegro, Herzegovina and southern Dalmatia.

The Serbs came under the influence of Orthodox missionaries from Constantinople, in the same way that Rome proselytised Croats in Dalmatia, but it was not until the late 9th century that the Serbian *župans* (patriarchs) fully accepted Christianity and Serbs as a whole started to relinquish their paganism. The first three centuries of Serb presence in the Balkans were characterised by conflict, with constant power struggles taking place between competing local princes. The first Serbian kingdom emerged in present-day Montenegro in the early 11th century when Stefan Vojislav set up the vassal state of Duklija and began to bring Serbian tribes under his control after renouncing his allegiance to Constantinople and pronouncing himself in favour of Rome. This state expanded to incorporate much of the territory of present-day Montenegro, Herzegovina and Albania, and in 1077, Zeta, as it had come to be known, became a kingdom under the auspices of Rome, with a Catholic ruler, Constantine Bodin, at the helm. After Bodin's death, the kingdom plunged into civil war and power shifted northwest to Raška. It was here that Serbia's first dynasty was founded in the 1160s under Stefan Nemanja – a 200-year dynasty that would go on to exert enormous military power as the fledgling Serbian state consolidated and expanded its territories within the Balkans.

The Nemanjić dynasty

The next two centuries are often looked upon as Serbia's golden age and above all as the period when the Serb's sense of national consciousness was forged, first by a pride in unhindered military success, then later by the bitter tears of defeat at Kosovo. This period of Serbian history has always been looked upon with great affection and self-esteem by Serbs, and with good reason: before the Nemanjić era, the Serbs were just a loose association of tribes; by the end of this period they shared a common identity, a national spirit and a sense of destiny that would sustain them through the difficult years to come. This was also the era when Serbia's close association with the Orthodox Church was at its peak. The Nemanjić dynasty brought a stability and confidence that nurtured the sense of Serbian statehood. It was also during this period that parts of Kosovo came under Nemanjić tutelage and became another component of the Serbian milieu.

Stefan Nemanja was succeeded by his middle son, also called Stefan, while his youngest son, Rastko, entered a monastery and took the name of Sava. The new King Stefan became embroiled in a feud with his elder brother Vukan, who sought papal support for his claim to the crown. The Hungarian Catholic King Imre invaded and placed Vukan on the throne. The kingdom became Catholic for a brief spell but returned to Orthodoxy in 1204 when King Imre died, and Stefan regained the throne from his brother. The feud between the brothers was reconciled when Sava returned from Mt Athos with the mortal remains of their father, Stefan Nemanja, who would soon be venerated as Simeon, the first Serbian saint, and his body buried at Studenica, where he remains to this day. Sava was a clever diplomat and this was just one of many remarkable achievements.

In 1217 Sava sent an emissary to Pope Honorious III asking for his blessing and for 'the royal wreath' for his brother Stefan. The pope acceded to Sava's wishes and King Stefan came to be known from now on as the 'First Crowned'. This was a tremendous boost for the Serbian monarchy, as to receive the papal blessing was the medieval equivalent of international recognition. Sava's work was still unfinished: having dealt with the Catholic Church in Rome, he now turned his attentions to the Byzantines. In 1219, he visited the exiled Byzantine Emperor Theodore I Lascaris in Nicaea and secured autocephaly (self-appointing autonomous status) for the Serbian Orthodox Church. Naturally, the first archbishop to be appointed was Sava himself. Like his father before him, Sava went on to be canonised after his death in 1236.

Many other members of the Nemanjić dynasty chose the priesthood as an alternative, or reclusive conclusion, to their reign. As well as Stefan Nemanja choosing to end his days at Mt Athos as a monk, his son Stefan the First Crowned also died there. Following this tradition, Stefan the First Crowned's son and successor Radoslav chose to abdicate after six years on the throne and died as a monk named John. The unique religious identity that the Serbs had by now claimed for themselves expressed itself in other ways than just a royal propensity for the priesthood. The most obvious expression of this was the extent of church building that took place throughout the kingdom. Serbian monasteries that date from the golden age of Nemanjić rule include Durđevi Stupovi near modern-day Novi Pazar, Studenica and Hilander on Mt Athos in Greece.

The next generation of Serbian kings – Radoslav, Vladislav and Uroš I – were altogether less impressive and marked a period of stagnation in the state. These leaders were far more dependent on neighbouring states like Hungary, Bulgaria or Byzantium than the Nemanjić dynasty had been. However, when Uroš I's son Dragutin married a Hungarian princess and abdicated to become a monk in favour of his younger brother Milutin, the Hungarian King Ladislaus IV handed over lands in northeastern Bosnia, together with the regions of Srem and Macva and the city of Belgrade, all of which became part of the Serbian state for the first time. Under Milutin (who became King Uroš II) Serbia grew in strength, mainly through his many diplomatic marriages (he was married five times, to Hungarian, Bulgarian and Byzantine princesses). Uroš II Milutin went on to build a large number of churches, some of which remain as the finest examples of medieval Serbian architecture: the Gračanica Monastery in Kosovo, the St Archangel Church in Jerusalem and the Cathedral in the Hilandar Monastery on Mt Athos. Milutin was succeeded by his son Stefan 'Dečanski' (who became Uroš III) who expanded Serbian territory east as far as Niš, and south to include parts of Macedonia, and who went on to build the Visoki Dečani Monastery in Metohija, thereby earning his monastic sobriquet.

It was Stefan Dečanski's son Dušan, born in 1307, who would go on to become the greatest and most powerful of all the Nemanjić kings, although he engineered his own succession in something of an unorthodox manner. Dušan seized power from his father and had him incarcerated in the fortified town of Zvečan, and in 1331 Dušan was crowned as King of Serbia shortly after his father had been strangled on his own orders. Stefan Dečanski was buried in Visoki Dečani, the monastery he had started to build, and whose work was continued by his patricidal son. Dušan went on to be the greatest of the Serbian monarchs but, unlike his father who was to become celebrated as a saint at his Dečani Monastery resting place, he would never be canonised due to the part he played in his father's death. Dušan's rule was celebrated chiefly for two achievements. Firstly, there was the short-lived empire that he expanded quite spectacularly in just a few short years. Secondly, there was the legal code he introduced in 1349 that gave his name the epithet 'the lawgiver'. The legal code dealt partly with religious matters but was also devoted to the most common crimes of the day like bribery, theft and forgery. The punishments it meted out were severe – cruel even – but no worse than anywhere else in Europe in the medieval period.

By the time of Stefan Dušan's death in 1355, the Serbian kingdom had expanded considerably from what it had been just 200 years before. Now, the Serbian Empire stretched from the Danube south as far as the Peloponnese, and Serbian armies stood at the gates of Salonica, poised to expand their empire further east towards Constantinople. At this stage, Serbia's territory included Macedonia, all of Bulgaria and parts of northern Greece – the most powerful nation in the Balkans. But with the death of Stefan Dušan came a sudden and drastic decline of the nation's fortune. Quarrels divided the empire when two brothers, Vukašin and Jovan Uglješa, feudal landowners from Macedonia, tried to usurp power from Uroš, Dušan's rightful but weak successor. Vukašin was declared king under the nominal sovereignty of Emperor Uroš, and ruled in the south before being killed along with his brother at the Battle on the Marica River in 1371. Uroš IV died soon after in the same year and, with no sons to his name, this was effectively the end of the Nemanjić dynasty.

After the Battle on the Marica River, that which was left of Serbian lands was divided up between a number of feudal landlords. It was around this time that Prince Lazar, who claimed kinship to the Nemanjić clan, started to come into view. Lazar had lands in central Serbia and parts of Kosovo and, after expanding his territories by seizing land on the Bosnian border, was starting to emerge as one of the most powerful of the lords that ruled over Serbian territories. He also had great support from the Church who viewed Lazar as a suitable leader for restoring the Serbian kingdom to its former glory. The Church also thought that Lazar would be able to reconcile the Serbian Church with the Orthodox patriarchy in Constantinople, which had broken relations with the Serbian Orthodox Church on the occasion of Dušan's coronation. Lazar achieved this reconciliation and as his power grew started to consider himself as 'the ruler of all Serbs'. This was not quite correct, of course, but it did demonstrate the scope of his ambition.

With none of Stefan Dušan's successors able to maintain the impetus that he had set up during his reign, coupled with sudden, violent advances of the Turks from the south, disaster was on the horizon. The empire's swift demise led the way to a catastrophic downfall that is still remembered today as Serbia's darkest hour. In 1371, the Turks fought and defeated the Serbs for the first time at a battle on the river Marica in what is now Bulgaria. Then, in 1389, Prince Lazar grouped together the nation's forces for a last-ditch attempt to repel the advancing Turks at the Battle of Kosovo Plain (see box, *1389 – The Battle of Kosovo*). To say that this was nothing more than a decisive battle is to underestimate its continuing importance in the Serbian psyche. In many ways, the defeat at Kosovo Polje ('Field of blackbirds') was a defining moment in Serbian nationhood. The battle was not completely one-sided – the Turkish sultan perished on the battlefield, along with many Turkish troops – but the defeat marked a turning point for a state that was already in decline.

Ottoman rule

A large-scale Serb migration north to Hungary and west to the Adriatic began soon after the defeat at the Battle on the Marica and continued with the loss at the Battle of Kosovo in 1389. An unstable period followed, with a shrinking nation that was ruled jointly by Prince Lazar's son, Despot Stefan Lazarević, and by his cousin, Đurađ Branković, who moved the state capital to the newly built fortified town of Smederevo on the Danube. The final fall came in 1459, when Smederevo fell into Turkish hands. This brought a northern migration on a much larger scale.

Fear of the Ottomans was tangible enough and, as the Ottoman Empire was a strict

1389 – THE BATTLE OF KOSOVO

Although the Battle on the Marica River of 1371 was probably a greater military defeat, and the event that most significantly led the way for Turkish subjugation of the Serbs, it was the events of June 28 1389 on the Field of Blackbirds (*Kosovo Polje*) in Kosovo that held and still holds the greatest sway on the Serbian psyche. It is hard to think of a parallel European example, in which a specific military defeat is taken as such a defining moment in a nation's history. For Serbs, the failure to hold back the Turkish tide at Kosovo Polje was a noble defeat, something which is considered both a tragedy and a source of national pride, the misfortune of an overwhelmed nation bravely defending its freedom.

There are few hard facts about what really happened on the battlefield. It is true that numerous epic poems were composed later on praising the valour of those taking part but this is myth-making rather than any detached first-hand account. What is certain is that on the Serbian side the main contingents were led by Prince Lazar and Vuk Branković, along with Bosnians under the command of Vlatko Vuković. There were probably mercenaries involved too, on both sides of the lines. Lazar and Sultan Murad both certainly died on the battlefield, while Vuk Branković, Vlatko Vuković and Beyezid, Murad's son, all survived. The notion that the defeat was the death knell of the medieval Serbian state is not really correct. For a start, the Turks did nothing to consolidate their victory: almost as soon as the battle was over they retreated to Edirne (Adrianople), which was their capital at that time, and it would be another 70 years before they pushed north in earnest. What is also in doubt was whether or not it was such a clear-cut defeat. Some initial reports from Kosovo seem to have celebrated the battle as a victory against the Turks rather than the other way round. Whatever the facts, what has had far more bearing on the Battle of Kosovo's place in Serbian consciousness is the myth and legend that followed the event to give it metaphysical meaning – the epic poems that celebrate the battle and the need for sacrifice, and the promotion of Lazar as a cult figure.

Islamic theocracy, religious persecution was rife. The sultan handed over large tracts of Serbian land to Muslim knights and some Serbs converted to avoid subjugation as serfs or *rayah*. Many did not however, and the Turks took tens of thousands of Christian Serbs into slavery, dragging many of them from their lands to serve Ottoman masters in Constantinople. The Turks targeted the Serbian aristocracy in particular, determined to wipe out the *župan* social elite that headed the *zadruge* (loose family groups that associated as clans). Many left the urban centres where they had previously lived, preferring to withdraw to the mountains where they could eke out a living by cattle breeding and farming.

What was resented more than anything else under Turkish rule was the ongoing recruitment and increasing power of the Janissaries. Originally, the Janissaries were Muslim converts who had been forcibly taken from Christian families when they were children, to be trained as the elite troops of the Ottomans. Although they began as a military instrument of the sultan's will, with time the Janissaries became a powerful and self-determining elite that protected its own power and influence with quite spectacular savagery and cruelty. They imposed taxes and exploited the peasantry to such a degree that they ended up being more hated than the Turks themselves.

Belgrade itself did not finally succumb until 1521, when it was finally besieged and burnt down by Sultan Suleiman the Magnificent. It remained in Turkish hands until 1717 when it was conquered once more by Prince Eugene of Savoy.

Over the next few centuries there were many Serbian uprisings against Turkish rule, some more effective than others. In 1594, during the Austrian–Turkish War (1593–1606), an insurrection was staged in the Banat north of the Danube, a region now in Vojvodina province. The Turkish sultan responded by skinning alive and hanging the Serbian patriarch, Teodor, before bringing the relics of St Sava to Vračar near Belgrade to be burned because the figure of St Sava had adorned so many of the rebel flags. This desecration was considered to be an unimaginably sacrilegious act by all Serbs, and even by many Muslims equally devoted to the saint who had something of a reputation as a miracle worker.

During the Great War between Turkey and the Holy Alliance (1683–90), Austria, Poland and Venice incited the Serbs to rebel once more. Insurrection spread throughout the western Balkans from Montenegro to the Danube basin but the Austrians soon withdrew their support. As the Austrians withdrew from Serbia, they invited the Serbs to travel north with them, to live alongside them in their territories. For many Serbs, this was the lesser of two evils, and faced with choosing between certain Turkish vengeance and a life in a Christian, albeit Catholic, imperialist state, many chose the latter. Large areas of southern Serbia were depopulated as a result of this and the Turks used the opportunity to proselytise Raška (the Turkish *Sandžak*), Kosovo and Metohija, and parts of Macedonia. This widespread conversion explains much of Serbia's present-day religious demographic.

Shortly after this mass movement north, another important episode took place when Serbian territories became the battleground for another Austrian–Turkish war launched by Prince Eugene of Savoy in 1716. Once again, the Serbs sided with Austria and, after a peace treaty was signed in Požarevac, Turkey lost control of its possessions in northern Serbia and the Danube basin, as well as in northern Bosnia, parts of Dalmatia and the Peloponnese.

Serbian uprising

By the turn of the 19th century, the Ottoman leadership was corrupt, profligate and in decline, and the Janissaries, who originally had been selected and trained by the Turks, had become an unruly and self-perpetuating elite that were a law unto themselves. As the years of Turkish domination progressed, small-scale resistance to Ottoman rule, and especially to the Janissaries and the *spajis* – Turkish cavalry units of similarly rapacious character – started to emerge. This came in the form of rebel bands called *hajduks*. These had started to form in the 15th century but became far more numerous and troublesome during the later years of Turkish domination. The name translates literally as 'brigands' but the *hajduks* of Ottoman Serbia are more popularly viewed as guerrillas or Robin Hood-type folklore heroes – bandits with a political agenda. It was the actions of the *hajduks* that inspired the first larger-scale rebellion against the Turks in the **First National Uprising** of 1804.

This, the first of two national revolts, was headed by a pig-farmer from the Šumadija region called Đorđe Petrović, commonly known as Karađorđe ('Black George'). The rebellion started early in 1804, when Janissaries executed up to 150 Serbian local leaders or *kneze* in an operation they termed, 'The Cutting Down of the Chiefs'. This action was viewed as a pre-emptive strike against those who were plotting against them but all it really achieved was to precipitate a widespread rebellion. Karađorđe was elected leader and the rebels soon managed to liberate most of the Belgrade *pashalik* (district) from Janissary control. At first, the Serbs were joined by many from the Muslim population, who suffered as much from the excesses of the

'BLACK GEORGE'

Karađorđe – 'Black George' – was a colourful figure who could best be described as brave, determined and uncompromisingly violent. When he was not killing Turks he was murdering members of his own family as a way of setting examples for his followers. Early in the campaign, he had his stepfather killed for refusing to stop fighting when a tactical withdrawal had been ordered; later on, he had his brother hung on a charge of rape, and suspended the body from the gate of his house as a warning to others. Despite, or perhaps because of, this violent streak Karađorđe went on to found a royal dynasty, a remarkable achievement for an illiterate pig-farmer of peasant stock. There are those that accuse Karađorđe of cowardice, saying that he should not have fled when the Turks got the better of him; others would contest that he was merely making a tactical withdrawal to regroup his forces before renewing his campaign, and that he was a warrior, not a diplomat, and so would brook no negotiations with the enemy. Like many other Serbian leaders he died a violent death, murdered by the command of Miloš Obrenović, the founder of Serbia's rival dynasty, when he returned to the fray during the second uprising.

dahis – the Janissary commanders – as anyone else, but this co-operation turned to bloodshed later on when it became clear that the Serbs were rebelling not just against Janissary tyranny but against all aspects of Turkish rule. Under Karađorđe, the Serbs demanded complete autonomy, which alarmed the Turkish rulers to the extent that they set up an Ottoman army to fight them. By now, the rebels had made contacts with semi-independent Montenegro and had sent a delegation to Russia to seek assistance.

The Ottoman army was beaten soundly at Ivankovac in August 1805, and, after two years of fighting, Belgrade was liberated on January 8 1806. Karađorđe, with his army of about 25,000 rebels, found the city in ruins. It was soon rebuilt and went on to become the capital of the territories that made up newly liberated Serbia. A fledgling Serbian government (the *Praviteljstvujušči Sovjet*) had its first assembly there in 1807; by 1811, the first ministries had been set up.

By the end of 1806, the Russians too had joined the fight on the Serbian side. This support encouraged the Serbs to fight on to try and reclaim more of their past territories. However, within a few weeks, the Russians had signed a treaty with the Turks and their short-lived support fell away. Fighting resumed between the Turks and the Serbs in 1809, who again received a moderate amount of help from the Russians. But once again, this was not going to be long-lived as Russia was soon going to need all of its military might in its own territories due to the sudden appearance of Napoleon Bonaparte and his armies in the Russian homeland.

A short time afterwards, the Russians and Turks signed another peace treaty together, which specified that Serbia would return to Ottoman rule on the condition that amnesty be given to all participants in the insurrection. This was rejected outright by the Serbs, and Karađorđe, along with thousands of others, fled north across the Danube to safety in the Habsburg provinces. The Turks, never ones to forgive and forget, soon took vengeance: hundreds of villages were sacked, and thousands of Serbs, particularly women and children, were taken into slavery. In 1813, the city of Belgrade, which had enjoyed just a few years of freedom, was conquered once again by the Turks.

The **Second National Uprising** of 1815 was led by Miloš Obrenović, a veteran of the first campaign, who, after the first rebellion's failure, rather than fleeing north with Karađorđe had tried to make a deal with the Turks instead. Although the Turks offered Obrenović a local position of limited power, it soon became clear that such a deal was untenable. In 1814, one of Karađorđe's former commanders attempted to start up a fresh rebellion but this was soon quelled. However, in the wake of the brutal reprisals that followed, new plans were hatched for another, more ambitious, uprising. This attempt was far more successful, and by mid July 1815, Obrenović's rebels had succeeded in liberating most of the Belgrade *pashalik*.

The Turks were more wary this time, influenced by events abroad: Napoleon had just been defeated at Waterloo, and they were concerned that the Russians, now free from the threat of French invasion, might join the fight on the part of the Serbs. Consequently they were willing to do a deal with Obrenović. Obrenović was undoubtedly a brave commander in battle but, unlike Karađorđe, he was also skilled in the art of diplomacy, and this helped in his negotiations with the Turks. He negotiated for the Belgrade *pashalik* to become autonomous to the extent that the Turks would remain only in the towns and forts of the province, and that only Serbian chiefs would have the right to collect taxes from now on. As he sought these concessions he cleverly managed to undermine the power of the Turks in other ways, such as in encouraging Serbs from the south to move to Belgrade, which resulted in many Turks being obliged to sell their houses and land at prices far below their real worth.

In 1817, Karađorđe sneaked back into Serbia, but Obrenović, doubting the former commander's motives, had him murdered by his agents. Karađorđe's head was duly stuffed and sent to the sultan – an act prompting the beginning of a feud between the two families that would last for almost 100 years.

Miloš Obrenović turned out to be as avaricious as the Turks when it came to tax collecting, and his increasingly oppressive rule prompted seven uprisings against him between 1815 and 1830. Nevertheless, it was a progressive and prosperous time for the capital. Many new buildings were constructed in Belgrade during this period: Princess Ljubica's *konak*, the cathedral and the king's palace complex at Topčider. Great scholars and educators also emerged during this period; like Dositej Obradović, who became minister of education and opened the Great School, the country's first institution of higher education, and Vuk Karadžić who collected epic poems, developed the Cyrillic alphabet for modern Serbia and single-handedly reformed the Serbian language. Influenced by these innovators, Belgrade soon became a centre for literary activity: in 1831 the first printing press was opened, and in 1837, the first bookshop. Soon after, newspapers would be printed in the city for the first time. It was a rapid advance from Ottoman stagnation and, from the 1830s onwards, Serbia started to develop an identity that was more akin to central European society than to that of a peripheral province of a flagging empire. The days of foreign rule were numbered. Belgrade's familiar minarets started to disappear as mosques were taken down following the Turkish exodus. Ottoman soldiers left Belgrade for the last time on April 18 1867. The Principality of Serbia received full international recognition at the Congress of Berlin in 1878 and the Kingdom of Serbia was proclaimed four years later.

The Balkan Wars of the early 20th century

Serbia in the latter part of the 19th century was ruled by a dynasty descended from Miloš Obrenović, with the exception of Prince Alexander Karađorđević who reigned from 1842–58 and was the son of Karađorđe. A coup d'etat in 1903 brought Karađorđe's grandson to the throne with the title of King Petar I. Petar had received a European education, and had been influenced by liberal ideas, especially those of John Stuart Mill. He introduced a democratic constitution and initiated a period of parliamentary government that encouraged political freedom.

This new-found political freedom was interrupted by the outbreak of liberation wars in the region, and the whole of the Balkans region underwent rapid change as new Balkan states were created in the vacuum left by the Turks. With full backing from King Petar I, the League for the Liberation of the Balkans from Turkey was set up, in which Bulgaria, Greece, Serbia and Montenegro all co-operated to drive the Turks from the region. The **First Balkan War** of 1912 was short and successful and forced the Turks to concede both Macedonia and Kosovo to Serbia. However, the new allies soon fell out over Macedonia, and Bulgaria attacked both Greece and Serbia in its attempt to claim sole possession. This led to the **Second Balkan War** of 1913, in which Romania entered the affray on the side of Greece, Serbia and Montenegro. The war ended in the same year with the Treaty of Bucharest, an agreement that was unsatisfactory on all sides, especially to the Slavs of Macedonia who now found themselves divided. Serbia though, came out of it reasonably well, having acquired western Macedonia as part of the settlement.

By 1914, Turkish domination in the region had finally ended for good but now there were fresh problems of national sovereignty to have to deal with. Bosnia-Herzegovina had been part of the Ottoman Empire but was governed by Austria since its annexation in 1908. Discontent here caused a number of pan-Slavic movements to agitate for union with Serbia, something that greatly worried the Austrians. The assassination of the Austrian prince, Archduke Franz Ferdinand in Sarajevo on June 28 1914 gave the Austrians the excuse they needed to attack Serbia, first politically, then militarily. The assassin had been Gavrilo Princip, a Bosnian Serb and member of the 'Black Hand' and 'Young Bosnian' nationalist movements. The Serbian government had no connection with Princip or his co-assassins but in July the Austrians invaded regardless, after first having imposed an impossible ultimatum. This single Bosnian incident had immediate repercussions in a Europe that was already embroiled in territorial disputes and military allegiances: World War I had begun.

World War I

The Serbs fiercely defended their country from the Austrian invasion but after several major victories they were eventually overpowered by the joint forces of Austria-Hungary, Germany and Bulgaria. The army had to withdraw from its national territory by marching across the Albanian mountains in winter to the Adriatic, suffering dreadful losses along the way. What was left of the army regrouped on the island of Corfu before returning to fight on the Salonica (Thessaloniki) front alongside the other forces of the Entente – Britain, France, Russia, Italy and the United States. Even on the horrific scale normally expected of World War I casualty figures, the Serbian losses were appalling. By the end of the war Serbia had lost 1,264,000 of its men: 28% of its pre-war population of 4,529,000, and 58% of its total male population. Such a devastating loss could never be fully recovered from.

As war ended and eastern Europe reshaped itself, Serbia became incorporated as just one component in a greater South Slav nation. On December 1 1918, the Kingdom of Serbs, Croats and Slovenes came into existence, which united the territories of these three republics along with Bosnia-Herzegovina and Macedonia. This short-lived federation would become the blueprint for the future Yugoslavia.

The Yugoslav state of the inter-war years 1918–39

The post-World War I state had come into existence, under Western supervision, as a monarchy headed by Prince Aleksandar Karađorđe. Inevitably, having a Serbian monarch in power soon led to accusations of Serbian dominance. When the constituent states of the new kingdom met to draw up a constitution in 1921, the

Croats, led by Stefan Radić, refused to vote on any of the proposals and returned to Zagreb. As a result, a very centralist constitution favoured by the Serbs was drawn up: the Croat withdrawal had merely exacerbated matters and made the new constitution more Belgrade-centred than it might have been had the Croats participated. Radić was assassinated in 1928 by a pro-Serbian Montenegrin. In January of the following year, Aleksandar (now King Aleksandar after the death of his father King Peter I), perturbed by the attempts to promulgate a workable constitution, banned all political parties, dissolved parliament and imposed a Royal Dictatorship, renaming the country Yugoslavia. In Serbian, *yugo* means south, and so this new name simply meant, 'land of the South Slavs' – a term that carried none of the baggage of Serb–Croat rivalry.

The Royal Dictatorship was an unmitigated disaster, which solved none of the existing problems as it failed to bring any Croats into positions of power. Instead, many Croats, frustrated by their lack of power, were now joining an underground nationalist movement led by a lawyer, Ante Pavelić. This organisation – the Ustaša – had fascist leanings and its supporters wanted to rid themselves of the Serbian king in any way possible. King Aleksandar I was assassinated on a visit to France in 1934 by a member of VMRO, an extreme nationalist organisation in Bulgaria that had close links with the Ustaša. VMRO had plans to annex lands along the southern and eastern Yugoslav borders and sympathised with the Ustaša cause, which had its own territorial aspirations.

Aleksandar's son, Prince Peter, was just ten years old at the time of his father's death and so authority passed instead to the assassinated king's brother, Prince Paul. Under Paul, ever fearful of more Ustaša-style killings, anti-separatist repression was

JOSIP BROZ TITO

Tito was born Josip Broz in 1892 in Kumrovec, northwest Croatia, then part of the Austro-Hungarian Empire. He was the seventh child of Franjo and Marija Broz; his mother, a Slovene and his father, a Croat. His first job at age 15 was as a locksmith's apprentice. In 1910 he joined both the Union of Metallurgy Workers and the Social Democratic Party of Croatia and Slavonia, both of which contributed to developing his political awareness. From the autumn of 1913, Tito served in the military and at the outbreak of World War I was sent to Ruma in Vojvodina.

During his time in the Austro-Hungarian army he was arrested and briefly imprisoned in Petrovaradin Fortress for distributing anti-war propaganda. He was subsequently released and sent to fight against the Russians. In 1915 he was badly injured by a grenade from a Russian howitzer at Bukovina. After months in a Russian prison hospital, Tito was sent to a work camp in the Urals where he was arrested again in 1917 for organising demonstrations of prisoners of war. He later escaped from the camp and went to join the demonstrations in St Petersburg of July of that year. Here he was arrested once more and locked up in the city's Petropavlovsk Fortress for three weeks before being sent to a prison camp in Kongur from where he escaped to enlist in the Red Army at Omsk. In the spring of 1918 he applied for membership of the Russian Communist Party.

After his wartime adventures in revolutionary Russia, Tito returned to Yugoslavia to become a member of the Yugoslavian Communist Party. In 1934 he became a member of its Central Committee in the Political Bureau, adopting the nickname 'Tito'. World War II came and, following the alignment of the Yugoslav crown with the Nazis in 1941, Tito called for armed resistance.

rife, which further exacerbated the rift between the Croats and a Serbian monarchy that favoured its own.

At around the same time another political force was emerging in Yugoslavia – the Communist Party – a political force that had already succeeded in uniting the Soviet Union, a vastly more disparate nation, earlier in the century. The unifying appeal of communism was undeniable: the party won a number of seats in the early municipal elections in both Serbian Belgrade and Croatian Zagreb but they were forbidden to enter parliament, being proscribed, along with trade unions, from the national government. This denial of power drove the Yugoslav Communist Party further underground, where it regrouped and forged links with the Soviet Union. A leader eventually emerged in the form of Josip Broz, who had been imprisoned for his beliefs but had worked in Moscow with the Third International on his release (see box, *Josip Broz Tito*). In 1939, Josip Broz was elected chairman of the Yugoslav Communist Party. Later to be better known as Tito, Josip Broz would go on to play a crucial role in uniting the resistance against Nazi occupation before modelling the country's destiny in the post-war years that followed.

World War II

At the breakout of World War II, Yugoslavia found itself surrounded by hostile countries. Hitler was pressuring Yugoslavia to join the Axis powers so, after a period of neutrality, the regent, Prince Paul, decided to align his government with the Nazis. This prompted rebellion from many quarters, with massive protests in Belgrade on March 27 1941. A group of air force officers, supported by the communists, arrested

Between 1941 and 1945 he was the Chief Commander of the National Liberation Army, better known as the Partisans, and became entrenched in the bitter, three-way war between Partisans, Nazis (both German and Croatian Ustaše) and Royalist Chetniks.

After victory finally came in 1945, Tito became both prime minister and minister of foreign affairs of the new communist republic. He followed the hardline Soviet example for a while but in 1948, after a serious rift with Stalin, he decided that Yugoslavia should follow its own path and started to develop ideas for a non-aligned version of socialism. In 1961, along with Egypt's Gamal Abdel Nasser and India's Jawarhalal Nehru, he co-founded the Non-aligned Movement. Tito became president of Yugoslavia on January 13 1953; on April 7 1963 he was named 'president for life', which he remained until his death in May 1980.

Tito died in a clinic in Ljubljana, Slovenia on May 4 1980. His funeral was a spectacular and solemn occasion that drew world leaders of every political persuasion. In Western eyes, Tito's greatest strength was his ability to maintain unity throughout the country and hold the various factions together. Following his death, the glue that held the federation together seemed to start becoming unstuck and within ten years ethnic divisions and conflict had grown to the extent that civil war was inevitable. Tito's admirers would say that it was his political genius and powerful personality that held Yugoslavia together for so long; his critics would declare that it was by manipulation and political repression. The real truth is, no doubt, somewhere between the two.

His grave is at the mausoleum in south Belgrade called 'The House of Flowers' (*Kuća cveća*) although it no longer receives the silent, awestruck lines of pilgrims that it used to.

Prince Paul and replaced him on the throne with Prince Peter, who was still a teenager. The reaction from Berlin was to bomb Belgrade, which the Nazis carried out with great ferocity on April 6 1941. This was followed by a land invasion of both German and Italian forces. Peter, now King Peter II, fled with his government to exile in London. Belgrade was occupied just a few days later on April 12.

The country was divided up between the Axis powers. Germany took most of Slovenia, Italy annexed Montenegro and the Adriatic coast, while Bulgaria occupied much of Macedonia. Meanwhile, Croatia and Bosnia-Herzegovina combined to become a Nazi puppet state, called the Independent State of Croatia (NDH), with the head of the Ustaša fascists, Ante Pavelić, a natural choice as its leader. Serbia was occupied by German troops, apart from its northern territories, which were annexed by Axis Hungarians, and parts of eastern and southern Serbia by Bulgaria. Kosovo and Metohija were mostly annexed by Albania, which at that time was being sponsored by fascist Italy. Croatia's autonomous territory was enlarged and the regime adopted an extreme policy of racial purification, a repugnant and peculiarly Balkan feature of war that would reappear half a century later during the break-up of Yugoslavia. Over two million Serbs lived in this territory at the time, together with many other minorities like Roma. Enthused by the Nazi model, the Independent State of Croatia established extermination camps where they committed genocide on 750,000 Serbs, Jews and Roma over the next three years. Such were the excesses of the Ustaša that even some Nazis baulked at the zeal with which their Ustaša compatriots went about their murderous handiwork.

The lust for genocide displayed by the Ustaša, and the presence of a ruthless German occupation force, prompted Serbian resistance on a large scale. Two very different resistance groups emerged. One of these was the Chetniks, who were pro-Serbian but devoutly royalist and anti-communist, and headed by Colonel Dragoljub Mihailović. The Chetniks were supported by King Peter's government in exile in London. The other resistance group – the Partisans – was pro-communist and led by Josip Broz Tito. Most Ustaše were Croats, but by no means all, and many Croats chose to join the resistance struggle, particularly later on in the war. The Partisans, in particular, would draw fighters from all over Yugoslavia, even if the bulk of their support was Serbian. The Partisans, after all, had a post-war agenda that went beyond simply liberating the country from the Nazis and returning to the previous status quo.

The first Chetnik acts of resistance to occupation met with savage reprisals from the Nazis, which led to an extended period of relative inactivity in which Mihailović tried to accommodate the Germans, although he stopped short of active collaboration. In contrast, the Partisans under Tito's leadership fought an all-out struggle and, despite suffering dreadful losses, went on to have far more success. Many non-communists joined the struggle on the Partisan side once it became clear that their opposition was more effective than that of the Chetniks. The Partisan and Chetnik leadership met up on several occasions in the early years of the war but each time, Mihailović rejected any idea of joint resistance. Inevitably, this led to an armed struggle between the two resistance armies: a Chetnik–Partisan civil war broke out between the two factions in November 1941 and lasted until liberation in October 1944. With the Croatian Ustaša as a common enemy of both, this led to a three-way struggle, another depressingly common feature in Yugoslavia's history that would emerge again later in Bosnia-Herzegovina in the 1990s.

Despite the distraction of internecine warfare with the Chetniks, Tito's Partisans continued to harangue the Germans during 1942 and 1943. They were often on the run from the Nazis' far superior military machine: at one time, forced to retreat from Croatia into the mountains of Bosnia and Montenegro; then later, obliged to undergo a spectacular withdrawal along the Sutjeska valley, carrying their wounded along with them. In the areas that they successfully liberated they set up pockets of de facto government, the AVNOJ, which although a direct challenge to the royalist government in exile, received great local support in areas freshly liberated from Axis control.

A British military mission under Brigadier Fitzroy Maclean was sent in September 1943 to support Tito's Partisans. The British had always wanted to encourage anti-Nazi resistance in the Balkans but initially it had been a matter of debate which of the two factions they should support. At first, influenced no doubt by the presence of the Yugoslav king in London, and a general distaste for communism, the British had supported the Chetniks, but after a meeting with other Allies at Tehran they decided to withdraw all support for Mihailović and to provide material aid to Tito instead. This additional support greatly helped the Partisan cause and considerable advances were soon made. There was an unsuccessful attempt to kill Tito at his island headquarters at Vis, but this was thwarted and the Partisans proceeded to systematically force the Axis armies out of the Balkans during the early months of 1944.

With the end of the war in sight, Tito saw the necessity for making plans for the future. Tito, always a shrewd leader, knew that when liberation came there would immediately be an internal struggle for political dominance in the post-war nation. He fully understood that there were two possible endgames: either his preferred communism, or the return of King Peter from London and royalist rule. He met secretly with Churchill, and then flew immediately afterwards to Moscow to meet with the Soviet leadership. The outcome of this second meeting was to invite Soviet troops into Yugoslavia so that they could participate in the inevitable liberation that would soon come about.

The Partisans, together with Soviet Red Army units, entered Belgrade on October 22 1944. By early spring of the following year they were in full control of all Yugoslav territory. Yugoslavia was liberated from Nazi rule but the human cost had been appalling: in just five years, nearly one-tenth of the nation's population, an estimated 1,700,000 Yugoslavs, had perished, either in combat, in reprisals or in the concentration camps that targeted not only Jews but also Serbs, Roma and many others who did not fit in with the notion of an Aryan 'master race'. In a few short years, Belgrade had run the whole gamut of political fortune. It had at first been neutral, then briefly pro-Alliance before being bombed comprehensively by the Germans; it was then occupied by the Nazis for three years before being bombed yet again, this time by Allied forces. When Tito's Partisans and their communist supporters marched into the capital that autumn day in 1944, perhaps its citizens had every right to be a little sceptical about any sort of lasting peace.

Tito's Yugoslavia

Tito reached an agreement with King Peter's government in exile in which he was given temporary authority as a leader. By the end of 1945, elections were held throughout the country. The Communist Party, which was still technically illegal, stood as the People's Front and won 90% of the vote for the Federal Council. Such a landslide victory resulted in royalist members of Tito's provisional government resigning, while the king remained in exile and Mihailović was executed, along with many Chetniks and other troublesome opponents.

Socialist Yugoslavia was established as a federal state made up of six republics – Serbia, Croatia, Bosnia-Herzegovina, Macedonia, Slovenia and Montenegro – together with two autonomous regions within Serbia itself – Vojvodina and Kosovo-Metohija. A Soviet-style constitution was drawn up as Tito immediately instigated a number of reforms. Industries were nationalised, large estates were confiscated and

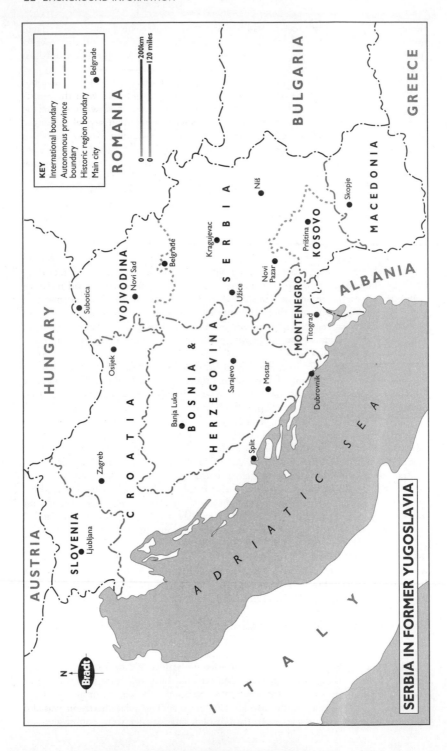

SERBIA IN FORMER YUGOSLAVIA

redistributed, there were currency reforms, and the first Five Year Plan, emphasising the need to develop Yugoslavia's industrial base, was started. At this stage, Yugoslavia was still closely linked with the Cominform, the Soviet-controlled organisation of east European communist states. This membership guaranteed financial aid for the country with its pro-Soviet policies. Things changed quite dramatically however in 1948, when, because of his differences with Stalin, Tito severed his links with the Soviet Union. Already he had begun to develop his own ideas about how the country's foreign policy should operate, and had resisted Soviet pressure on several important issues. Yugoslavia were expelled from the Cominform and there followed a tense period when it seemed quite likely that the Soviet Union would invade Yugoslavia in order to bring it into line. Tito refused to waver, however, even when the Soviets started to shell the country from its 'friendly' satellite states of Bulgaria and Albania.

Having rejected Stalin's hardline and inflexible brand of communism, Tito went it alone with his own vision of socialism. He instigated a federal system, which gave each of the constituent republics individual autonomy for its internal affairs. Another innovation, introduced in 1950, was the introduction of self-managing workers' councils in industry, with producers' councils operating on a regional level.

Although Tito himself was no stranger to odd bouts of autocracy, especially during his early years in power, his brand of socialism was generally far more democratic than that practised throughout the rest of eastern Europe. Tito felt that he had much to offer other non-aligned countries that did not embrace the full-on communism of the Soviet Union. In 1961, the First Conference of Non-aligned Countries was hosted by Belgrade. With continued reforms, and a determinedly non-aligned approach, Tito steered Yugoslavia into becoming a reasonably prosperous and liberal state, which reached its zenith in the 1960s and 1970s. There were a few problems along the way, as Tito did not always quite receive the unfailing support he would have liked – as in many other parts of Europe, there were widespread student riots in 1968 – but overall, he was a respected leader who was genuinely popular with most of his own people and, from the viewpoint of the Western democracies, a preferable choice to any hardline alternative. Much of his popularity was down to his persuasive powers of unification, and perhaps his greatest achievement of all was to successfully unite Yugoslavia's diverse population in a post-war climate in which the scars of ethnic conflict were still fresh. This unification would not be permanent however; it would not be long before the wounds and violent memories of World War II would be resurrected in many people's minds.

Tito's death and its aftermath 1980–91

When Tito died in May 1980, many commentators predicted imminent economic collapse. Tito had achieved much on the strength of his personal charisma and his skill in dealing with problems of nationalism. Before his death, Tito had laid down conditions for a power-sharing leadership that would ensure the survival of the federation and avoid the emergence of any dictator-like figures. The presidential authority was to change yearly from one republic to the next thus avoiding concentrating power in any particular region.

The predictions came true: within five years Yugoslavia had accumulated a massive foreign debt, had 60% inflation and was suffering from high unemployment throughout the republic. Membership of the Communist Party started to decline and many critics were arguing for modernisation and liberalisation of the economy. The Party, without Tito at the helm, was starting to become something of a behemoth that could only respond to criticism by clamping down on such dissidents.

Ironically, this same period of economic decline and political stagnation was also Yugoslavia's heyday as a tourist destination. Tourism, along with large loans from

Western banks, became a lifeline for the Yugoslav economy. As package-tour operators searched for alternative destinations to Spain, Italy and Greece, Yugoslavia became increasingly popular, and by the 1980s millions of northern European tourists were coming each summer to Yugoslavia's Adriatic coast to swim, sunbathe and enjoy bargain prices. The income from this did much to prop up Yugoslavia's flagging economy but it was not enough in itself.

At the same time as this economic decline, regionalist dissatisfactions were starting to emerge once again. Some Croats were suspicious of what seemed to them a Serbian dominance in Yugoslav politics. The Slovenes too, were starting to resent being dragged down economically by central government – Slovenia had always been one of the most prosperous republics of the federation, and a region which looked more to central Europe than to the Balkans. Most worrying was the situation developing in Kosovo-Metohija, Yugoslavia's poorest and most-overlooked province, where the Albanian majority had been demanding autonomy for many years. With Tito dead, and a growing dissatisfaction with federalism, the seeds of secession were planted for the full-scale civil war that would tear the country apart in the 1990s.

The break-up of Yugoslavia 1991–2000

By 1991, the tensions between the six republics had grown to crisis point. Slovenia was the first to withdraw from the federation, after fighting a brief war of independence, followed by Croatia. Both countries were soon recognised internationally as bona fide nations. The Slovenian secession occurred without too much bloodshed but Croatia, which was still home for many Serbs, saw the reappearance of an extreme nationalist movement that echoed the Ustaša of World War II. The Serbian minority that was mostly concentrated in the Krajina and Slavonia regions suffered greatly in the face of Croatian nationalist oppression. Even after 1992, when a United Nations protection force was enlisted to protect Serbian interests, the Serbs in Croatia continued to leave in droves, sometimes because they were burned out of their homes, but often simply because of a well-founded fear of the consequences if they remained. By 1995, over 200,000 Serbs had left Croatian soil to become refugees in Serbia.

A parallel crisis developed in Bosnia-Herzegovina. With an evenly mixed population of Catholic Croats, Orthodox Serbs and Muslim Bosniaks, Bosnia-Herzegovina had its own special problems. The Croats and Muslims wanted to secede from the federation (although not necessarily together), while the Bosnian Serbs wanted to remain tied to Belgrade. Bosnia's independence was recognised internationally in 1992, much to the chagrin of the Belgrade government who feared for the future of Serbs in Bosnia. Fighting raged between all three factions – Serbs, Croatians and Bosnian Muslims – from April 1992 until the signing of the Dayton Peace Accord in November 1995.

With Macedonia, newly independent as well, it left just two of the former republics – Serbia and Montenegro – to constitute what was by now a severely eroded Yugoslavia. Belgrade was still unwilling to let go of the idea of federation and announced, in April 1992, the establishment of the new Federal Republic of Yugoslavia, a creation made up of these two remaining countries, which from now on would each have their own president and legislature.

Even a new Yugoslavia composed of just two republics was fraught with difficulties, and in 1998, Kosovo, the region which everyone expected trouble to emerge from, erupted into violence. The cause of the disunity here was just as predicted: Serbia still had Kosovo, which was still an autonomous province, and which still had a majority Albanian population that still wanted full independence.

Given its history, its ethnic make-up, its years of neglect and the degree of ethnic violence that was emerging from every corner of the Balkans, it was only a matter of time before bloodshed spilled over into Kosovo. In 1998 the Kosovo Liberation Army (KLA), supported by many of the ethnic majority Albanians, came out in open rebellion against Serbian rule. President Milošević sent in Serbian troops to quell the uprising and, as the Serbs became embroiled in civil war in Kosovo, international pressure grew in demanding that he withdraw. NATO attempted to bring the two sides together in peace talks in early 1999. Representatives of the KLA signed a deal in Paris on March 18, but the Serbs chose to boycott the event. Finally, NATO launched air strikes against Serbia on March 24 1999. On June 3 1999, Milošević accepted a peace plan brought by EU and Russian envoys that required withdrawal of all forces from Kosovo and the entry of an international peacekeeping force under UN mandate. Serb forces started to leave the province a week later, and NATO halted the bombardment of Serbian territory. Russian peacekeepers entered Kosovo for the first time on June 11, and a day later, NATO troops crossed the border.

Slobodan Milošević had already been active in Serbian politics for some time, having been president since 1989. There had been protests against him in 1996 because of his rejection of opposition victories in municipal elections. Reeling from the failure of the Kosovo campaign and the humiliation of NATO bombing, the Serbs were becoming increasingly disenchanted with Milošević and what they perceived as bullyboy tactics. In April 2000, more than 100,000 Serbs assembled in central Belgrade to listen to opposition leaders call for early general elections: a defiant act which prompted Milošević to set presidential, parliamentary and local elections for September of that year. Opposition candidate Vojislav Kostunica won by 48.22% to 40.23%, but a second round was called as neither candidate had an absolute majority. Kostunica's supporters accused the federal election commission of fraud and rejected the result. This rejection set in motion a campaign of strikes and civil disobedience that finally forced Milošević to relinquish power. On October 6, he conceded defeat and Kostunica was sworn in as president the following day.

Serbian politics post-Milošević

In January 2001, three months after Milošević's involuntary step down from power, the Serbian Parliament overwhelmingly approved a reform government headed by Zoran Đinđić, head of the Democratic Party. A rift soon started to develop in the second half of 2001 between the new Serbian Prime Minister Zoran Đinđić, a keen reformer, and the new president Vojislav Kostunica, a conservative who had been in favour of Milošević going on trial in Belgrade, rather than The Hague as Đinđić had wanted. In August 2001 Kostunica's Democratic Party of Serbia pulled out of the government in protest over alleged corruption charges and, in the June of the following year, all 45 deputies belonging to Kostunica's party walked out of parliament in protest at the prime minister's decision to replace 21 of the party's members for absenteeism.

In February 2003, under pressure from the UN, the country changed its name from Yugoslavia to Serbia and Montenegro, although by now, Montenegro, having been persuaded by the EU to forgo independence for the time being, was a somewhat reluctant partner in a loose federation with its larger neighbour. A precondition of this was that there would be a vote in 2006 on the future of the combined state – Montenegro may well go it alone at some stage in the future.

The following month, in March 2003, Zoran Đinđić was assassinated in Belgrade while stepping out of his car. Those guilty of his murder have not yet been positively identified, although organised crime syndicates – in particular the so-called 'Zemun Clan' led by Milorad 'Legija' Luković – Albanian separatists and even revenge-

THE RISE AND FALL OF SLOBODAN MILOŠEVIĆ

Slobodan Milošević was born in Požarevac, Serbia, of Montenegrin parents on August 20 1941. His first career was as a banker with the Beogradska Banka, with whom he served as their official representative in New York for a while. He had joined the Communist Party when he was 18 years old and gave up banking to enter politics full-time in 1981 when he took over as head of the local communist organisation in Belgrade. He emerged as a leading force in Yugoslav politics in September 1987 when he replaced Ivan Stambolić as party leader in the Serbian section of the League of Communists of Yugoslavia. He went on to be elected president of Serbia by the National Assembly in May 1989 and a month later, on the 600th anniversary of the Serbian defeat at the Battle of Kosovo, gave a rousing speech to a huge crowd at Kosovo Polje, in which he promised the Kosovo Serbs his protection and full support. As president, Milošević presided over the transformation of the League of Communists into the Socialist Party of Serbia in July 1990, and the adoption of a new Serbian constitution in September of that year. The new constitution provided for the direct election of a president with increased powers. In December 1990, it was Milošević who went on to win the presidency. The new constitution also abolished Kosovo's autonomous status, a move that pleased the Serbs who lived there but which enraged many Albanians.

Milošević's rise to power coincided with the growth of nationalism that followed the collapse of communism throughout eastern Europe. In Yugoslavia, part of this nationalism could, no doubt, be attributed to Milošević's centralist tendencies that created a fear of Serb domination in the other republics. When Croatia and Bosnia-Herzegovina (along with Slovenia and Macedonia) seceded from the federation, the Serb minorities in both of these former Yugoslav republics called for self-determination to remain part of what was, by now, a Yugoslavia with a mainly Serb population. Civil war soon broke out in both Croatia and Bosnia-Herzegovina. The Serb cause was supported politically and militarily by the Yugoslav government during this period and Milošević sent Yugoslav Federal Army troops into action in both countries to assist the Serb militias fighting to unite their portions of Bosnia and Croatia with Serbia to form a 'Greater Serbia'.

Under Milošević, Yugoslavia had been suffering from trade sanctions imposed by the United Nations since 1992. By agreeing to sign the Dayton peace agreement in November 1995, and withdrawing his active support for the Bosnian Serbs, Milošević got the sanctions lifted. But Milošević's troubles were not over. Student demonstrations broke out in the winter of 1996, following reports of fraud in local elections. This badly damaged his reputation at home. In June 1997, when the constitution of Serbia prevented him from being president for the third time, Milošević assumed the presidency of the Yugoslav Federation (by now just Serbia and Montenegro remained anyway).

Following its loss of autonomy in 1990, the situation in Kosovo deteriorated

seeking Milošević supporters have all been suggested as prime suspects. To replace Đinđić, Zoran Zivković was appointed as the new Serbian prime minister on March 18 2003.

In the aftermath of the assassination the government imposed a 42-day State of Emergency and a crackdown on organised crime designated 'Operation Sword'. Four thousand people were arrested as a result, not just as suspects in the assassination but throughout the 1990s as Albanian separatists sought independence in the face of increasing state repression. In February 1998, Milošević ordered Yugoslav military forces into Kosovo to join Serbian police as part of a hardline crackdown on the separatists. A succession of violent encounters between Serbian police and Albanian Kosovars culminated in full-scale civil war in the province. Hundreds of ethnic Albanians were killed and hundreds of thousands more left the province as refugees to Albania, Montenegro or Macedonia. In the brutal cycle of war, the Kosovo Serb population continued to suffer too as reprisals were taken out against them. Western support was firmly on the side of the Albanian population and Milošević was threatened with military attack if he did not withdraw his forces from the province. The subsequent NATO air strikes increased his popularity to some extent but he was eventually forced to pull out.

On May 27 1999 Milošević was indicted for war crimes and crimes against humanity in Kosovo. Following the elections in September 2000, Milošević's rejection of a first-round opposition victory led to mass demonstrations in Belgrade on October 5 and the complete collapse of his authority as leader. Vojislav Koštunica took office as Yugoslav president the following day.

Milošević was arrested on April 1 2001 on charges of abuse of power and corruption and later on June 28 was handed over to the United Nations International Criminal Tribunal to face his war crimes charges. After his transfer, the original charges were upgraded by adding charges of genocide in Bosnia, as well as further war crimes in Croatia. The trial began in The Hague on February 12 2002 with Milošević providing his own defence while at the same time refusing to recognise the court's jurisdiction. The trial which continues, ad infinitum, has to prove the case that he had command responsibility in Croatia and Bosnia, at least de facto, as holding the post of Serbian president at the time means that, technically, he was formally not in charge.

Some critics of the tribunal argue that the trial is just a showcase to justify the bombing actions of NATO in 1999 and the thinly disguised US sponsorship of Albanian terrorists/freedom fighters such as the KLA. At the time of writing, Milošević remains in The Hague, the trial continually delayed by the call for witnesses and his extended periods of illness.

Whatever the extent of his crimes is, portraying Slobodan Milošević as a straightforward nationalist is probably doing him a disservice. During the war in Bosnia and in the period immediately after Dayton he was often criticised by genuine hardline nationalists like Vojislav Šešelj, and it was not until 1998 that Šešelj and his Radical Party agreed to join in a coalition with him.

What is without doubt is that Milošević's personality is that of a highly stubborn traditionalist, devoted to his equally stubborn wife Mira, his childhood sweetheart, and highly moral in his own peculiar way. He is also quite manifestly a skilled manipulator; whether or not he is proven guilty as charged remains to be seen.

also in connection with other murders, kidnappings and drug-related crimes. At the same time, the remains of Ivan Stambolić, the former Serbian president who went missing in August 2000, were found and charges were made against, among others, Slobodan Milošević, his wife Mirjana Marković and Milorad 'Legija' Luković.

Serbia had been without a president since Milan Milutinović's term finished in December 2002. Serbian Parliament Speaker, Nataša Mičić, stepped in as acting

President and two attempts were made to elect a new president in 2002 but both were declared invalid because voter turnout failed to reach the required 50%. A third attempt on November 16 2003 failed yet again, largely due to a boycott by opposition parties.

Parliamentary elections took place in December 2003, with the ultra-nationalist Serbian Radical Party winning 82 seats and more votes than any other party with 27.8% of the vote. Overall turnout was 58.8%. Although they topped the poll the nationalist Radical Party were not strong enough on their own to form a government and so a coalition was necessary. The election's outcome was welcomed by EU observers but Serbia was still without a president.

The election of the new president took place in June 2004. Because of repeated low turnouts of the past the 50% minimum was abolished – after three previous attempts it was essential that one be elected this time. The two main candidates for the presidency were Tomislav Nikolić for the Radical Party and Boris Tadić for the Democratic Party. All the early polls suggested that it would be the Radical candidate who would win but in the end it was Boris Tadić, the former minister for defence, who was sworn in as president in July 2004.

ECONOMY

Serbia's economy is slowly stabilising after more than a dozen years in the wilderness. The problems started around 1991 when secession by Croatia, Slovenia and Macedonia meant that Serbia had to radically rethink its economic framework, which previously had been centrally planned with the focus of power in the capital. With secession came the loss of much of its manufacturing base that had favoured Croatia and Slovenia; the revenue from package tourism, too – enormously important to the pre-war Yugoslav economy – had come mostly from the Adriatic region of Croatia but, with the advent of war, tourism ceased to be a reality anywhere in the region for many years. Fortunately, the Vojvodina region continued to be the most productive agricultural region in the whole of the Balkans, and raw materials were still being unearthed from the coal mines in the southeast and the mineral mines of Kosovo. Nevertheless, the unhappy break-up of the Yugoslav federation meant that Serbia's economy soon became deficient in terms of raw materials, manufacturing base and a market for its goods. Successive wars and sanctions compounded the problem until a point was reached in the mid 1990s when inflation reached the world's highest-ever figure – a staggering 600,000% – that eclipsed even that of pre-war Germany (see box, *Hyperinflation – the 500 billion dinar banknote*). Serbia, shunned by most of the world, had reached a point where some of its people were living in conditions of almost Third World-style poverty. Many of those that could leave – the young and well-educated – did so, which left a skills shortage that further inflamed the situation. Finally, when popular protest finally brought the regime of Slobodan Milošević to its knees in late 1999, the widespread protest was fuelled as much by dissatisfaction with the dire shape of the economy as it was by political and ideological rejections of Milošević's plans for a greater Serbia.

The coalition government that followed Milošević inherited an economy shattered by war and nearly a decade of sanctions. The Serbian government has since taken several bold economic decisions: stabilising the dinar, streamlining the tax system and reforming the banking sector. In 2001 Yugoslavia became eligible for interest-free loans from the World Bank and a credit of US$540 million was authorised to contribute towards political, economic and social reforms. In 2003, the European Union granted €242 million in aid to Serbia and Montenegro, €229 million of which was destined for Serbia. With corruption and organised crime steadily on the wane, foreign investment slowly increasing and what looks to be a far more stable government in power, the current mood is one of quiet optimism.

HYPERINFLATION – THE 500 BILLION DINAR BANKNOTE

Inflation in Milošević's Yugoslavia became so acute that in December 1993 the central bank introduced a 500 billion dinar banknote as the country's economy plummeted into total chaos. The banknote appeared only a week after the first 50 billion dollar bill had been released into circulation, and ten days after the 5 billion dinar denomination had been introduced. When the new 11-zero bill was released into circulation on the morning of December 23 it was worth approximately US$6; by the same evening its value had halved. Already, the pavements of Belgrade were awash with discarded banknotes that even the destitute could see no point in picking up. For many Serbs, the colourful new bill, with its portrait of the children's poet Jovan Jovanović Zmaj on the front, represented their income for the coming month. It was just enough to buy ten loaves of bread, four ounces of meat, a gallon of milk or two dozen eggs. The release of the note coincided with the government announcement that it would slash nine zeros from the dinar in one week's time on New Year's Day, and came only three months after the central bank had already removed six zeros off the dinar in a futile attempt to control galloping inflation that peaked at 600,000%.

It is difficult to comprehend inflation of this order. These days people become concerned when inflation goes above 3%; that is, 3% *per year*: at its peak in 1990s Yugoslavia, inflation ran as high as 3% *per hour*.

PEOPLE

Even without including the autonomous provinces of Vojvodina and Kosovo-Metohija, the population of Serbia is surprisingly varied in its ethnicity. When these two provinces are included in the picture, it soon becomes clear that Serbia today is anything but a homogeneous population, with Serbs representing just 66% of the total population, Albanians 17% and a diverse mix of Hungarians, Romanians, Croatians, Bulgarians, Ruthenians, Slovaks, Vlachs (see box, *The Vlachs* on page 31) Roma and others making up the remaining 13%. Notwithstanding this, the Serbs are the most populous group across the country, apart from in Kosovo and Metohija where Albanians have a 90% majority, and in the parts of Vojvodina that have a large Hungarian or Romanian element.

Serbs

The origins of the Serbs (and the Croats) are unclear. One school of thought states that the Slavs were a group of tribes living in the Carpathian Mountains region, close to what is now the Romania–Ukraine border, and that they were driven from these lands by raiding Avars and Bulgars. Others contend that the Slavs came from the Caucasus region and were escaping from the clutches of an Iranian elite. Evidence for this second theory is supported by the records of Greek geographers who wrote, in the 2nd century AD, of an Iranian tribe called the *Serbi* or *Serboi* living on the banks of the river Don, but Professor John Fine, a foremost historian on the region, suggests that even if the first Serbs and Croats were actually Iranian, the Iranians quickly became assimilated into a society that was clearly Slavic, despite the non-Slavic origins of its ruling class. Whatever their true origin, the Slavs, unlike the other raiding tribes, came to stay; they settled in the territories depopulated by warfare and clung tenaciously to their new-found lands.

Differentiation took place as some tribes occupied the lands along the Adriatic littoral, to become the Croats, while others filled the niche available in the depopulated lands below the Danube. The two tribes had much in common, particularly in their unique social organisation: both Serbs and Croats lived as large, extended family groups (*zadruge*) governed by a patriarch or chieftain (*župan*). The Serbs especially, would maintain this unique form of social organisation, even during the long, oppressive years of Turkish domination.

To understand what constitutes the Serbian character, it is probably best to consider the way that Serbs see themselves. Proud, generous, strong-willed, brave: these are all adjectives that few Serbs would find argument with. Other terms like violent, paranoid, self-pitying, profligate and xenophobic, might well be more contentious. Whatever constitutes its exact make-up, it is undeniable that the Serbian character is strongly individualistic with an enormous love for home, family and nation. As for racial stereotypes, the so-called 'victim' mentality that Serbs are said to suffer from is undoubtedly more the result of years of isolationism than any generic, deeply embedded psychological trait.

Rebecca West was clearly a great fan of the Serbs and writes fondly of them in *Black Lamb and Grey Falcon*, her epic pre-war journey through Yugoslavia. Unlike the Croats, whom she considered to be caught at odds between their inner Slavic souls and outward Western aspirations, she repeatedly observed that Serbs were proud, honest and completely in touch with their warrior roots. She quotes (in French) from a book by the Serbian author, Mičić:

> La ciel serbe est couleur d'azur
> Au dedans est assis un vrai dieu serbe
> Entouré des anges serbes aux voix pures
> Qui chantent la gloire de leur race superbe

Albanians

The Albanians, which make up the great bulk of the population in Kosovo and Metohija, are a non-Slavic people descended from the ancient Illyrians. The date of their appearance in medieval Serbia is a matter of contention but there is little doubt that by the 15th century, when Ottoman advances drove many Christian Serbs north to safety, many land-hungry Albanians moved in to fill the void and colonised much of Kosovo and Metohija.

Albanians speak an Indo-European language that has developed from Illyrian. They are mostly Muslim – nominally at least – a result, perhaps, of their willingness to go along with the religion of the presiding power of the day. Many Albanians converted to Islam during Ottoman rule in order to be given the same status as Turks, and also in the hope that religious brotherhood with the rulers would give them a degree of protection from their Greek and Serbian enemies. The Albanian saying, 'Where the sword is lies religion', speaks clearly of such pragmatism.

Serbian–Albanian relations were not always so fractious if we are to believe Rebecca West in her reflections in *Black Lamb and Grey Falcon*. She remarks that, 'We noted again the liking that most Serbs now feel for the Albanians, who during the Turkish occupation were their most constant tormentors', although perhaps she is a little too ingenuous in her estimation of Serb forgiveness. Such forgiveness has never featured very strongly in Balkan history, whatever the ethnicity of the offended group.

Roma

The Roma in Serbia arrived in the Balkans some time around the 10th century after a slow migration west from India. Throughout their history in the region they have

THE VLACHS

Although there is some controversy about their origins, the most commonly held view is that the Vlachs are a Romanised pre-Slavic group who survived the Slavic onslaught in the Balkans during the 6th century AD. With the arrival of the Serbs, first as raiders, then later as settlers, they took to the hills or migrated to the Balkan fringes. These nomadic clansmen moved around the Balkans in the wake of the rise of urban centres. The Vlachs, with their large herds of sheep, goats and cattle would service the cities, driving their flocks over long distances whilst taking advantage of seasonal grazing lands along the way. In Roman times they provided cheese to many parts of the empire. The Latin tongue they developed over the centuries of doing this became preserved as Vlachs took to more mountainous areas during subsequent Slavic invasions. Centuries later, the Vlachs were practising transhumance over vast areas, spurred on by the Byzantine taxation system, which was far easier to evade when constantly moving. Later colonisation encouraged the Vlachs to maintain this way of life when the Turks persuaded them to keep to their nomadic lifestyle as the expanding Ottoman cities of the Balkans had great demand for the cheese, milk, wool and leather they provided.

Despite many being later assimilated by the Serbs and taking up their language and culture, many others kept true to their traditions, speaking a Latin-based language that is close to modern Romanian. Modern-day Vlachs in Serbia are generally integrated into mainstream society and seem little different to ordinary Serbs although they still retain elements of their language and tradition.

The most populous enclaves of Vlachs in Serbia today are the villages of the Homolje Mountains in the east, near to the Romanian border, but even in this region they do not form a majority. The southern, or Aromanian, Vlachs that live in Kosovo, Macedonia and Montenegro appear to be a separate group without any Romanian ties. The writer, Noel Malcolm, in his book *A Short History of Kosovo* puts forward the somewhat controversial theory that both of the Latinised tribes – Romanians and Vlachs – have their origins in Kosovo and adopted their northern territories after a gradual northerly migration. It is hard to establish how many genuine Vlachs there are in Serbia today: in a 1948 census, nearly 100,000 declared themselves to be Vlachs but this number dwindled to a third of this by 1954, and to a negligible 1,369 by 1961. This decline probably reflects a lack of ethnical commitment more than other factors like migration. Clearly, many had recovered their Vlach identity by the 2002 census when 39,953 registered themselves as such. One of the several annual events celebrated by the Vlachs is the 'Slatina gathering', which takes place in the village of that name to the east of Bor every year.

remained, for the most part, outside mainstream culture, having little bearing on political and social systems of the countries they lived in, regardless of whether they were feudal, socialist or capitalist. Persecution and racial discrimination has always been a feature of life for eastern Europe's Roma but this turned to genocide during World War II when Nazis and fascist Ustaše collaborated in their murder.

Serbia's Roma population are no worse off – perhaps even slightly better off – than their kinsmen in other parts of eastern Europe. That, however, is not saying very much. Like Roma everywhere they are a disadvantaged and disenfranchised section of the population who live beyond the reaches of any state aid, such that may exist. A limited number have become integrated into Serb society to follow professional careers but for the most part Serbia's Roma live in poor conditions eking out an existence at society's fringes. Few Roma get to enjoy the benefit of a full state education (unlike other minorities in Serbia, Roma children are not taught in their native language); consequently, many are illiterate. With many suffering from the diseases and poor health that are associated with substandard living conditions it is hardly surprising that average life expectancy is well below the national average.

The former Yugoslavia had one of the largest Roma populations in eastern Europe with an estimated 1981 population of 850,000. Life was marginally better in the pre-war period before the break-up of the federation. Under the Yugoslavian constitution, Roma had, theoretically at least, an equal status with other ethnic groups in the federation. In practice, things were not so equitable, but at least they were recognised as being a constituent people of the republic. Since the break-up, Roma have become even more disadvantaged, suffering greater discrimination in employment, social services and education, as well as having to endure the privations of a trade embargo that has affected them disproportionately.

In recent years, many Roma have migrated from rural poverty to Serbian cities for a better life that rarely materialises. Many of them have had no choice but to move, and a large number of Roma have arrived as refugees in central and northern Serbia as a result of ethnic cleansing in Kosovo by the Albanian majority. In Serbia, the Kosovar Roma, who may number as many as 30,000, are considered to be internally displaced people rather than bona fide refugees, which excludes them from many basic rights and benefits. In neighbouring Montenegro, they have fared better and been afforded true refugee status.

To see the depressing makeshift huts that line the railway tracks leading into Belgrade's central station, or to visit 'Bangladesh', the disused pig farm outside Novi Sad that has served as home to a Roma community of 200 for the past 30 years, is to witness conditions that bring to mind Third World shanty towns or Brazilian *favelas*, and serves as a reminder of their position at the bottom of the social heap. But, despite their lowly status, and the rising incidence of skinhead racist violence against them, Roma are grudgingly admired in some quarters. In particular, they are lauded for their skill as musicians, and Roma wedding bands always have plenty of work. Some musicians of Roma descent, like trumpet player Boban Marković, have gone on to become household names with a reputation that extends beyond national boundaries.

Other minorities

Vojvodina has more minorities than any other Serbian province, with a total of 37 ethnic groups represented. The minorities in Vojvodina are far less visible than Kosovar Albanians or Roma and are generally fully integrated into mainstream Serbian society even though many of them still maintain their own traditions. The most numerous of these groups are Hungarians, who make up about 4% of Serbia's total population and over 14% of that of Vojvodina, and who constitute a large proportion of the citizens in northern towns like Sombor and Subotica. The Hungarian influence in these northern towns is quite palpable, with the Hungarian language widely spoken and prevalent in newspapers, advertisements and street signs. The architecture, music and food of northern Vojvodina are also heavily influenced by Hungarian culture. Of the other minorities in Vojvodina, ethnic Romanians are numerous in the northeastern villages of the Banat, as are Slovakians, Croatians and Ruthenians in other parts of the province. Hungarian, Romanian and Slovakian are taught as the first language in some of the schools of this region, along with Serbian.

Other minorities in this most ethnically diverse part of the country include Germans, Montenegrins and Ukrainians.

Refugees and the internally displaced

One of the realities of life in post-Milošević Serbia is the large number of refugees that remain in the country as a result of ethnic persecution or conflict. Depending on the source of the data, there are estimated to be between 350,000 and 800,000 refugees and internally displaced persons (IDPs) living in camps or makeshift accommodation throughout Serbia. The refugees originate from former Serbian enclaves in Croatia like Krajina or Slavonia, or from non-Serbian parts of Bosnia-Herzegovina, while the internally displaced persons are either ethnic Serbs or Roma from Kosovo-Metohija. Many of these arrived in Serbia with just the clothes on their back, and despite a limited amount of state and foreign aid have often found it difficult to adapt to their new circumstances. Often this is as much to do with cultural differences as it is a consequence of the trauma they have already suffered. In some cases, refugee Serbs, such as rural Krajina farmers, find that they have little in common with the communities they find themselves in, and that acceptance by their host communities, who themselves have suffered economically as a result of sanctions and war, is often begrudging. This is especially true of displaced Roma from Kosovo.

According to a 2001 census carried out by the Serbian Commissariat for Refugees in co-operation with the UNHCR, the majority of the refugees (63%) are from Croatia, with a smaller and declining percentage from Bosnia-Herzegovina (36%) as some refugees start to return to their homes there. In both cases, about 60% of refugees and IDPs have opted for integration into the State Union of Serbia and Montenegro. Within Serbia there are over 400 registered collective centres that accommodate over 30,000 people, two-thirds of whom are refugees and the rest, IDPs from Kosovo-Metohija. At least another 10,000 live in unregistered collective centres, while many more live with relatives and friends. The greatest numbers of refugees are housed in Belgrade, Vojvodina and in the municipalities of Loznica and Šabac in western Serbia. Most of those displaced from Kosovo-Metohija have become spread right across Serbia, in Belgrade, Kraljejo, Kragujevac, Niš, Smederevo, Kruševac, Leskovac, Vranje and Kuršumlija.

In many ways the IDPs are the worst off, because as they originate from within Serbia's national boundaries in Kosovo-Metohija they do not qualify as bona fide refugees. Consequently, they receive little of the meagre state and foreign aid that is available to refugees from beyond Serbia's borders.

Another important demographic factor that needs to be considered is the large-scale exodus of many of Serbia's young professionals to Europe, Australia and North America during the 1990s, which has resulted in a skill shortage in the country, particularly in areas like health and education.

LANGUAGE

Standard Serbian is one of the eastern variants of the Central-South Slavic language that was previously referred to as Serbo-Croat; Croatian is a western variant of the same. It is an Indo-European language that is closely related to other Slavic languages like Russian, Czech or Polish, although modern Serbian, because of the long Ottoman occupation of the region, also contains a considerable number of words of Turkish origin. The Serbian language, which is based on the Shtokavian dialect, is spoken primarily in Serbia and in the Republika Srpska of Bosnia-Herzegovina, in addition to Serb communities abroad in cities such as Chicago, Melbourne and Toronto.

Serbian, in its written form, uses both a Latin and a Cyrillic alphabet of 25 consonants and five vowels, the Latin form being adjusted by the use of standardised diacritical accents to render it phonetically accurate. The Cyrillic alphabet is based upon an earlier form that was first devised by St Cyril in the 9th century, later to be refined by St Kliment at Ohrid, Macedonia. Cyrillic may look intimidating at first, but given the ubiquitous nature of Cyrillic signs on display it soon becomes familiar enough, at least in its upper-case form. Using either alphabet, written Serbian is completely phonetic, with none of the unvoiced letters or variants in pronunciation that confound foreign students of English. Foreign names are also transcribed phonetically, so that well-known English names can appear unfamiliar when they are seen in their Serbian form, such as *Džon Mejdžor* for John Major, or *Đordž W Buš* for a certain US president. The Cyrillic alphabet is still widely used throughout Serbia (perhaps a little less in Vojvodina where Latin-script Hungarian is common) and has enjoyed something of a revival since the break-up of Yugoslavia and the rise of Serbian nationalism, with the use of Cyrillic serving as a clear way of distinguishing Serbian from closely related Croatian and Bosnian that use only the Latin alphabet. For information on pronunciation and a brief vocabulary, together with a comparison of the Cyrillic and Latin alphabets, see *Appendix 1: Language*.

Under Tito, Russian was the main foreign language taught in Yugoslav schools but that has long been replaced by English, a language that most under-30s know at least a little of. This secondary school tuition, coupled with the influence of growing up on a diet of Western rock music and Hollywood movies, has resulted in many young Serbs, in Belgrade especially, having an impressively fluent command of the English language. German is also quite widely spoken or understood in some quarters, often by older Serbs or Kosovar Albanians who learned it while working abroad in Germany or Austria.

The northern Gheg dialect of Albania is the first language of all Kosovar Albanians, while minorities such as the Hungarians and Romanians in Vojvodina also learn to speak, write and read in their own native languages as well as in Serbian. Most of Serbia's Roma community speak their own Roma language among themselves, although there is so much variation between dialects spoken in different parts of Serbia that they may be mutually unintelligible. Although Roma does have a written form, very few Roma speakers are able to read or write in this language even though they may be fully literate in Serbian.

RELIGION

The majority religion in Serbia is Orthodox Christianity, with an ethnic Slav Muslim majority in the Sandžak region of southwest Serbia. In Kosovo, approximately 90% of the current population are Muslim Albanians. There are also Catholic (mostly Croatian) and Protestant (mainly Hungarian) minorities in the north of the country.

Serbia started to become Christian in the 7th century with the encouragement of Byzantine missionaries and, although some pockets of paganism resisted for longer, most of the country was Christian by about AD790. For the next 200 years, religious influence fluctuated between Rome and Constantinople until 1054, when the Eastern Orthodox Church finally broke with Rome over the issues of the primacy of the pope and the language of the creed. For the next 165 years, all of Serbia's archbishops were appointed by the Patriarchate of Constantinople, but in 1219 the Serbian Orthodox Church separated from the Eastern Orthodox Church when Stefan Nemanja's youngest son Sava succeeded in negotiating with Constantinople for autocephalous status. Sava, who was later canonised like his father before him, became the first archbishop of this newly established Church.

Serbian monasteries

The period of the Nemanjić dynasty saw a proliferation of church and monastery building as successive rulers sought to mark their time in power with new construction projects. Many of Serbia's most noteworthy religious buildings date from this 'golden age' in the years before Ottoman subjugation, from the late 12th century to the early 1400s. The monastic churches that were built during this period represent some of the finest achievements of the Byzantine era, both in terms of the architecture itself and the richly coloured decorative frescos they contain.

King Stefan Nemanja was responsible for the building of the monastery of Studenica in the latter part of the 12th century. His son Stefan the First Crowned was responsible for the construction of Žiča in 1208, which became the seat of the newly established Serbian Archbishopric, while the monastery of Mileševa was founded by King Vladislav in 1234 to become one of the most important Serbian spiritual centres in the 13th century. During the reign of King Stefan Uroš (1243–76), the centre of the Serbian Church was moved to the Church of the Holy Apostles at Peć, which was completed about 1250, because it was considered that Peć was not only closer to the centre of the Serbian state but it was also less vulnerable to raids from the north. King Uroš I also founded the monastery of Sopaćani close to the source of the Raška River. Several members of the Nemanjić family were buried in the monastery, including Stefan the First Crowned, under the gaze of some of the finest medieval frescos.

Gračanica, perhaps the most spiritually important of Serbia's surviving medieval churches, was founded by King Milutin Nemanja close to what is now Priština in present-day Kosovo, while his son, King Stefan Uroš III, went on to initiate work on the Church of the Ascension at Dečani south of Peć, alongside his own son and heir, Stefan Dušan, who saw its completion. Both monasteries could be described as the jewel in the crown of medieval Serbian architecture: Gračanica for its grace; Dečani for its imposing form as well as its wealth of medieval paintings. Later monasteries belong to the so-called Morava style. Before perishing on the battlefield at Kosovo Polije, King Lazar built Ravanica in 1370, where his body still rests today; he also founded Ljubostinja in 1388, together with Princess Milica, who entered the monastery after Lazar's defeat in the following year. The monastery of Manasija with its massive defensive towers and walls was founded by Despot Stefan Lazarević between 1407 and 1418.

CULTURE
National folklore

There are many facets of Orthodox religious practice that are central to Serbian culture even for individuals who are not especially religious. One of the most important of these is the custom of celebrating *slava*, a practice not followed by any other Slavic groups. *Slava*, which might best be translated as meaning 'the praise', is the celebration of a patron saint. Each family celebrates its own saint, who is considered to be its protector. A particular *slava* is inherited from father to son and the occasion brings families together as each household, in sharing the same *slava*, is obliged to celebrate the event together. In special cases, such as migration abroad, family members may stage the event separately but as a rule it takes place under one roof, that of the family patriarch.

During a *slava* the family home is open to anyone who wishes to drop by. It is considered untraditional to actually invite guests outside the family, but visitors are welcomed if they come of their own free will. To be turned away from a Serbian home during a *slava* is unheard of as this would bring disgrace to the household. The *Krsna slava* ritual involves the breaking of bread and the lighting of a candle by a priest. A prayer is said over the *koljivo* - ground cooked wheat – the third of the three ingredients central to the *slava* ceremony (the Serbs have a thing about the number three). Incense is burned and everyone present is blessed with holy water before the priest blesses and cuts the bread in the sign of the cross. The bread is then rotated by the family patriarch, his godfather and the priest before everyone assembled sits down for a meal. Of the various saints' days, the most commonly celebrated are those of St Nicholas (*Nikoljdan*) on December 19, St George (*Đurđevdan*) on May 6, St John the Baptist (*Jovanjdan*) on January 20 and St Archangel Michael (*Arandjelovdan*) on November 21.

The custom of *slava* is believed to date back to the late 9th century when Serbs were first Christianised. It is thought that each of the Serb tribes adopted its collective saint protector around this time and this is borne out by *slava* variations according to geographical regions. Another commonly held belief, which does not necessarily contradict this, is that the custom of *slava* is a remnant from pre-Christian paganism and that *slava* was a syncretic adaptation in which the qualities of the old Serbian gods found sustenance in the personalities of the new Christian saints. Occasionally, a new *slava* is adopted when it is believed that a particular saint has facilitated deliverance from an affliction such as an illness, in response to prayer.

As well as individuals and families, various communities such as villages, cities, organisations, political parties, institutions and professions, Belgrade's own *slava* is on Ascension Day, which takes place on a Thursday, 40 days after Easter each year.

Christmas is celebrated in a different way to the West. Orthodox Christmas Eve is two weeks later than its Western counterpart, falling on January 6, its date according to the Gregorian calendar. Tradition dictates that early on Christmas Eve morning the head of the family should go to a forest to cut *badnjak*, a young oak sapling, which is then brought to church to be blessed by a priest. The sapling is then stripped of its branches and burned in the family fireplace. Rather like the burning of a yule log in Britain, this is clearly a ritual that has pagan origins. These days, with many Serbs living in cities at some distance from the nearest forest, the ritual is remembered by the Church dispensing the oaks themselves. The floor of the church, and sometimes the home, is covered with straw to remind of the stable where Jesus Christ was born. The Christmas meal usually consists of roast piglet and the sweet ground wheat *koljivo*, but the most important item on the table is *česnica*, a special loaf that contains a coin. Whoever gets the coin is considered to be especially lucky for the forthcoming year. Presents are not distributed at Christmas as in the West but are given instead on the *slava* of St Nicholas on December 19. Under communist rule it became more traditional to give presents on New Year's Day, which follows shortly after.

Easter is probably a more important event in the Orthodox calendar and a time when even many non-believers attend church for midnight mass on the night of Good Friday. Again, the timing of the Gregorian calendar means that it usually takes place later than Easter in western Europe. On this night, attendance of the mass is accompanied by much jollity afterwards and the drinking of *šljivovica*.

The painting of eggs is another Serbian Easter custom that still survives, especially in Vojvodina, and which takes place the week before Easter. During this week, whole families become engaged in painting hard-boiled eggs red and sometimes decorating them, although this is a later tradition. The painting of the eggs symbolises the renewal of life and one egg remains on the family altarpiece throughout the coming year. The red colouration is thought to frighten away the devil.

National costume

Little evidence remains today of the varied styles of national dress once worn in different parts of Serbia, although Belgrade's Ethnological Museum has an excellent collection that is well worth seeing. In Kosovo, many Albanian men still wear the egg-shaped white skullcap that identifies them as Ghegs, the same as those in northern Albania. Similarly, some older Albanian and Turkish women in Kosovo still wear the baggy trousers that identify them as Muslims. All across Serbia, many older women wear headscarves, regardless of religion.

In rural areas of Central Serbia, some older men still adopt the *šajkača*, the narrow, black or grey cap that used to be worn right across the country by Orthodox Serbs, but *opanak*, the traditional shoes with turned-up toes that used to be worn are now only usually sported by waiters in national restaurants. In the cities, and in Belgrade especially, Serbians are as fashion-conscious as anywhere else in Europe, if not more so.

ART AND ARCHITECTURE
Serbian religious art and architecture
The fine Christian art produced in the period of Nemanjić rule represents the apex of artistic achievement in medieval Serbia – an era of great creativity that might be compared to the Italian Renaissance that was yet to come. The monasteries built during this golden age were deliberately located in inaccessible spots around the country. Part of the reason for this was defensive, but it was also important to ensure that the monks who lived in them were able to follow a purely contemplative life away from all worldly distractions. With the arrival of the Turks in the first half of the 15th century, many of these monasteries were either converted into mosques or completely demolished, as the biblical scenes displayed in the lush frescos offended the Ottoman sensibility with its Muslim proscription on representing the human image. Consequently, many frescos were simply plastered over to hide the offending images; in many cases this plaster remained firmly in place until restoration was possible in the 19th and 20th centuries after the final withdrawal of the Ottomans had taken place.

As with all Orthodox churches, Serbian churches differ in layout from those of the Catholic and Protestant faiths. Instead of a nave or choir, there is a *naos*, a central area for worship that might be of a square or round plan, which is usually topped by a dome, a symbolic representation of Heaven above. The congregation always stands for the liturgy – there are no seats – and the central, public part of the church is separated from the apse by means of an iconostasis, a tall screen, usually made of wood that is decorated with elaborate carving and numerous icons of the saints. What characterises the Orthodox Church, in particular the medieval Serbian Orthodox Church, is the use of frescos to decorate the walls. These are far more than ornamental flourishes; they are there to show the congregation the heavenly kingdom that they can aspire to, to bring to life the Gospels and the lives of the saints for what would formerly have been an almost entirely illiterate congregation.

In medieval Serbia the art of fresco painting was developed to a high art form, but there were strict conventions that had to be adhered to. The images portrayed were considered to be representations of Christ's manifestation on Earth and so there was little scope for wild experimentation. However, regional stylistic differences did develop over time, both in the style of architecture and in the visual art on the walls.

The earlier Serbian monastery churches were built in what is referred to as the **Raška School**. This style, seen in the early Nemanjić monasteries, takes its name from Raš, the capital of the early Serbian kingdom. During this period, the Serbian Church was distancing itself from Byzantium and starting to lean more to the West, which explains the undeniable Romanesque influences that can be seen in the monasteries built at this time. The Romanesque influence is apparent in features such as animal and floral decoration around portals, and scenes such as nativities or *pietàs* carved in high relief in the lunettes above doors and windows. A good example of this East–West fusion of styles is the fresco of the *Crucifixion* at Studenica, in which the iconography is clearly Byzantine yet the rendering of the head of Christ, with eyes closed and head on one side, recalls the work of painters of the Pisan School. The Studenica paintings are impressive but a lighter and more personal style had developed by the time the frescos of Mileševa were laid out. These were done under the patronage of King Vladislav, whose portrait appears in the narthex of the monastery church. The paintings here are highly varied: the head of the *Virgin of the Anunciation* is delicate and tender, like an Italian Renaissance portrait, while the angel's head from the scene of the *Resurrection* reflects a more eastern influence. Possibly the best of all of the religious art of this period comes from Sopoćani. Some of the works from here, like the *Dormition of the Virgin*, are particularly striking because of the large number of figures represented in the painting and the elaborate detail of the architectural background in the scenes. The Raška churches, which were always stone-built, although they were sometimes faced in marble, characteristically have no aisles, but just a central apse with side transepts below a raised dome. The most prominent examples of the Raška style that still survive today are, in chronological order: Studenica, built in 1209, Žica (1219), Mileševa (1237), Morača (1252), Peć (1263), Sopoćani (1265), Gradac (1275) and Arilje (1295).

The continued expansion of Serbia under King Milutin in the late 13th century led to new architectural influences. From the late 13th century until the defeat by the Turks in 1389, a new style flourished: the **Serbo–Byzantine School**. This style reintroduced some of the Byzantine features that had been neglected by the Raška School. The cruciform shape was replaced with a cross-in-square plan; cupolas were introduced around domes; external sculpting was spurned; façades utilised coloured bricks and stones to create a striped effect: the overall effect was much more oriental in appearance than before. The frescos of the Serbo-Byzantine School portrayed a broader choice of subject matter and adopted a more narrative style, depicting figures in mythical landscapes, the lives of saints, and Serbian royalty in addition to the more familiar scenes from the Gospels. By the early years of the 14th century a new realism had crept in that suggested that painters might be using life models from the neighbourhood as a basis for their portraiture.

It was also at about this time that painters started to put their name to their handiwork. One of the most important painters from this period, who worked on a whole series of King Milutin's projects between about 1295 and 1310, was a man called Astrapas, whose best work appears in the church of Bogdorica Ljeviška at Prizren. The most extensive frescos from this period are found at Gračanica and Dečani in Kosovo. At times, quality is sacrificed for sheer abundance: at Dečani, for example, there are a total of 46 scenes from Genesis, 43 from the *Passion* cycle, 26 from the *Last Judgement*, and a *Calendar* with a scene for every day of the year. Existing churches of the Serbo-Byzantine School include Gračanica, built in 1320, and Dečani (1350), both in Kosovo.

The death of King Stefan Dušan in 1355 heralded the start of a decline in Serbia's fortunes, while the momentous defeat at the Battle of Kosovo in 1389 brought about a Serbian retreat northwards to the relative safety of the Morava valley. This withdrawal gave birth to another architectural style – the **Morava School** – that combined elements of both of the two previous schools. Churches kept their domes and multiple cupolas and their striped brickwork, but animal and vegetable motifs, that echoed the style of the Raška School, were added in low relief on windows and doors. The Morava churches were tall and quite large but, overall, the churches were simpler and less ostentatious than their antecedents. The painting style had now been developed to reflect the influence of both previous schools, combining Raška-style restraint with Serbo-Byzantine dynamism. The colouring is naturalistic, and the compositions are elegant, often with architectural backgrounds; the figures, tall and imposing with refined faces. This new style was intimate and tender, very much at odds with the realities of the day, as if there had been a conscious effort to take the

Above Mosaic at Karađorđe
Mausoleum, Oplenac (LM)

Right Žlča Monastery,
central Serbia (LM)

Below Window detail of mosque
at Turkish fort, Niš (LM)

Above Sićevačka Gorge and highway, near Niš, southeast Serbia (LM)

Left Traditional farm building of west Serbia, Sirigojno, Zlatibor region (LM)

Below Long-eared owl, *Asio otus* (MU)

human spirit beyond the reaches of the terror that lay at Serbia's door. The principal churches of the Morava School were built over a relatively short period of time: Ravanica (built in 1377), Rudenica (1403–10), Ljubostina (1405), Manasija (1407–18) and Kalenić (1413).

The Ottoman advance northwards announced an end to monastery-building in Serbia as the country came under Muslim rule but later, in the 16th century, new monasteries started to emerge in the Fruška Gora hills in Habsburg-controlled Vojvodina. These monasteries, the most famous of which are Krušedol, Hopova and Vrdnik, were built with a strong sense of nostalgia for Serbia's earlier golden age, and display features from all of the previous schools in their design.

Art in the Ottoman era
With the Muslim injunction on representation of the human figure, many of the skills developed by the medieval fresco painters were soon lost to history. The Ottomans imported architects and builders from Turkey to build mosques, or convert existing churches. Unfortunately many of these collapsed with disuse, or were destroyed outright, when the Turks finally came to leave. Ottoman rule left its imprint in later Serbian architectural style when, in the early 19th century, many Turkish style *konaks* were built in Belgrade. However, most of those which made it to the next century were destroyed in the Nazi bombings of 1941.

Art in the 18th and 19th centuries
The churches that were built in the early 18th century were influenced by an eastern baroque tradition but by around 1750 Western influences were starting to feature once more. From the end of the 18th century to the 1880s, Serbian art was closely tied to that of Vienna. The art of portrait painting, which had started to become popular in the previous century, was in the ascendant, and although the work of the Viennese masters was closely studied, artists like Arsa Teodorović and Konstantin Danil succeeded in infusing Viennese classicism with a distinctive Serbian character. As the 19th century developed, a Romanticist tendency appeared in Serbian art. Serbian Romanticism went on to reach its peak in the work of Đura Jakšić who was influenced by the use of chiaroscuro in paintings by artists such as Rembrandt. Up until the late 19th century, landscape had always played a subordinate role in Serbian artwork but it was during this Romantic period that paintings with pure landscape themes started to appear, usually as a digression by portrait painters such as Steva Todorović and Novalk Radonović.

After 1870, a generation of painters educated in Munich heralded a new phase in Serbian art, one in which pure landscape was accepted as an independent art form. Influenced by a range of ideas from various European schools, still lifes and village scenes now became respectable subject matter. Two prominent artists from this time, both Munich-trained, were Miloš Tenković and Đorđe Krstić.

By the end of the 19th century, Serbia was striving to establish itself as an equal member among sovereign European states. Many artists were forced to compromise their artistic sensibility with the requirements of patrons who wished to glorify Serbia's history in the eyes of Europe. For this, large, pompous paintings showing idealised scenes from Serbia's past were required, which gave birth to patriotic canvasses such as *The Great Migration under Arsenje III Carnjević 1690* by Pavle Jovanović (1896) and *The Entry of Tsar Dušan into Dubrovnik* by Marko Murat (1900).

Modern art
From 1900 until the end of World War I, painters like Milan Milanović and Branko Popović were under the spell of French Impressionism, but in the years

that followed Serbian art became heavily influenced by a wider range of styles. Artists like Nadežda Petrović became acquainted with the work of painters like Van Gogh, Munch and Kandinsky, and subsequent artists such as Veljko Stanojević, Milan Konjović and Ignjat Job, experimented with the genres of Constructivism, Cubism and Surrealism. By the 1930s, a new form of Expressionism had been returned to that concerned itself more with regional identity and ethnicity, an example being Petar Lubarda's painting *The Gusle Player* (1935), which depicts a peasant musician playing a folk instrument.

After 1945, many of the new tendencies that were emerging on both sides of the Atlantic in the 1950s – neo-Surrealism, action painting etc – had their counterparts in Tito's Yugoslavia, even if they were a little self-conscious and unoriginal at times. As elsewhere in post-war eastern Europe, much creativity was constrained by the requirements of Socialist Realism, which did not always make for great art. Following the split with the Soviet Union, politically driven art became less of a compulsion and artists were free to explore the abstract. By about 1970, Conceptual Art had become an important new direction in Belgrade and Novi Sad.

Because of Tito's post-war split with the Soviet Union, the tradition of Socialist Realist **sculpture**, so abundant elsewhere in the Communist bloc in the 1950s and 1960s, is not particularly well-represented in Serbia, although there are a number of imposing military monuments scattered throughout the country, the most notable being the war memorial at Avala by Ivan Meštrović. Croatian-born Meštrović (1883–1962) was heavily influenced by the Vienna secession movement and met Rodin at the turn of the century while studying in Paris. He developed an epic style that was very much his own and went on to produce some of Yugoslavia's most memorable monuments, the most notable Serbian examples beyond that at Avala being the *France* and *Messenger of Victory* monuments that stand in Belgrade's Kalemegdan Park.

LITERATURE
Poetry
The oral tradition has always been strong in Serbia: in World War I, a Serbian general roused his troops into action by speaking of the emperor Dušan; in World War II, some Partisan groups took an oath of loyalty identical to the one Karađorđe used for his troops at the time of the First Serbian Uprising. From the time of the defeat at Kosovo field in 1389, Serbian heroic poetry has been an oral tradition in which epic poems are memorised and handed down from one generation to the next. This remained an oral tradition until Vuk Karadžić, the great Serbian philologist and scholar, collected many of the epic poems and transcribed them to paper in the 19th century. The rich and lyrical works collected by Karadžić soon attracted considerable attention from devotees of the Romantic Movement. Serbian epic poetry was translated into English, French and German, and both Goethe and Walter Scott were sufficiently enthused to translate the same classic work called *Hasanaginica*.

The themes of these poems mostly concern heroic battles, bravery, morality and the exploits of Serbian monarchs. Naturally, many of them are based upon the Battle of Kosovo. These are not written as a cycle but as separate poems that observe the battle from different viewpoints, which, when read together, have a cohesive quality. Other poems deal with Prince Marko, a heroic figure with a magic horse, animal cunning and a prodigious thirst for wine, who manages to kill numerous Turks on the battlefield and outwit those who escape his sword. Later heroic poems deal with the Serbian uprisings and the activities of the *hajduk* outlaws, and even with events from World War I and II. Much of the poetry, however, deals with themes of nationhood and belonging:

Whoever is a Serb and Serbian born,
Serbian his blood and his lineage,
Who has come not to fight at Kosovo,
By his own hand shall he bring forth nothing:
Neither golden wine nor fine white meat,
There shall be no harvest from his lands
Nor in his house children of his blood.
While his race lives, they shall waste away.

The popularity of Vuk Karadžić's translations and the introduction of Belgrade's first printing press in the mid 19th century encouraged Serbia to develop its own tradition in literature. During this period, the indefatigable Karadžić translated the New Testament, the Montenegrin bishop and poet Njegoš published *The Mountain Wreath*, and poems by the Romanticist Branko Radičević were printed, together with the philological treatise *The War for the Serbian Language and Orthography* by Đuro Daničić. In the wake of this literary renaissance, a new generation of poets started to appear, the most notable being Jovan Jovanović Zmaj (1833–1904) who went on to leave a massive legacy of literature that incorporated a wide range of themes and genres.

The Serbian novel

The modern Serbian novel began with Borisav Stanković (1867–1927) who explored the contradictions of man's spiritual and sensory life in his 1910 work *The Tainted Blood*. This was the first Serbian novel to receive praise in its foreign translations. A little later, in the period between the wars, Expressionism appeared as an avant-garde movement in literature, just as it had done so in painting and music, when *The Manifesto of the Expressionist School* by Stansilav Vinaver was published in 1920.

Following World War II, the narrative form of the novel, which has always been important in Serbian literature given its oral traditions and epic poetry, was developed and perfected by Ivo Andrić (1892–1975), a Bosnian Serb, who to this day, remains probably the most famous writer from the former Yugoslavia. His most famous works are those of the trilogy published in 1945: *The Bridge on the Drina*, *The Travnik Chronicle* and *The Spinster*. By the time Andrić received the Nobel Prize for Literature in 1961, he had become the most commonly translated Serbian writer ever. A contemporary of Andrić, who dealt with similar themes but especially in the struggle between opposing principles, and between authority and the individual, was Mesa Selimović (1910–82). Selimović's novels, *Death and the Dervish* (1966) and *The Fortress* (1970), both deal with these themes in a historical framework; in the first case in the form of a narrative about a Muslim cleric in the 18th century, and in the second, from the viewpoint of an educated man in the 17th century.

From the 1960s onwards, many Serbian writers became as preoccupied with the form of their work as they were with the content. Experimentation continued with varying success: novelists like Bora Čosić (born 1932) baffled many readers with his constant interplay of construction and deconstruction in his massive novel *The Tutors*. Others, like Borislav Pekić (1930–92) and Danilo Kiš (1935–89) were more successful, Kiš in particular with his 1976 novel about the Stalinist purges, *A Tomb for Boris Davidović*, which brought him international acclaim for his skilful interweaving of fiction and documentation. Another writer from this period was Croatia-born Slobodan Selenić (1933–95) who became Belgrade's Poet Laureate. Selenić's major work *Fathers and Forefathers* is firmly of the psychological conflict/inner monologue school, and spans 50 years of Belgrade life as it covers the fortunes of an Anglo-Serb family and more generally the 20th-century struggles of the Serbian people.

Perhaps the most groundbreaking and innovative of all of the post-war Serbian novelists is Milorad Pavić (born 1929) whose most famous work *Dictionary of the Khazars* (1984) has been widely acclaimed by critics at both home and abroad. This novel, which is not really a dictionary or a historically faithful tract on the Khazars, is quite unique and recognised by many as a post-modern masterpiece. In this 'dictionary', Pavić challenges the usual temporal sequence of the narrative by making a random order reading of the text possible, even desirable. The text, which claims to be a reprint of the surviving fragments of a 1691 dictionary, purports to offer parallel sources from three civilisations and three religions – Christian, Muslim and Jewish – that offer an interwoven account of the Khazars, an ancient people about which very little is known. The allure of the text is its interplay between knowledge and fantasy, and the real and the possible, and the non-linear narrative allows the reader to follow numerous, labyrinthine hyper-textual links between the three accounts at whim. The book works as a type of mystery novel that seeks to answer two questions: to which religion did the Khazars convert, and why at regular intervals do representatives of the three religions come together to try and solve this first question?

The twist is that the first question cannot be answered as clues in the text point to each of the religions believing that it alone was the one ultimately chosen by the Khazars. The coming together of the representatives ends in destruction, and the search for synthesis is seen to be a utopian pipedream. On one level at least, *The Dictionary of the Khazars* can be seen as an allegorical account of Serbian (and Yugoslav) history and the necessity of simultaneously looking at the past from different perspectives. The *Dictionary* makes the case for the post-modern contention that, like the polemicists of the Khazar accounts, attempts at synthesis inevitably lead to destruction as no single 'meta-narrative' – Khazar religion or unified Yugoslavia – will suffice.

CINEMA

The first motion picture ever shown in Serbia was in a Belgrade café called 'At the Golden Cross' on June 6 1896. This was just six months after the first demonstration of moving pictures in Paris. The first permanent cinema was opened in 1909 in Belgrade at, appropriately enough, the city's Hotel Paris. By World War I there were 30 permanent cinemas in Serbia, together with many other travelling ones.

The early films were all of French origin but in the autumn of 1911 Svetozar Botorić, the owner of the Paris picture theatre, engaged a French cameraman to make the first Serbian feature film *Karađorđe*, a historical drama about the life of the leader of the First Serbian Uprising. Other works soon followed but production came to a halt with the outbreak of World War I. In the 1920s, several film companies set up in Belgrade to create newsreel and documentary films as well as a few feature films. The most ambitious and successful of the films made before World War II was the 1932 production of *With Faith in God*, directed by Mihaljo Popović.

From the end of World War II right up until 1991, the Yugoslavian film industry was centralised in Belgrade with Serbia being responsible for at least 50% of the output in the Yugoslav federation. From 1953 onwards several films were made in co-production with foreign countries like Austria and Norway, and the first colour feature was made in 1957. Throughout the 1960s, Serbian film was dominated by the work of Aleksandar Petrović, who won the Grand Prix at the International Film Festival at Cannes for his 1967 film *I Met Some Happy Gypsies Too*. A new generation of younger film directors started to appear in the middle of the 1970s, like Goran Paskaljević (*The Beach Guard in Winter*, 1976 and *The Dog Who Liked Trains*, 1977) and Slobodan Sijan (*Who's That Singing Over There?* 1980).

THE CINEMA OF EMIR KUSTARICA

Emir Kustarica made his first feature-length debut with the much-acclaimed *When Father Was Away on Business* (1985) but his first big international success was with *Time of the Gypsies* (1989). The film, originally titled *Dom za vesanje* ('A house for hanging'), is remarkable for its revolutionary use of non-professional actors, its Roma-inspired musical soundtrack (music by Goran Bregović) and for having a dialogue in the Roma language throughout. The film 'reads' like a magical realist novel: a sad, joyous, helter-skelter of a film with humour, pathos and romance all jumbled together with elements of surrealism. It combines elements of road movie, gangster film, romantic comedy and rites-of-passage, 'feel good' classic, as if Fellini and the Coen brothers both had a hand in its making.

With this and subsequent films like *Black Cat, White Cat* (1998) Kustarica was both applauded and reviled for his portrayal of Roma as picaresque characters. Kustarica was inspired to make *Time of the Gypsies* after reading an article about Roma involvement in child trafficking, one of the sub-plots of the film. He describes it as follows... 'the film is just like the typical suit of a Gypsy. Under his shirt he wears three T-shirts of different colours, his trousers seem to come from another planet...It is a film where everything mixes...The cinema being pulled about between video, television, music, literature, it can only have a strange form.'

The Roma theme was taken up again in 1998 with *Black Cat, White Cat* (*Crna mačka, beli mačor*), which once more was full of larger-than-life characters and was, if anything, even more chaotic than *Time of the Gypsies*, with wonderful surreal images like that of a brass band tied up in a tree playing their instruments, and a pig attempting to eat a rusting Yugo.

Between the making of these two films, Kustarica worked on his most ambitious, and most controversial project yet, *Underground* (1996) – a film that attempted to encapsulate the history of Yugoslavia (and in particular that of Serbia) between the period 1941–92. Although this was, once again, a spectacular roller-coaster of a movie, it would be fair to say that it was not entirely successful and the plot gets a little lost near the end. Again he had his critics. This time he was accused of being an apologist for Serbia's excesses in the Balkan conflicts of the early 1990s. Kustarica, a Bosnian Muslim by birth (although he would probably say Yugoslav), left Sarajevo for Belgrade at the beginning of the siege of that city. Many could not forgive him for what they saw as jumping ship.

His films have also been hugely influential in their music, which has always been composed and recorded by either Goran Bregović or by himself and his No Smoking Orchestra (he started out as a bass player in this band, while Bregović was a guitarist in another Yugoslav rock band). Several tunes from his films will be familiar to any Serbia visitor: the beautiful Roma anthem 'Ederlezi', and 'Mesečina' and 'Wedding Čoček' from *Underground* – tunes that are always requested of brass bands at Serbian weddings. His latest film *When Life was a Miracle* (*Zivot Je cudo*), not yet released in English at the time of writing, is based on a story centred around the Mokra Gora railway in the Zlatibor region of western Serbia.

With the disintegration of the former Yugoslavia, Serbian cinema suffered less than the other republics as it had been operating more or less independently for some time. Despite war and sanctions, film production was not halted, and new directors started to emerge alongside an older generation that was still directing films like *The Origin of the Forgery* (director Dragan Krešoja, 1991) and *Tito and Me* (Goran Marković, 1992). Ironically, it was at about this time that, despite its international pariah status, Serbian cinema was starting to receive plaudits from the foreign film community for the quality of its productions. One director who would go on to develop this international reputation made a great impact around this time with a film called *Time of the Gypsies* (1989). This was Emir Kustarica, who won Best Director at the Cannes Film Festival in 1989 and best foreign film at Sweden's Guldbagge Awards (see box, *The Cinema of Emir Kusturica*).

MUSIC

Serbia has a rich and varied **folk music** culture that draws influences from as far away as Hungary and Turkey and beyond. Much of this is still relatively unknown to the outside world, as Serbia's musical traditions have not received as much attention as other eastern European countries like Bulgaria or Romania.

Geography plays some part in explaining the prevailing influences. In the far north of Vojvodina, Hungarian traditions are strong: many of the songs are sung in Hungarian and instruments like cimbalom and *tamburica* are used alongside the more traditional violin and accordion. In the Šumadija region of central Serbia, a popular instrument is the *frula*, a small recorder-like flute. There is even a *frula* festival devoted solely to this instrument in July in the village of Prislonica near Čačak. In Kosovo, a musical tradition akin to that of the Ghegs in northern Albania predominates, with the widespread use of bagpipes, hand drums and clarinet. A popular dance throughout the country is the *kolo*, a village circle dance which is a great leveller and allows participants from all walks of life – young and old, educated and unschooled, male and female – to take part.

Traditional music is currently enjoying something of a renaissance in Serbia and it is starting to reach wider audiences now that go-ahead recording companies like B-92 are recording both established performers and new talent, and releasing their CDs internationally. Artists that are beginning to get an international reputation include: Lajko Felix, an ethnic Hungarian violinist from Subotica; singer Svetlana Spajić-Latinović from western Serbia; Bokan Stanković, a bagpipe player from eastern Serbia; and Earth-Wheel-Sky Ensemble, a Roma group from Vojvodina led by Olah Vince. All of these have toured throughout Europe but still remain close to their musical roots.

Serbia's **Roma** community have had an enormous effect on the development and propagation of music styles throughout the country. Roma, undaunted by mere tradition and unfettered by the attentions of the folk-music police, have always been musical magpies and regularly perform a seamless repertoire that is a happy hybrid of traditional dance tunes from all over the region, as well as pop tunes, nationalist anthems, film music and even television commercials. Some aspects of Roma music have become more respectable of late, particularly the **brass-band music** that has been developed by musicians in the villages of Serbia's southeast and which has encouraged a plethora of non-Roma imitators in its wake. The annual Guča Trumpet Festival (see box, *The Guča Trumpet Festival* in the *West and Southwest Serbia* chapter) is a showcase for these, and the venue where now-famous Roma performers like Boban Marković first made their name. The most popular style played by these bands is called *čoček*, a fast 2/4 dance that is performed better when lubricated with a few glasses of *šljivovica*.

TURBO-FOLK – WORTHY FUSION OR MUSICAL NIGHTMARE?

Turbo-folk emerged as the sound of 1990s Serbia as an unholy fusion of nationalist folk tunes and techno dance music: an unlikely meeting of Western pop culture, traditional values, state-controlled media and criminality. Its genesis was partly down to Slobodan Milošević's firm grip on the media during that period. Those in power recognised what they termed newly composed folk music (*novokomponvana narodna muzika*) or 'neo-folk' was more in keeping with the new order than Western rock music. Neo-folk fused traditional musical styles with new lyrics and modern arrangements and, like country and western, to which it could be comfortably compared, songs about patriotism and national pride were the order of the day. Songs with anti-communist and royalist themes, dating from World War II and firmly underground during Tito's socialist era, were resurrected, and new ones were written along the same lines.

Turbo-folk was the natural development of this, adapting already existing commercial forms and combining them with neo-folk using the latest technology. Turbo-folk appropriated images of a consumer lifestyle, beats from Western dance music and traditional Serbian folk tunes. Unlike the obvious agitprop of neo-folk, turbo-folk was escapist and all about love and romance. Turbo-folk videos, which were shown endlessly on TV Pink and TV Palma during the 1990s, celebrated the glamour of the criminal elite, with beautiful, scantily clad women and a spirit of defiant optimism. Rather than condemn it or replace it with gentler neo-folk propaganda, Milošević actively encouraged the constant stream of turbo-folk on the airwaves during this period; in his own words, it 'eliminated alternatives'.

Although village brass bands have always been popular in rural Serbia the popularity of the films of Emir Kusturica, like *Underground* and *Time of the Gypsies* with their brass-band soundtracks has brought about an enormous revival of interest in the form and brought about a crossover influence between the Roma bands and ethnic Serb musicians. Prior to 1990, most Serb bands would try to shun any Roma influence but, increasingly, they are now embracing it. Nowadays, there are ethnic Serb bands from Šumadija playing a very Roma-influenced repertoire, while ensembles of non-Slav brass players from as far away as Toronto or New York are producing *ćoček* music that is authentic enough to be warmly applauded at Guča.

Unlike the Roma tradition, other musical experiments that have fused Serbia's folk music with other forms have not always been as successful. In the Milošević years, a new musical hybrid raised its ugly head to attain large-scale popularity. This was so-called **turbo-folk**, a noisy dance music characterised by deeply sentimental lyrics sung by pneumatic, scantily clad young women to sugary folk tunes backed by industrial-strength techno rhythms. If the mere idea of this sounds bad, then the reality is worse. Imagine the Prodigy performing 'Edelweiss' with a Julie Andrews vocal, then throw in the worst sentimental excesses of bad country and western to complete the picture. In the wild, wartime days of the 1990s, the jackhammer rhythms of turbo-folk provided a soundtrack for the 'live today–die tomorrow' lifestyles of Belgrade's shady underworld of racketeers, hoodlums, gun-runners, gangsters, hardline nationalists and paramilitary Rambo figures. The spirit of turbo-folk is that of a sort of Balkan version of gangster rap – but without the rap. One of the most famous and, it has to be said, the best, singers in the turbo-folk tradition is Svetlana Raznjatović, better known to her fans as Ceca, the widow of gunned-down gangster and militant nationalist Željko 'Arkan' Raznjatović. Although she is equally famous for her marriage, her good looks and her dodgy business associates, she is actually a talented singer. Ceca is still enormously popular in Serbia and has recently made something of a comeback following the embarrassment of a rather messy embezzlement charge.

In the field of Serbian **rock music** there is perhaps less cause for excitement. During the 1970s and 1980s Yugoslavia produced many competent, if somewhat derivative, rock groups whose musical influences clearly came from the other side of the Atlantic. With sanctions, war in Croatia, Bosnia and Kosovo, and then the final indignity of NATO bombing, it is easy to see why a nation's youth might wish to look beyond the usual fertile ground of American rock and MTV for its influences. This is not to say that Western-influenced pop music stopped dead in its tracks in the 1990s, as since that time some highly individualistic (and politically attuned) groups like Darkwood Dub and Eyesburn have emerged, as well as Celtic music oddities like the Orthodox Celts, Belgrade's answer to the Pogues. Enthusiasm for boy bands is thankfully absent from the scene; currently, the biggest foreign names in Serbia are performers like Roni Size, Asian Dub Foundation, Goldie, Tricky, Morcheeba and Primal Scream.

Serbia has a small but enthusiastic **jazz** scene that rarely ventures beyond the city limits of Belgrade or Novi Sad. That being said, the standard of musicianship is usually very good and it is well worth attending one of Belgrade's jazz clubs if you are not allergic to cigarette smoke or late nights. A jazz artist who attempts to combine jazz and traditional music in a sort of Balkan jazz-folk **fusion** is saxophonist Jovan Maljoković. Another fusion artist in a very different vein is Boris Kovač from Novi Sad. What he and his Ladaaba Orchestra play is not folk, or jazz, or rock but something akin to Balkan *tango*, a highly theatrical chamber music that Kovač likens to a palm court orchestra playing a gig on the night before the apocalypse.

Practical Information

WHEN TO VISIT

Serbia has a climate similar to the rest of southeast Europe, although it rarely gets as hot as Greece during the summer months or as cold as Romania in winter. Unless a skiing vacation is planned, winter is not a good time to visit: it will be cold and wet, perhaps snowing, and many of Serbia's less expensive hotels have inadequate heating. The summer months are rarely oppressively hot, although it can become quite sticky in Belgrade during the dog days of August.

Generally speaking, the best time to visit is anytime between late spring and early autumn. Depending on personal interests, it is a good idea to try and make your visit coincide with particular events that are taking place throughout the country ie: for music fans this might be during the Exit Festival (Pop and Rock) that is held in Novi Sad during July, the Dragačevo Trumpet Festival (Gypsy brass bands, world music) that takes place at Guča in western Serbia every August, or the Belgrade Music Festival – BEMUS (Classical) that is hosted by the capital in October. Alternatively, you may wish to time your visit to coincide with religious and cultural celebrations like Orthodox Easter, which can be an enjoyable time to visit. Overall, May, June and September are probably the most perfect months, although May and June are also marginally the wettest. In the countryside, early to mid October can be a delight, still reasonably warm but with golden autumn colours, and this is a superb time for energetic outdoor activities like walking or cycling. Hotel accommodation and public transport can be at a premium at certain times of year like Easter, or during the Belgrade Book Fair in October, but as a rule this presents few problems. The one thing that you can be certain of, for the time being at least, is that wherever you go and whenever you choose to visit Serbia, it will not be overrun with tourists. Enjoy this while it lasts.

PUBLIC HOLIDAYS AND FESTIVALS

January 1	New Year's Day
January 7	Orthodox Christmas Day
February 15	Statehood Day
May 1 and 2	Labour Days
April/May	Orthodox Easter
	(2005: Good Friday, April 29 – Easter Monday, May 2
	2006: Good Friday, April 21 – Easter Monday, April 24
	2007: Good Friday, April 6 – Easter Monday, April 9)

The following are also considered to be holidays but are working days:

January 27	St Sava's Day
April 27	Statehood Day
May 9	Victory Day
June 28	St Vitus's Day

Individual towns and cities have their own *slava* day, which is treated as a holiday.

The most commonly celebrated *slava*s are those of St Nicholas (*Nikoljdan*) on December 19, St George (*Đurđevdan*) on May 6, St John the Baptist (*Jovanjdan*) on January 20 and St Archangel Michael (*Arandjelovdan*) on November 21. *Đurđevdan* is of particular importance to Serbia's Roma and Vlach communities and St Vitus's Day on June 28, being the anniversary of the Battle of Kosovo, is a meaningful date for many Serbs, especially those with strong nationalist concerns.

In rural areas, country fairs are held during traditional feast days (*zavetina*) at certain times of year, the most popular time being at Whitsun and on Ascension Day (*Spasovdan*), which occurs 40 days after Easter.

HIGHLIGHTS

Serbia has always been overlooked by visitors to the southeastern Europe region; this was even the case during the heyday of Yugoslav tourism in the 1970s and 1980s. It is difficult to understand why this is, as the country has plenty to offer: an interesting, although admittedly not beautiful, capital city that boasts a rich cultural life, with excellent restaurants and nightlife; quiet, rural market towns that still cling to traditional ways; and a countryside that is characterised by lush green hills and forested mountains, with age-old monasteries hidden away in remote valleys. Perhaps the current lack of foreign visitors should be seen as an advantage as, in this case, low tourist numbers equate to low prices. Serbia remains one of the cheapest countries in Europe, apart from hotel prices, which are about average for the region. The people are friendly; the food is good, wholesome and organic for the most part, due to the lack of fertilisers and pesticides used. Public transport connections are reasonable too, although a car is useful for visiting more out of the way places like some of the monasteries. Compared with other destinations in the same region, Serbia is currently untouched by the crowds, high prices and indifferent service that are starting to characterise parts of the Adriatic coast. Put simply, now is a great time to visit.

Belgrade is worth at least a couple of days if your interests are cultural and historical; if you are of a more hedonistic persuasion then you will need longer, as Belgrade has one of the best restaurant, nightclub and music scenes in all of southeast Europe. Much the same can be said of Novi Sad too, which offers a slightly more refined and second-city version of the same, although the city can easily be visited as a long day trip from the capital. Other Serbia highlights might include a trip along the Danube to see Golubac Castle, the archaeological finds at Lepenski Vir and the Iron Gates at Đerdap. Further options might be a monastery tour to see some of Serbia's hidden gems like Studenica or Manasija; a tour of some Hungarian minority towns in Vojvodina like Subotica and Sombor with their ornate secessionist architecture; or hiking among the forested hills of Zlatibor or Kopaonik national parks. Railway enthusiasts will enjoy taking part in one of Belgrade's summer steam excursions or travelling along the intriguing 'Šargan Eight' line. In the south, the cities of Novi Pazar and Niš have a reasonable amount to see and both can serve as good bases for visiting the hinterland. Old Turkish towns like Pirot or Vranje are also worthy of a day's visit. As an alternative to touring the country, there is also much to be said for basing oneself in Belgrade for the duration of a visit, especially if it is a fairly short one – Serbia is not a large country and many places of interest can be reached by travelling just a few hours from the capital.

TOURIST INFORMATION

The **National Tourist Office of Serbia** (NTOS) have their headquarters at Dečanska 8, 11000 Belgrade (tel/fax: 3342 521, 3232 685, 322 1068; email: ntos@yubc.net). They have an informative website at www.serbia-tourism.org. Their main branch in **Belgrade** is in the underpass by the Albania Tower at the bottom end of Knez Mihaila, and also at Knez Mihaila 18. They also have a counter for information in the International Arrivals lounge at Belgrade Surcin Airport (tel: 601 555). NTOS have information centres at many of the land border crossings into Serbia: from Hungary at Bački Breg, Kelebija and Horgoš; from Romania at Vatin and Kaluđerovo; from Macedonia at Preševo; from Croatia at Batrovci and Bezdan; from Bosnia-Herzegovina at Sremska Rača, Badovinci, Trbušnica and Mali Zvornik. NTOS are normally helpful and courteous, answering enquiries and offering a range of maps and illustrated booklets.

Many regional towns and cities have their own tourist office and/or information websites, which are referred to in the appropriate chapter.

Most NTOS offices outside Serbia are associated with JAT Airlines, the national carrier.

UK 7, Dering St, London W1R 9AB; tel: 020 7629 2007, 7409 1319, 7495 1323; fax: 0207 629 6500; email: sales@jatlondon.com

Rest of Europe
Austria Kruger Strasse 2/7, 1010 Vienna; tel: +431 512 3657, 512 3658, 512 3659; fax: +431 512 3657; email: jat@vienna.at

France 11 Rue Vignon, Paris 75008; tel: +33 1 42 66 32 39, 66 32 57; fax: +33 1 42 68 03 89

Germany Kurfuerstenstrasse 126/II, 10785 Berlin, Room 414; tel: +49 30 213 2003, 217 7362; fax: +49 30 218 5514; email: jat-berlin@t-online.de. Hochstrasse 48/1, 60313 Frankfurt/M; tel: +49 69 20 756, 20 956; fax: +49 69 284 263; email: jatfrankfurt@aol.com

Greece Voucouretiou 4, 10654 Athens; tel: +30 1 322 8067, 322 6372, 327 6492, 322 3675, 323 6492; fax: +30 1 322 6653; email: JAT-Athens@otenet.gr

Israel 2, Rothschild Bd, Tel Aviv; tel: +9 723 516 95 50; fax: +9 723 516 95 51

Italy Via Pantano 2/III, Milan; tel: +39 02 866 859; fax: +39 02 865 271

Russia Kuznjecki Most 3, Moscow; tel: +70 95 921 2846, 928 2101; fax: +70 95 292 3857

Switzerland Limmata Vai 6 2/II, 8001 Zurich; tel: +41 1 258 8787; fax: +41 1 258 8788

TOUR OPERATORS
UK
This is currently an area of development in which operators will hopefully involve themselves more in the next few years. For the time being, there is a rather limited choice of organised tours that visit Serbia.

Balkan Holidays Ltd Sofia House, 19 Conduit St, London W5 2BH; tel (free): 0500 245 165 for brochure request, 0845 130 1114 for reservations; email: res@balkanholidays.co.uk; www.balkanholidays.co.uk. Organises 1-week skiing holidays based in Kopaonik between December and March. For the time being, flights are to Belgrade, then a long coach transfer to the resort. With the recent reopening of the airport at Niš it is likely that this will soon be used in preference over Belgrade, resulting in a much shorter transfer time. Costs are between £409 and £719 per person for half-board depending on the time of the season and the standard of accommodation chosen. No single supplements are charged. The prices for ski-lift passes and ski hire are comparatively inexpensive when compared with those paid in the more traditional resorts of France, Italy or Switzerland.

Regent Holidays 15 John St, Bristol BS1 2HR; tel: 0117 921 1711; fax: 0117 925 4866; email: regent@regent-holidays.co.uk; www.regent-holidays.co.uk. Organises 3-day city breaks to Belgrade throughout the year. Costs are between £369 and £485 per person for flights, hotel and breakfast. Transfers from the airport to hotel are £40 extra.

Thomson Ski Tel: 0870 888 0254; email: info@thomson-ski.co.uk. This company added winter ski packages to Kopaonik to their catalogue in the 2004/5 season, offering accommodation in a choice of 2-, 3- or 4-star hotels at the resort and flights from Gatwick airport to Belgrade.

US

In the United States, specialised tours with an interest in folklore are arranged every year by Cheryl Spasojević, a Serbian-speaking American, who leads a two-week tour to Serbia each summer. The tour includes a three-day folk-dance camp and visits to folk festivals, village museums and traditional craft centres. She can be contacted at:

Folklore Treasures of Serbia c/o Cheryl Spasojević, 17626 68th Av West, Edmunds, WA 98026-5636; tel: (425) 745 1785 in winter, or at Cheryl Spasojević, Selo Vuckovica, 34240 ZP Knic, Serbia; tel: (034) 591 306; email: cspaso@eunet.yu after March 2.

General Tours 53 Summer St, Keene, New Hampshire 03431; tel: 1 800 221 2216; fax: 603 357 4548; email: info@generaltours.com; www.generaltours.com. Visit Serbia briefly (twice) on their deluxe Eastern European Odyssey Cruise, which sails from along the Danube from Budapest to the Black Sea at Constanta then back to Vienna. Prices are from US$3,159 including flights from the United States.

Grand Circle Travel Tel (free): 1 800 321 2835; email: online@gct.com. Offers a 13-day Danube cruise to the Black Sea via Serbia from May to October that call in at Belgrade and Novi Sad. Prices start at US$1,995.

Kutrubes Travel 328 Tremont St, Boston, MA 02116; tel: 1 800 878 8566, 617 426 5668; fax: 617 426 3196; email: adventures@kutrubestravel.com; www.kutrubestravel.com. Organises 7-day tours to Serbia for US$860 per person double occupancy, based on a group of 6 travellers; for a group of 4, it is US$985 per person; for 2, US$1,215. This price includes tour service, bed and breakfast and transfers but excludes air fares from the United States. They can also arrange individualised custom tours.

Canada

Adria Travel 828 Notre Dame Av, Winnipeg, Manitoba R3E OM5; tel: 204 982 1200; email: info@adriatravel.ca. Have a Serbia monastery tour among their various Balkan offerings.

Belgium

Transnico International Av Montjoie, 114-B-1180 Brussels; tel: +32 2 3444690; fax: +32 2 3465665; email: transnico.international.group@skynet.be; www.transnico.com. Train enthusiasts may be interested in the steam railway tours that are offered in Serbia and Kosovo each year.

Germany

FarRail Tours Email: mail@farrail.com; www.farrail.net. Organises trips to visit steam railways and tramways of Serbia and Bosnia-Herzegovina.

Intra Express Hobby-und-Studienreissen GmbH, Burgherrenstrasse 2, D-12101 Berlin; tel: +4930 785 3391; fax: +4930 785 9208; email: intraex@t-online.de. Run week-long tours to visit tramways in Croatia, Bosnia and Belgrade in the summer. They require groups of a minimum of 30 participants. The cost is around €900 per person.

Serbia

Putnik is the state tourist agency that as well as booking tickets can organise excursions and longer tours. They arrange ski accommodation packages at Kopaonik from January to March, and at Tara and Zlatibor between December and March. Their main Belgrade office is at Dragoslava Jovanovića 1; tel: 3232 911, 3230 699, 3240 022; fax: 3342 278, with another branch at Terazije 27; tel: 3232 473. The company has recently been bought by a Serbian-American who is keen on modernising the company.

Belgrade Sightseeing is a tour guide service run by Branko Rabotić MA, a Belgrade-based polymath, who offers a wide range of year-round itineraries, from a three-hour walking tour of the capital to a week-long monastery tour of central

Serbia. Prices are available on request but should be in the order of €80 and up for the Belgrade Highlights Tour, which includes a Belgrade sightseeing tour by car and a walking tour; from €200 for the Belgrade Treasures Tour, which is a five-day/four-night package that includes two Belgrade walking tours and a full-day tour of Vojvodina; and start at €300 for a seven-day Belgrade and Serbia Explorer Tour that includes Belgrade sightseeing and walking tours, a full-day Vojvodina tour, a full-day tour to Manasija and Ravanica monasteries and a full-day tour to Topola and Oplenac. All tours include guide services, transport and transfers from the airport but not accommodation or meals. Mr Rabotić is an experienced and knowledgeable guide who speaks Serbian, English and Greek. In addition, Belgrade Sightseeing also provides hotel booking and airport transfer services. The website is also very informative, with Serbian-language and hotel-booking links. Contact details: Mr Branko Rabotić MA, 11000 Belgrade, 14 Decembra 33; tel/fax: 446 1153; GSM (+38163) 854 2648 (calls to GSM from inside Serbia 063 854 2648); email: rabotic@EUnet.yu; www.rabotic.tripod.com.

Hiking and bicycling trips of between two and seven days in the mountains of southeast Serbia can be organised by **ACE Cycling and Mountaineering Centre** (B Krsmanovica 51/8, 18000 Niš; tel/fax: 64 2476 311; mobile: 64 1847 287; email: info@ace-adventurecentre.com). They have several standard packages available: a seven-day hiking and biking trip in southeast Serbia that includes hiking to the highest peaks of the Stara Planina and Suva Planina ranges and cycling along quiet, country roads, or a seven-day cycling tour of monasteries in central Serbia. Both are fully supported and cost around €450 per person for double occupancy, which includes six nights half-board in a three-star hotel, five lunches, transportation from Belgrade, bicycle use and the service of two guides. They also offer a range of weekend cycling and hiking tours in the Niš region, and can tailor bespoke tours to customers' requirements.

Village@dventure (email: village@ptt.yu; www.villageadventure.co.yu) specialise in running rural tourism projects in small villages in the Mt Zlatibor region of western Serbia and the Šumadija region of central Serbia. They offer a hands-on approach where guests are invited to lend a hand mowing the hay or milking the cows if they wish, or to simply enjoy the bucolic surroundings and fresh farm produce. The appeal is that of a quiet rural retreat where guests can immerse themselves in traditional country ways in an unspoiled natural environment. All of the villages are good bases for walking. Depending on the accommodation chosen and the size of the group, it costs between €120 and €200 per person for bed and breakfast and between €150 and €220 for full board for a week's stay; for a fortnight, it is between €200 and €260 for bed and breakfast and between €240 and €300 for full board. This includes airport transfers from Belgrade. They can also arrange hunting and fishing trips and accommodation on a stud farm.

Novi Sad-based **Magelan Corporation** (tel: +381 21 420 680, +381 21 424 524; email: office@magelancorp.co.yu; www.magelancorp.co.yu) offer a range of services and tours, from one-day Fruška Gora excursions to 11-day tours of Serbia and the Montenegrin coast. Their four-day eco-adventure tours in Vojvodina require a minimum of six participants and cost from €335 per person. Magelan Corporation also organise birdwatching excursions under the auspices of knowledgeable Serbian ornithologist Dragan Simić. These range from one-day visits to the Čarska Bara wetlands, Gornje Podunavlje alluvial forest, Delibalto Sands or Dubovac wetlands to eight- or ten-day tours that take in a wide range of habitats: spring migration tours that run in late April, autumn migration tours in mid August, and breeding season tours from late May to June. Costs range from between €350 and €450 per person, which includes full-board accommodation for the duration of the trip, transport and the services of an English-speaking guide.

In the town of Valjevo, 100km southwest of Belgrade, the **Amala Summer School** offers residential courses in Roma and Serbian music, dance and language during July and August. Seven-, ten- and 14-day courses are offered, in which participants are totally immersed in Serbian and Roma culture, staying in a Serbian–Roma household, eating traditional food and witnessing traditional daily life. Professional music teachers and performers conduct daily lessons for voice, violin, accordion, percussion and bass, and excursions are made to family celebrations in nearby villages. Serbian language and dance are taught at a variety of levels, while the Roma language classes are designed primarily for beginners. The cost for a week's dance or language tuition is €550 or €950 for a fortnight; for music or singing classes, €600 for a week, €1,050 for a fortnight. Combinations of dance, music and language study are also possible at a slightly higher price. The cost covers lessons, accommodation, traditional home-made food and visits to Roma weddings or other celebrations, as well as transportation from Belgrade and back. Optional excursions beyond the immediate area are available at weekends. To secure a place it is necessary to complete the application on the Amala website and pay a non-refundable deposit of €150 on acceptance. Details at www.galbeno.co.yu; enquiries can be made to amala@galbeno.co.yu.

RED TAPE

The good news is, as of May 31 2003, most foreign visitors no longer require visas for a short stay in the country. Passport holders of the following countries may stay in Serbia for a period up to **90 days without the requirement of a visa**: Andorra, Argentina, Armenia, Australia, Austria, Azerbaijan, Belgium, Bolivia, Canada, Chile, China (for purposes of business only), Costa Rica, Croatia, Cuba, Cyprus, Czech Republic, Denmark, Ecuador, Egypt (diplomatic passports only), Estonia, Finland, France, Georgia (for business purposes), Germany, Greece, Guinea, Iceland, Ireland, Israel, Italy, Kyrgyzstan (for business), Latvia, Liechtenstein, Lithuania, Luxembourg, Malta, Mexico (180 days), Monaco, Mongolia (for business), Netherlands, New Zealand, North Korea (for business), Norway, Peru, Poland, Portugal, Russian Federation (for business), San Marino, Seychelles, Singapore, Slovakia, Slovenia, South Korea, Spain, Sweden, Switzerland, Tajikistan (for business), Tunisia, Turkmenistan (for business), United Kingdom, United States of America and Vatican City.

The following are granted **30 days visa-free** stay in Serbia: Albania, Belarus, Bosnia-Herzegovina, Bulgaria, Hungary, Macedonia (60 days), Romania and Turkey (for diplomatic, special and official passports only).

For those requiring a visa, an application should be made at one of Serbia's foreign embassies where the applicant will be required to produce a valid passport, a letter of introduction (this can be organised through a Serbian tourist agency or a business contact), a return ticket, proof of funds and evidence of medical cover for the duration of the stay.

Funds in excess of €2,000 should be declared on arrival in the country as, in theory at least, failure to do this could result in confiscation on leaving Serbia.

EMBASSIES OF SERBIA AND MONTENEGRO ABROAD

United Kingdom 28 Belgrave Sq, London SW1X 8QB; tel: +44(0)20 7235 9049; fax: +44(0)20 7235 7092; email: londre@jugisek.demom.co.uk; www.yugoslavembassy.org.uk
United States of America 2134 Kalorama Rd, NW Washington, DC 20008; tel: +1 (1) 202 332 0333; fax: +1 (1) 202 332 3933, 332 5974; email: info@yuembusa.org; www.yuembusa.org
Albania Skender Beg Building 8/3-II, Tirana; tel: +35542 23 042, 232 091; fax: +35542 32 089; email: ambatira@icc-al.org

Australia 4 Bulwarra Cl, O'Malley, ACT 2606, Canberra; tel: +61(0)2 6290 2630, 6290 2948; fax: +61(0)2 6290 2631; email: yuembau@ozemail.com.au

Austria Rennweg 3, 1030 Wien; tel: +431 713 2595, 713 2596, 712 1205; fax: +431 713 2597; email: ambasada@scg-diplomat.at; www.scg-diplomat.at

Belgium Av Emile de Mot 11, 1000 Bruxelles; tel: +322 647 5781, 647 2652, 647 2651, 649 6545, 649 8349; fax: +322 647 2941; email: ambaserbiemontenegro@skynet.be

Bosnia-Herzegovina Obala Marka Dizdara 3a, 71000 Sarajevo; tel: +38733 260 090, 260 080; fax: +38733 221 469; email: yugoamba@bih.net.ba

Bulgaria Veliko Trnovo 3, 1504 Sofia; tel: +3592 946 1635, 946 1633, 946 1636; fax: +3592 946 1059; email: ambasada-scg-sofija@infotl.bg

Canada 17 Blackburn Av, Ottowa, Ontario K1N 8A2; tel: +1(0)613 233 6289, 233 6280, 565 9263; fax: +1(0)613 233 7850; email: diplomat@yuemb.ca; www.yuemb.ca

Croatia Pantovcak 245, Zagreb; tel: +3851 457 9067, 457 9068, 4573 330, 4573 334; fax: +3851 457 3338; email: mailto:ambasada@ambasada-srj.hr

France 54 Rue de la Faisanderie, 75116 Paris; tel: +33(0)1 4072 2424, 4072 2410; fax: +33(0)1 4072 2411, 4072 2423; email: ambasadapariz@wanadoo.fr

Germany Taubert Strasse 18, D-1 4193 Berlin; tel: +49(0)30 895 7700, 895 770222; fax: +49(0)30 825 2206; email: info@botschaft-smg.de

Hungary Dozsa Gyorgy ut 92/b, H-1068 Budapest VI; tel: +361 322 9838, 342 8512, 352 8847, 322 1436, 322 1437; fax: +361 322 1438, 352 8846; email: ambjubp@mail.datanet.hu

Israel 10 Bodenheimer St, 62008 Tel Aviv; tel: +972(0)3 604 5535; fax: +972(0)3 604 9456

Italy Via dei Monti Parioli 20, 00197 Roma; tel: +3906 320 0796, 320 0890, 320 0805, 320 0959; fax: +3906 320 0868; email: amb.jug@flashnet.it

Japan 4724 Kitashinagawa, Shinagawa-ku, Tokyo; tel: +81(0)3 3447 3571, 3447 3572; fax: +81(0)3 3447 3573; email: embassy@embassy-serbia-montenegro.jp

Macedonia St Pitu Guli 8, Skopje; tel: +3892 3129 298, 3131 299, 3128 422, 3129 305; fax: +3892 3129 427, 3131 428; email: yuamb@unet.com.mk

Netherlands Groot Hertoginnelaan 30, 2517 EG The Hague; tel: +70 363 2397, 363 2393, 363 6800; fax: +70 360 2421; email: yuambanl@bart.nl; www.users.bart.nl/~yuambanl

Romania Calea Dorobantilor Nr34, Bucarest; tel: +4021 211 9871, 211 9872, 211 9873; fax: +4021 210 0175; email: ambiug@ines.ro

Russian Federation Mosfiljmovskaja 46, R–119285 Moscow; tel: +7(8)095 147 4106, 147 9008, 147 4105, 147 4108; fax: +7(8)095 937 9615, 147 4104; email: mailto:ambasada@aha.ru

Slovenia Slomskova 1, 1000 Ljubljana; tel: +3861 438 0111, 438 0110; fax: 1386 434 2688, 434 2689; email: ambasada.scg.ljubljana@siol.net

South Africa 163 Marais St, Brooklyn 0181, PO Box 13026 Hatfield 0028, Pretoria; tel: +2712 460 5626, 460 6103, 346 4139, 246 6191; fax: +2712 460 6003; email: info@sgembassy.org.za; www.sgembassy.org.za

Spain Calle de Velasquez 162, E-28002 Madrid; tel: +3491 563 5045, 563 5046, 564 2250, 562 6040; fax: +3491 563 0440; email: Madrid@embajada-yugoslavia.es; www.embajada-yugoslavia.es

Switzerland Seminarstrasse 5, CH-3006 Bern; tel: +4131 352 6353, 352 6354, 352 6355; fax: +4131 351 4474; email: info@yuamb.ch; www.yuamb.ch

Turkey Paris Caddesi 47, PK28 Kavaklidere, TR-Ankara; tel: +90312 426 0236, 426 2432; fax: +90312 427 8345; email: yugoslav@tr.net

Registration with police

All foreigners visiting Serbia are obliged to be registered with the police. This is normally done automatically by hotels on checking in. You will be registered anew each time you change hotels and given a registration card when you check out. If you are staying somewhere privately, or camping, then it is up to you or your hosts to ensure that you are registered with the police within 12 hours of arrival and to report any subsequent change of address within 24 hours. This may seem a mere formality but it is important to do so, as you may be asked to provide the necessary registration documents when you leave Serbia.

This requirement is likely to change in the near future. There was talk of compulsory registration with the police being relaxed in 2004 but at the time of writing no one seemed very certain about this and hotels were still providing the documentation.

Foreign embassies in Serbia

A list of these is given in the *Belgrade* chapter.

GETTING THERE AND AWAY
By air

Several airlines serve Belgrade directly. These include the national carrier JAT Airways, British Airways, Air France, Alitalia, Austrian Airlines, ČSA Czech Airlines, KLM, Lufthansa, Malev, Olympic Airways, Swiss and Turkish Airlines. The low-cost airline Snowflake also has regular flights from Denmark. At Belgrade's Surcin Airport, Terminal 2 deals with all international traffic, with domestic flights using Terminal 1. Although Belgrade handles nearly all of Serbia's international traffic, Niš Airport also has a limited number of international flights and is looking to expand in the near future.

From the UK

There are direct flights to Belgrade with JAT from Heathrow every day except Monday, and British Airways, which flies to Belgrade five times a week with flights that leave Heathrow in the morning to conveniently arrive in Belgrade about midday. The return flight leaves early afternoon to arrive at Heathrow by mid afternoon. There are also BA flights three times a week between London Gatwick and Priština in Kosovo. The best prices for both BA and JAT are from about £140 return including tax, although it may be difficult to get this price during busy holiday periods or at short notice. BA flights can be booked online at www.ba.com. JAT also has two websites that give information on flight times and prices but which do not permit online booking: www.jat.com and its London-based site www.jatlondon.com. One agent in London who deals exclusively with flights to the Balkans is Nada Parausić-Martinez at Hipnos Travel, 116c Lots Road, London SW10 0RJ; tel/fax: 020 7349 9758; email: offers@hipnos.com.

Fom Europe

JAT has direct flights that connect Belgrade with Amsterdam, Athens, Banja Luka, Berlin, Brussels, Copenhagen, Düsseldorf, Frankfurt, Göteborg, Hamburg, Hanover, Istanbul, Kiev, Larnaca, Ljubljana, London, Malta, Munich, Moscow, Paris, Prague, Sarajevo, Skopje, Sofia, St Petersburg, Stockholm, Trieste, Vienna, Warsaw and Zurich. The best-connected of these are Paris with 15 flights a week, Skopje with 13 and Zurich with 22 weekly connections.

There are also limited services to the Middle East, with Beirut, Cairo, Damascus, Tel Aviv, Tripoli and Tunis all being served by JAT. In a category all of their own, which cannot adequately be described as being either domestic or international destinations, there are six flights a day from Belgrade to Podgorica and Tivat with JAT and Montenegro Airlines that link Montenegro with the capital.

From the US

There is a direct flight to Belgrade from New York with JAT that flies overnight twice a week on Thursday and Saturday evenings. Other than this, it is necessary to connect a transatlantic flight in one of the European hubs like London, Paris or

Amsterdam. Air fares from the east coast of the United States to Belgrade start at about US$600 return.

For international flights, Belgrade Airport charges all adult passengers a departure tax of 800din, although this is usually included in the ticket price with JAT services. This tax applies even in transit. Flights to Montenegro that go via Belgrade are charged the domestic tariff of 200din or €3, but on the return journey passengers must pay the international rate of 800din or €11.

To save money, it is possible to combine a cheap budget airline flight with a train or bus journey through to Serbia. For example, by taking a cut-price Ryanair flight to Trieste in Italy, or Graz or Klagenfürt in Austria, and then continuing the journey through Slovenia and Croatia, or Hungary, by train or bus. It is unlikely that great savings will be made by doing this, especially if sleepers need to be booked, but it is a good way of seeing more of the region. Budget flights to eastern Europe continue to fly closer and closer to Serbia but, for the time being at least, do not quite reach it. However, with the introduction of inexpensive easyJet flights to both Budapest and Ljubljana, a combined flight and overland option has become all the more feasible.

By train

To travel all the way to Serbia by train from Britain requires time, money and planning. It is actually cheaper to fly, but the following may appeal to rail buffs. The first stage is to take the 12.09 Eurostar from London Waterloo to Paris Gare du Nord, arriving at 15.59. This costs from £59 return (one-way fares are actually more expensive!). At Paris Gare du Nord you then walk to the nearby Gare de l'Est and travel overnight on the 'Orient Express' (the real one, not the tourist train), which leaves Paris at 17.47 and arrives Vienna at 08.30. This section of the journey costs from £120 single, £240 return for a bed in a six-berth couchette, the cheapest option. From Vienna you take the 'Avala' straight through to Belgrade, which leaves Vienna at 10.07 and arrives in Belgrade at 20.15, costing approximately £60 one-way, £80 return. To book this, you can use a number of UK agencies, like Deutsch Bahn's UK office (tel: 0870 243 5363) or Rail Europe (tel: 0870 5848 848).

A better bet is to travel by rail to Serbia from somewhere rather nearer, perhaps in combination with a low-budget flight. Belgrade can be reached directly by train from all of the surrounding countries, as well as some beyond. From Zagreb the fare is about €14, and the journey takes six hours. From Venice via Zagreb the overnight journey to Belgrade costs €104, including a €13 couchette supplement. It is possible to save €30 by buying a ticket from Venice–Zagreb and then getting off when the train arrives in Zagreb in the early morning to buy a fresh ticket through to Belgrade. There is plenty of time to do this as the train remains in Zagreb station for almost an hour as the carriages are split between those that will go on to Budapest and those that continue to Belgrade, but it does mean that you must forsake an early morning lie-in in your couchette. The overnight express leaves Venice about 21.00, reaches the Slovenian border about midnight, the Croatian border about 04.00, and arrives in Zagreb just after 05.00. It finally reaches Belgrade about 12.30. Direct services are also available from Ljubljana: an overnight service leaves Ljubljana about 21.00 and arrives in Belgrade early the next morning.

Rail connections are also good with Budapest to the north, and go via Novi Sad, Subotica and the Hungarian border at Horgoš, although the journey is not really long enough to be convenient for an overnighter. Direct routes also exist between Greece, Romania, Turkey, Macedonia and Bulgaria and Belgrade, although the railway route between Sarajevo and Belgrade is rather circuitous and it is generally better to travel between Bosnia-Herzegovina and Serbia by bus. From Montenegro, there is a convenient overnight service between Bar and Belgrade by way of the Montenegrin capital, Podgorica. This journey can also be done during the daytime to make the most of the stunning scenery along the way.

By bus

There are direct bus routes to Serbia from all over western and northern Europe. For the longer journeys, given the cost and the time involved, flying is probably a more attractive option. **Eurolines**, which in Serbia are operated by the **Lasta** bus company (www.lasta.co.yu), run services between Serbia and Austria, Benelux, Bosnia-Herzegovina (and Republika Srbska), Croatia, Czech Republic, Denmark, France, Germany, Greece, Hungary, Macedonia, Slovakia, Slovenia, Sweden and Switzerland. Another company, **Srbija Tours International** (Lička 3, Belgrade; tel: 3619 576, 3611 576, 3614 545; fax: 3618 227; email: office@srbija-tours.com) operates services to various destinations in Germany. Some sample fare and frequencies for Lasta-Eurolines are given below.

From Germany
Munich–Belgrade: 8 times a week, €55 one-way, €75 return
Berlin–Belgrade: 6 times a week, €95 one-way, €170 return
Frankfurt–Belgrade: 3 times a week, €90 one-way, €150 return

From France
Paris–Belgrade: twice weekly, €97 one-way, €130 return
Lyon–Belgrade: twice weekly, €92 one-way, €120 return
Marseille–Belgrade: twice weekly, €107 one-way, €184 return

From Austria
Salzburg–Belgrade: twice weekly, €40 one-way, €65 return

From Benelux
Amsterdam–Belgrade: twice weekly, €118 one-way, €193 return
Brussels–Belgrade: twice weekly, €102 one-way, €174 return

From Bosnia-Herzegovina
Banja Luka–Belgrade: 7 daily, 17 Bosnian marks one-way

From Slovenia and Croatia
Ljubljana–Novi Sad: daily, €27 one-way, €37 return
Ljubljana–Belgrade: daily, €31 one-way, €44 return
Zagreb–Belgrade: daily €22 one-way, €38 return
Dubrovnik–Belgrade: 6 times a week €26 one-way, €45 return
Split–Belgrade: 6 times a week, €27 one-way, €45 return

From Scandinavia
Malmö–Belgrade: once a week, €114 one-way, €174 return
Göteborg–Belgrade: once a week, €120 one-way, €190 return
Göteborg–Kladovo: once a week, €125 one-way, €196 return
Copenhagen–Belgrade: once a week, €113 one-way, €199 return
Copenhagen–Kladovo: once a week, €126 one-way, €212 return

International bus tickets can be booked at various agents in the country of origin: in Germany, at any branch of Deutsch Touring; in France at the Eurolines bus stations, which in Paris is found at 28 Avenue General de Gaulle; tel: (01) 4972 5151, (01) 4972 5166; fax: (01) 4972 5161. In Sweden, at Agency 'Top Tourist', Helsingborg; tel: (042) 132 720, (010) 661 2290. In Croatia, at 'Otisak Tours', Put Plokite 57, Split; tel: (021) 524 852. In Slovenia, at 'Kompas-Hertz', Celoveska 206; tel: (061) 573 532. In Austria, at 'Blagus Reisen', Richard Strauss strasse 32, Vienna; tel: (1) 610 90. In Belgium, at 'Anjo Travel', Jos Reusenlei 46, Borsbek; tel: (3) 366 1666. The Lasta head office in Belgrade is at Železnička 2; tel: 625 740.

By ferry

Ferries from Bari to Bar operate an overnight service six days a week in summer, four in winter; from Ancona they run twice a week in summer, once in winter. Serbia is landlocked but a frequent ferry service operates between Ancona and Bari in southern Italy and Bar in Montenegro from where trains and buses are available to continue through to Serbia.

By private car

With Serbia's landlocked position surrounded by a total of seven other countries excluding Montenegro, it is little surprise that there are many options available if you are driving your own vehicle. From Hungary, there are **crossing points** at Bački Beg, Bezdan, Kelebija, Subotica and Horgoš, and from Romania at Srpska Crnja, Zrenjanin, Vatin, Vršac, Kaluđerovo, Bela Crkva, Đerdap and Kladovo. From Bulgaria, crossings exist at Mokrinje, Negotin, Vrška Čuka, Zaječar, Gradina, Dimitrovgrad, Strezimirovci, Ribarci and Bosilegrad; and from Macedonia at Prohor Pčinjski, Bujanovac, Preševo, Đeneral Janković, Globočica and Uroševac. Croatian border crossings are at Batrovci, Bačka Palanka, Bogojevo, Odaci, Bezdan, Sombor and Šid, while land crossings across to Bosnia-Herzegovina are at Sremska Rača, Sremska Mitrovica, Badovinci, Trbušnica, Loznica, Mali Zvornik, Ljubovija, Bajina Bašta, Kotroman, Čajetina, Uvac and Priboj. There are also border crossings between Albania and Kosovo at Čafa Pruit, Đakovica, Vrbinca and Prizren, but these cannot be recommended in the current climate. Some of the borders of Kosovo with Macedonia should also be treated with caution and referral made to the current FCO recommendations. All of the crossings listed are open around the clock.

Insurance policies from countries that have signed the Vehicle Insurance Convention are fully valid, but citizens of other countries must purchase an **insurance policy** when entering Serbia. Green Card cover can be issued for drivers of the following countries: Great Britain, Germany, France, Czech Republic, Norway, Turkey, Denmark, Romania, Croatia, Hungary, Bulgaria, Macedonia, Bosnia-Herzegovina, Slovakia, Moldova, Cyprus, Albania, Andorra, Greece, Spain, Austria, Iceland, Sweden, Belgium, Ireland, Switzerland, Finland, Italy, Netherlands, Luxembourg, Portugal and Tunisia. Drivers who have insurance policies issued in countries other than these will be required to purchase a short-term insurance policy of about €80 per month for a passenger car. Whatever your country of origin, it may be hard persuading immigration officials that a particular policy from any of these countries is valid for Serbia (it should state it clearly on your document, or you should have a covering letter) and they may try and insist that you purchase compulsory insurance anyway.

On entering Serbia, drivers with foreign registration plates have to pay motorway road tolls at a higher premium. Tolls are as follows: from Novi Sad to Belgrade on the E75, 360din; from Novi Sad to Subotica on the E75, 360din; for the section of the E75 from Belgrade to Niš, 930din; for the E75 from Niš to Leskovac, 210din; and on the E70 from Belgrade to Šid, on the Croatian border, 430din. These tolls may also be paid in euros.

In the case of breakdown or emergency, the roadside service of the **Automobile and Motorists Association of Serbia and Montenegro - AMS SCG** (formerly known as *Auto-moto savez Jugoslavije* – **AMSJ**) – is available for assistance and the towing or transport of damaged vehicles (telephone: 987). If a vehicle with foreign licence plates is abandoned, it should be reported to the local AMS SCG unit so that a certificate may be released. Similarly, if a foreign tourist enters Serbia driving a vehicle with damaged bodywork, they should receive a certificate from the officials at the border crossing that clearly evaluates the extent of the damage. In the case of a traffic accident, the **Traffic Police** (*Saobraćajna policija*) should be summoned (telephone: 92), who will then issue an accident report.

By river transport

Sadly, no international public river transport currently plies the Danube, Tisa or Sava waterways, although some international cruises transit Serbia en route to the Black Sea. For those in a position to pilot or charter their own boats – or paddle a canoe – international crossings exist along the river Tisa at Kanjiža and the Danube at Bezdan, coming from Hungary; at Veliko Gradište, Prahovo, Kladovo, Donji Milanovac, Tekija and Golubac, coming from Romania; at the ferry across the Danube from Croatia near Vajska and the internal river transport customs posts at Apatin, Novi Sad and Belgrade.

One interesting but very challenging option would be to join in on the **Tour International Danubien** that takes place every year along the river Danube, and which traverses Serbia as part of a 2,080km kayak journey from Ingolstadt, Germany to Silistra, Bulgaria. The tour leaves Germany in late June and arrives in Serbia at Apatin at the end of July before taking a further 16 days to cross the country. Daily stages are on average 43km long, allowing plenty of time for sightseeing in the towns passed by. The Canoe Federation of Serbia organises the tour within Serbia's boundaries and provides camping and free food along the way – ideal for a cheap, albeit highly energetic, holiday. It is also possible to canoe just sections of the route and there may even be a chance of finding a place in someone else's canoe for part of the tour. For information, tel: 354 1145; email: kajakss@eu.net.

HEALTH

Health insurance is highly recommended. As a foreigner, visitors do not have access to Serbia's public health system and most would doubtlessly prefer the services of a private clinic anyway. Many doctors who work in these private clinics will have been educated abroad and thus able to speak English – a great comfort in times of illness. Also, the standard of care in most private clinics is reasonably high. Some medications may not be as freely available as at home, and so it is important that the visitor brings along a sufficient supply of any necessary medication that they are dependent upon.

On the whole, Serbia is a healthy place; the greatest health danger that visitors are likely to encounter is probably an unacceptable degree of passive smoking in public places.

The following immunisations are recommended, depending on the nature of a visit. In all cases, these are of low to moderate risk, and some only really apply to extended visits to more remote areas of the country. If you are planning an extended stay it is wise to visit your doctor or a reputable travel clinic at least four weeks before travel.

Routinely you should be up to date with tetanus and diphtheria, which is now given as a combined vaccine that lasts for ten years. Hepatitis A vaccine (eg: Havrix Monodose, Avaxim) is also recommended as standard. A single dose gives protection for a year. This can be extended for up to 25 years by having a follow up booster dose of vaccine.

Other vaccines are only recommended for trips of one month or more. These are typhoid, polio, rabies and hepatitis B. The latter two vaccines are compromised of three doses that can be given over 21 days if time is short.

Travellers wishing to visit more rural parts of Serbia from late spring to autumn should take precautions against tick-borne encephalitis. This disease, as the name suggests, is spread by the bites of ticks that live in long grass and the branches of overhanging trees. Wearing long trousers tucked into boots, hats and applying tick repellents can all help. Likewise, checking for ticks after forays into grassy areas is sensible. Any ticks should be carefully removed with tweezers avoiding damage to the mouth part. Medical help should always be sought as soon as possible even if the tick is safely removed. Vaccine stocks in the UK are scarce, but if available should be taken if advised by a doctor. The course is comprised of three doses that can be given over 14 days. Receiving vaccination does not mean that you should not go for medical help in the event of being bitten.

There is concern in some circles about the use of **depleted uranium** in Kosovo and Serbia during the recent conflicts. There is some evidence that its use leads to a greater incidence of leukaemia and other cancers. Whatever the reality of this is for the people who live here, visitors who visit Serbia for a short period have absolutely nothing to fear.

Up-to-date information on Serbia's current health concerns can be found at:

MASTA (Medical Advisory Service for Travellers Abroad) Keppel St, London WC1 7HT; tel: 09068 224100. This is a premium-line number, charged at 50p per minute.
Boots Travel clinics
The Department of Health in the UK
Centers for Disease Control 1600 Clifton Rd, Atlanta, GA 30333; tel: 877 FYI TRIP; 800 311 3435; www.cdc.gov/travel. This organisation is the central source of travel information in the USA. Each summer they publish the invaluable Health Information for International Travel which is available from the Division of Quarantine at the above address.

Food and drink
Most food in Serbia is healthy, organic and hygienically prepared. Meat is rarely served very rare, which minimises the risk of picking up parasites and developing intestinal complaints. Tap water is perfectly safe for consumption. Some of the home-made liquor that may be offered to the visitor in parts of rural Serbia should be treated with caution but to refuse it outright might appear rude.

SAFETY
This is an area where Serbia's perceived image as a lawless, mafia-controlled haven for unreconstructed war criminals needs to be addressed. The reality is in fact very different. Western war correspondents during the Yugoslav wars of the 1990s used to sardonically refer to Serbia as 'Mordor!', as if it were an unutterably dark and menacing state. However, the reality is a far cry from any goblin-infested land of despair. Even Serbia's largest city Belgrade feels very safe indeed when compared with London, Paris or New York. In fact, it seems the sort of city where anyone – young or old, male or female – can walk around safely at any time of day or night. The Western (British) disease of aggressive binge drinking does not seem to exist here; instead, the streets seem calm and civilised, with well-behaved young people crowding the pavements or drinking coffee at outdoor tables. If this all sounds too good to be true, the statistics bear it out: robbery and violent crime *are* rare, which is not to say that visitors should be complacent as opportunist thieves exist everywhere, and perhaps should be expected in a country that has suffered continual economic hardship for such a long period. As in any city, you should avoid seemingly deserted streets and parks late at night.

As long as you keep away from large public demonstrations, and avoid the few unfortunate areas where there are obvious ethnic tensions, Serbia is very safe indeed.

The UN-administered province of Kosovo fluctuates in terms of safety recommendations, and the divided community of Kosovska Mitrovica has always been a flashpoint best avoided (there is little to see there anyway), but even here during calmer times, the ongoing FCO advice to 'avoid unless a visit is essential' can appear a little overcautious. Nevertheless, the British FCO advice (at www.fco.gov.uk) should be consulted prior to any visit and its counsel taken seriously.

WHAT TO TAKE
A visit to Serbia does not require the same sort of preparation as a trip to the Amazon rainforest but a few hard-to-find items may prove useful. Any personal medication should be brought along, as it may be imprudent to assume that a supply will be readily available in Serbia. Spectacle-wearers will probably not need reminding that they should bring along a spare pair, and their own prescription sunglasses, essential in the summer glare. A pocket torch (flashlight) is always a good idea too, although power cuts are no longer a feature of Serbian life. A plug adaptor (two-prong, round-pin) will enable you to use your own electrical devices whilst in the country, and, in considering such devices, a shortwave radio is probably the most useful in terms of its size-to-satisfaction ratio. American 110-volt electrical devices will require an adapter to use the 220-volt European current.

Photographers should ensure that they bring enough film along, especially if they require professional-quality slide film, which is very hard to find outside of Belgrade. Although the number of foreign bank-friendly ATMs is on the increase, it is best to back up plastic with a reasonable supply of cash too – euros preferably, but dollars or sterling will suffice – as it can sometimes be hard to find an ATM that works outside of the larger cities.

Insect repellent is a good idea as mosquitoes can be a pain in summer, even in Belgrade. Kalemegdan Park can be particularly bad around dusk on a warm summer's night and the application of a repellent with a high 'deet' content is a wise precaution.

As for clothing, be prepared for cold in winter, early spring and late autumn, and anticipate the possibility of rain, even in the summer months, by bringing along a cagoule or an umbrella.

MONEY AND BANKING
Currency
The official monetary unit of Serbia is the **dinar**, usually abbreviated as din. At the time of writing, there were approximately 112 dinar to the pound sterling, 80 to the euro, and 60 to the US dollar. In recent years, the Serbian dinar has become a reasonably stable currency. Thankfully, the days of hyperinflation of the early 1990s are a thing of the past, and it is no longer necessary to push along wheelbarrows of multiple-zeroed banknotes in order to make a simple purchase (see box in *General Information* chapter: *Hyperinflation – the 500 billion dinar banknote*).

The Serbian dinar is divided into 100 **para**, although these are almost never used. Banknotes come in denominations of 10, 20, 50, 100, 200, 1,000 and 5,000din; coins are 50 para (rare), and 1, 2, 5, 10 and 20din. Current Serbian currency shows a nation still in transition: older coins and banknotes say 'Yugoslavia', whereas those from 2003 onwards are denoted 'Serbia' even though their designs are similar to the older notes.

Foreign nationals may take a maximum of 120,000din in or out of the country in 1,000din banknotes or smaller. However, it is important to remember that the Serbian dinar is not used in either Montenegro or Kosovo, where the euro is the official currency. It is hard to exchange Serbian dinars at a reasonable rate in either of these places, and virtually impossible beyond, although dinars may be exchanged in some of the banks in Szeged, just across the Hungarian border.

Exchange rates vary very little between **banks** and **exchange offices** (*menjačnica*) and so it is not really worthwhile shopping around. As well as the usual manned outlets, in Belgrade and the large cities there are also money exchange machines that accept euros, dollars or pounds sterling; you are required to feed your notes into the machine, which will then, hopefully, provide the correct equivalent in Serbian dinars.

Serbia is still predominantly a cash economy even though electronic banking is starting to catch up. Foreign exchange of **cash** can be performed at banks and post offices throughout the country, as well as at numerous small exchange offices where the transaction is usually quicker. Euros usually get the best rate. **Travellers' cheques** are a little harder to change: branches of Raiffeisenbank or Komercijalna banka are probably the best bet, but beware of high commission charges. For Eurocheques, branches of ProCredit Bank are probably the best bet. Neither personal nor travellers' cheques can normally be exchanged for goods in shops, so credit cards make far more sense.

Banks are generally open from 08.00 to 19.00 on weekdays and from 08.00 to 15.00 Saturdays. In Belgrade, some banks and post offices are also open on Sundays, one being the Komercijalna Banka at Trg Nikole Pašića 2 (tel: 3234 087), which is open on Saturdays from 08.00 to 20.00, and on Sundays and holidays from 09.00–15.00.

The most widely accepted credit cards are VISA, closely followed by MasterCard, and cash can be withdrawn from ATMs bearing these symbols, as well as cash advances being given in banks throughout the country. Maestro and Electron debit cards may also be used where the symbol is displayed. American Express and Diners Club are not so well accepted, although they may be used in payment for goods in some shops, top hotels and car rental agencies. Currently, there are no Diners Club or American Express-linked ATMs anywhere in Serbia. It is worth remembering that, even for the payment of goods with MasterCard, you will need to know your PIN code.

Electronic banking is moving swiftly forwards in Serbia but it is inevitable that there may be some hiccups: some ATM machines may not recognise foreign cards and, in a worst-case scenario, may even swallow your card. To be on the safe side, it is probably wise to carry more than one type of card if at all possible; say, two different credit cards – VISA and MasterCard – as well as a debit card.

ATMs that accept MasterCard/EuroCard/Maestro include those of Delta Banka, Komercijalna Banka, Nova Banka and Eksim Banka, although not all branches of Komercijalna Banka have ATM machines. Branches of Société Generale have ATMs that accept MasterCard/Maestro/Cirrus. Cash advances against MasterCard, EuroCard or Maestro may also be made at any branch of Delta Banka. For VISA, there are far more options and, as well as having numerous ATMs, branches of Vojvodanska Banka will allow you to withdraw money against your card at those branches that lack one.

Emergency help numbers for credit cards: VISA (011) 301 1550; MasterCard (011) 301 0160; Diners Club (011) 344 06 22; American Express card holders may be able to receive help from the emergency service of Komercijalna Banka (011) 308 0115.

For those arriving by plane, there is an ATM at the arrivals hall (downstairs) of Belgrade's Surčin Airport, which will accept VISA, VISA Electron, VISA Plus, MasterCard, Maestro and Cirrus cards.

The best way to arrange a fast transfer of funds from abroad is to make use of the services of Western Union Serbia (www.wu.co.yu). Whatever the currency your money is sent in, you will receive it in euros. All Serbian banks are members of SWIFT, and so another alternative for money transfer is to open a bank account in Serbia then arrange for a transfer. A SWIFT transfer will take between two and seven business days to come through.

Budgeting

Serbia is an inexpensive country; cheaper than its immediate neighbour Bosnia-Herzegovina, considerably cheaper than Croatia or Slovenia, and even noticeably less pricey than Montenegro. On any reckoning, Serbia remains one of Europe's last bargains: food, drink and transport are all very good value, and consumer items like clothing and CDs can be purchased at a fraction of their cost in western Europe. Accommodation is not quite such a bargain, although this too is rarely prohibitively expensive. This situation may change in the next few years as more private hotels come onto the market. Serbia is slowly emerging from a tradition of faceless, state-run hotels that were not required to compete against each other. Consequently, although some real bargains do exist, on the whole, many Serbian hotels can seem a little overpriced considering what they have to offer in terms of facilities and service.

For some idea of costs: a meal with wine, depending on the exclusiveness of the establishment, will cost between 300 and 1,200din; an espresso coffee, 20–40din; a beer, 50–80din. A bus journey of 100km will cost about 150din, the equivalent train journey cheaper (and slower) at about 90din.

In cafés and run-of-the-mill restaurants, it is customary to round up the total rather than adding a percentage. In smarter establishments, 10% would be considered more than adequate. It is not necessary to tip taxi drivers although, naturally, any gratuity offered will be gladly accepted.

GETTING AROUND

The most popular and practical means of getting around the country is by **bus**. There are frequent departures that run between most towns and, from Belgrade in particular, numerous services that radiate out of the capital to quite obscure parts of the country. Most towns of any size have a purpose-built bus station that will have left-luggage and snack facilities. Timetables of departures and arrivals are shown on large boards, usually in Cyrillic. Tickets can be bought in advance from booths inside the bus station and on some routes they can sell out quickly, particularly during public holidays or on village fair or *slava* days. Buses that run between major centres like Belgrade, Novi Sad or Niš are so frequent that it is often unnecessary to buy a ticket in advance, although the caveat about holidays still applies. Buses are usually quite comfortable with reasonable leg room, and seat reservations are honoured, but additional standing passengers are often taken on board once a journey is in progress and some buses can become uncomfortably crowded and stiflingly hot in summer.

Trains are an alternative on some routes, although the Serbian railway network has deteriorated over the past two decades as a result of poor maintenance, lack of investment, management/trade union clashes and war damage. The Serbian government's own website pulls no punches in describing the parlous state of its railways, informing us of 'Telecommunication equipment at a very rudimentary level,' and that '50% of railway stations are equipped with signalling-safety devices manufactured by Siemens over 30 years ago'. What this tells us about the remaining 50% is open to speculation. Currently, there are future plans in store for EU assistance to be provided through the European Agency for Reconstruction. At the time of writing, however, most of these improvements were still in the planning stage.

In practical terms, trains are invariably cheaper than the bus option but they are usually slower and more prone to breakdown. For comparison: there are about 30 buses a day from Belgrade to Novi Sad, which cost between 200 and 300din, depending on whether or not it is an express service, and taking between 1½ and 2½ hours; by train, there is a more limited choice of only eight services, the cost is less than the bus but it will take between 2½ and 3½ hours to cover the same distance unless you take one of the international express services, which cost more. Serbian trains do come into their own on longer journeys, such as the overnight services to neighbouring capitals like Sofia or Bucharest, or the wonderfully scenic journey down to the coast at Bar in Montenegro. Sleepers should be booked as far in advance as possible.

Overall, trains are a good way to travel if you are not in any great hurry. The common perception is that Serbian trains generally leave on time but arrive at their destinations late. Certainly, they are a good way to meet people, especially on longer trips.

Information on trains can be gathered from Yugoslav Railways (Jugoslovenske železnice), Nemanjina 6, 11000 Beograd; tel: 361 4811, 361 6722; fax: 361 6802; email: posta@yurail.co.yu; www.yurail.co.yu, or from individual railway stations. In Belgrade tel: 636 493, 641 488 (06.00–22.00), 629 400, 645 822 (24-hour service), 688 722 (for car train and sleeping cars); in Novi Sad tel: 443 178; in Niš tel: 364 625, 369 78; in Subotica tel: 555 606. As well as at stations, tickets can also be booked through travel agents such as Putnik.

By car
Car rental is available in towns and cities throughout the country, although Belgrade and Novi Sad have the widest choice of agencies – see individual chapters for details. Driving is reasonably straightforward, and takes place on the right – mostly. Most main roads are in reasonable condition, although minor roads in the countryside can be in quite poor repair with pot-holes and loose stones. Because of the preponderance of blind corners and the occasional speed-crazed local, driving at night in rural areas can sometimes prove to be a nerve-wrecking experience that is probably best avoided.

In order to drive in Serbia you must have an international driver's licence and a Green Card (international insurance). The wearing of seat belts is compulsory and traffic police are keen to impose fines for failing to do this, as they are for any infringements of the speed limit. Foreign licence plates are more likely to attract the attention of traffic police who can be quite zealous in their work. Spot penalties for minor infractions are usually 1,500din. The speed limit is 120km/h (75mph) on highways, 100km/h (62mph) on secondary roads and 60km/h (37mph) in built-up areas. For vehicles with a trailer the limit is 80km/h. There are many speed cameras and traffic police to check on this. The police do not possess radar guns but they are still happy to wave down drivers if they suspect them of speeding. The maximum permissible amount of alcohol in the blood is 0.05%. Children under 12 (and adults 'affected by alcohol') are not permitted to sit in the front seat next to the driver. Foreign cars must bear the appropriate country designation sticker, which unfortunately will single it out for special attention from the police, and from petty thieves when it is parked. Petrol (gasoline) is fairly expensive at around 50din (€0.90) a litre for premium and unleaded, and 42din (€0.80) for diesel. Petrol stations along main roads and in cities are usually open 24 hours a day.

Road conditions vary throughout Serbia but are generally worse in the south of the country. The main E-75 motorway heading south peters out between Niš and Leskovac, to continue along a pot-holed ordinary road from here on.

Road tolls are charged on the major trunk roads – foreign-registered cars pay a premium, about 2½ times more than nationals. Paying in euros, you will be charged 20% commission – see *Getting there and away* section for details.

The Automobile and Motorists Association of Serbia and Montenegro (AMS SCG), at Ruzveltova 18, 11000 Belgrade (tel: 401 699; fax: 419 888; email: info@amsj.co.yu; www.amsj.co.yu) forwards details on traffic information and road conditions on a daily basis to other European motor organisations, and the AMS SCG International Alarm and Information Centre at the same address (tel: 9800 for 24-hour service) can supply traffic information and other information on touring. For

CYCLING IN SERBIA

Dutch biker Ivo Miesen, who in 2002, cycled through Serbia from the Hungarian border to the Montenegrin coast, offers the following advice:

I started cycling just north of the Yugoslav–Hungarian border, in the town of Szeged. From Novi Sad to Smederovo I followed the Danube valley, then diagonally through Serbia and Montenegro to the Durmitor Mountains. From the Durmitor Mountains through the valley of the Žeta to Podgorica. With the benefit of hindsight, I would not take the Novi Sad–Belgrade main road again, and Belgrade is only to be cycled in when it's really necessary. It would have been better if I had gone directly south after crossing the border between Szeged and Subotica. Another option for those with less time would be to go south from Novi Sad and stick close to the Bosnian border.

I used a variety of maps. For planning, I used the Freytag & Berndt Yugoslavia and Macedonia map at 1:500,000. This map lacks detail. Slightly better is the 'Serbija' map of the AMCC at 1:535,000. It gives a little more detail, and lots of altitude information in its colour schedules. This was the main map for my trip. The Novi Sad & Vojvodina map at 1:270,000 is hardly better than the AMCC map. All of the maps are unreliable and conflicting. Not all of the roads on the map exist; sometimes the information is outdated; sometimes roads not yet built are shown.

I used a standard touring bike, a Koga Miyata Alloy Randonneur. Being nine years old, and having suffered many blows, it was to be its last trip. For tyres, I used Swallow City Marathon 35-622 at the front and Michelin Tracer 32-622 at the back. As a spare, I took a Panaracer Tour Guard 32-622. The gearing was standard, with 28-38-50 front rings and a 12/28 seven-speed cassette. Both rear racks and lowriders were by Tubus, with two large Karrimor panniers at the rear and two Karrimor universals (30l) at the front. A Karrimor barbag and a standard sports bag on top of the rear rack completed the luggage. Since the weather in April can be both mild and cold, I took full winter kit, as well as summer clothes. I also took a large duffel bag and a transport bag for my bike. The estimated combined weight of the bike and luggage was between 40 and 45kg.

In the Danube valley and the lower mountain ranges, I either camped wild or stayed with local friends. In the mountain ranges, the opportunities for wild camping were limited, as most flat land was already in use. Wild camping is not very well known among the local population, so it can be hard to get permission to camp on somebody's land.

Before I set out, I did not know what to expect. So I prepared for the worst, deliberately not taking anything with me that might arouse unnecessary interest. None of these precautions was needed. There were no safety issues resulting from the various wars in the region. Serbia was spared from groundwar, so the danger of landmines is negligible. There might be stray bombs near some bombed sites, so don't dash through the undergrowth in those places. Traffic safety depends on the region. I regard the Novi Sad–Belgrade main road and the city of Belgrade as unsafe in regards to traffic. Elsewhere it's OK.

In mid April the weather was a bit wet and cold. I guess that May/June and September/October would be the best months for the region.

help on the road, dialling 987 will summon the road assistance service of the AMS SCG. To summon the traffic police in the case of accident, dial 92.

Other Serbian motoring organisations include:

Automobile and Motorists Association of Serbia Ivana Milutinovica 58, 11000 Belgrade; tel: 4443 904; fax: 451 078
Automobile and Motorists Association of Vojvodina Arse Teodorovica 15, 21000 Novi Sad; tel: 616 533, 20 039; fax: 20 039

Cycling in Serbia definitely offers great potential, particularly if main roads are avoided. Cycling in Belgrade itself is not recommended due to heavy traffic and drivers' unfamiliarity with the habits of cyclists. See box: *Cycling in Serbia.*

City transport

Local bus transport serves all urban areas throughout the country, with additional trolleybus and tram services operating in some of the larger towns and cities. There is usually a flat fare for any journey along a particular route. Routes can be hard to decipher at times: often they are only given in Cyrillic, or they rely on obscure landmarks to denote the route that only a local would know. More often still, bus routes are not written down at all and exist only inside the minds of the driver and local passengers. It is always best to ask fellow passengers: state your preferred destination clearly and confirm this with the driver when you enter the vehcle. Depending on the size of the vehicle, you either pay the driver on entry or, as is sometimes the case in articulated trolleybuses, you pay a conductor at a little counter in the rear part of the vehicle. Fares are invariably cheap.

Sometimes it is easier to take a taxi, which abound in every Serbian town. Apart from the sharks that haunt the airport and railway stations in Belgrade, taxi drivers are usually honest and helpful, although you should always agree on a price at the outset if there is no obvious sign of a meter.

ACCOMMODATION

The hotel situation in Serbia is similar to that of other eastern European countries surfacing from long years of indifferent state control; perhaps it is even a little behind most of the others. One of the main troubles with the Serbian hotel industry is the lack of choice outside of the ubiquitous, mid-price, state-owned range. Away from Belgrade, there are usually just one or two of this type of hotel in each town, with a few motels strung along the trunk roads to complement them.

The majority of Serbian hotels can be characterised as large, concrete landmarks in which charm and personality have been sacrificed for size and space. Too often they are massive concrete and steel edifices that enclose expansive lobby areas carpeted in wrinkled polyester and lit by the few 50-watt bulbs that have not yet expired in the dusty chandeliers. With cavernous restaurants that serve institutional food, and dark bars that often have a mens' club atmosphere, they can seem more geared up to the needs of business conventions rather than individual travellers. But, on the plus side, they are always clean and, because they are invariably large, it is nearly always possible to find a room without reservation, although singles can sometimes be elusive.

Prices vary, but can range from quite good value for money to seriously overpriced. Generally speaking, it is hard to find anywhere for less than €15 single or €22 double. A residence tax of 60din a day applies to all hotel rates, which is sometimes, but not always, included in the price quoted. A television set nearly always comes as standard, although it will probably not be wired for cable channels and you may need to do a little judicious fiddling with the aerial socket if you want to catch that late-night movie on Pink TV. Check-out time is usually at noon.

Breakfast is usually included, and will normally consist of a combination of bread, jam, ham and eggs – especially eggs. Although coffee or tea may be offered, this may well mean a milky beverage that contains only homoeopathic quantities of coffee, or a tepid infusion of herbs. If you hanker for something more familiar – a cappuccino, an espresso or a pot of English Breakfast – then you will probably be charged extra. If breakfast is not included then you are usually better off going to a café or snack bar instead, as the breakfast sitting in many hotel restaurants just seems to be an opportunity for the waiting staff to practise their scowls.

The star system is only a rough indicator of quality; in some cases it can seem purely academic and there are even instances where single-star hotels outshine those bearing three. With five stars, things start to become more predictable – and far more expensive. A good rule of thumb is to knock off a star to get some idea of the western European equivalent.

Beyond the middle ground, there are few real luxury hotels, and few decent budget options or pensions for the more impecunious traveller. Hopefully this will change in the future as more independently financed hotels are set up, and as more people offer private accommodation in their homes. For the time being, signs that offer *SOBE* – a room in a private house – are a rarity in Serbia, as the tradition has not yet caught on in the same way as it has on the Adriatic coast of Croatia or at resorts like Ohrid in Macedonia.

At the time of writing, some of Serbia's more desirable state hotels were being taken into private ownership, which will probably mean both improved standards and increased prices in the future. A few purpose-built, privately owned hotels have already set up in business, and the indications are that others will follow this trend if these prove successful.

Useful sites that list hotels throughout Serbia are at www.hoteli-srbije.co.yu and www.hotels.co.yu.

There is a mere handful of **hostels** in Serbia that offer cheap, dormitory-style accommodation. Currently, they have just two in Belgrade, one in Kladovo and one in Novi Sad. These can be booked through Hostelling International, Ferijalne Savez Beograd, Dom Mladost, Makedonska 22, Belgrade; tel: 323 1268; fax: 322 0762; www.hostels.org.yu.

Official **campsites** in Serbia are few and far between, and when they do exist they are actually places with cabins and limited space for tents. Wild camping is possible although not widely practised. It is best to be out of sight of a road and/or ask a landowner's permission to erect a tent.

EATING AND DRINKING
Dining out

Serbian cuisine is similar to that of other Balkan countries, with a few specialities that it can claim for its own. The long Ottoman occupation has clearly had some influence, especially in the wide range of grilled meats available. In fact, Serbs enjoy eating meat in as many ways as they can think of cooking it. This passion for animal flesh is reflected in a cuisine that, whilst both tasty and wholesome, can be daunting for vegetarians and health-food aficionados.

Although there are hints of the Mediterranean in the cooking, most Serbian food is on the heavy side: lard is used extensively instead of olive oil and there is a tendency towards greasiness. This is not the whole picture, of course. While meat is enjoyed in quantity at every possible opportunity, so are fresh vegetables, and, in a country where fresh, unadulterated produce is still a fact of life – fertilisers and pesticides are rarely used – it is possible, with a little careful selection, to eat well whatever one's personal dietary tastes might be. If you are vegetarian you will need to declare, '*Ja sam vegetarijanac*' if you are a man, or '*Ja sam vegetarijanka*' if female. It's probably better to be more specific and say, '*Ne jedem meso*' – 'I don't eat meat' – perhaps adding, '*Ne jedem pilece meso, ribu ni šunku*' – 'I don't eat chicken, fish or ham' – to be on the safe side.

The problem with eating out in Serbia is often a matter of understanding exactly what is on offer, as menus are often written in Cyrillic and hard to decipher. There is also the phenomenon of overly optimistic menu-writing in which the items listed merely reflect the chef's familiarity with sophisticated cuisine rather than his ability or willingness to produce it.

A typical meal might consist of *kajmak* – a sort of salty, cream-cheese spread – with bread to start, then a grilled meat like *ćevapčići* with a salad. Fresh fruit is as likely to conclude a meal as any sweet dish. While wine is often chosen to accompany a meal, something stronger like a glass or two of *šljivovica* might well precede it as a high-octane aperitif. For many Serbians, lunch (*ručak*) is the main meal of the day, followed by something a bit lighter for dinner (*večera*). As well as 'national food', foreign and international cuisine is also available in some of the larger towns and cities. Italian food is especially popular, as evidenced by the numerous pizza and pasta restaurants even in small towns throughout the country. More exotic cuisines like Indian, Mexican or Thai can generally be found only in Belgrade. So-called 'national food' is itself fairly variable and shows an undeniable Hungarian influence in the north of the country.

For starter courses, smoked meats are a popular choice, with *dalmatinski pršut*, a lightly smoked ham, or *užicka pršut*, a hard, smoked beef, frequently offered on menus. Another meat preserve, *pihtije*, a dish of jellied pork or duck with garlic, tastes much better than you might imagine. A dip that can be spread on bread in the same way as *kajmak* is *ajvar*, spiced peppers and aubergine, which are chopped and seasoned with vinegar, oil and garlic, a little like the Arab dish, *baba ghanoush*.

For the main course, the most popular meat dishes are *pljeskavica* (meat patties, usually a mixture of pork, beef and lamb, sprinkled with spices, then grilled and served with onion), *ražnjići* (shish kebabs of pork or veal), *ćevapčići* (spiced minced meat kebabs), *leskovački ćevapčići* (kebab with peppers), *mesano mesto* (mixed grill), *karađ orđe snićla* ('Black George's schnitzel), *medljoni* (veal steak), *ćulbastija* (grilled veal or pork), *prasetina na ražnju* (spit-roast suckling pig), *jagnjetina na ražnju* (spit-roast lamb), *jagnjece pecenje* (roast lamb), *kapama* (lamb stew), *kolanica* (leg of suckling pig) or *kobasice* (sausages). Other Serbian dishes combine meat with vegetables, as in *sarma* (minced beef or pork mixed with rice and stuffed inside pickled cabbage leaves), *podvarak* (roast meat with sauerkraut), *punjene tikvice* (courgettes stuffed with meat and rice), *đuveč* (pork cutlets baked with spiced stewed peppers, courgettes, tomatoes and rice) and *punjene paprike* (peppers stuffed with minced meat and rice).

Accompaniments to the above might include a *šopska salata* (chopped tomatoes, onions and cucumber with grated white cheese), a *mešana salata* (mixed salad – rather variable) or a *srbska salata* (tomatoes, onions, peppers and parsley); alternatively, you might choose something cooked like *paprike* (roast peppers) or *prizoli* (vegetables).

Fish (*riba*) dishes can be very good but generally are far more expensive, as fish has to be brought a considerable distance from the coast. There are some restaurants where you make your selection from specimens swimming around in a large tank, which introduces a personal touch to the proceedings that not everyone is comfortable with.

As well as seafood, freshwater fish are widely available too, and just as popular, especially *pastrmka* (trout) and *saran* (carp). One tasty freshwater fish dish that appears on menus throughout the north of Serbia is *alaska čorba i paprikas*, a fiery-red fish stew that incorporates vast quantities of paprika pepper. Traditionally, this is a festive dish prepared out of doors in large cauldrons over campfires but it is also available as a standard menu item in many restaurants, especially in Vojvodina.

For dessert, if you still have room after battling through a typical Serbian culinary onslaught, there is usually a choice of seasonal fruit, along with less healthy options like *doboš torta*, a Hungarian-style cake or *baklava*, a layered flaky pastry filled with nuts and oozing with syrup. All you need now is a *turska kava*, another *šljivovica* and a good lie down.

Snack food

Some of the tastiest food in Serbia is the snack food that is sold on the street and from bakeries. Apart from the ubiquitous *pljeskavica, senvić* and hamburger outlets, there are also many small hole-in-the-wall establishments that sell *burek* (cheese or meat pies, sometimes with apple to cut the grease a bit; with cheese is *burek sa sirom*, with meat, *burek sa mesom*; they are also made with potatoes, *krompiruča* – very heavy and filling – or with mushrooms, *pecurke*). *Burek*, which is of Turkish origin, is often eaten with yoghurt, and is more usually on sale in the mornings. Other popular snack choices are *gibanica* (a sort of cheese and egg pie baked with filo pastry), *zeljanica* (similar to *gibanica* but with spinach, rather like the Greek dish *spanikapita*), a mouth-watering, flaky cherry strudel called *pita sa višnjama* and sometimes a range of mini pizzas. All of these are cheap and delicious, and an excellent choice for breakfast or a snack; servings are generous, so they can be quite filling.

Sweets and pastries

Sweet tooths are well catered for in Serbia. Many *slastičarnica* (confectioners) offer table service and fresh coffee, together with a tantalising selection of delicious cakes (*torta*) and pastries (*kolač*) to choose from: the strudels (*štrudla*) in particular, are to die (but not diet) for. *Štrudla na jabukama* is apple strudel, and *Štrudla na trešnjama* is filled with cherries. Ice-cream (*sladoled*) is as popular as it is in Italy and is available in just as many flavours from numerous street-corner *slastičarnica*. Another Serbian favourite is pancakes (*palačinken*); most towns have at least one dedicated *palačinkanica* that offers pancakes with a range of inventive sweet and savoury fillings. However, all of these calorific treats belong to imported central European or Italian traditions (Turkish in the case of *baklava*); the only dessert that is exclusively Serbian and does not owe anything to foreign cuisine is the luxury version of a country dish called *žito*, a kind of creamed wheat porridge that is flavoured with nuts and raisins and served with whipped cream.

Hot beverages

Unless it says otherwise, coffee means strong thick Turkish coffee (*Turska kava*), although many Serbs, like the Greeks, prefer to believe that they invented the drink themselves. Sugar is added at the beginning of the brew and so it is customary to specify the amount of sweetening that you require. If you do not specify then it will invariably come semi-sweet. The relative proximity to Italy has meant that most establishments now have espresso machines and so can conjure up a convincing *espresso* or *cappuccino*. It is probably best not to ask for an *americano* as this will just lead to confusion. Tea (*čaj*) is also available but it is usually fairly weak and insipid. For tea with milk, ask for *sa mleko*, with lemon, *sa limun*. Speciality and herb teas are also popular.

Alcoholic drinks

Most Serbian wines are drinkable and some are actually very good. The best are probably the white wines (*bela vino*) that come from the Sremska Karlovci region in Vojvodina, but Serbia has a range of wines that come from various grape-producing regions such as Vršac and even Kosovo. Most red wines (*crni vino*) come from Montenegro. Wine can be bought in restaurants and cafés by the bottle, by the glass or in carafes of various sizes. In a supermarket, a bottle of a decent domestic wine will cost something in the order of 200–600din; in a restaurant, maybe double this.

Serbians are proud of their wines but probably more enthusiastic about the range of alcoholic spirits they produce. Experimentation with these products can be something of an adventure. *Šljivovica* is a sort of brandy traditionally made from plums, but *rakija*, which is normally a spirit made from grapes, tends to be used as a generic term for any sort of strong liquor. *Konjak* is, as its name implies, cognac, and *Lozovaca*, another form of grape brandy. There are proprietary brands of all of these spirits available at low prices, as well as home-distilled versions of the same that range from palatably fruity to downright dangerous. For Serbian home brewers, there is a sort of unwritten kudos attached to distilling a spirit so high in alcohol content that it is better suited to paint removal purposes rather than as a refreshment offering for unsuspecting foreigners. An annual *šljivovica* festival takes place in the small town of Kolvinj near Novi Sad, which boasts a wide range of home-produced spirits made from various fruits and vegetables. Attend it at your peril.

At least beer (*pivo*), both draught and bottled, is always an alternative. The most popular brand is Jelen, but BIP (Beogradska Industrija Pivara), BG (Beogradsko Pivo) and Montenegrin Nikšićko are also widely available; Karlovačko brand is not recommended. German-style draught beer is also sometimes on sale and often heavily advertised. Imported bottled beers like Amstel and Heineken, some of which – to my taste at least – seem inferior to many of the domestic brands on offer, are always more expensive, and their popularity seems to owe more to their being a status symbol than anything to do with flavour.

Non-alcoholic drinks

A wide range of bottled fruit drinks are available, as well as the real thing in season. *Sok od pomorande* is orange juice; *sok od jagode*, strawberry; and *sok od jabuka*, apple juice. Although tap water is generally safe to drink, mineral water (*mineralna voda*) is easy to find.

SHOPPING

Shops in Serbia are normally open 08.00–20.00 from Monday to Friday, 08.00–15.00 on Saturdays, closed on Sundays. There is often a long lunch break from noon until mid afternoon. Grocery stores keep longer hours: usually 06.30–20.00 in the week, 06.30–18.00 on Saturdays, and 07.00–11.00 on Sundays. Many supermarkets stay open longer than this, until late in the evening. It may come as a surprise to some but there is no lack of consumer goods, as supermarkets stock most of the items that you might expect to find at home.

The best place to buy souvenirs is, without a doubt, Belgrade. Leather goods, needlework and embroidered textiles are all good value, as are CDs and computer software, although the legality of these items may be in question. Lace can be a good deal too, especially when bought in the countryside; the quality is usually very good. Some food items, like smoked sausages and chocolates, are inexpensive and make good gifts, as do bottles of *šljivovica* or Vojvodina wine. For more traditional souvenirs like handicrafts the best place to look is in one of the capital's souvenir emporiums – see the *Belgrade* chapter. Fans of naïve art and folk pottery may wish to visit the villages where these are produced, such as Jagodina south of Belgrade, or Kovačica in the Banat. However, it is unlikely that the goods on sale will be that much cheaper, even at the point of origin.

ARTS AND ENTERTAINMENT

Belgrade is very much the cultural capital when it comes to the arts, although Novi Sad has a thriving scene too, particularly in music and theatre. All manner of musical events – folk, rock, world music, jazz and classical take place in the capital throughout

MAKING THE BEST OF YOUR TRAVEL PHOTOGRAPHS
Nick Garbutt and John R Jones
Subject, composition and lighting
As a general rule, if it doesn't look good through the viewfinder, it will never look good as a picture. Don't take photographs for the sake of taking them; film is far too expensive. Be patient and wait until the image looks right.

People
There's nothing like a wonderful face to stimulate interest. Travelling to remote corners of the world provides the opportunity for exotic photographs of colourful minorities, intriguing lifestyles and special evocative shots which capture the very essence of a culture. A superb photograph should have an instant gut impact and be capable of saying more than a thousand words.

Photographing people is never easy and more often than not it requires a fair share of luck. Zooming in on that special moment which says it all requires sharp instinct, conditioned photographic eyes and the ability to handle light both aesthetically and technically.

* If you want to take a portrait shot, it is always best to ask first. Often the offer to send a copy of the photograph to the subject will break the ice – but do remember to send it!
* Focus on the eyes of your subject
* The best portraits are obtained in the early morning and late evening light. In harsh light, photograph without flash in the shadows.
* Respect people's wishes and customs. Remember that, in some countries, candid snooping can lead to serious trouble.
Never photograph military subjects unless you have definite permission.

Wildlife
There is no mystique to good wildlife photography. The secret is getting into the right place at the right time and then knowing what to do when you are there. Look for striking poses, aspects of behaviour and distinctive features. Try not only to take pictures of the species itself, but also to illustrate it within the context of its environment. Alternatively, focus in close on a characteristic which can be emphasised.

* Photographically, the eyes are the most important part of an animal – focus on these, make sure they are sharp and try to ensure they contain a highlight.
* Look at the surroundings – there is nothing worse than a distracting twig or highlighted leaf lurking in the background. Although a powerful flashgun adds the option of punching in extra light to pep up the subject, artificial light is no substitute for natural light, and should be used judiciously.
* At camera-to-subject distances of less than a metre, apertures between f16 and f32 are necessary to ensure adequate depth of field. This means using flash to provide enough light – use one or two small flashguns to illuminate the subject from the side.

Landscapes
Good landscape photography is all about good light and capturing mood. Generally the first and last two hours of daylight are best, or when peculiar climatic conditions add drama or emphasise distinctive features. Never place the

horizon in the centre – in your mind's eye divide the frame into thirds and either exaggerate the land or the sky.

Equipment

Keep things simple. Cameras which are light, reliable and simple will reduce hassle. High humidity in many tropical places, in particular rainforests, can play havoc with electronics.

For keen photographers, a single-lens reflex (SLR) camera should be at the heart of your outfit. Remember you are buying into a whole photographic system, so look for a model with the option of a range of different lenses and other accessories. Compact cameras are generally excellent, but because of restricted focal ranges they have severe limitations for wildlife.

Always choose the best lens you can afford – the type of lens will be dictated by the subject and the type of photograph you wish to take. For people, it should ideally have a focal length of 90 or 105mm; for candid photographs, a 70–210 zoom lens is ideal. If you are not intimidated by getting in close, buy one with a macro facility, which will allow close focusing.

For wildlife, a lens of at least 300mm is necessary to produce a reasonable image size of mammals and birds. For birds in particular, even longer lenses like 400mm or 500mm are sometimes needed. Optics of this size should always be held on a tripod, or a beanbag if shooting from a vehicle. Macro lenses of 55mm and 105mm cover most subjects and these create images up to half lifesize. To enlarge further, extension tubes are required. In low light, lenses with very fast apertures help (but unfortunately are very expensive).

For most landscapes and scenic photographs, try using a medium telephoto lens (100–300mm) to pick out the interesting aspects of the vista and compress the perspective. In tight situations, for example inside forests, wide-angle lenses (ie: 35mm or less) are ideal. These lenses are also an excellent alternative for close ups, as they offer the facility of being able to show the subject within the context of its environment.

Film

Film speed (ISO number) indicates the sensitivity of the film to light. The lower the number, the less sensitive the film, but the better quality the final image. For general print film, ISO 100 or 200 fit the bill perfectly; under weak light conditions use a faster film (ISO 200 or 400). If you are using transparencies just for lectures then again ISO 100 or 200 film is fine. However, if you want to get your work published, the superior quality of ISO 25 to 100 film is best. Try to keep your film cool – it should never be left in direct sunlight (film bought in developing countries is often outdated and badly stored). Fast film (ISO 800 and above) should not pass through X-ray machines.

Different types of film work best for different situations. For natural subjects, where greens are a feature, Fujicolour Reala (prints) and Fujichrome Velvia and Provia (transparencies) cannot be bettered. For people shots, try Kodachrome 64 for its warmth, mellowness and superb gentle gradation of contrast; reliable skin tones can also be recorded with Fuji Astia 100. If you want to jazz up your portraits, use Fuji Velvia (50 ISO) or Provia (100 ISO), although if cost is your priority, stick to process-paid Fuji films such as Sensia 11.

Nick Garbutt is a professional photographer, writer, artist and expedition leader, the year, at a variety of venues that range from small clubs and theatres to the cavernous halls of the Sava Centre. In October each year the capital is host to **BEMUS**, a classical music festival, while the annual **Belgrade Guitar Arts Festival** that takes place in April attracts internationally famous names like John Williams, among others.

Belgrade is not always the centre of Serbia's musical universe, however: **EXIT**, the country's largest rock and pop event, which is held each July, actually takes place in Novi Sad, just outside the city in the environs of Petrovaradin Fortress by the Danube. Not to be outdone by this, Belgrade stages a similar but smaller festival (**ECHO**) on an island beach by the Danube a few weeks later, while the city of Niš makes use of its Ottoman Fortress as the location for **Nišomania**, its own version of the same. Numerous folk music events take place throughout the country in the summer months; most of these are small, local affairs, with the obvious exception being the massive, and very hectic, **Guča Trumpet Festival** that is held in Central Serbia in August.

Both Belgrade and Novi Sad have an enthusiastic theatrical scene that stages productions by both classical and contemporary writers. As for films, the latest Hollywood blockbusters hit the screens of the capital and Serbia's larger cities shortly after their release. The visual arts are best represented in Belgrade, where, as well as occasional retrospectives by established artists, many exhibitions of new work are staged throughout the year.

Further details can be found in the appropriate chapters, and an up-to-date list of cultural events is available at www.serbia-tourism.org.

PHOTOGRAPHY
Beware of unwittingly taking photographs of military installations. Also, photographing any obvious war damage does not always go down well with the authorities nor with proud civilians.

It can be hard to find decent quality slide film outside Belgrade, and very difficult to find professional-quality film, ie: Fuji Velvia, even in the capital. Take enough film and spare batteries to last for the duration of your trip.

MEDIA AND COMMUNICATIONS
Newspapers
Serbia's biggest-selling daily newspaper is *Večernje Novosti*, closely followed by *Glas Javnosti*, *Blic* and *Pobjeda*. All of these Belgrade-based dailies are probably the most influential, if not the most serious. The oldest and probably most prestigious is the 100-year-old *Politika*. This was the flagship of serious journalism before the collapse of communism, and later became a mouthpiece for Milošević's propaganda. After Milošević was ousted, the newspaper drew closer to Kostunica's opposition. Currently it is owned by the German WAZ group.

Of the various news weeklies, *Vreme* is probably the most highly thought of, although its future remains in jeopardy because of low circulation figures.

All of the above newspapers are in Serbian only. It is usually possible to find day-old copies of some of the international press like *The Times* or the *New York Herald*, and possibly French, Italian and German newspapers too, in the bookshops and postcard booths along Kneza Mihaila in Belgrade.

Television
Serbia's state television network, RTS, was considered so powerful during the Milošević years that its headquarters became a legitimate target for NATO bombers in the 'war of propaganda'. Today, RTS has a much smaller share of the media, with the

B92 – A SHORT HISTORY

Radio B92 started life in May 1989 as a temporary student radio station. It was not long before it made an impact with its unusual mix of music and independent news reporting. Over the next few years B92 was shut down four times by the authorities for its role in the opposition movement. The first time was in 1991 when B92 disc jockeys encouraged people out onto the streets to take part in demonstrations against Milošević's regime. In 1993 they joined forces with seven other Serbian stations to form the Association of Independent Electronic Media (ANEM). By 1996, when even larger anti-Milošević demonstrations were hitting the streets, B92 had expanded beyond radio programmes to publishing and CD production, had launched Belgrade's first internet service provider, Opennet, and had even set up its own cultural centre, Cinema Rex. B92 was closed for the second time in December 1996, which prompted it to switch its news bulletins to its website. Because of its high profile, it was allowed to broadcast again after only two days, the result of much national and international pressure.

In April 1999, extensive NATO air-raids on Serbia resulted in a massive clampdown from a government that would brook no dissent. B92's name and broadcasting frequency, together with its premises, were hijacked by the regime. In order to disseminate information about the domestic situation in Serbia to the world at large it was necessary to put full reliance on the internet, which allowed B92 journalists to tell the truth as they saw it, without the mask of state censorship, but with the fear that all independent journalists felt in the face of the state-sanctioned violence against them. Soon the website was attracting over one million hits a day.

The radio station was back on the air in August 1999, this time as B2-92, using a borrowed frequency and premises. They branched out briefly into TV production before being closed for the fourth and final time in May 2000. This was the signal that drove them firmly underground and a guerrilla-like existence of secret premises that changed almost daily. Radio and television productions were sent to other ANEM members around the country by way of satellite, and radio stations just over the border in Bosnia and Romania were used for transmissions.

Instead of folding under pressure, B92 diversified even further, promoting two concert tours around Serbia that encouraged voting in the forthcoming autumn elections. The resulting turnout led to a victory for the democratic parties, widespread anti-regime protests and the long-awaited downfall of Milošević on October 5 of that year. On that same momentous day, B92 TV started broadcasting for the first time alongside its sister radio station.

With the return of democracy B92 continues to play a key role in ANEM, which now has a total of 58 radio and 37 television stations across Serbia, Montenegro and Kosovo. One of ANEM's bravest initiatives is to launch the Truth, Responsibility and Reconciliation project, which aims to acknowledge and lay open the horrors of the previous decade by means of television and radio programmes and international conferences, and to move Serbia forward into a new era of peace, tolerance and cultural richness.

For a more detailed history of B92 and its role during the Milošević period consult Matthew Collin's book, *This is Serbia Calling: Rock 'n' Roll Radio and Belgrade's Underground Resistance* (Serpent's Tail, 2001).

most popular TV channel currently being independent RTV Pink, another erstwhile apologist for the Milošević regime. RTV Pink is characterised by brash and noisy programming that tends to favour loud music, scantily clad dancers and vapid soap operas. It was through RTV Pink that turbo-folk first came to the attention of the Serbian public, pumped out as a glitzy patriotic sop to the masses during the troubled years of sanctions, civil war and isolation. Another privately owned, commercial station run along similar lines to Pink, is BKTV, which is the television interest of the Brača Karić media company. Both Pink TV and BKTV are owned by figures once close to the old regime: Zeljko Mitrović and Bogoljub Karić respectively.

In Kosovo, the Albanian-language channel TV Kosova is owned by the German Bertelsmann group. Given that it was formerly in the hands of the Miloševićs' daughter, Marija, TV Kosova has undergone a volte-face in recent years, from a pro-Belgrade state mouthpiece to a far more pro-Albanian position with NATO sympathies.

RTV Pink has, at times, strayed beyond the boundaries of good taste to broadcast content that could by any standards be considered offensive. It has been accused of promoting a culture of stereotypes and intolerance, continuing the tradition it began while maintaining the previous regime by offering a false image of reality and Serbian society. In 2003 RTV Pink broadcasted a prime-time 'entertainment' show called It Cannot Hurt, which promoted a very misogynistic outlook in which women were depicted as being little more than sex objects, with constant reference being made to the necessity for their being submissive to men. Following these broadcasts, a lawsuit was filed on November 20 2003 to the Second District Court in Belgrade signed by 55 women NGOs and other individuals. This was the first court proceeding to be filed according to a new law on public information, which prohibits hate speech in article No 38. Shortly after, on December 10, the International Day of Human Rights, posters appeared around Belgrade declaring, 'Yes it hurts, because violence starts with insults'. Controversial broadcasting is sometimes less a case of political correctness and more a matter of copyright. In 2004 one independent TV channel, Enigma, found itself in trouble with the authorities when it broadcast a pirated version of The Lord of the Rings: The Two Towers just weeks after its European premiere. What was truly scandalous was the poor quality of the tape: it had been videotaped directly from a cinema screen.

In contrast to the chauvinism and old-regime leanings of some of the other independents, TV B92 is an independent television station that grew out of a radio station, B2-92, which was very critical of the old regime. Although it does not have anything like the market share of Pink TV, which has 30%, or BKTV with about half this, B92 wields a disproportionate amount of influence thanks to its perceived integrity and the international respect it earned for its anti-Milošević stance during the late 1990s. (See box, B92 – A Short History).

Radio

There are over 1,000 private radio stations throughout Serbia, a number that is way beyond the optimal for a small, relatively poor country. This, along with television and the printed media, reflects a rather cluttered media landscape.

As well as two stations on state-run RTS Radio, prominent broadcasters are:

Radio Barajevo on FM 105.9 MHz
From Novi Sad, **Radio 021** on 92.2 MHz
Radio Index from Belgrade
Radio B2-92 with live news radio on Real Audio and MP3

English-language broadcasting can be heard on the **BBC World Service**, which can be received on short wave at 6195 and 9410 kHz mornings and evenings; 12095 kHz throughout the daytime.
Voice of America on 9760 and 6040 kHz

The BBC also relays broadcasts on FM in Albanian, Serbian, English and Turkish from Priština, Kosovo, on 98.6 kHz

Internet news and information sources
ANEM www.anem.org.yu
BETA www.beta.co.yu
B92 www.b92.net
Belgrade Media Centre www.mediacenter.org.yu
Independent Journalists' Association – IJAS www.nuns.org.yu
Serbian Unity Congress www.suc.org is a non-profit international organisation representing the Serbian Diaspora.
www.Emperors-Clothes.com is an English-language internet magazine with an occasionally controversial, pro-Serb stance that often challenges the analysis of the Western press.
Tanjug www.tanjug.co.yu

Internet providers
BeoTeNet www.beotel.yu
Bits www.bitsyu.net
EUnet Yugoslavia www.eunet.yu
MemoData www.memodata.net
SezamPro www.sezampro.yu
YUBC Net www.yubc.net

Internet cafés are now reasonably widespread throughout Serbia. The locations of some of these are given in individual chapters, although the situation is that of constant mushrooming and closing down. Internet charges are reasonable, generally in the order of 60din per hour.

Telephones
Halo telephone cards can be bought from post offices and kiosks at 150, 200 and 300din value. They work in the more modern orange phones, which conveniently have buttons to change foreign-language settings. Calls can also be made directly from post offices, where you are directed to a booth and pay for the call when you have finished. The code for dialling abroad from Serbia is 99; you then dial the country code then the city and the recipient's number. To phone Serbia from abroad, you must first dial the international access code (which is usually 00), then 381 for Serbia; then you dial the city code (11 in the case of Belgrade) and the number. Mobile phones in Serbia all begin with 06 (063 for Mobtel, 064 for Telekom Srbija). The Serbian mobile phone network is currently being developed and undergoing privatisation, which should see an improvement from what is currently a rather ragged service.

City codes Belgrade (0)11, Novi Sad (0)21, Niš (0)18
Serbian online telephone book www.telekom.yu
Important phone numbers Police 92, Fire department 93, Ambulance 94

Post
The basic Zip code for Belgrade is 11000. Post offices are open 08.00–20.00 weekdays, 08.00–15.00 Saturdays. In Belgrade, some may be open on Sundays. The cost of sending

a postcard to elsewhere in Europe is 35din. Letters cost 35din for those weighing less than 35g, 41din for up to 45g and then the tariff increases with 10g increments. Post from Serbia to the United Kingdom takes between a week and ten days. All of the major express courier companies like DHL and FedEx have offices in Belgrade.

BUSINESS

Many Serbian entrepreneurs are keen to develop business links overseas, especially with western Europe. After years of feeling that they were out in the cold, there is a begrudging confidence that things might finally be moving forwards economically and that burgeoning Serbian business interests will have a chance to play in the international field. It has not been easy: whereas most eastern European countries have experienced teething pangs in converting a communist state monopoly to a free-market economy, Serbia has had civil war and economic sanctions to deal with as well. There are still vestiges of the old way of doing things and, despite ongoing privatisation, a lingering feeling that good service is not a commodity in itself. But this is changing rapidly, as state ownership of many enterprises is privatised and foreign companies start to move in. While it would be foolhardy to claim that the business climate of the 1990s, where corruption and nepotism counted for more than business skills and hard work, has changed completely, by and large, doing business in Serbia today is little different from anywhere else in eastern Europe. Serbian entrepreneurs like to take their time, and to impress: business in Serbia is often conducted over a large shared meal or, more likely, after it; inevitably, the host will pick up the bill.

- The Serbian Chamber of Commerce and Industry has lots of useful advice for businesses wishing to invest in Serbia at www.pkj.co.yu/en.
- Company reports on Serbian companies can be obtained from the Chamber of Commerce by paying €80 per company into either of the following and sending a copy of the payment to their fax: 3248 754 or 3225 903.
- Eksimbanka, a/c no: 9359258 10, SWIFT code: EKBEYUBG, through Deutsche Bank F/M, SWIFT code: DEUTDEFF.
- Komercijalna Banka, a/c no: 935966200, SWIFT code: KOBBYUBG, BLZ 99900, through the intermediary of Deutsche Bank Ag F/M FR Germany, SWIFT code: DEUTDEFF, BLZ 50070010.
- Information on facts and figures, regional data, and rules and regulations that affect businesses in Serbia are available at www.invest-in-serbia.com.

Foreign banks that have branches in Belgrade include:

HVB Rajićeva 27–29; tel: 3204 500
Micro Finance Bank Gospodar Jevremona 9; tel: 3025 625
National Bank of Greece Kralja Petra 22–24; tel: 3281 498
Raiffeisenbank Resavska 22; tel: 3202 121
Sociéte Generale Vladimira Popovića 6; tel: 3111 515

CULTURE
Cultural dos and don'ts

Perhaps it should go without saying that any discussion of politics in Serbia may well invite argument from some quarter. The future of Kosovo, in particular, is a very tricky topic. Opinion is frequently divided in Serbian politics, but rarely are the arguments in clear-cut opposition. Rather, there are many grey areas, and to disapprove of the past Milošević regime is not the same thing as condoning the NATO bombing. This is not to say that discussions of politics should be avoided –

that would be impossible anywhere in the Balkans – but simply that it is best to have an open mind and listen, and to offer opinions only when they are asked for. Serbians are only too aware of the problems facing their country, and do not take warmly to foreign smart alecs who claim to know all the answers. The same might be said of conversations about Serbian football teams too.

Serbians take a pride in their reputation for hospitality and will defend it to a fault. When paying the bill in a restaurant it is customary for the host to pay the whole bill. This is done regardless of the host's financial standing, and in most circumstances foreigner visitors are automatically considered to be guests. Often the bill is paid surreptitiously to avoid protest. The idea of breaking a bill down so individuals can pay for their own share of food and drink is unheard of. Similarly, if you are invited to have something to eat or drink, even if it is just a cup of coffee, it is always best to accept graciously. To refuse something proffered in this way can cause offence as it may give the impression that you are behaving in a haughty manner.

Eating and drinking is a serious business in Serbia, as is the conversation and toasting that punctuates a meal. When sharing a toast with someone it is imperative that you look into their eyes as you do this. To avoid eye contact is considered disrespectful or, at best, weak.

If you are able to speak Serbian it is inadvisable to do this in Kosovo unless you are in an exclusively Serb enclave as doing so could attract unnecessary attention and even violence.

Dress should be conservative and respectful when visiting churches, monasteries or mosques; no shorts, short skirts or flip-flops.

Homosexuality is tolerated, officially at least, but open displays of same sex affection are frowned upon and could even provoke a hostile reaction.

Interacting with local people

Many of Serbia's younger generation speak and understand English, but a few words of Serbian go a long way and, with the exception of most of Kosovo, will always be well received. Older people may speak German or French instead. Indeed, in poorer enclaves like Kosovo or southern Serbia, German speakers are quite plentiful as so many of them worked abroad as *Gastarbeiten* when they were younger. Away from the cities it may be harder to find people who share a common language but with hand gestures, patience and a dictionary or phrasebook, it is always possible to communicate at least on a rudimentary level.

If you are staying with a Serbian host, any offers of cash will probably be swept aside, but small gifts of a non-monetary nature will be gladly accepted. Suitable gifts might be books, flowers, foreign magazines or clothing items like T-shirts with foreign logos. Business cards, family photographs and postcards of home are always appreciated.

Although, as a foreigner, they will probably draw the line at handshaking, most Serbians will be impressed if you adopt their custom of planting three kisses on alternating cheeks, a practice that takes place between both men and women. However, this is a custom that takes place mainly between family members and close friends and so it may be best to let them initiate you into this to spare any potential embarrassment. The number three is of great significance to Serbs. One Serbian expression goes, 'God helps three times', and even the National Tourist Office have adopted 'Three times love' as their slogan.

Nicotine and caffeine are the twin fuels of Serbian youth culture, with alcohol sitting firmly in third place. In Serbia, tobacco smoking is less of a habit and more a way of life, as is the frequent consumption of strong coffee. Non-smokers will just have to grin and bear it.

GIVING SOMETHING BACK

Several charities work in Serbia doing their best to alleviate the suffering of refugees and displaced people. Serbia's Roma community, given the straitened circumstances in which they often find themselves, are frequently targeted as being an especially deserving cause. The Roman Catholic charity **CAFOD** (Romero Close, London SW9 9TV, United Kingdom; tel: +44 20 7733 7900; fax: +44 20 7274 9630; email: cafod@cafod.org.uk) does much good work in this field: helping to educate Roma children, providing a counselling service for refugees, and assisting Roma families in getting access to clean water, medical treatment and the basic necessities of life.

Save the Children UK is also active in Serbia, most notably in working with local Roma non-government organisations to improve educational achievement for Roma children. They can be contacted by writing to them at FREEPOST NAT7383, Witney OX29 7BR, United Kingdom, or via their website at www.savethechildren.org.uk.

In contrast to the previous two, the **BLAGO Fund** concerns itself primarily with Serbia's cultural heritage, especially its Orthodox churches and monasteries. The BLAGO Fund state that their mission is to preserve and promote Serbian treasures that tie together past, present and future. One of their current projects is to save the frescos of Mileševa Monastery, which are in urgent need of conservation. They receive considerable patronage from the Serbian Orthodox Church and the Serbian diaspora overseas, particularly in the United States. Donations can be made to: Serbian Unity Congress, PMB 352, 17216 Saticoy St, Van Nuys, CA 91406-2103, USA.

Another organisation with connections with the Serbian Orthodox Church is **United Orthodox Aid** (www.unitedorthodoxaid.com), which encourages volunteers to visit Serbia in order to collect information about the immediate technical needs of hospitals, schools and refugee camps. They are particularly interested in obtaining surplus medical equipment from abroad for use in Serbian hospitals, as well as sourcing unwanted computer and IT hardware for schools and refugee camps. United Orthodox Aid is keen on employing the services of those who have expertise in the funding of small charities and start-up business enterprises. Enquiries can be made by mailing them at webmaster@unitedorthodoxaid.com, or writing to United Orthodox Aid, The Beeches, 33 Albion Hill, Loughton, Essex IG10 4RD. Donations can be made directly to this address or by downloading their donation form at: www.unitedorthodoxaid.com/forms/donationform.htm.

Hope and Aid Direct are a British concern that organise convoys twice a year to take supplies to help refugees and displaced people in Serbia and other Balkan countries. Their motto is, 'We take aid, not sides'. They are always interested in taking on more volunteers and can be contacted at www.hopeandaiddirect.org.uk.

Those who would prefer to help Serbian wildlife might be interested in the activities of the **League for the Ornithological Action of Serbia and Montenegro** (LOASM), whose goal is that of protecting birds, their habitats and sites through the involvement of people, and is dedicated to educating the people of Serbia and Montenegro in the importance and enjoyment of birds. For information, write to: Liga za ornitolosku akciju Srbije i Crne Gore, 51 Njegoseva Street, 11000 Beograd; or directly to the LOASM chairman, Dragan Simić, at goingbirding@yahoo.com.

More specific still is the **Birds of Prey Protection Fund** (www.vulture.org.yu) dedicated to the conservation of diurnal and nocturnal raptors in Serbia and Montenegro. The most significant project undertaken by the BPPF was Save the Griffon Vulture Campaign which increased the dwindling population of this species to become the biggest flock in the central Balkans. For information, get in touch with them at: Fond za zastitu ptica grabljivica, 29 novembra br 142, 11000 Beograd; tel: 764422, ext 152; fax: 1761433; email: grifon@ibiss.bg.ac.yu.

For those interested in voluntary work, **Young Researchers of Serbia (YRS)** is a non-profit, non-governmental organisation whose main aims are education and exchange as well as work with young people. It works as an umbrella organisation, gathering together 27 clubs and societies from universities and towns across Serbia, and is interested in fostering scientific creativity in youthful volunteers. Its activities are diverse: scientific projects, work in youth camps, humanitarian work and environmental education. A small participation fee is payable. YRS can be contacted at: Bulevar umetnosti 27, 11070 Novi Beograd; tel: 311 1314, 311 6663; fax: 311 6653; email: misvss@eunet.yu; www.mis.org.yu.

MISCELLANEOUS

Serbia is one hour ahead of GMT and, in spring, adds an hour on for summer time, the same as the UK.

Public toilets are uncommon but may be found at markets and bus or train stations; the facilities in cafés or restaurants are usually a better bet. There is usually a small charge made for the privilege but this does not guarantee cleanliness. Men and women's facilities are often marked in Cyrillic, with **М, МУЩКИ**, Muški for men, and **Ж, ЖИНСКИ**, or Ž, Ženski for women.

Electrical power is 220 volts, 50Hz. Plug sockets are the standard European two-prong, round-pin type. Power cuts are fairly rare these days.

Wild boar

SERBIA

NATIONAL TOURISM ORGANISATION OF SERBIA

Tourism Organisation of Serbia:
your one stop source for all travel information on Serbia

www.serbia-tourism.org

Part Two

The Guide

KEY TO STANDARD SYMBOLS — Bradt

—·—·—	International boundary
------	District boundary
------	National park boundary
✈	Airport (international)
✈	Airport (other)
✚	Airstrip
🚁	Helicopter service
▬▬	Railway
----------	Footpath
--🚢--	Car ferry
--🚢--	Passenger ferry
⛽	Petrol station or garage
🅿	Car park
🚌	Bus station etc
→	One way arrow
M	Underground station
🏠	Hotel, inn etc
Å	Campsite
♦	Hut
♀	Wine bar
✗	Restaurant, café etc
✉	Post office
☎	Telephone
e	Internet café
✚	Hospital, clinic etc
🏛	Museum
🐘	Zoo
ℹ	Tourist information
$	Bank
♦	Statue or monument
∴	Archaeological or historic site
🏛	Historic building
🏰	Castle/fortress
✝	Church or cathedral
♣	Buddhist temple
🏠	Buddhist monastery
♣	Hindu temple
٢	Mosque
⚑	Golf course
🏃	Stadium
▲	Summit
△	Boundary beacon
◉	Outpost
⊠⊠	Border post
⌂	Rock shelter
□—○—□	Cable car, funicular
)(	Mountain pass
○	Waterhole
✳	Scenic viewpoint
✿	Botanical site
♤	Specific woodland feature
🎋	Lighthouse
≈	Marsh
♈	Mangrove
⤳	Bird nesting site
∭	Waterfall
✳	Source of river
⤢	Beach
⤳	Scuba diving
⤳	Fishing sites

Other map symbols are sometimes shown in separate key boxes with individual explanations for their meanings.

Belgrade Београд

INTRODUCTION

Telephone code: 011

The first thing anyone will tell you about Serbia's capital is
that it does not live up to its name – Belgrade, or rather,
Beograd (the 'White City'), is anything but white. Rather, it is
mostly a utilitarian grey, the colour of concrete, which looks its
dreary worst under a leaden, winter sky and only marginally
more cheerful in spring sunshine. This stereotypical Eastern-
bloc greyness is deceptive though, because although the grim
monoliths of New Belgrade's high-rises and the Roma shanty town
that clings haphazardly alongside the railway tracks do their best to
dispirit the first-time visitor, the city has far more to offer than these
initial impressions might suggest.

For a start, there is the Kalemegdan Fortress perched high above the town,
overlooking the confluence of the Sava and Danube rivers. The 18th-century fortress
is impressive enough but it is the ample green space of the parkland and gardens that
surround it that holds most year-round appeal for Belgrade's citizens. Nudging the
park to the south and east is Stari Grad, the Old City, with its cathedral, secessionist
buildings and a few, and now sadly rare, Ottoman remnants. Running through the
elegant streets that lead down to the city's more prosaic commercial centre is
pedestrianised Kneza Mihaila – a constant stream of humanity, particularly in the
evening when Belgrade's younger citizens take their place in the Balkan equivalent of
the *korso*, the southeast European evening promenade.

Such is the cosy and intimate scale of this older part of Belgrade that it is only when
you reach the splendid art nouveau edifice of the Hotel Moscow on busy, traffic
laden Terazije at the bottom end of Kneza Mihaila, having passed Trg Republike
(Republic Square) and Trg Studentski (Students' Square) along the way, are you
reminded that you are in a large capital city; a city that has, perhaps inevitably given
its recent history, become a little battered and careworn in places. However, those
expecting to find a bomb-damaged, war-ravaged city on its uppers may be
disappointed – despite the extensive damage done by the NATO bombing of 1999,
little physical evidence remains of this today. Similarly, the mood on the streets is
upbeat. To those in the know, Belgrade is party city; a calm, dignified party that
shows style, finesse and an undeniable joie de vivre.

HISTORY

The first evidence of settlement comes from Zemun, across the Danube from Old
Belgrade. At Zemun, formerly a separate town but now effectively a Belgrade suburb,
archaeological evidence has been found to suggest that the banks of the Danube were
first settled here about 7,000 years ago. The Celts were the first to colonise the
opposite bank, on a bluff overlooking the confluence of the Danube and Sava rivers,

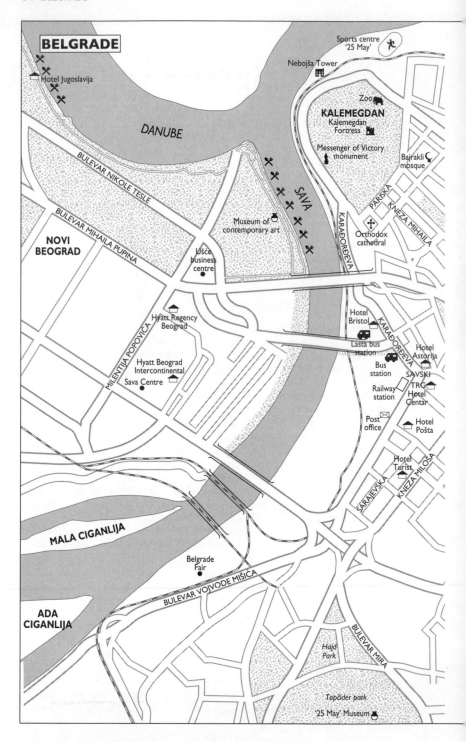

BELGRADE

Sports centre '25 May'

Nebojša Tower

Hotel Jugoslavija

Zoo

KALEMEGDAN

Kalemegdan Fortress

DANUBE

Messenger of Victory monument

Bajrakli mosque

BULEVAR NIKOLE TESLE

SAVA

PARSKA

KNEZA MIHAILA

BULEVAR MIHAILA PUPINA

Museum of contemporary art

Orthodox cathedral

KARAĐORĐEVA

NOVI BEOGRAD

Ušće business centre

Hotel Bristol

KARAĐORĐEVA

Hyatt Regency Beograd

Lasta bus station

Hotel Astorija

MILENTIJA POPOVIĆA

Hyatt Beograd Intercontinental

Sava Centre

Bus station

SAVSKI TRG

Railway station

Hotel Centar

Post office

Hotel Pošta

Hotel Turist

SARAJEVSKA

KNEZA MILOŠA

MALA CIGANLIJA

Belgrade Fair

ADA CIGANLIJA

BULEVAR VOJVODE MIŠIĆA

BULEVAR MIRA

Hajd Park

Topčider park

'25 May' Museum

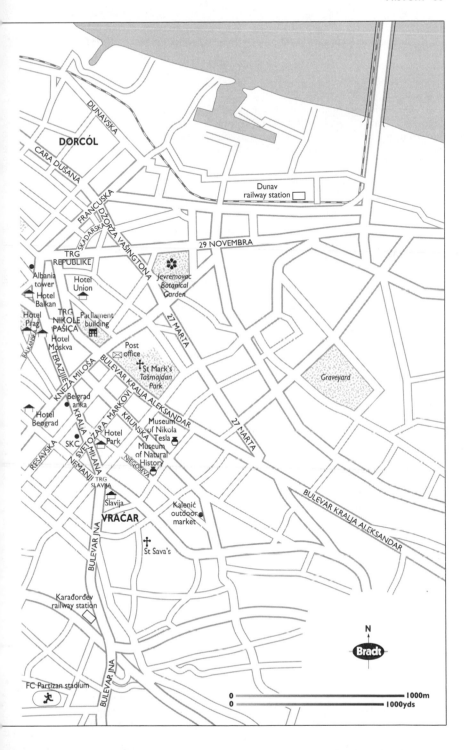

founding the settlement of Singidinum in the 3rd century BC. The next to come were the Romans, who arrived in the 1st century AD and remained for the best part of the next 400 years. With their typical flair for disciplined road-building, the Romans provided the route and some of the foundations for present-day Kneza Mihaila, Belgrade's first and, in the hearts of its citizenry at least, still most-important thoroughfare.

Huns, Goths and Avars took turns at occupying the city before the Serbs arrived to make Belgrade their capital in 1403, having fled their southern territories after a momentous defeat at the hand of the Turks at the Battle of Kosovo in 1389. The Serbian occupation continued with interruption for the next century or so until the ever-advancing Ottomans captured the city from the Hungarians in 1521, in whose hands it remained until 1842 when a final Turkish withdrawal allowed it to become the capital of a newly liberated Serbia. Later, as the first of several regional federations were formed, Belgrade became the capital of the short-lived Kingdom of Serbs, Croats and Slovenes created at the end of World War I. With the establishment of the larger, and far more ambitious, federation of Tito's socialist Yugoslavia at the end of World War II, it was only natural that Belgrade should become the new capital.

Belgrade's vital position has been both a blessing and a curse; its strategic vantage point at the confluence of two great rivers, and its position as a sort of crossroads between northern and southern Europe has led to it being attacked, sacked, plundered and bombed numerous times during its long history – at least 20 times in fact. Even as late as the end of the World War II Belgrade was still a relatively small country town, and a great deal of that which remains is, in fact, a pragmatic, if not always aesthetically pleasing, response to the appalling devastation unleashed by Nazi bombers during 1941. Much of what you see today is the result of this post-war reconstruction: a very necessary response to the widespread homelessness and migration to the city in the years that followed the creation of the new socialist state.

PRACTICAL INFORMATION
Arrivals and departures
Belgrade's Surcin Airport (code: BEG; for enquiries, tel: 601 555/605 555) lies 20km west of the city. After passing through immigration you enter the arrivals hall that has a money exchange, an ATM machine and a tourist information counter. Waiting for you both inside the arrivals hall and outside in the car park will be any number of taxi drivers, all delighted to be of service. However, it is probably best not to entrust any of these stubble-chinned knights of the road with the responsibility of taking you into town as the taxi syndicate that operates out of the airport is something of a racket and, like many other airport-based operations the world over, it serves as a poor ambassador for the profession. Taxis are fairly priced in Belgrade, even cheap; but not here. The airport taxi drivers will conjure a price of between €15 and €30 to go into town, depending on how malleable you appear to be; the real cost, using the 'broken' meter, should be something more like €8 for the 30-minute journey. Better then to walk straight past them, smiling enigmatically as if you know their game, and catch either city bus 72, which leaves every 20–30 minutes from outside the main terminal building and terminates at Zaleni Venec close to Terazije and Kneza Mihaila, or the official JAT bus that departs every hour from 07.00–20.00, and which will take you to Hotel Slavija at Trg Slavija downtown, stopping in Novi Beograd and the railway station (probably the most useful stop for most of Belgrade's hotels) along the way. The city bus costs just 20din, the JAT bus, 120din. If you have too much luggage to consider this, and really do require a taxi, then you can get the tourist information counter at the arrivals hall to phone a legitimate one for you. Decide on this before you leave the arrivals hall, as once you have left it you cannot get back in.

Above Playing chess on Danube walkway, New Belgrade (LM)

Right Karadorde statue and St Sava Church, Belgrade (LM)

Below Pontoon bridge across to Lido Beach, New Belgrade (LM)

Above Roma with horse and hay cart, Niš (LM)
Right Slano Kopovo nature reserve (LS)
Below Haystacks in Šumadija region, central Serbia (LM)

Getting a taxi to take you from the city centre to the airport for a fair price is far easier. Once again, you could take the bus: JAT buses leave from the Hotel Slavija on the hour from 05.00 until mid evening. The airport's departures lounge possesses all of the services that you might expect and a last chance to buy a souvenir bottle of *šljivovica* or that essential *Best of Ceca* CD.

Bus and rail terminals

Arriving by train or bus brings you right into the city centre itself, as both the **main railway station** (Železnička Stanica Beograd) and the **central bus station** (Beogradska Autobuska Stanica, **БАС** in Cyrillic) lie next door to each other on busy Karađorđeva, one of Belgrade's main thoroughfares. Both stations possess a *garderoba* – a left-luggage office – and currency exchange facilities, and there is also a small tourist office at the entrance to the train station (open 07.00–21.30). Currently there are no ATM machines at either of the stations but both have exchange offices for cash.

Unless you have elected to stay in New Belgrade across the river, it will be a relatively short, uphill walk from here to your chosen hotel. The taxis parked up in front of the stations are more likely to agree to use their meter than those at the airport but if they do not agree to this, then it is easy enough to flag down one that is passing. The fare to any of the central hotels should be no more than €2. Alternatively, any one of trams number 2, 11 or 13 passing right to left in front of the station will take you up to Kalemegdan Fortress, a short distance from Studentski Trg. The fare is 20din if you pay the driver or 12din if you buy a book of tickets from one of the snack booths at the bus station beforehand. Be aware that the tram may be crowded and could be a trial if you are carrying much luggage.

International services to and from Serbia terminate and depart from the main railway station, although some trains may stop at suburban stations as well. Through-tickets may be bought on services to Zagreb, Budapest, Ljubljana, Thessaloniki, Skopje and Bucharest, or even to more far-flung destinations like Moscow or Istanbul. The main domestic line runs north to Subotica in Vojvodina, and south to Bar on the Montenegrin coast.

The railway station has a slightly neglected and, depending on the time of day, sometimes deserted feel to it. To some extent, the atmosphere is that of a service in decline. The bus station is altogether livelier and handles far more domestic traffic. Generally, there are more buses than trains running to any given destination, and the bus network is considerably more wide-ranging anyway, serving every corner of Serbia and Montenegro. In addition, there are international buses, mainly used by migrant workers, which run as far as Germany and Istanbul. As a general rule, trains are slower but cheaper than buses.

In planning your exit from Belgrade, either station will give you an opportunity to get to grips with the Cyrillic alphabet – timetables that use Latin script are rarer than hens' teeth in Serbia – although the train station does have boards in Latin script announcing *Dolasci* – arrivals – and *Polasci* – departures. Be sure to check though, as some of the listed trains may not actually exist.

For information and reservations:

Bus station Tel: 636 299
Railway station Tel: 636 493

Getting around – city transport

Belgrade has a comprehensive bus and tram network, which is cheap but invariably crowded at rush hour. The most useful routes for visitors are those that run between the old town and the bus and railway stations – the aforementioned numbers 2, 11 and

13 – as well as those that connect Trg Slavija with Kalemegdan – numbers 19, 21, 22 and 29. Do not neglect to buy a ticket and make sure that you get it cancelled in the machine on board as you will run the risk of having to pay a fine if caught. A ticket purchased in bulk from a booth costs only 12din. It costs 20din if you pay the driver.

Another useful service is the bus route that runs between Pijaca venac by McDonald's, just down from the Hotel Moscow, and New Belgrade. Buses 15, 84 and 706 run from here across the river Sava and along Bulevar Nikole Tesle to reach the waterfront at the Hotel Jugoslavija and Zemun, an area rich in floating cafés and restaurants.

For many, taxis are a better option. Not only are they extremely cheap but their appeal is strengthened with the knowledge that, with the exception of the airport-based operators, cab drivers in Belgrade are usually honest and helpful. A typical fare for a short city ride is 100din. There are a few cowboys of course, but a genuine registered taxi can be recognised by a clear plastic sign on the roof, a functioning meter, and a sticker in the window displaying its rates. They are marginally more expensive at night and on Sundays. Dependable companies which may be called up are: **Alfa** (tel: 444 1113), **Alo** (tel: 532 2888), **Bell** (tel: 235 1212), **Beogradski** (tel: 9801), **Beotaxi** (tel: 970), **Lux** (tel: 324 8888), **Palma** (tel: 316 2020), **Plavi** (tel: 555 444), **Pink** (tel: 9803), **Naxi** (tel: 157 668), **Zeleni** (tel: 324 6088) and **Žuti** (tel: 9802).

Car rental

Avanco rent-a-car Trmska 7; tel: 243 3797; fax: 344 0412 (08.00–16.00); mobile: 381 64 184 5555 (00.00–midnight); email: avaco@yubc.net; www.avaco.co.yu. Their office is located off Bulevar Revolucije, with cars from €25 per day for long-term hire, more for shorter periods. Minimum age is 21, requiring at least two documents with a photo and a deposit of €500–1,000.

Avis (www.avis.co.yu) have branches at: Bulevar Kralja Aleksandra 94 (tel: 433 3140), Obilićev venac 25 (tel: 620 362), Hotel Intercontinental (tel: 311 2910), Maksima Gorkog 32 (tel: 457 677) and at Belgrade Airport (tel: 605 690).

Budget Hotel Hyatt Regency, Milentija Popovića 5; tel: 137 703, and at Belgrade Airport; tel: 601 555, ext 2959.

Eminence rent-a-car 29 Novembra 15; tel/fax: 3239 603; mob: 381 63 397 266. Have cheap rates for long-term hire (Yugo or Zastava).

Ineco have branches at Topličin venac 17 (tel: 639 319), Trg Republike 5/IX (tel: 622 361) and Belgrade Airport (tel: 601 555 ext2732).

Putnik-Hertz have two city branches: one at Kneza Miloša 82 (tel: 641 566) and the other at Belgrade Airport (tel: 600 634).

YUTim rent-a car (previously Kompas Hertz); tel: 672 155, 692 339; fax: 609 730; email: yutimrac@eunet.yu; www.yutim.co.yu. They have three branches: Bulevar Nikole Tesle 3, Hotel Jugoslavija and Belgrade Airport.

Airline offices

Aeroflot Braće Jugovića 21; tel: 322 5814
Aerosvit Nikole Spasića 3; tel: 328 3430
Air India Bulevar Mihajla Pupina 10g; tel: 133 551
Alitalia Terazije 43/I; tel: 324 5000
Austrian Airlines Terazije 3/III; tel: 324 8077
British Airways Kneza Mihaila 30/IV; tel: 328 1303
CSA Prizrenska 2; tel: 3614 592
Emirates Kneza Mihaila 6/VI; tel: 624 435
JAT Bulevar Umetnosti 16; tel: 311 4222
KLM Kneza Mihaila 30/III; tel: 328 2747
Lot Terazije 3/VII; tel: 322 8640

Lufthansa Terazije 3/VII; tel: 322 4974
Malev Kneza Mihaila 30/II; tel: 626 377
Montenegro Airways Kneza Mihaila 23/I; tel: 628 002
Olympic Airways 29 Novembra 12; tel: 3226 800
Qantas Sremska 4a/I; tel: 639 166
Royal Jordanian Starine Novaka 3; tel: 3222 214
Swiss Terazije 3/III; tel: 3030 140

Tourist offices

The main branch of the helpful **Tourist Organisation of Belgrade** (TOB) is down
the underpass at the bottom of Kneza Mihailova in Terazije Passage near the Albanija
building (tel: 635 622; fax: 635 343). It is open Monday to Friday 09.00–20.00,
Saturday 09.00–16.00, and closed on Sundays. There is a smaller branch nearby at
Kneza Mihaila 18 (tel: 064 8181 016), which is open Monday to Friday 09.00–20.00,
Saturday 09.00–18.00 and Sunday 11.00–17.00, and another at the Central Railway
Station with a useful exchange office next door (tel: 3612 732, 3612 645; open daily
07.00–21.30, Sunday 10.00–18.00). In addition, TOB have a counter at Belgrade
Airport (tel: 601 555 or 605 555, ext 2638), which, in theory at least, is open daily
between 09.00 and 20.00. The Sava Centre in New Belgrade, Milentija Popovića 9
(tel: 698 031) has its own branch, which is open daily 09.00–20.00, Saturday
09.00–15.00 and closed Sundays.

All of these can issue city maps, hotel listings and a copy of *Welcome to Belgrade*
magazine, as well as advise on current events in the city. Their *This Month in Belgrade*
booklet is also useful. TOB has its own useful and informative website at
www.belgradetourism.org.yu.

Local tour operators

The **Tourist Organisation of Belgrade** run a couple of good-value bus tours: a
city sightseeing tour that leaves every Saturday at noon, lasting 90 minutes and costing
150din, and a three-hour guided tour to the Vinča archaeological site that leaves on
Saturdays at 11.00 and costs 230din. Both tours depart from near their head office at
Trg Nikole Pašića.

Putnik (www.putnik.co.yu) is the main travel agency and tour operator that
operates throughout Serbia. Although previously state-owned, its operations have
now been bought up by a Serbian-American with a view to modernisation. In
Belgrade, Putnik has its main office at Terazije 27 (tel: 323 2911; fax: 323 4461). It
can arrange both domestic and international bus and train tickets as well as providing
a range of tour services. There are other branches at Dragoslava Jovanovića 1 (tel: 323
1905) and at Trg Nikole Pašića 1 (tel: 334 5619) as well as a branch near to the bus
station on Milanova Milovanovića.

In addition to Putnik, both **BAS** at the bus station (tel: 638 555) and **Turist Biro
Lasta** (opposite at Milovana Milovanovića 1; tel: 641 251) sell bus tickets. Train
information and tickets may be obtained from the English-speaking staff at **KSR
Beogradturs**, Milovana Milovanovića 5 (tel: 641 258), avoiding the crush and
possible communication difficulties at the station itself. They do not charge
commission. They also have a branch at Dečanska 21 (tel: 323 5335).

Belgrade Tourist Guide Association (Kalemegdan Fortress Information
Centre, tel: 354 7865; fax: 622 452) is a collective of trained multi-lingual guides who
can guide you around the fortress or further afield in the city or beyond. Their prices
start at about 1,500din for a 90-minute fortress tour.

Belgrade Sightseeing provides an efficiently run tourist service headed by
Branko Rabotic, a licensed guide who speaks English, Serbian and Greek. Mr

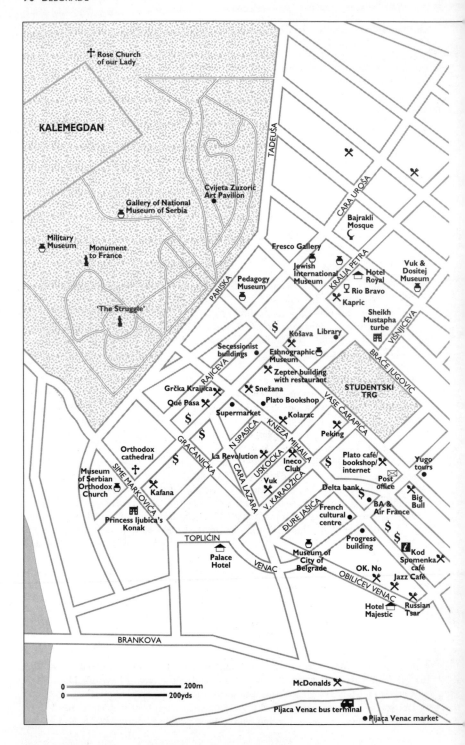

† Rose Church of our Lady

KALEMEGDAN

Cvijeta Zuzorić Art Pavilion

Gallery of National Museum of Serbia

Military Museum

Monument to France

'The Struggle'

TADEUSA

CARA UROSA

Bajrakli Mosque

Fresco Gallery

PARISKA

Pedagogy Museum

Jewish International Museum

KRALJA PETRA

Hotel Royal

Rio Bravo

Kapric

Vuk & Dositej Museum

Sheikh Mustapha turbe

VIŠNJIĆEVA

Košava Library

BRAĆE JUGOVIĆ

Secessionist buildings

RAJIĆEVA

Ethnographic Museum

Zepter building with restaurant

STUDENTSKI TRG

Grčka Kraijica

Snežana

VASE ČARAPIĆA

Qué Pasa

Plato Bookshop

Supermarket

N SPASIĆA

Kolarac

KNEZA MIHAILA

Peking

GRAČANIČKA

La Revolution

USKOCKA

Ineco Club

Plato café/ bookshop/ internet

Yugo tours

Orthodox cathedral

CARA LAZARA

Vuk

Post office

Big Bull

Museum of Serbian Orthodox Church

SIME MARKOVIĆA

Kafana

V. KARADŽIĆA

Delta bank

BA & Air France

Princess ljubica's Konak

ĐURE JAŠIĆA

French cultural centre

Progress building

Kod Spomenka café

TOPLIČIN

Palace Hotel

VENAC

Museum of City of Belgrade

OK. No

Jazz Café

OBILIĆEV VENAC

Hotel Majestic

Russian Tsar

BRANKOVA

| 0 | 200m |
| 0 | 200yds |

McDonalds

Pijaca Venac bus terminal

Pijaca Venac market

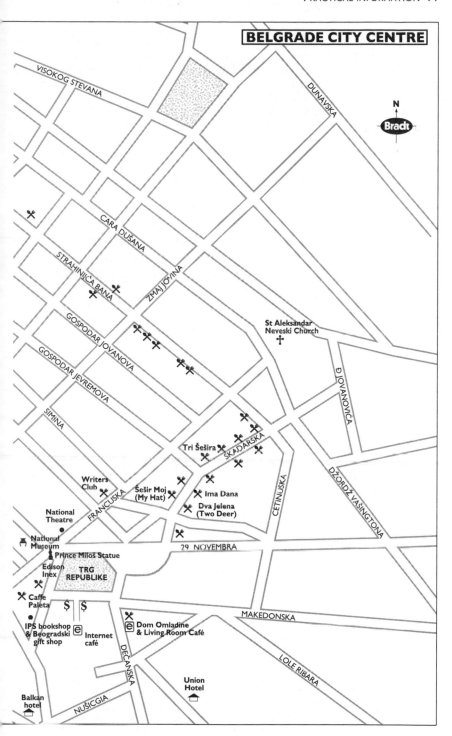

BELGRADE CITY CENTRE

Rabotic is very knowledgeable about Belgrade's history and organises a range of private city tours and guided walks, as well as multi-day excursions further into the Serbian countryside. City walking tours begin at about €30 per group. He can also arrange airport transfers and provide an interpretation service. His office is at 14 Decembra 33; tel/fax: 446 1153; mob: 063 854 2648; email: rabotic@Eunet.yu. He hosts an informative website at: http://solair.eunet.yu/~rabotic.

Jolly Travel (Kneza Miloša 9; tel: 323 2393; fax: 334 1843; www.jolly.co.yu) can arrange tours, both in Belgrade and beyond, and assist in organising car hire and booking airline tickets. English, French, Italian, Spanish, Greek and Russian are all spoken. City-centre tours start from 1500din per group.

Pleasure river cruises

River services between Belgrade and other Serbian towns used to run in the past and there is some hope that pleasure cruises may restart in the next year or two.

The **Tourist Organisation of Belgrade** runs local river cruises during the summer months, beginning at the quay by the Hotel Jugoslavija. The boats sail past Lido Beach in Zemun, around Veliko Ratno Island in the confluence of the two rivers, and past the May 25 Sports Centre in Dorćol; then they turn south to pass Kalemegdan Fortress and the Orthodox cathedral, heading under the Sava River bridges as far as Ada Ciganlija Island before returning north past the Museum of Contemporary Art to the quay. Boats leave at 16.00 and 18.00 on weekends, and at 18.00 during the week; there is no service on Mondays. The trip takes approximately 90 minutes and costs 250din for adults, 125din for children aged six to 14, and free for children less than six years old. They also run occasional night-time trips with onboard music and refreshments.

Steam railway trips

On some summer weekends, excursions with the *Romantika* steam train take place between Belgrade and Sremska Karlovci, near Novi Sad. The *Romantika* departs from Belgrade at 08.30 and returns to arrive back there at 19.50. The Magelan Corporation Tourist Agency of Novi Sad (see *Vojvodina* chapter) arrange tours that can be pre-booked to meet the train at Sremska Karlovci, visiting the Peace Chapel, the Krušedol and Gregteg monasteries and the museum house at Neradin. A lunch is also included. Return train tickets cost between 320 and 450din, depending on class; for children between four and 14, 250din. The excursion costs 790din for adults, 490din for children.

Another summer steam excursion operates in summer between Belgrade and Smederevo, leaving Belgrade at 08.15 and arriving in Smederevo at 10.45, where a tour can be arranged of the town and its museums before the train returns to Belgrade at 19.00, arriving at 21.30. A lunch can also be booked at a traditional restaurant 5km from the town with transport to and from provided.

For the precise dates of these weekend excursions enquire at a TOB office. The tours can be booked at several travel agents, including branches of Putnik and KSR Beogradturs and Agencija Romantika Travel at Balkanska 52–54 (tel: 683 056, 683 046).

Maps and guides

One of the most useful city maps is the Belgrade map in the pocket-sized *Autoatlas-Srbija i Crna Gora/Beograd* published by M@gic M@p, which contains a useful 1:880,000 Serbia-Montenegro map together with a detailed city map at 1:20,000 and a gazetteer for both. Another good map is the *Beograd city map 1:20,000* published by Intersistem Cartography. Both of these are readily available at the postcard kiosks and bookshops along Kneza Mihaila. The Tourist Office of Belgrade produce their own

1:20,000 city map based on the Intersistem map, which shows museums, churches and other tourist sights, together with an inset city transport map.

The TOB, and some bookshops, also sell the *Belgrade Tourist Guide* by Ljubica Corović for around 700din. Although this is rather out of date in terms of practicalities it serves as an excellent guide to Belgrade's historical landmarks.

WHERE TO STAY

Virtually all of Belgrade's hotels are state-owned and, although some may have obliging and enthusiastic staff, many tend to perpetuate the stereotypes of the socialist-era school of management. The majority are geared more towards expense account-funded business conventions than to the tastes of foreign tourists. Nevertheless, they are invariably clean and adequate, if, at times, lacking in character. There is a degree of overlap between the prices and facilities offered in the mid-range and budget categories listed below. The stars awarded in each category should be taken with a liberal pinch of salt, particularly at the bottom end of the market. There is residency tax to pay of 60din a day that cheaper hotels tend to include in the price but more expensive ones usually do not.

As a rule, budget travellers are not well catered for, although there are a couple of real bargains that should be reserved in advance. During busy periods such as the October Book Fair, budget-priced rooms are particularly hard to find. It is usually safer to book well ahead. Solo travellers suffer from the disadvantage that single rooms are sometimes small and cramped, often less than half the size of a double but inevitably more than half the price.

Luxury

Hyatt Regency Beograd★★★★★ Milentija Popovića 5; tel: 301 1182; fax: 311 2234; email: admin@hyatt.co.yu; www.regency.belgrade.hyatt.com. This is one of Belgrade's top hotels, 1km from the city centre in Novi Beograd, next to the Sava Congress Centre, a modern concert and conference venue. Mostly used by embassies for visiting VIPs and high-flying businessmen. The Hyatt boasts a massive marble lobby area that resembles a temple. Elegant rooms, with excellent views of central Belgrade from upper floors, good restaurants, fitness centre with swimming pool, disabled facilities. Breakfast is not included in the basic price. The hotel has a total of 308 rooms and suites for €120–220; also, 43 apartments and suites with prices on request.

Beograd Inter-Continental★★★★★ Vladimira Popvica 10; tel: 311 3333; fax: 311 1402; email: ihcbegha@eunet.yu. The other top hotel, close to the Hyatt, and one with real historical connections for Balkans buffs. Currently this is disowned by the Inter-Continental chain, perhaps because of some of its more sinister associations. This was where gangster, bank-robber, national hero and alleged war criminal Arkan was gunned down. His wife, turbo-folk star Ceca, was shopping in one of the hotel's fashion boutiques at the time. For the morbidly curious, Arkan was sitting outside the Rotisserie restaurant on an aubergine-coloured leather banquette at the moment of his demise. Don't let this put you off staying there – Arkan was hardly a typical guest. Enormous lobby, several restaurants, sports centre, swimming pool, nightclub, tennis courts. A very good buffet breakfast is included in the price. Altogether, the hotel has a total of 415 rooms and suites, some non-smoking, at rates of US$170–380 per room.

Slavija Lux★★★★★ Svetog Save 2; tel: 2450 842; fax: 344 2931; www.jat.com. Located 1km south of the city centre and railway station, towering over the thunderous traffic circling Slavija Square, and looking more like an office block than a place to sleep, this is notably more downmarket than those listed above. Owned and run by JAT, the national airline, the 'Lux' has a careworn feel to it, and a brown-panelled ambience that has a distinct KGB flavour. Double rooms range between 7,300 and 9,200din; apartments, 12,200–13,400din.

Aleksander Palas★★★★★ Kralja Petra 13–15; tel: 3305 300, 3305 326; fax: 3305 334. The Aleksander Palas is a recently opened, privately owned luxury hotel that is under the same ownership as the adjoining Que Pasa? restaurant. Perfectly situated close to the Orthodox cathedral, Kalemegdon Park and the pedestrian shopping street of Kneza Mihaila, the Aleksander Palas offers just nine luxurious apartments with facilities such as king-size beds, cable TV, DVD, internet lines and home cinema system. Each apartment has a bedroom, cosily furnished living room and bathroom. Bathrooms come complete with state-of-the-art shower cabins that include Turkish bath and Finnish sauna facilities. Apartments cost between €150 and €350 per night, depending on season.

Upmarket

Best Western M★★★★ Bulevar JNA 56a; tel: 3972 560; fax: 309 5501; www.bestwestern.com. 4km from the city centre, in a wooded residential area close to the FC Red Star football stadium, this is, perhaps, best suited to business travellers and those travelling in groups or with their own transport. This modern, comfortable hotel, near the quiet, upmarket Dedinje area, joined the Best Western group in 2000 when it was completely overhauled and renovated. Conference halls, nightclub, restaurant, aperitif bar, parking facilities. The 'M' has 156 spacious rooms at 3,300–7,440din, and 11 suites, 8,240–9,400din.
Jugoslavija★★★★ Bulevar Nikole Tesle 3; tel: 600 222; fax: 691 230. In New Belgrade, on the banks of the Danube, 3km from the city centre. An excellent location if you intend to spend a lot of time visiting the numerous floating restaurants, cafés and nightclubs moored nearby. There is another Arkan connection here, in that he allegedly used to own the hotel's casino. This may or may not account for NATO bombing it in 1999, destroying the swimming pool, conference hall and some of the rooms. The Chinese Embassy nearby was also famously hit in the same raid. This vast complex houses restaurants, cocktail bars, a post office, a hair salon and souvenir shops. Disabled facilities. There are 165 rooms at 2,100–6,000din; 20 apartments at 12,000din.
Le Petit Piaf★★★★ Skadarska 34; tel: 303 5252; fax: 303 5353; email: office@petitpiaf.com; www.petitpiaf.com. Le Petit Piaf is a privately owned central hotel that first opened for business in September 2004. It is situated in the heart of Skadarlija behind the house of the writer and painter Đura Jaksić. For the time being the hotel has a bar, a restaurant and 2 terraces but it is looking to expand and in the future plans to include a wine bar, a national restaurant, conference facilities and a beauty centre. There are 7 double rooms and 5 suites, each with cable TV, internet access, direct phone lines and air conditioning. Rates are €130–230 for single occupancy and €156–276 for double. Most credit cards are accepted.
Majestic★★★★ Obilićev venac 28; tel: 636 022; fax: 328 4995; email: majestic@eunet.yu; www.majestic.co.yu. The Majestic enjoys an excellent, central location just off pedestrian-only Kneza Mihaila and close to a concentration of bars, clubs and restaurants. Some of the rooms have been recently renovated. The Majestic has a restaurant, a coffee shop, a summer terrace and garage. The hotel has 76 rooms in total (46 singles, 26 doubles and 4 triples) at 3,200–7,000din. Also, 6 large apartments with rooftop terrace at 7,000din.
Metropol★★★★ Bulevar Kralja Aleksandra 69; tel: 323 0911; fax: 323 2991; email: metropol@sezampro.yu. The Metropol is a pleasant 1950s hotel, 1km from the city centre, next to Tašmajdan Park. This hotel had plenty of prestigious visitors in the 1960s and 1970s but its popularity has now been eclipsed somewhat. Marble lobby with an attractive aperitif bar, restaurant, garage, café, hairdresser, travel agency, guarded parking. The Metropol has a total of 216 rooms at 2,100–6,000din, as well as 6 suites at 12,000din.
Moskva★★★★ Balkanska 1; tel: 686 255; fax: 688 389; email: hotelmoskva@absolutok.net; www.hotelmoskva.co.yu. Right in the heart of the city, the Hotel Moskva is actually one of Belgrade's most beautiful buildings with a very attractive art nouveau façade and lots of period charm. This well-appointed hotel, built in 1906 and reconstructed in 1973, is one of central Belgrade's better-known landmarks. There are genuine antiques in some of the rooms, while

others are rather more prosaically furnished. The lobby is deceptively small, but the rest of the hotel is airy and spacious with high ceilings. Restaurant, aperitif bar, banquet hall, patisserie, business lounge, limited parking. There is an enormous, atmospheric coffee shop at street level. There are 132 rooms in total, with singles starting at €55 and doubles from €80. Triple rooms and apartments are also available.

Palace★★★★ Topličin venac 23; tel: 185 585, 637 222; fax: 184 458; email: office@palacehotel.co.yu; www.palacehotel.co.yu. Another of the older city-centre hotels, this one dating back to the 1920s. The Palace has an elegant façade, brightly lit at night, and two restaurants (the Classic in the lobby, and the Belgrade Panorama on the sixth floor that offers excellent city views) as well as bar, exchange office, casino, garage with car wash service and all standard business facilities. The hotel has been recently privatised, with most rooms now refurbished or renovated; 70 rooms, 3,670–5,340din, and 15 suites, 6,640din.

Zlatnik★★★★ Slavonska 26, Zemun; tel: 3167 511; fax: 3167 235; email: office@hotelzlatnik.com; www.hotelzlatnik.com. Zlatnik is a privately owned hotel located in Zemun, 7km from Belgrade city centre. This modern, recently built hotel has 2 restaurants, a conference hall and business centre, a gift shop and an aperitif bar. All rooms have air conditioning, cable TV, internet access and safe deposit boxes. Both garage parking and non-smoking rooms are also available. Singles cost €120; doubles €146; apartments €160–296. Most credit cards are accepted.

Mid range

Astorija★★★ Milovana Milovanovića 1a; tel: 645 422; fax: 686 437; email: astorija@astorija.co.yu; www.astorija.co.yu. The Astorija is located opposite the train and bus stations in a noisy, uninspiring part of town. The hotel has a restaurant, coffee shop, bar and parking spaces for its guests. The Astorija has 81 rooms in total, at prices between 1,160 and 1,860din.

Balkan★★★ Prizrenska 2; tel: 687 466; fax: 687 543. This is another central hotel, directly opposite the Moskva. An old-fashioned atmosphere pervades the Balkan with its smoky lobby area, smallish rooms and 1970s décor. The hotel has a restaurant and a coffee shop but the facilities across the road at the Moscow are more inviting. 1,270–2,070din per room.

Excelsior★★★ Kneza Miloša 5; tel: 323 1381; fax: 323 1951. This is located close to the Parliament building, with restaurant, coffee shop and small conference hall. A total of 80 rooms at prices between 2,000 and 3,000din; suites go for 4,500din.

Kasina★★★ Terazije 25; tel: 323 5574/5; fax: 323 8257; http://kasina.stari-grad.co.yu. The Kasina has a very central location, close to Balkan and Moskva on Terazije, one of Belgrade's busiest thoroughfares. The single rooms are quite small but the doubles are good value. Good bar with a choice of beers. No private parking. All 84 rooms have recently been renovated. Singles cost €33; doubles, €55. There are also a few well-renovated apartments.

Nacional★★★ Bežanijska kosa bb; tel: 601 122; fax: 601 177; email: nacional@bitsyu.net; www.hotelnacional.co.yu. Located 8km from the city centre on the E-70 highway, and reasonable value for those with their own transport. The Nacional boasts a restaurant, aperitif bar and conference hall. There is parking for guests. Rooms cost 1,200–1,800din.

Park★★★ Njegoševa 4; tel: 323 4723; fax: 323 3029; www.park.stari-grad.co.yu. The Park lies about 1km from the city centre, within walking distance of the Belgrade Palace, the Student Cultural Centre, and the Nikola Tesla and Natural History museums, in a street full of designer cafés and bars. Some of the lower rooms may be noisy due to rush-hour traffic. The hotel has its own restaurants, bar and garage. There are 34 single rooms at 2,780din, and 95 doubles at 4,600din.

Prag★★★ Narodnog fronta 27; tel: 361 0422; fax: 361 2691. Located in a small street halfway up the hill between the station and the old town, the Prag has its own restaurant, exchange office and bar. 116 rooms, 1,360–2,720din.

Putnik★★★ Palmira Toljatija 9; tel: 697 221; fax: 692 534. In Novi Beograd, 4km from the city centre. In keeping with its surroundings, the Putnik is a large concrete edifice with plenty of parking space. It has a restaurant, café-bar and exchange office. Rooms cost 1,560–2,520din; apartments, 3,300din.

Royal ★★★ (formerly **Toplice**, pronounced: *Taup-leetse*) Kralja Petra 56; tel: 634 222, 626 426; fax: 626 459; email: toplice@net.yu; www.hotelroyal.co.yu. Still referred to by its (unfortunate) former name by some, this is actually Belgrade's oldest existing hotel, dating from 1886. The hotel has a superb location on a quiet street that runs across the top of Kneza Mihaila, close to many restaurants and bars, museums, Kalemegdan Park and Belgrade's solitary mosque. The Royal has its own restaurant, lobby bar (with cheap beer) and exchange facilities. This is a good inexpensive three-star choice but it is sometimes full so book well ahead. All of the reception staff speak English and vary in the welcome they provide from quietly courteous to frosty. Do not set too much store by the promise of a TV set in each room: they do exist but may not function in quite the way you might expect. 105 rooms: singles 1,050–1,560din, depending on facilities; doubles, 1,370–2,150din. Room rates include a rudimentary breakfast of eggs, coffee and bread, served in the basement restaurant.

Skala Zemun★★★ Bežanijska 3, Zemun; tel: 196 605; fax: 190 724. 6km west from the city centre in Zemun, a separate town that effectively serves as a suburb of Belgrade. This small hotel is privately run, with quiet, well-furnished rooms grouped around a covered courtyard. It has its own restaurant and garage. There are 16 rooms at 2.760–4,140din, and 2 suites for 4,830din.

Slavija 'A'★★★ Svetog Save 1; tel: 450 842; fax: 431 517. This hotel is the poor relation of the Slavija Lux, and a fine example of dubious '3-star' categorisation. Like its more luxurious twin – the tower next door – the Slavija 'A' is owned by JAT and the hotel serves as the drop-off and departure point for airport buses. The 'A' boasts restaurants, conference halls, casino, hair salons, exchange office, but is generally neglected and shoddy, and, according to those who know about these things, one of the worst hotels in eastern Europe. The Slavija is a good choice for connoisseurs of Cold War nostalgia, and it may also be of value to novelists and film makers wishing to conjure up the atmosphere of Tito's 1960s Yugoslavia. Still, at least it has plenty of rooms in a crisis, with singles and doubles available at 1,860–4,260din, and even apartments at 3,660–5,460din.

Splendid★★★ Dragoslava Jovanovića 5; tel: 323 5444; fax: 324 3298; email: reservation@splendid.co.yu; www.splendid.co.yu. A city-centre location, with small, smoky lobby and attached café-bar, parking and exchange office, but no restaurant. Splendid by name and splendid by nature if you can trust the sign by the door that proclaims, 'You can touch the star with us'. You can also get your legs shaved in the salon next door should the urge take you. A cluster of travel agencies are located nearby, including Putnik, whose staff make good use of the hotel's lobby bar; 18 singles and 31 doubles, 1,760–3,520din per room.

Srbija★★★ Ustanička 127c; tel: 289 0404; fax: 489 2462. This is another businessman's hotel, 4km from the city centre, with restaurant, bar, parking, disabled facilities and non-smokers' room. No credit cards are accepted. Rooms cost 1,070–1,540din.

Turist★★★ Sarajevska 37; tel/fax: 361 1862; email: office@hotel-turist.co.yu; www.hotel-turist.co.yu. Another of the small concentration close to the railway station, and more geared towards businessmen than tourists, despite the name. Facilities include restaurant, coffee bar with terrace, conference hall and parking. Single rooms cost 1,360–3,000din; doubles, 2,480–4,600din.

Union★★ Kosovska 11; tel: 3248 022, 172, 054, 056; fax: 3224 480. 5 minutes' walk from Trg Republike and the Serbian Parliament, this is a comfortable, well-kept hotel with helpful, friendly staff. The Union has spacious, good-value doubles but relatively small singles. The hotel's restaurant has live music some nights. Parking is available. Singles cost 1,950din; doubles, 3,200–3,950din; triples, 4,800din; apartments, 4,900–5,900din.

Budget

Beograd★★ Nemanjina 6; tel: 645 199; fax: 643 746. Another one located near the railway station, the Beograd is rather basic and in need of renovation. It has a restaurant and bar; 77 rooms in total: singles, 1,160din; doubles, 1,720din; triples, 2,480din.

Bristol★★ Karađorđeva 50; tel: 631 895; fax: 637 453. Close to the bus station, with a restaurant, souvenir shop and bar. Credit cards are not accepted. Single rooms cost 1,250din; doubles, 2,250din.

Centar★★ Savski Trg 7; tel: 644 055; fax: 657 838. Not to be confused with the 'Central' below, the Centar is directly opposite the railway station, so handy for late-night/early-morning connections. The hotel has a dark, dingy brown lobby with helpful reception staff. It is quite basic and very 1970s in style, but reasonable value for the money. Because of its low price this hotel tends to get block-booked for months on end but, if you can get in, singles go for 910din, doubles for 1,380din.

Central★★ Glavna 10, Zemun; tel/fax: 191 712. This is located 6km from central Belgrade and so is only 'central' in the sense of being in the middle of Zemun. The hotel has a restaurant; credit cards are not accepted. When I enquired about a room here the woman at the reception desk was very friendly but pointed out that the hotel had no heating – an important consideration in the cold winter months. 10 single rooms at 800din; 18 doubles at 1,300din; triples at 1,950din; two apartments at 1,700din.

Dom★★ Kralja Milutina 54; tel: 685 696; fax: 683 872. The Dom is situated away from the city centre, across the road from the Russian Embassy. No credit cards are accepted. Singles go for 900din; doubles, 1,500din; triples, 1,760din; apartments, 2,840din.

Hotel N★★ Bileceka 57; tel/fax: 3972 183; email: office@hotel-n.co.yu; www.hotel-n.co.yu. At 5km from the centre, in the quiet suburb of Voždovac, this is also a long way out. With its own restaurant, parking and coffee shop, it claims: 'Your pleasure is our idea.' Single rooms cost 1,410din; doubles, 2,200din; triples, 2,355din; apartments 2,870din.

Pošta★★ Slobodana Penezića Krcuna 3; tel: 361 4260; fax: 643 961. As its name implies, this is found opposite the post office, over the road at the side of the railway station. The Pošta is a fairly basic hotel with its own inexpensive restaurant. No credit cards are accepted. Single rooms can be had for 1,100din; doubles, 1,600din.

Slavija 'B'★★ Svetog Save 1; tel: 2450 842; fax: 2431 517. The same as Slavija 'A' but with rooms that are considered to be 1 star less according to their highly optimistic grading system! This is rumoured to have been closed down recently – or it may simply be a ploy of the management to fill the more expensive rooms first.

Taš★★ Beogradska 71; tel: 324 3507; fax: 323 8027. Located to the east of the city centre, above a sports centre, this offers restaurant, casino and parking amongst its facilities. Singles are 1,800din; doubles, 2,520din.

Hostels

Slavija Hostel Svetog Save 1; tel: 323 1268. This is not really a hostel at all but if you book this at the Hostelling International office (Ferijaini Savez Beograd, Makedonska 22, second floor; tel: 324 8550; fax: 322 0762), and already have HI membership, you will be entitled to a 'B' grade, 2-star room at the Slavija Hotel. Only 4 rooms are available: singles, US$11.50; doubles, US$23.

Jelica Milovanović Krunska 8; tel: 323 1268; fax: 322 0762; www.hostels.org.yu. This hostel has a good central location, close to the Parliament building. It should be booked in the same way as above as you are supposed to be a member of Hostelling International to stay here. However, an International Student Card might just do the trick. This is a good deal if you are here at the right time of year. The hostel is clean and newly renovated, and has 3–4 bedded rooms with showers, and 4–8 bedded rooms without. In the 3- or 4-bed rooms it costs €11 per bed; in the 4–8 bed rooms, €9 per bed. Group bookings can also be made at €9 per bed. There are also 4 private rooms – 2 singles and 2 doubles – at a slightly higher rate. Reception is open 08.00–12.00 and 17.00–2300. The hostel is open sporadically, mostly during holiday periods: from Dec 22–Jan 13, Mar 1–4, May 1–7 and Jun 22–Aug 31.

Three Black Catz Nušićeva 8. This small, unofficial hostel is just off Terazije, 200m from Trg Republika at the very heart of the city. The Three Black Catz is basically just a 6-bed dormitory and a communal living room. Facilities include DVD and cable TV, and the youthful staff can advise on clubs and bars in the city. The hostel offers security lockers, internet access, free coffee and the use of a kitchen. With dormitory beds, no curfew and 24-hour reception it is squarely aimed at younger travellers and represents good value if you do not crave privacy or object to the slightly hugger-mugger atmosphere of the place. Reservations can be made online at the following websites if you search for 'hostels in Yugoslavia', then 'Belgrade': www.bootsnall.com or www.hostelworld.com. Bed with breakfast costs €12 per person.

Private accommodation

This is hard to find in Belgrade. There may be a few individuals hanging around the railway station who sidle up and offer you the option of private rooms. Great discretion should be shown as these may turn out to be poor value: run-down and at a considerable distance from the city centre – perhaps in one of the jerry-built *bloks* of Novi Beograd. At least check the room out first before committing yourself or handing any money over.

It is much more likely that you will not be offered anything at all. Unfortunately, Belgrade – indeed all of Serbia – has not yet caught on to the trend of providing cheap private rooms or *sobe,* a custom far more prevalent in Croatia and on the Montenegrin coast. Hopefully, this will change at some stage in the future: Serbia needs more affordable, decent-quality accommodation.

Camping

Auto-kamp 'Košutnjak' Kneza Višeslava 17; tel/fax: 555 127. This is close to Topčider Park, to the south of the city centre. They are not really geared up for individual campers but have bungalows available for 960–2,800din. The site is in a pleasant, leafy suburb and has plentiful sports facilities.

The nearest campsite outside the city is at **Dunav** at Batajnički put, Zemun, 12km northwest of the city centre. They charge 90din to camp, 90din for a car and 120din to be connected to an electricity supply. They also have bungalows to rent for 900din.

WHERE TO EAT AND DRINK

> We ate too large a lunch, as is apt to be one's habit in Belgrade, if one is
> man enough to stand up to peasant food made luxurious by urban lavishness
> of supply and a Turkish tradition of subtle and positive flavour.
>
> Rebecca West, *Black Lamb and Grey Falcon*

Belgrade abounds with restaurants, cafés and bars for all tastes and pockets. Cheapest and most plentiful are the ubiquitous fast food places, where, although the produce may be familiar in some – McDonald's and the like – there are many more that demonstrate a particularly Balkan slant on what constitutes fast food: *čevapčići, burek, pljeskavica* etc. In contrast, restaurants serving slow food – and they can be very slow – can be considered as serving either Serbian or foreign cuisine, only occasionally both. Most of the 'foreign' cuisine is actually Italian, although Belgrade has a few representatives from all over the globe. It should be noted that the smarter restaurants, especially those of the Serbian 'national cuisine' variety, are considered more as suitable venues for a fine evening out than merely as places to take the necessary calories on board; after all, that is what fast food is for. With large family groups enjoying quality time eating, drinking, talking, smoking and singing together, restaurants are seen as places to linger, let your hair down and enjoy life.

Despite the Serbian fixation for meat, vegetarians need not despair even if they cannot expect too much in the way of variety. Reliable standbys like *gibanica*, *srpska* or *šopska* salad are nearly always available. Dedicated non-smokers, on the other hand, may find life difficult: in the tobacco-friendly world of Belgrade's restaurants, the air is often smog-thick with plumes of Marlboro Lite. The concept of passive smoking has yet to catch on in the Balkans, where non-smokers are considered to be a touch eccentric. At least in summer you can usually sit outside.

Restaurants tend to be clustered in certain areas of the city, as do the café-bars. In the old city, many cafés, bars and restaurants line the pedestrian thoroughfare of Kneza Mihaila, as well as the side streets that lead off from it. In particular, Obilićev venac, by the Metropol hotel, has almost totally given itself over to trendy theme-bars, the haunt of young folk mostly, and the place to be seen sipping your cappuccino. Many of the bars also serve light snacks: pancakes, sandwiches, ice-creams and the like. For heavier fare, there is a dense concentration of Serbian 'national' restaurants running all the way along the short length of Skardarska, although this area is much busier during the summer months than the rest of the year. Similarly, the lines of boat restaurants moored along the Danube and Sava tend to be most active when nights are warm and at their shortest. Generally speaking, they open relatively late and stay open until the early hours. A little further afield, and a pleasant choice for a summer's evening, is the neighbouring town of Zemun with its own dense concentration of fish restaurants lining the river frontage there.

In the business-oriented part of the city, restaurants are more spread out and generally more geared to the lunchtime trade, although there are notable exceptions to this. Even here, there are pockets of activity that lure people out in the evening, an example being the concentration of stylish café-bars along Njegoševa close to the Park hotel.

Restaurants

Alexander Cetinjska 15; tel: 322 7401. This is actually a beer garden, but it also serves a wide range of light dishes and is a good choice for lunch on a warm day.

Amigo Mladena Stojanovića 2a; tel: 663 366. This is a Mexican-style restaurant in the Dedinje area.

Bardova Mitropolita Petra 8; tel: 761 045. A steakhouse that makes its own beer, and which doubles as a cabaret club at weekends. Open 11.00–01.00.

Beogradska panorama On the 6th floor of Hotel Palace, Topličin venac 23; tel: 186 866. As you might expect, there is an excellent city view from up here. Open 19.00–01.00.

Big Bull Vasina 9; tel: 18 30 88; fax: 63 41 56. There is a clue in the name: this is one for meat eaters. In fact, Big Bull is so meat-oriented that the entrance is actually through a butcher's shop, which guarantees freshness at least. Seating is at large bench tables in a cellar with simple, modern décor. Excellent grilled meats like *ćevapčići* and *pljeskavica*. Good service and very reasonably priced, with main courses at 125–400din.

Byblos Kneginje Zorke 30; tel: 064 610 6542. Close to the Slavija roundabout, Byblos is a Lebanese restaurant that specialises in *mezze* dishes.

Dača Patrisa Lumumbe 49; tel: 781 009. This is hidden away in the city's northeastern suburbs but comes recommended by many. The décor and layout is that of a traditional Serbian rural home, both inside and out. Waiters dress in Serbian costume and there is a gift shop where you can buy souvenirs like Serbian headgear and pottery. Foodwise, it offers a wholesome range of authentic Serbian and Montenegrin dishes at very reasonable prices. Helpings are very large, served in rustic clay dishes, and there is a whole range of fruit-flavoured *rakija* to experiment with. It is always best to book a day ahead here. Open daily 10.30–midnight, but closed on Mondays.

Danubius Oslobođenja kej 57, Zemun; tel: 617 233. This waterfront café-restaurant in Zemun serves *riblja čorba*, fish and grilled meats, all at very reasonable prices. There are several similar restaurants close by, like **Sharan** and **Kafana-Restoran Venecija**, that also serve fish dishes in a riverside setting.

Dva Jelena Skadarska 32; tel: 3234 885; fax: 3238 363. One of many 'national cuisine' restaurants on this street, the 'Two Deer' is an institution that dates back to 1832. Two large, smoky dining halls with wooden panelling cater mostly to large noisy groups. Like all Skadarlija restaurants, it is a tad overpriced – you pay for the atmosphere. The waiters are of the old school and tread a broad line between attentiveness and indifference. The musical accompaniment to your meal is optional – well almost. Don't be in too much of a hurry. Open 09.00–midnight.

Edison Inex café Trg Republike 5; tel: 621940. On the 2nd floor above the Edison Inex coffee and cake shop is an unnamed pizzeria. The sign simply says: '*Restoran-Picarija-Postlastičarnica*'. Good views over the square. The service is friendly and attentive and the pizzas are quite reasonable at around 300din.

Focaccia, Milentilja Popovića 5 (Hyatt Regency hotel); tel: 301 1143. Located in one of Belgrade's smartest hotels and, as you might expect, one of Belgrade's most elegant restaurants too, with a very good selection of international wines. If you are really pushing the boat out, expense-wise, you could do far worse than eat here. Alternatively, having Sunday brunch here is a relative bargain. Open 19.00–23.00.

Grčka Kraljica (Greek Queen) Kneza Mihaila 51; tel: 638 963. As the name suggests, there is a vaguely Hellenic theme to the food here. There is a pleasantly bright dining room inside, or you can eat outside and observe the evening *korso* along Kneza Mihaila. Open 09.00–midnight.

Il Borghetto Skadarska 11; tel: 324 2940. This is a rare Italian place on this street dominated by national restaurants, and one of the best in the city. Open 10.00–midnight.

Indian Palace Ljubićka 1b; tel: 444 3226. Well away from the city centre, in the suburb of Dušanovac, this stylish restaurant serves the sort of mouth-watering northern Indian food that is familiar to British taste buds. Despite an awkward location, this restaurant is a very worthwhile target for curry addicts. Open 12.00–midnight.

Kalemegdanska Terasa Belgrade Fortress, Mali Kalemegdan; tel: 328 2727. This is a fine, and fairly pricey, restaurant for those who like to surround themselves with history while they eat. A smart restaurant with a fairly strict dress code ie: no shorts and sandals. Live music is provided some nights. Open 12.00–01.00.

Kapric Kralja Petra 44; tel: 625 930. This smart pasta place, just off Kneza Mihaila, is one of Belgrade's top Italian restaurants. Prices are quite reasonable for the quality of food that is offered.

SOME SKADARLIJA RESTAURANTS

Dva bela goluba 29 Novembra 3; tel: 3239 079

Skadarlija Cetinjska 17; tel: 3234 983. Just off Skadarlija but with a similar ambience. Open 11.00–01.00.

Zlatni bokal Skadarska 26; tel: 3234 834. Open 11.00–01.00.

Šešir moj Skadarska 21; tel: 3228 750. With slow service that verges on the indifferent, 'My Hat' has a reasonable choice of dishes for vegetarians. It is open 09.00–01.00.

Tri šešira Skadarska 29; tel: 3247 501. Another with a 'hat' theme, the famous 'Three Hats' is one of the oldest and best restaurants on this street. Try proja (traditional corn bread) with kajmak. Open 11.00–01.00.

Konoba Skadarska 36; tel: 3235 986

Bevanda Skadarska 36a; tel: 3234 179

Ima dana Skadarska 38; tel: 3234 422. This is considered by some to be the best of the lot. The waiters here seem less jaded and grumpy than some in Skadarlija. 'Karađorđe's steak' is a speciality of the house.

Kimono Simićeva 16; tel: 369 2077. A Japanese restaurant – and probably the only one in the city – for those in need of a sushi fix.

Klub Knjiizevnika Francuska 7. This place, The Writers' Club, is an institution that dates back to the Tito era when Belgrade's government-approved literati would meet here to discuss metaphors over *kajmak* and glasses of *šljivovica*. The entrance to this grand stucco mansion is through a gate on the street that has a plaque next to it that reads: 'Association of Literary Translators of Serbia'. The dining room is downstairs. White-jacketed waiters help to complete the impression of a bygone age. The roast lamb with potatoes is heartily recommended. No literary credentials required.

Kolarac Kneza Mihaila 46; tel: 638 972, 636 987. Many meaty Serbian choices at low prices are available in this restaurant favoured by locals and family groups. There is a menu in English if you ask for it. The waiters have a tendency to give you one or two items that you did not ask for, otherwise good value and good, solid food.

Košova Kralja Petra I 36; tel: 628 281, 627 344. A small atmospheric and cheerful *trattoria* with 2 small rooms on different levels, located just off Kneza Mihaila, near the Royal hotel. The menu offers authentic Italian food, including pastas and pizzas, as well as meat dishes like goulash. Excellent selection of home-made breads, and good salad dishes too. The service is friendly and attentive, and prices are moderate. Open 10.00–01.00.

Snežana Pizzeria/Cafeteria Corner of Kneza Mihaila and Kralja Petra. Serves a variety of pizzas for 250–400din, draught Svetlo or Nikšićko beer, and a range of fancy flavoured coffees and juices. They also do good cappuccino and delicious cherry strudel, which could serve as the basis for a sumptuous breakfast.

Mamma Mia Resavska 70; tel: 687 683. Italian obviously, and Belgrade's only 4-star Italian restaurant; close to the British Embassy. Open 08.00–midnight.

McDonald's Brankova; tel: 630 105. There are 9 McDonald's in Belgrade, and this branch of the familiar icon of our globalised world sits on a terrace above Zeleni venac, the terminus for many of the city's bus routes. The view over the confluence of the Danube and Sava rivers is actually very good and the food is … well, McDonald's. Being an all-American icon is not always an advantage: during the 1999 NATO air-raids this same building was partially vandalised in a pique of anti-Western sentiment. On a more positive note, there is air conditioning and a no-smoking policy in operation inside.

Orao 29 November 28; tel: 322 8836, 322 4231. This pizzeria provides a wide range of both national and Italian dishes that are good value and come with prompt service. The outside terrace, however, is extremely noisy with the constant stream of heavy traffic thundering down this major thoroughfare. There is another branch at Bulevar Kralja Aleksandra 142; tel: 444 3031, 444 1606. Both restaurants offer 24-hour service.

Peking Vuka Karadića 2; tel: 181 931. Not surprisingly, the Peking is a Chinese restaurant, ideal for those hankering to order their food by numbers. As well as Chinese specialities like pork in sweet and sour sauce, it also serves Serbian dishes. This is rated as a 4-star restaurant, so it is fairly expensive. Open 11.00–23.00.

Perper Omladinski brigade 18a, Novi Beograd; tel: 606 046. This is considered by some aficionados to produce the best grilled meat in Belgrade. Try *leskovacka mućkalica* – spicy grilled pork with vegetables. Open 12.00–01.00.

Polet Kralja Milana 31; tel: 3232 454. On the corner with Njegoševa, close to the Park hotel, this has good, inexpensive seafood dishes but the service is slow.

Porto Francuska 52; tel: 322 5624. Porto is a high-class seafood restaurant with marine specialities like octopus salad and fish in salt. Prices are on the expensive side. Open 12.00–01.00.

'?' (Znak Pitanje) Kralja Petra I 6; tel: 635 421. The '?' is actually one of very few 19th-century buildings still standing in the city but, instead of being a museum piece, it remains an authentic local restaurant, refreshingly un-themed and without a hint of pretence. If there is any theme at all, it is 'brown', with brown window frames, brown furniture and brown food.

To top it off, faded sepia (brown) photographs of Old Belgrade decorate the walls. By way of contrast, small vases of dead wildflowers sit on each of the tables and the roughly white-washed walls are covered in watercolour paintings of the Primitive School – very primitive indeed – possibly the work of an inventive infant. To eat, you sit on low wooden chairs around, equally low, wooden tables. The waiter, with slicked-down hair and wearing a double-breasted jacket two sizes too big for him, has a broad but mischievous smile, and looks as if he might have just come from a hasty court appearance. There is a battered English menu of sorts and the food, the usual range of Serbian grilled meat and salads, is filling, wholesome and encouragingly cheap. The whole experience is so unforced and authentically Serbian that you feel that you could be in an Emir Kustarica film. Any minute you expect the door to fly open and a gaggle of white geese to enter, flapping their wings in a flurry of feathers as they are pursued by a Roma brass band. Open daily 07.00–23.00. It does not serve food on Sunday evenings.

Que Pasa? Kralja Petra I 13–15; tel: 3284 764; www.que-pasa.co.yu. On the way down the hill towards the '?', this could not be more different in character if it tried. And it does try. Que Pasa? is a smart, trendy café-restaurant with a self-conscious Spanish/Latin-American theme. Light snacks or more substantial meals are available, like pancakes and *tortillas*. This is very much a haunt of Belgrade's beautiful people, with fairly high prices to match. The numerous monitors showing Fashion TV tend to be quite distracting and obtrusive. Occasionally, live music provides a more harmonious accompaniment. Open 09.00–02.00.

Resava Resavska 24; tel: 3233 192. This is another high-class Italian restaurant on this street of the same name. Open 12.00–midnight.

Šangaj Ustanička 149; tel: 4888 407. The name (Shanghai) has been slavicised; the food is Chinese.

Skala Bežanijska 3, Zemun; tel: 196 605. This Zemun restaurant is in a large basement and specialises in game dishes.

Srpska Kafana ('Serbian Tavern') Svetogorska 25; tel: 3247 197. This is a centrally located Serbian restaurant with an authentic atmosphere.

Studio B Masarikova 5; tel: 361 3886. This is discreetly hidden away on the 5th floor of the Beogradjanka ('Belgrade Girl') building with a lush, albeit slightly dated, interior. A cheap, set lunch menu is available.

Tabor Bulevar Kralja Aleksandra 348; tel: 412 464. Tabor is a 4-star Serbian restaurant that has live music for its diners. Open 10.00–01.00.

Trandafilović Makenzijeva 63; tel: 430 230. This is another city restaurant that specialises in Serbian food.

Vuk Vuka Karadžića 12; tel: 629 761. Good grilled meats on a pleasant, breezy summer terrace just off Kneza Mihaila.

Zepter Club Kralja Petra 32; tel: 3281 414; fax: 418 3988. Unusual for Belgrade, this is a stylish, post-modern restaurant located in the courtyard of the metal and glass, post-modern Zepter building. Zepter Club serves international food at quite reasonable prices.

Zorba Corner of Starine Novaka and 27 Marta; tel: 337 6547. Zorba is a small Greek taverna with very reasonable prices.

Bars and cafés

Belgrade has a tradition of 'hobby bars' where enterprising individuals set up small intimate watering holes for themselves and their friends to use but where visitors are always welcome to drop in. They tend to come and go quickly in equal measure so the best you can do is ask around and get local advice. Listed below are some of Belgrade's more permanent institutions.

Ben Akiba Nušićeva 8. If this place is still going then it is well worth checking out. This small 'hobby bar' is tucked away in a converted flat up an alleyway just off Terazije. There are paintings by local artists hung on the wall and a large selection of unusual cocktails to choose from.

Café Centro Terazije 28. Located close to the Hotel Moskva and next door to a 24-hour supermarket, this is more like a bakery than a café, with a fine selection of cakes, pastries and savoury snacks. Good for a light lunch or a snack. Open 07.00–midnight.

Caffe Paleta Trg Republika 5; tel: 633 027. Located next door to the IPS bookshop in the Dom štampe (Press building), with comfortable armchairs and a stainless-steel bar in the corner, Caffe Paleta has a relaxed atmosphere, with a mixed crowd of young couples, weary shoppers and garrulous intellectuals.

Caffe OK.no Obilićev venac 17; tel: 629 072. Next door to the Jazz Café, this establishment, one of several trendy cafés on this street, is a real curiosity with its mining nostalgia theme. Even the doors on to the street have pick-axes for handles and, once inside, the extensiveness of the coal mine theme becomes apparent, with faux ventilation ducts and pit props, miners' lamps hanging from the ceiling, and tools suspended on the walls. Not surprisingly, everything is painted black to enhance the subterranean atmosphere. The only false note, apart from a thankful lack of coal dust, is the presence of *Vogue*-style photos on the wall that feature attractive young models in various states of undress. The music is loud Serbo-house, but it is still possible to hold a conversation. With a wide range of beers, juices, coffees and cocktails, you can have draught *pivo* for 70din, or a Multiple Orgasm for 250din. Open 09.00–02.00. Also on this street are **Identico Caffe**, **Irish pub**, **Caffe Hardy**, **Café Ulaz** and **Stress-Stress**.

Edison Inex Trg Republike 5; tel: 621 940. This is just one of several cafés that look out on to Belgrade's most famous square. A large, two-storey place that is always busy with shoppers taking a break and young couples meeting on dates, this has a wide selection of sticky, sweet cakes to choose from, and a Pizzeria upstairs. Located on the opposite side of the square, closer to the equestrian statue, is **Kod Spomenika** Caffe/Poslastičarnica, with a similar selection and prices.

Guli Skadarska 13; tel: 3237 204. This is a bar in Skadarlija with a wide range of cocktails to choose from. Open 11.00–01.00.

Jazz Café Oblićev venac 19; tel: 328 2380. As the name says, the musical focus is jazz in this relaxed hangout, which has modern art on the walls and wooden benches to sit on. Occasionally, live music is staged here. Open 10.00–02.00.

Jump Café Njegoševa 10; tel: 323 9860. Jump is one of several smart designer cafés along this street by the Park hotel. Open 08.00–01.00, Sunday 10.00–01.00.

La Revolucion Uskočka 66; tel: 269 8888. The iconic image of Che Guevara identifies this place: a Cuban/Mexican theme-bar with excellent Latin music. Inside, the bare brick walls are covered with black-and-white photographs of Che, Castro, Zapata and other revolutionary leaders. The ceiling is vaulted and there is an upstairs galley with additional seating. In keeping with the Cuban theme, the waiters all sport Che T-shirts and red 'pioneer' neckerchiefs. Coffees, beers, spirits and cocktails are available, all at reasonable prices, with draught beer going for 60din a glass. La Revolucion has occasional live (mostly Latin) music.

Living Room Café Makedonska 22; tel: 324 8202. Effectively, this has taken over half of the lobby of the Dom Omladine Centre, a venue for films, theatre and live music; the rest of the space is taken up by a book and record shop. This is a good meeting place, with large windows looking out on the street and real espresso coffee. Being in such a large space means that it is less smoky than average. There is also a cavernous pool hall downstairs and a noisy internet café above. Open 09.00–01.00, Sunday 17.00–01.00.

Parlament Obilićev venac 27; tel: 627 880. Around the corner from the others on the Obilićev venac strip and next door to the Russian Tsar, Parlament offers a considerable range of coffees, cocktails and ice-creams.

Plato Akademski plato 1; tel: 635 010. On the square next to Belgrade University's philosophy faculty, hence the name, and located above an eponymous bookshop, this is one of Belgrade's most well-known institutions: a dark, trendy coffee-bar that attracts a mostly young crowd, not just university students. Plato is also very popular with foreign visitors and is usually crowded, despite being a little more expensive than most of the competition. A wide range of beers, cocktails, coffees, ice-creams and pasta-based light meals is available, as well as a few vegetarian options. The music is a mixture of drum 'n' bass and Latin, with live jazz at weekends. Tables spread outside onto the square in summer.

Plum Inside the Millennium Shopping Centre, off Oblićev venac; tel: 184 176. This is a multi-levelled coffee bar that spirals upwards alongside the stairwell of a smart shopping mall mostly given over to designer clothing. Hermetically sealed-off from the streets outside, you could be anywhere in the developed world, in fact Belgrade seems an unlikely choice. Depending on your outlook, you might consider this either glamorous or pretentious. Open, along with the shops, from 09.00 to 21.00.

Red Skadarska 17; tel: 850 1676. A convenient bar that serves good cocktails on a street that is mainly devoted to restaurants.

Rio Bravo Kralja Petra I 54; tel: 628 612. Named after a John Wayne film, this Western-style saloon bar has wooden swing doors and wall-mounted cartwheels. It serves a wide range of beers, whiskies and cocktails, and is less popular with cowboys than you might imagine. Open 11.00–02.00, Sunday 17.00–02.00.

Ruski Car (Russian Tsar) Obilićev venac 28; tel: 633 628. Close to Trg Republike, this large, elegantly faded café is identified by its name in Cyrillic only, but it is hard to miss as the building that dominates the corner of Kneza Mihaila and Obilićev venac. The interior is smoky, with dusty chandeliers, faded Regency pink décor and portraits of Russian tsars on the wall. This establishment continues to be highly popular, as it always has been throughout the best part of the 20th century, even during wartime – it is referred to twice at the beginning of Kustarica's cinematic epic, *Underground*. Beer, coffees, juices, ice-creams and a wide selection of fruit teas are available. In summer, the outside tables spread over a considerable area pleasantly shaded by trees.

Scena Strahanića bana 17; tel: 185 336. Found in a basement along 'Silicone Valley', Scena doubles as an Italian pizza place, but at night it is filled mostly with young people who come to drink beer and cocktails in the bar here. Open weekdays 12.00–01.00, Saturdays 12.00–05.00, Sundays 17.00–05.00.

Simbol Oblićev venac 27. This café-bar's name is written using a combination of Roman letters and … symbols. Wine bottles line the walls.

The Three Carrots Knez Milosa 16; tel: 683 748. An Irish pub, and Belgrade's first Hibernian representative. Its name apparently derives from an error in translation, as it was originally intended to be something to do with shamrocks. The Three Carrots has a vaguely faux-Paddy interior, and is frequented by the city's young crowd as well as by expatriates and embassy staff. Both Guinness and tasty pub snacks are served.

Triangle Kralja Petra 4a. A trendy café-bar next door to the '?' providing a considerable culture shock if you visit both establishments one after the other.

Zu-Zu's Obilićev venac 21; tel: 635 906. Another of the designer cafés on this street; currently, this is very much the 'in' place.

Snack bars and takeaways

These are everywhere throughout the city with similar prices and quality. A few usefully located ones are indicated below.

Ruski Car (corner of Obilćev venac and Kneza Mihaila) is a café-bar institution. There is a busy take-away counter on the Kneza Mihaila side, selling excellent, freshly made snacks: *pljeskavica, gibanica, pita višne, pita krompir* and so on.

Amica (Skadarska 40c) is a *palačinkarnica*, located in a basement at the bottom of Skadarska, that has a wide range of cheap and delicious pancakes with both sweet and savoury fillings.

Burek i Pecivo (Nemanjina 5) is open mornings only, but ideal for breakfast if you have to catch a train. It is close to the railway station and the Hotel Beograd.

In the Old Town, near the top end of Kneza Mihaila, there is the handy **Sarajevska pite i burek** on the east side of Kralja Petra I at number 34, by the junction with Uzun Mirkova. Also, there is **Grill Park**, a fast food hut that has good *pljeskavica* for 90din, on Balkanska, at the top of the park, opposite the lobby entrance of Hotel Moskva.

Around the corner from the Plato café and bookshop at Vase Čarapića 29 the **Plato Giros** fast food outlet sells Greek-themed fast food like *giros* and *souvlaki* for about 100din apiece. It is open weekdays and Saturdays 08.00–04.00; Sundays 12.00–04.00. Closer to the park and opposite the Košova restaurant on Krala Petra 43 is the **Tweety** chicken sandwich shop, while the **Košova** restaurant itself has a counter selling pizza slices to take away.

Good ice-cream is available everywhere throughout the city and especially along Kneza Mihaila, where it comes in a huge variety of flavours for 15din a scoop.

For cakes, the pastry shop in the **Hotel Moscow** is highly recommended with its staggering range of cream-rich *torte*.

In Zemun, the **Lido Pizzeria** on Karađorđev Square next to McDonald's does good sandwiches and snacks. Also the **Pinocchio Pancake Parlour**, on the same square, is recommended.

ENTERTAINMENT AND NIGHTLIFE

It may come as a surprise, but Belgrade offers some of the best nightlife in eastern Europe, with a constantly changing, finger-on-the pulse, club scene that is sufficiently hip to attract international (actually, mostly British) performers and DJs as notable as Goldie or Tricky. Despite the privations of recent years, and low wages that make clubbing prohibitively expensive for locals, the Serbian capacity for nightlife remains legendary. Dispense with any notions of a dreary, retrograde city locked into a grey, post-Yugoslav recession, Belgrade is up there with the best of them.

The focus for nightlife is spread throughout the city: much of the activity takes place on boats and rafts (*splavovi*) moored along the Danube and Sava. There is also a dance club located on one of the beaches of Ratno Ostrvo (War Island), a short ferry ride from New Belgrade, where you have the opportunity to dance in the sand underneath the stars. Other pockets of nightlife lie closer to the Old Town, near the top of Kneza Mihaila, at the top end of Kneza Miloša and along Resava. A recent development is the concentration of cafés, bars and clubs that have mushroomed along Strahinića bana, a street popularly known as 'Silicon Valley' due to the hordes of surgically enhanced young women who are said to frequent the area at night. This is a bit of a misnomer, as the vast majority of Belgrade's womanhood has no need for cosmetic surgery and would not choose it even if they could afford to, which they cannot.

Note that there is a certain amount of crossover between these listings for cafés, bars and clubs: some restaurants have live music and double as night-time hot spots and so there is not always a clear division, although the opening hours should give a clue as to how lively they become at night. With such a constantly evolving scene, venues come and go in terms of popularity. You may find that a previously acknowledged venue has vanished without trace by the time you get there. Make enquiries about which places are currently in vogue.

Perhaps the best policy is simply to take a taxi to a promising area, Bulevar Nikole Tesle along the Danube riverfront for example, and then just follow your ears and instincts. The music that you hear will be a good indication of the crowd it attracts: house and techno will lure young ravers; gypsy bands, an older, more mixed demographic; while the frenetic strains of turbo-folk might indicate the presence of young 'businessmen' ('gangsters' is such a strong word) and their silicon-enhanced molls. A few reliable suggestions are offered below.

Clubs and music venues

Akademija Rajićeva 10; tel: 627 846. A club near the north end of Kneza Mihaila that plays mostly guitar-based indie music, but which also has different theme nights. This is the place where Serbia's post-communism music scene really kicked off in the late 1980s.

Aundergraund Pariska 1a; tel: 328 2524. Romantically located in the 18th-century catacombs beneath Kalemegdan Fortress, this is one of the city's top clubs, with an enormous dancefloor, famous DJs, deafening house music and strobe lighting. For the faint-hearted, there are also quieter sitting areas away from the dance action. Open from 22.00–04.00.

Beggars Banquet Resavska 24; tel: 334 6168. Taking its name from a Rolling Stones LP, this is a club with live rock music.

Bizzare Zmaj Jovina 25; tel: 639 428; www.cafebizzare.cjb.net. Bizzarre is a café–bar with loud music, pinball machines, candle-lit tables and disorienting red light. There is usually a live DJ on Friday and Saturday nights. Open 10.00–02.00.

Bus Abadareva 1b; tel: 334 0671. This is a huge place that really does resemble a bus depot. The centrepiece is the red London double-decker that houses the DJ. Surprisingly, the music played is not necessarily 'garage'. Bus is at its most lively on weekend nights but has discounted prices on Tuesdays.

Crazy Svetogorska 14; tel: 334 6727. This has live music virtually every night.

Ellington's Milentija Popovića 5 (Hyatt Regency hotel); tel: 311 1234, ext 8178. Ellington's is a very smart jazz club inside Belgrade's top hotel. Jam sessions take place from time to time at weekends. Open 21.30–02.30.

Havana Nikole Spasića 1; tel: 328 3108. This is a café-club on weekdays, playing jazz and Latin music. On Fridays and Saturdays, there is a resident DJ and the emphasis shifts towards techno and house.

Klub studenata tehnike Bulevar Kralja Aleksandra 73; tel: 37 0890. As its name implies, this is a student club, with cheap drinks, house music and a youthful clientele. Live rock bands frequently perform here.

Libre! Džorđe Vašingtona 40; tel: 322 5445. This is a Cuban-themed bar and nightclub that becomes very lively on weekend nights. Open 10.00–01.00, Sunday 17.00–01.00.

Liquid Njegoševa 6; tel: 323 8164. Liquid is a pleasant, modern bar during the daytime that becomes a drum 'n' bass venue on weekend nights. Open 09.00–01.00.

Make-Up Francuska 40; tel: 329 0095. A bare-bricks bar with live music on a tiny stage area every night apart from Mondays. It becomes very crowded at weekends, which is perhaps part of its attraction for many. Open 10.00–02.00.

Mondo DC Takovska 34; tel: 324 5437. Currently this is one of Belgrade's most prestigious clubs, which has guest appearances by world-famous DJs most weekends.

Nana Koste Glavinića 1; tel: 650 875. This club does not get going until very late, but then it continues until dawn.

Oh! Cinema In winter, at Gračanička 18; tel: 627 059. In summer, at Kalemegdanska Terasa; tel: 328 4000. Note the two different locations: at Gračanička, it is in a hall decorated with cinema posters; at the fortress, on an outside terrace. Both venues have live music and tend to keep going later than many of the other clubs. Open 21.00–05.00.

Sargon Pariska 1a; tel: 063 667 722. This is another club located inside the Kalemegdan caves with a good atmosphere and music mostly from the 1980s and '90s.

Temple Music Bar Nikole Spasića 3; tel: 627 457. A live venue where the emphasis is on jazz.

Tramvaj Rusveltova 2; tel: 340 8269. To be found just down from Vukov Spomenik, towards Novo Groblije on Rustelova. Good draught beer, with live musicians performing most nights of the week.

Xinogoga Rabina Alkalaja 5, Zemun; tel: 316 1800. An unusual venue for a club: a disused synagogue in Zemun.

Zvezda Kneza Mihaila 51; tel: 328 2989. For the time being, this is one of the city's top clubs.

Floating restaurants, cafés and nightclubs

Acapulco Bulevar Nikole Tesle bb; tel: 784 760. With its Mexican associations on the tenuous side, this raunchy raft close to Hotel Jugoslavija is a prime location for turbo-folk, with all of its comic and less savoury manifestations. A night here is an interesting specatacle, but probably not for those of a nervous disposition. You will be pleased to hear that guns are not allowed inside. Open 12.00–03.00.

Amphora Bulevar Nikole Tesle bb; tel: 699 789. This is possibly the smartest and most exclusive of all of the *splavovi* along here. A smart dress code is enforced.

Asterix Ušće 1; tel: 311 2219. This is one of several floating pizzerias along the waterfront.

Bahus Bulevar Nikole Tesle; tel: 673 437. An expensive floating restaurant behind the Hotel Yugoslavija that is air conditioned in summer and heated in winter. The emphasis is on fresh fish. You can study their menu online at www.bahus.co.yu. Bahus refers to the Greek god of indulgence rather than any pre-war German school of art. Open 10.00–01.00.

Bangkok As the name suggests, the Caffe Club Restoran Bangkok provides Thai food in a restaurant on the waterfront north of Hotel Jugoslavija in the direction of Zemun.

Bibis Bulevar Nikole Tesle bb; tel: 319 2150. Bibis is one of the most popular of the *splavovi* café-nightclubs along the riverfront just south of the Hotel Jugoslavija. This one has photos of famous sportsmen on the walls and is patronised by good-looking athletic types. Open 10.00–02.00. Similar upmarket places close by are: **Amsterdam**, **Monza** and **Danus**.

Black Panther Savski kej. This is a lively place and one of the best venues in the city to see and hear Roma music performed.

Bleywatch Kej oslobođenja, Novi Beograd; tel: 319 1228. Another *splavovi* close to the Hotel Jugoslavija.The name is a Serbian-English pun that combines '*Baywatch*' – Pamela Anderson's former dramatic vehicle – with *bley*, the Serbian equivalent of 'chilling out'.

Dunav Boat restaurant, located close to the Bangkok restaurant approaching Zemun.

Exil Savski kej. One of many nightclubs on the Sava River. With dance music, a lively atmosphere and a resident disc jockey.

Palma Pizzeria-restaurant. This is next to the pontoon bridge that crosses the Sava to Lido Park. It has live music in the evenings.

Sound Savski kej. Sound is another trendy and popular club along the Sava riverside in New Belgrade, with its own local DJ and house music.

Live music

In addition to the clubs listed above, there are frequent live performances by jazz artistes and pop groups at the Youth Cultural Centre **Dom Omladine** at Makedonska 22 (tel: 324 8202). Bigger, internationally famous names tend to play at the **Sava Centar** in New Belgrade.

Many pubs, clubs, café-bars, restaurants, and even bookshops, put on live music in the evenings. For gypsy musicians, you can be pretty much guaranteed hearing something in the 'national' restaurants along Skadarska, as some have their own resident musicians on hand to serenade customers. For pop music or jazz, try some of the more upmarket pubs and cafés; they often advertise what is coming up with fly posters.

For classical music, try to find out what is coming to the **Guarnerius**, a beautifully restored recital hall near Trg Republike at Džorde Vašingtona 12, or alternatively at the national theatre, **Narodno pozorište**, in Zemun.

Occasional concerts are also staged by the various cultural institutes, particularly the **French Cultural Institute** on Knez Mihaila and the **Spanish Cervantes Institute** nearby. The **Fresco Gallery** has a small concert hall that occasionally puts on performances by classical musicians and vocal groups, as does the **Ethnographic Museum**.

Best of all during the warm summer months is the impromptu singing, playing and circle dancing that sometimes takes place in Kalemegdan Park. These are not professional performers, just ordinary people enjoying themselves. You will just have to follow your ears and hope to get lucky.

The **ECHO** pop music festival is Belgrade's own response to the success of Novi Sad's EXIT. It now takes place annually in late July. Recent artists have included Morcheeba and Sonic Youth. The festival takes place on the Lido, the beach on the uninhabited island in the middle of the Danube and Sava confluence. Access is across a pontoon bridge from the Novi Beograd–Zemun waterfront and special boat services are also laid on. The event lasts for five days and tickets are cheap, costing around €25. Four music stages present a mixture of musical styles – rock, reggae, techno – some with DJs, others with live bands performing. Being Belgrade, acts start late and finish even later, with many festival goers not bothering to arrive before midnight. For further information on line-up and ticket sales check the website at: www.echofest.com.

For fans of classical music, **BEMUS**, the Belgrade Music Festival, is held annually in October, with many international artistes and orchestras performing at a range of venues throughout the city. Information on what's on can be found at: www.jugokoncert.co.yu/srpski/bemus.

Theatres
There are plenty of Serbian-language productions but very little in the way of English. It may be worthwhile contacting the following:

National Theatre (Narodno pozorište) Francuska 3; tel: 3281 333
Atelje 212 Svetogorska 21; tel: 3247 342
Beogradsko dramsko pozorište Mileševka 64a; tel: 423 686
BITEF teatar Skver Mire Trailović; tel: 3220 643
DADOV Dure Salaja 6; tel: 3243 643
Madlenianum Opera House Glavna 32; tel: 316 2533
Pozorište na Terazijama Trg Nikole Pašića 3; tel: 3234 037
Slavija teatar Svetog Save 16; tel: 436 995
Teatar T Bulevar Kralja Aleksandra 77a; tel: 2421 314
Zvezdara teatar Milana Rakića 38; tel: 419 664

Cinemas
The **Muzej Kinoteke** at Kosovska 11 next to the Union Hotel (tel: 324 8250) shows classic films. They print a monthly programme of what is coming up, and have the same information available on their website at: www.kinoteka.org.yu.

Elsewhere, Belgrade's cinemas show all English-language films with their original dialogue and Serbian subtitles. The following is an abridged list of city cinemas.

20 Oktober I/II Balkanska 2; tel: 678 182
Academic City Bulevar AVNOJ-a 152a; tel: 698 222
Akademija 28 Nemanjina 28; tel: 361 1644
Art Bioskop 'Museum' Uzun Mirkova 2; tel: 328 1888
Balkan Braće Jugovica 16; tel: 3343 491
Dom kulture 'Studentski Grad' Bulevar AVNOJ-a 179; tel: 691 442
Dom Omladine Makedonska 22; tel: 324 8202
Dom Sindikata Trg Nikole Pašića 5; tel: 323 4849
Dvorana KCB Kolarćeva 6; tel: 621 174
Fontana Pariske komune 13; tel: 602 397
Jadran Trg Republike 5; tel: 624 057
Jugoslavija Bulevar Mihaila Pupina; tel: 676 484
Kosmaj Terazije 11; tel: 322 7279
Kozara Terazije 25; tel: 323 5648

Mala Kozara Ivana Ribara 91-93
Mali Odeon Kneza Miloša 14-16; tel: 643 280
Millennium Kneza Mihaila 19; tel: 064 110 7304
Narodna biblioteka Srbije Skerlićeva 1; tel: 643 355
Odeon Narodnog fronta 45; tel: 643 355
Palas Sumadija Turgenjevljeva 6; tel: 555 465
Roda Intermezzo Cineplex Požeška 83a; tel: 545 260
Sava Centar Milentija Popovića; tel: 311 4851
Tuckwood Cineplex Kneza Miloša 7; tel: 323 6517
Zvezda Terazije 40; tel: 687 320

Casinos

You can try your luck and get a taste of the Belgrade gambling (under)world at the following:

Aleksandar at Čumićevo sokaće 55; tel: 3243 111, Bulevar Kralja Aleksandra 158; tel: 458 393, Terazije 43; tel: 3230 681 and at 29 Novembra 1; tel: 334 6060
Aleksandar, Hotel Metropol Bulevar Kralja Aleksandra 69; tel: 3230 911, ext 223
Fair Play at the Hotel Kasina, Terazije 25; tel: 323 3613
Slavija Hotel Slavija, Svetog Save 1-9; tel: 444 4632
London Kralja Milana 28; tel: 688 530
Fun Uskočka 4; tel: 328 3060

Cultural centres

These have foreign-language libraries and newspapers and sometimes stage art exhibitions and musical or theatrical events in the evenings.

American Information Centre Knez Miloša 50; tel: 645 999
British Culture Centre Terazije 8; tel: 3023 800
Canadian Cultural Centre Kneza Miloša 75; tel: 644 666
French Culture Centre Zmaj Jovina 11; tel: 630 666
German Culture Centre – Goethe Institute Kneza Mihaila 50; tel: 622 823
Italian Culture Centre Njegoševa 47/III; tel: 344 2229
Russian House Narodnog fronta 33; tel: 642 178
Cervantes Institute (Spanish) Čika Ljubina 19

Sports
Football

The most popular spectator sport is of course football. This is taken very seriously, with fans swearing loyalty to one or other of the main teams at an early age. It can be difficult obtaining tickets for a high-profile international game or a local derby.

The three main teams, and their corresponding home grounds, are listed below.

FC 'Crvena Zvezda' Ljutice Bogdana 1; tel: 662 341; www.fc-redstar.net. Arkan was so devoted to this team (aka Red Star Belgrade) that he had a villa built for himself and his wife Ceca opposite the entrance gates. There is a perfect view of the pitch from the villa's roof turret but do not try asking to be let inside. The Red Star stadium is one of the largest in Europe, seating 54,000. Next door, at Ljutice Bogdana 1a, is the FC Red Star museum, which is filled with the team's silverware, as well as photographs and press cuttings concerning the club. Red Star's hardline supporters call themselves *Delije* ('heroes') – a name seen sprayed on walls across the city – and they are not to be messed with.
FC 'Partizan' Humska 1; tel: 648 222; www.partizan.co.yu. Originally recruited from the ranks of the Yugoslav army, this team used to be considered more pro-Tito, pro-Yugoslavia

than its main rival. Its supporters are called *Grobari*, 'graverobbers', a name which seems wholly appropriate whenever a derby takes place between Partizan and Red Star. By all accounts these matches are lively affairs and often feature fireworks used in ways not recommended by the manufacturer. Disappointment in a poor result is sometimes expressed by setting fire to the seats in the stands. Generally speaking, non-derby matches tend to have a little less of a Battle of Kosovo atmosphere about them.

FC 'Obilić' Gospodara Vučića 189; tel: 340 7426; www.fkobilic.com. This is the club that Arkan and Ceca eventually bought, having been rebuffed in their attempts of takeover at Red Star Belgrade. When they first obtained it in 1995, Obilić was an amateur club languishing in the Yugoslav third division. Arkan soon introduced new management techniques, bought promising new players from rival teams, and used strongarm tactics on those who did not see things his way. Numerous (apocryphal?) stories tell of opposing teams being intimidated into purposely losing matches, and of fellow gangster-managers coming to sticky ends. Such unorthodox chairmanship paid dividends, as by 1998 Obilić were playing in the UEFA Champions League and on their way to becoming Yugoslavian league champions. In 1999, when, as an indicted war criminal, it became impossible for Arkan to travel abroad anymore, Ceca took over the chairmanship of the club. Since then she has been accused of embezzling over £8 million from the transfer of FC Obilić players to other European clubs.

FC Radnički Tošin buna, Novi Beograd. Radnički are a second division side based in New Belgrade with a small, but fierce, skinhead fan base – a bit like a Balkan version of Millwall FC.

There is also a municipal stadium at Zemun, Ugrinovačka 80; tel: 615 944.

Basketball

Basketball is also immensely popular and the two main teams echo the names of Belgrade's football clubs: Crvena Zvzda ('Red Star') and Partizan. Their home courts are based at Kalemegdan Fortress. The 2005 European Basketball Championships are to be held partly in Belgrade, which will undoubtedly stir up a lot of interest for a sport in which Serbians and Montenegrins excel (see box, *European Basketball Championships 2005*). For basketball statistics and further information about the championships refer to the unofficial website at: www.Belgrade2005.com.

For more participatory sports action, Belgrade has a number of well-equipped sports centres:

Sports Centre 25 Maj Tadeuša Košćuška 63; tel: 182 242
Sports Centre Voždovac Crnotravska 4; tel: 660 826
Sports Recreational Centre Tašmajdan Ilije Garašanina 26–28; tel: 323 3048
Physical Culture Municipal Centre Deligradski 27; tel: 658 747
Sports Recreational Centre Banjica Crnotravska 4; tel: 669 211
Culture and Sports Centre Šumice Ustanička 125; tel: 488 3073

Swimming

In summer you can do what the locals do and swim from the beaches on Ada Ciganlija Island in the middle of the river Sava. There is also a discrete nudist beach here. Another beach is at the Lido opposite Zemun on the island in the middle of the confluence of the Sava and Danube rivers, which can be reached by walking across the pontoon bridge there.

Swimming pools

11 April Novi Beograd, Autoput 2; tel: 672 939, 671 547
25 May Tadeuša Košćućka 63; tel: 622 866
Košutnjak Kneza Višeslava 72; tel: 559 745
Tašmajdan Ilije Garašanina 26; tel: 324 0901

EUROPEAN BASKETBALL CHAMPIONSHIPS 2005

Quite reasonably, most Serbs consider themselves to have the best national basketball team in the world after the Americans. The former Yugoslavia always had a powerful side, one which famously even managed to defeat the all-conquering USSR team in 1975. Since the break-up of Yugoslavia, the national team of Serbia and Montenegro has gone on to win three European championships: Athens 1995, Barcelona 1997 and Istanbul 2001. This is on top of winning the world championships in the USA in 2003 and several medals at the Olympic Games.

Serbia's role as host has generated a great deal of excitement during the long years of build-up since 2001, both for the honour of being the host country and the high hopes the country has for the national squad retaining the title. The 2005 championships take place in Belgrade and three other cities – Novi Sad, Vršac and Podgorica in Montenegro – from September 16–25, with qualifying games for those not automatically eligible taking place throughout August. In Belgrade, games will be held at either the Belgrade Arena or the 'Pionir' sports hall, the shrine of Belgrade basketball as it describes itself. In Novi Sad, the 'Vojvodina' sports and business centre will be used (capacity 9,000) and in Vršac the brand-new Millennium Sports and Business Centre with a capacity of 3,600 will be utilised. During this period it is unlikely that café-bar conversations will ever stray far from the subject of tall young men in singlets.

Running

The **Belgrade 'Stark' Marathon** takes place every year in the second half of April, attracting up to 1,500 participants, including 70 international runners from 35 countries. There is also a 5km 'Race of Joy', in which up to 20,000 participants take part. A Children's Marathon starts at Belgrade Zoo a week before the main event.

SHOPPING

Belgrade is not as yet on any sort of widely recognised tourist trail and so traditional souvenir tat, all too common elsewhere in eastern Europe, is mercifully absent. There are, however, plenty of genuine handicrafts that are worth buying: embroidery, wickerwork, knitted garments and crochet work, in addition to copperware products and Serbian crystal. Sometimes, pieces of embroidery and crochet work are sold by women with small stalls along Kneza Mihaila. Leather products are also a real bargain, and the city is full of shoe shops selling high-quality footwear at bargain prices. As well as shoes, there are also leather suitcases, handbags and jackets worthy of consideration too.

For more place-specific souvenirs you might wish to consider the objects on sale at **Beogradski Izlog** (Belgrade Window) at Kneza Mihaila 6/Trg Republike 5 (tel: 631 721), which has a whole range of specialised calendars, notebooks, posters, postcards, T-shirts, glassware and tea mugs, all with a Belgrade theme. It is open 09.00–20.00 daily and 10.00–20.00 on Sundays.

In keeping with Belgrade's tendency to go out and stay out late, most of the shops, along Kneza Mihaila, including bookshops like **Plato**, stay open until late in the evening, until midnight in some cases.

For those nostalgic for the former Yugoslavia, all sorts of curiosities are on sale at the **Kalemegdan Information Centre** by the right-hand gate that leads to the central fortress. This Aladdin's Cave of communist kitsch, open from 10.00–16.00 and 10.00–20.00 on Sundays, includes Tito photographs and plaques, postcards, old books, inflationary, multi-zeroed bank notes and what must be the national collection of communist lapel pins amongst its treasures.

A fairly limited range of **postcards** is available throughout the city, both at pavement stalls and in bookshops, but the ones showing bomb-damaged Belgrade with typically Serbian, sardonic humour ('The children playground, designed by NATO' captioning a shot of boys frolicking in twisted wreckage; and, 'Sorry, we didn't know it was invisible - Greetings from Serbia' on a card showing a downed 'undetectable' F-117A spy plane) are becoming increasingly hard to find.

For those who like souvenirs with an ironic twist there are sometimes stalls along Kneza Mihaila or in Kalemegdan Park that sell nationalist items like *četnik* flags and Radovan Karadžić T-shirts and calendars. It is probably best to keep a straight face if you decide to buy any of these.

Other souvenir shops:

Ethno Center Ariljska 12; tel: 409 181
Etno magazin gral Zetska 13; tel: 3246 583
IPS Mamut Megastore Sremska 2; tel: 639 060
IPS Gifthouse Balkanska 14; tel: 688 933
Singidinum Kneza Mihaila 42; tel: 185 323
Zdravo Živo Terazije 15–28, opposite the Balkan hotel

For a wide range of **hand-made textiles**, including skirts, shirts, hats, kilims and table cloths, there is the showroom of the **Women's Textile Workshops Network** at Beogradska 44b; tel: 2438 088; fax: 437 913; email: wtwn@eunet.yu; www.wtwn.org.yu. The WTWN is a non-governmental organisation of women that encourages self-sufficiency and economic empowerment for its members. WTWN membership includes disadvantaged women from all over the former Yugoslavia: refugees, single mothers, low-income and unemployed women. All proceeds go to the artisans who make the goods on display.

Additionally, there are often women selling textiles from stalls along the middle section of Kneza Mihaila.

Many of the **art galleries** have copies of their work for sale, together with Serbian-language catalogues of the works on display. The **Ethnographic Museum** at Trg Studentski 13 (tel: 328 1888) also has a good gift shop.

Art sales galleries
107 Glavna 53, Zemun; tel: 611 485
12+ Vuka Karadića 12; tel: 632 450
Arheo Gospodar Jovanova 31; tel: 188 864
Ars Save Kovačevića 51; tel: 452 212
Artmedija Studentski trg 13; tel: 328 2060
Atrijum Simina 10a; tel: 626 431
Beograd Kosančićev venac 19; tel: 626 088
D/B Bulevar kralja Aleksandra 140; tel: 451 847
Dada Čumićevo sokače 54; tel: 324 2091
Fabris Milentija Popovića 23; tel: 311 2866
Lada Pop Lukina 1; tel: 188 595
Leonardo Vladimira Popovića 10; tel: 311 3333
Magica Milentija Popovića 9; tel: 311 4322
Mala Gallery Singidinum Uzun-Mirkova 12; tel: 622 582
Oda Milentija Popovića 9; tel: 311 4322

Pale Blagoja Parovića 25; tel: 547 405
Paleta Bulevar Mihajla Pupina 10; tel: 135 150
Parlament Palmotićeva 11; tel: 3238 295
Pero Milentija Popovića 1; tel: 311 3311
Radionica Duše Milentija Popovića 9; tel: 311 4322
Remont Makedonska 5 II/2; tel: 3344 171
Sebastijan Art Rajićeva 12; tel: 185 653
Singidunum Kneza Mihaila 42; tel: 185 323
Zvono Višnjićeva 5; tel: 625 243

For fans of naïve art, a wide range of paintings is available at **Naëve art - atelier Davidović**, Mihaila Pupina Bulevar 161/17, II floor, New Belgrade; tel/fax: 311 9453.

Close to Trg Republike on Terazije, **Yugoexport**, a department store still bearing the name of the now-deceased republic, is good for clothes. For smart, designer boutiques and a privileged, chi-chi atmosphere, there is the **Millennium Centre** shopping mall at Obilićev venac 16, just off Kneza Mihaila, which is open from 09.00–20.00. **City Passage**, Obilićev venac 20, which leads through to the Millennium Centre, has much of the same sort of thing. In New Belgrade, there is a similar range of exclusive boutiques in the cavernous **Sava Centre** building, Milentija Popovića 9. There is also a shopping centre at **Piramida**, Jurija Gagarina, Blok 44 in Novi Beograd.

Much of Belgrade's commerce is carried out in far less refined surroundings – either at the **street stalls** that line some of the main roads or at outdoor markets. Although they have tightened up recently, copyright laws in Serbia are lax, to say the least, and so 'genuine' Versace clothing, Cartier shoes, computer software and recent-release CDs and DVDs are often available at knockdown prices. The clothes packaging may look suspect, and the cover art on the CDs may be slightly blurry, but the chances are that if you cannot tell the difference then it is unlikely that anyone else will be able to do so either. Whether or not such facsimile items infringe copyright outside of Serbia is a moot point of course.

Markets

Belgrade's largest open-air market is at **Kalenić Pijaca**, at the bottom end of Njegoševa, within sight of the enormous dome of Sveta Sava Church. It is a dense warren of activity that is open every day but at its busiest on Friday and Saturday mornings. Every imaginable type of food produce is sold here: vast piles of seasonal fruit, heaving mounds of greens and onions, sheets of pastry dough, plastic bags of hand-made pasta, strings of peppers, rounds of cheese, hams, wooden tubs of *kajmak*, and enough garlic to dispatch any vampire straight back to Transylvania. With most of the stalls run by unhurried, cheerful women in headscarves, Kalenić is the spirit of the Serbian countryside transposed to the city. As well as food produce, and an adjoining area devoted solely to flowers, the market also has a section where chain-smoking Roma men sell a range of quite bizarre antiques – perhaps 'bric-a-brac' is a better term for the items on display here. Search amongst the broken 1940s wireless sets, World War II Partisan medals and broken watches for your own bargain. Haggling is quite acceptable.

There is another market selling similar produce, including antiques, every morning at the Sava Centre in New Belgrade.

Another market, which has less in the way of fresh produce but more cheap clothing and other items is at **Pijaca venac**, which is tightly contained beneath McDonald's and the city bus stops on Brankova. The market is housed in the area beneath the Chinese-looking, chequerboard towers; buildings which raised some controversy when they were first erected as they were considered by some to have some influence of the Croatian flag in their design.

Music

There are several CD shops on Kneza Mihaila that stay open until late at night, and which are responsible for providing the soundtrack for a walk along that street. The best selection of all is in the basement of the **IPS** shop at Kneza Mihaila 6/Trg Republike 5, which has a good range of folk, jazz, world and pop releases, as well as music DVDs. Serbian CDs cost around 500din, while those of foreign artists, 800–1,000din. The trade in bootleg CDs is not what it was but there are still street and market stalls that sell good-quality copies of popular titles for 150–300din.

Bookshops

Antikvarijat Kneza Mihaila 36; tel: 638 087
Beopolis Makedonska 22; tel: 322 9922
Ciklostil Kičevska 17; tel: 3441 900
Gecakon Kneza Mihaila 12; tel: 622 073
Plato Akademski plato 1; tel: 639 121
Skz Kralja Milana 19; tel: 323 1593
Stubovi Kulture Kneza Mihaila 6; tel: 632 384
Trojeručica Nušićeva 5; tel: 3224 234
Zepter Kralja Petra 32; tel: 328 1414

Foreign-language newspapers and books are available at **IPS**, Kneza Mihaila 6/Trg Republike 5 (tel: 328 1859), at the **Oxford Centre**, Dobračina 27 (tel: 631 021), and also at the **Plato** bookshop. The Plato branch on Kneza Mihaila has a much better selection than the one beneath the café on Akademski plato. The IPS shop has by far the greatest range overall, especially art and history books, and magazines.

OTHER PRACTICALITIES
Money and banking

ATM cash dispensers are now available at a number of locations in Belgrade, which is just as well as changing travellers' cheques can be quite a slow process. VISA, VISA Electron, MasterCard and Maestro are accepted by ATMs, although Plus does not seem to be widely recognised. Some machines will not accept VISA cards that have been issued by a foreign bank. Thankfully, this situation is constantly improving as new machines are installed.

American Express, Thomas Cook and VISA travellers' cheques can be exchanged at most banks, while Eurocheques can be cashed at the Micro Finance Bank. Generally speaking, branches of **Komercijalna banka** or **Raiffeisenbank** are the best bet. The commission charged for changing travellers' cheques may have quite a high flat rate and so it is probably more prudent to cash a fairly large amount at each transaction. For both cash and travellers' cheques the preferred foreign currency is the euro, closely followed by the US dollar. Cash can be easily exchanged at any bank or exchange office. There is no black market.

ATMs friendly to foreign-issued cards can be found at the locations listed below.

Branches of **Komercijalna banka** at: Svetog Save 14, Trg Nikole Pašića 2, Kralja Petra I 19–21, MERKATOR at Bulevar umetnosti 4, Bulevar Kralja Aleksandra 191, Voislava Ilića 62, Mekenzijeva 65, JAT at Bulevar Kralja Aleksandra 17, and RK Simpo, Svetonikolski Trg 2. In Zemun, there is a branch at Rajačićeva 2. Also at **Zepter banka**, Kneza Mihaila 41 – a particularly useful branch.

Other banks that offer over-the-counter exchange facilities in addition to those listed above include: **Agrobanka**, Sremska 3–5 (tel: 636 952); **Atlas banka**, Emilijana Josimovića 4 (tel: 3241 986); **Centrobanka**, Dalmatinska 22 (tel: 3228

807); **Delta banka**, Vladimira Popovića 8 (tel: 3010 180); **Jubanka**, Kralja Milana 11 (tel: 3230 685); **Micro Finance Bank**, Gospodar Jevremona 9 (tel: 3025 625); **Raiffeisenbank**, Resavska 22 (tel: 3202 100); **Vojvođanska banka**, Trg Nikole Pašića 5 (tel 323 0924); **Zepter banka**, Bulevar Mihajla Pupina 117 (tel: 3113 233); Kralja Petra 32 (tel: 328 1414); **National Bank of Greece**, Kralja Petra 22–24 (tel: 3281 498); **Novosadska banka**, Birčaninova 37 (tel: 3610 327); **Privredna banka**, Bulevar JNA 4 (tel: 657 064); **Sociéte Generale Yugoslav Bank**, Kralja Petra 14 (tel: 301 1607).

The Sociéte Generale listed above will also allow foreigners to open a bank account in Belgrade, as well as facilitating Western Union fast cash transfers (phone enquiries: 311 5525; email: transfer.novca@socgen.com). Western Union have a strong representation in Serbia and are probably the best way to have money sent from abroad. They have their own toll-free number with English-speaking operatives. Check for Belgrade locations at www.westernunion.com.

Foreign embassies

Albania Bulevar mira 25A; tel: 3065 350; fax: 665 439; email: albembassy_Belgrade@hotmail.com

Australia Čika Ljubina 13, tel: 624 655; fax: 624 029, 628 189, 3281 941 (Visas Department); email: austemba@eunet.yu; www.australia.org.yu

Austria Kneza Sime Markovića 2; tel: 303 1956, 303 1964, 635 955; fax: 635 606; email: OB@bmaa.gv.at

Belgium Krunska 18; tel: 3230 016, 3230 017, 3230 018; fax: 3244 394; email: embassy@belgium.org.yu

Bosnia & Herzegovina Milana Tankosića 8; tel: 329 1277, 329 1993, 329 1995, 329 1997; fax: 766 507; email: ambasadabih@yubc.net

Bulgaria Birčaninova 26; tel: 361 3980; fax: 361 1136; email: bulgamb@Eunet.com

Canada Kneza Miloša 7; tel: 306 3000; fax: 306 3042 (Consular section, tel: 306 3039; fax: 306 3040); email: bgrad@dfait-maeci.gc.ca; www.canada.org.yu

Croatia Kneza Miloša 62; tel: 3610 535, 3610 153; fax: 3610 032 (Consular section: Mirka Tomica 11; tel: 3613 592, 3670 076; fax: 3670 078); email: croambg@eunet.yu

Czech Republic Bulevar Kralja Aleksandra 22; tel: 3230 133, 3230 134; fax: 3236 448; email: belgrade@embassy.mzv.cz

Denmark Neznanog Junaka 9a; tel: 367 0443; fax: 660 759

Finland Birčaninova 29; tel: 3065 400; fax: 3065 375; email: finembas@eunet.yu

France Pariska 11; tel: 302 3500; fax: 302 3510 (Consular section, tel: 302 3561; fax: 302 3560) email: ambafr_1@Eunet.yu; www.france.org.yu

Germany Kneza Miloša 74–76; tel: 3064 300; fax: 3064 303; email: germemba@tehnicom.net (Consular section: Birčaninova 19A; tel: 3615 282/3615 290, 3615 323; fax: 3612 607; email: germcons@tehnicom.net)

Greece Francuska 33; tel: 3226 523; fax: 3344 746 (Consular section: Strahinjica Bana 76; tel: 3341 507, fax: 3344 746); email: office@greekemb.co.yu; www.greekemb.co.yu

Hungary Krunska 72; tel. 444 0472, 444 7479, 444 7039, 444 3739; fax: 344 1876; email: hunemblg@Eunet.yu

Israel Bulevar mira 47; tel: 3672 400, 3672 401, 3672 402, 3672 403; fax: 3670 304

Italy Birčaninova 11; tel: 306 6100; fax: 324 9413; email: italbelg@eunet.yu; www.italy.org.yu

Japan Geneksovi Apartmani, Vladimira Popovića 6, Novi Beograd; tel: 3012 800; fax: 311 8258

Macedonia Gospodar Jevremova 34; tel: 328 4924; fax: 328 5076; email: macemb@eunet.yu

Netherlands Simina 29; tel: 328 2332, 328 1147, 328 1148, 328 2127; fax: 628 986; email: info@nlembassy.org.yu; www.nlembassy.org.yu

Norway Užička 43; tel: 3670 404, 3670 405; fax: 3690 158; email: emb.belgrade@mfa.no
Poland Kneza Miloša 38; tel: 361 5287, 361 5297; fax: 361 6939; email:
ambrpfrj@Eunet.yu
Portugal Vladimira Gaćinovića 4; tel: 662 895, 662 894, 662 897; fax: 662 892; email:
embporbg@yubc.net
Romania Kneza Miloša 70; tel: 3618 327; fax: 3618 339 (Consular section tel: 3618 359)
Russian Federation Deligradska 32; tel: 657 533, 658 251, 646 068; fax: 657 845 (Consular
section, tel: 361 0192, 361 3964); email: ambarusk@eunet.yu
Slovak Republic Bulevar umetnosti 18, Novi Beograd; tel: 301 0000; fax: 301 0020, 301
0021; email: skembg@eunet.yu
Slovenia Zmaj Jovina 33a; tel: 328 4458; fax: 625 884
Spain Prote Mateje 45; tel: 344 0231; fax: 344 4203; email: embajada@sezampro.yu or
embespyu@mail.mae.es; www.spanija.org.yu
Switzerland Birćaninova 27; tel: 3065 820, 3065 825 (Consular section, tel: 3065 815); fax:
657 253
Sweden Pariska 7; tel: 3031 600; fax: 3031 601 (Consular section, tel: 627 047; fax: 3031
602); email: swedeemb@eunet.yu
Turkey Krunska 1; tel: 3235 431, 3235 432; fax: 3235 433; email: turem@eunet.yu
Ukraine Josipa Slavenskog 27; tel: 367 1516, 367 1781; fax: 367 1516, 367 1781 (Consular
section, tel: 664 896); email: ukr_yu@yubc.net
United Kingdom Resavska 46, tel: 645 055, 3060 900, 3615 660, 642 293, fax: 659 651
(Consular section, tel: 3061 070); email: ukembbg@eunet.yu; www.britemb.org.yu
United States of America Kneza Miloša 50; tel: 3619 344, 361 3041, 361 3909, 361 3928;
fax: 361 5489; www.usemb-belgrade.rpo.at

Communications

The **Main Post Office** is located on Tavoska 2, near Sveti Marko Church, while
the more conveniently located **Central Post Office** is at Zmaj Jovina 17. Other
branches are at: Slobodana Penezića Krcuna 2, Šumadijski Trg 2a, and at Glavna 8 in
Zemun. They are all open 08.00–20.00 daily.

The basic ZIP code for Belgrade is 11000.

Telephone calls can be made from all of the post offices above: the telephone
centre in the Main Post Office is open 07.00–midnight Monday to Friday and
07.00–22.00 at weekends; at the Central Post Office, calls can be made from
07.00–22.00 daily. A simpler solution may be to buy a Halo card for 200, 300 or
500din from a booth and use it at one of the red Halo street phones; 300din gets you
about 8–10 minutes to the UK.

An online telephone book for the whole of Serbia is available at www.telekom.yu.

Mobile phones networks

063 Mobtel Bulevar umetnosti 16; tel: 063 9863; fax: 063 311 311 or 063 97 97;
www.mobtel.co.yu
064 Telecom Srbija Makedonska 2; tel: 064 789; www.064.co.yu

Express mail couriers

BPS Koste Glavinića 2/L5; tel: 3691 815
DHL Omladinski brigade 86; tel: 318 1844
FedEx Express Autoput 22; tel: 314 9075
RGV Express Belgrade Airport; tel: 601 555, ext2409
TNT Cvijićeva 60; tel: 769 232
UPS Belgrade Airport; tel: 601 555, ext2112

Internet

Internet cafés are on the increase in the city. The following are a selection:

Belgrade Internet Club–Forum near the Hotel Prag at Balkanska 21; tel: 686 478; www.clubforum.co.yu. Open 24 hours a day.
Extreme on Beogradska (tel: 433 304) through the entrance by the Atlas Bank at IPS.
Internet Café Makedonska 4 (tel: 323 3344). This is a bit pricier than most at 90din per hour, but with a very fast connection. They also have a 'no smoking' section and a selection of drinks.
Maverik, Makedonska 22; tel: 322 2446. Inside the Dom Omladine Centre.
Akademski plato Tel: 303 0633. At the back of the Plato bookshop, underneath the café of the same name for 30din per half-hour.
Sezam Pro Skadarska 40c; tel: 322 7231
S-Soft Zetska 5; tel: 323 1560

Medical services

Clinical Centre of Serbia Višegradska 26; tel: 361 7777
Emergency Centre Pasterova 2; tel: 361 8444

Private clinics

Bel Medic Viktora igoa 1; tel: 3065 888. Open 24 hours.
Dr Ristić policlinic Narodnih heroja 38; tel: 693 287
Endotop Zmaj Jovina 6; tel: 634 630
HBO Medical Centre Bulevar Vojvode Stepe 347b; tel: 3972 666
Jevremova Gospodar Jevremova 41; tel: 328 1051
Medicom Braničevska 8/I; tel: 3443 781
Petković Clinic Maglajska 19; tel: 667 078

Dentists

AB Požeška 77/V; tel: 354 4299
Orthodent Strahinjića Bana 33; tel: 188 327
Sava dent Krunska 6a; tel: 323 8028
Super dent Sazonova 116a; tel: 404 350
Zepter Dental Clinic Kralja Petra 32; tel: 328 1414

There are **24-hour dentists** on duty at Obilićvenac 30; tel: 635 236, and Ivana Milutinovića 15; tel: 444 1413.

Pharmacies (24 hour)

Prvi maj Srpkih vladara 9; tel: 324 0533
Sveti Sava Nemanjina 2; tel: 643 170
Zemun Glavna 34; tel: 618 582

Other services

Police Tel: 92
Fire Department Tel: 93
Ambulance Tel: 94

PLACES TO VISIT
Stari Grad – the Old City

Many of Belgrade's most appealing landmarks lie within this comparatively small area. The Old City may be defined as being the part of the city that lies southwest of Dunavska, with its western boundary circumscribed by Karađorđeva and Kalemegdan Fortress, and its southern limit set by Brankova. Stari Grad's southeastern boundary is vaguer, but undoubtedly it extends as least as far as Skadarska, a leafy, cobbled street of restaurants serving up national cuisine. This haystack-shaped concentration of Belgrade's older buildings is bisected by Vase Čarapića, an important artery that connects Trg Republike, the spiritual heart of the city, with Kalemegdan Park by way of Studentski Trg. The pedestrian thoroughfare of Kneza Mihaila runs parallel to this.

Trg Republike (Republic Square) is as good a place as any to begin. This large, elongated square is flanked by the imposing neoclassical edifice of Narodni Musej – the **National Museum** – at its north side, with the **National Theatre** (built 1869) just across Vase Čarapića to the east. Dominating the part of the square that stretches up to link with Kneza Mihaila is **Dom štampe** (The House of the Press), a glass and concrete example of 1950s Socialist architecture and a window cleaner's nightmare. The square has been renamed recently as Trg Slobode – Freedom Square – but most simply refer to it as 'Trg'. A set of fountains divide the square at this side, stretching down to reach the **equestrian statue of Prince Michael Obrenović III**, who reigned from 1839 to 1868 and was widely hailed as a great liberator of Serbia from the Turks. The prince points steadily south, towards the lands that were still under Ottoman rule during his reign and which were yet to be liberated in the name of the motherland. The base of the statue has relief work which depicts episodes from the struggle against Turkish domination. This famous landmark is at the heart of the city and the statue has become an important meeting place for young Belgraders who say, 'kod konja' to each other ('Meet you at the horse'), which suggests that his steed has earned greater notoriety than the prince himself.

Not far from Trg Republike, leading off north from 29 Novembra, just beyond the National Theatre and opposite the post office there, is the tiny bohemian enclave of **Skadarlija**. This corner of the city was first settled by Roma in the 1830s who occupied the abandoned trenches in front of Belgrade's defensive walls. Their flimsy gypsy huts were replaced by more solid buildings in the middle of the century as the area became home to craftsmen and lower-rank bureaucrats. The street received its current name in 1872 in honour of the Albanian city of Shkoder and, by the turn of the 20th century, Skadarska Street had become a focus for the city's bohemian life and a haunt of Belgrade's artists, actors, writers and musicians. The writer Đura Jakšić lived here and his former home is still used as a poetry venue for occasional 'Skadarlija nights'. Belgraders like to compare Skadarlija with Montmartre in Paris but this is probably pushing things a bit. Effectively, the area consists of just one principal street, Skadarska, together with a couple of lanes that lead off it. There is a fountain near the top of the street that is a copy of the Sebilj fountain from the Baščaršija district of Sarajevo, a gift from that city to Belgrade and a reflection of friendlier times. Skadarlija does its level best to conjure up the atmosphere of bygone times in the city, albeit in a slightly self-conscious fashion. The street itself is picturesque enough – narrow, cobbled and leafy with plane trees – but its main attraction, particularly in summer, is the concentration of 'national' restaurants that are squeezed in along here. Running all the way down the street is a chain of old-time restaurants, all of which compete with each other to be the oldest, the most authentic, have the oddest name – My Hat, the Three Hats, the Two Deer, There Are Days etc – and host the best musicians. The appeal is there for both locals and visitors. Large groups of friends and extended families gather here to drink, eat and celebrate; tourists come to gawp at the spectacle of Serbs enjoying themselves and to absorb the bohemian atmosphere. The food is Serbian with frills: plentiful grease, grilled meat and kajmak. The formula is similar whichever restaurant you decide to patronise: slick waiters circulate with endless plates of meat as Gypsy bands surround diners at their tables and play for tips. For the price of a few euros the musicians will perform requests; for a bigger sum they will follow you along the street to your hotel or your parked car without missing a breath – a very gangster-cool thing to do if that is your inclination. Skadarlija can be a great night out, but it can also be a disappointment to those expecting to be seamlessly plunged back in time to witness some sort of bohemian Arcadia. The whole experience should not be taken too seriously: how much fun you have is really a matter of attitude. Skadarlija is certainly the 'real' Serbia, but it is also the closest that Belgrade comes to having any sort of tourist trap (see also under *Restaurants* in this chapter). There is a market, **Bajlonova pijaca**, and a line of florists running along Džorđa Vašingtona at the bottom end of the street. The Ottoman kiosk here is a replica of one from the Turkish quarter of Sarajevo and was given to the city as a gift of goodwill in 1989.

Returning to Trg Republike, and then continuing up Vase Čarapića, past the post office and the Plato café, you soon reach the quiet, green rectangle of **Trg Studentski**. This was originally a **Turkish graveyard**, which was later cleared to make way for a market place. When the Serbs took over the administration of the city the market area was transformed into a public park. The building facing the square at Studentski Trg 1 is the former residence of Captain Miša Anastesijević, an important 19th-century city merchant and business associate of Prince Miloš. The building, with a light-coloured fascia and red ornamentation, was built in 1863, and is a combination of Gothic, Roman and Renaissance styles. Today it is the seat of the rector's office of Belgrade University. The **Ethnographic Museum** stands on the square's northern side. Also on Trg Studentski, at the corner of Braće Jugoviće and Višnjićeva is the *turbe* **of Sheik Mustapha**, a Muslim holy man. This is one of the few Turkish monuments that still survives in Belgrade. It was built in 1784 as a mausoleum, and originally stood in the courtyard of a dervish monastery that has now completely vanished. Clearly, the sheik is still venerated in some quarters: when I visited the *turbe*, a group of Roma women were involved in kissing the locked doorway, posting dried flowers through the window, tying scraps of cloth to the metal grille and collecting plants from the grass outside.

Kalemegdan Park is nearby: a leafy, green refuge from the city, busy with strolling couples at any time of year, and situated on a bluff overlooking the confluence of the Sava and Danube rivers. The main path leading through it towards the fortress is lined with gift stalls and the stands of peanut vendors, while other walkways meander off into the shade of birch and chestnut trees. Busts of various national heroes stand on plinths at some of the intersections. Covering a total of 30ha, this is the biggest park in the city: a vast complex of fortifications and gardens that, as well as serving as a home for the Kalemegdan Fortress and Military Museum, also contains the Arts Pavilion, the Belgrade Zoo and the Cultural Monuments Protection Institute. From the park's higher reaches, marvellous views may be had of the Sava and Danube rivers below, the high-rise buildings of New Belgrade on the opposite bank, and the wooded countryside of the pancake-flat Pannonian Plain that lies north of the city limits, and which draws the eye to a hazy vanishing point far upstream. The view is best in the morning – or better still, in the early evening, when the *bloks* of Novi Beograd are silhouetted with the setting sun and the river gives off a silvery glow. Despite famous Viennese waltzes that claim a contrary colouration, the Danube's waters are resolutely brown at all other times. In the opposite direction, low hills stretch away to the south, towards central Serbia. It is at this time of day that Belgraders are most likely to linger here; strolling, talking, playing chess and sometimes singing and dancing in impromptu groups. It is also a favourite spot for courting couples, and quite rightly so: it is without doubt the city's most romantic spot.

Successive military powers at Kalemegdan had to respond to invasion and colonisation from both directions, and both northerners – Habsburg Austrians – and southerners – Ottoman Turks – held sway here at different times. In many ways, the fortress can be seen as a focal point for all Balkan history, the precise location where east clashes with west. By the same token it could be equally considered to be at the very edge of Europe itself; indeed, this was the case in the 18th and 19th centuries when the Austrian fortress was regarded by many as marking the very boundary of the civilised world.

The park was created in 1867 by Prince Mihailo Obrenović on the occasion of the fortress being handed back to the Serbs. The project was put in the hands of Emilijan Josivović, Belgrade's first urban planner. Originally, it only extended as far as the stone stairway leading up to the lower terrace but after 1931 the park was extended to include the upper city. The horse chestnut trees that were planted at this time have now reached full maturity and are a splendid sight when in flower in late spring.

Walking along the western pathway above the Sava River you soon come to the **Messenger of Victory** (*Pobednik*) monument, a landmark that was inaugurated in 1928 to commemorate the tenth anniversary of the breach of the Salonica front. This defiant and proud statue by Ivan Meštrović was originally intended to stand in the city centre but had to be relocated here due to prudish complaints about its full-frontal nudity and quite obvious masculine attributes. Now it stands looking west over the Sava River, its controversial feature pointing unashamedly towards New Belgrade and to Austria and Hungary beyond. As well as its more obvious manly charms, Meštrović's warrior figure has two symbols of Serbian nationhood incorporated in its design: in his right hand, the warrior holds a falcon to symbolise Slavic freedom, and in the left, a sword representing the defence of peace. Belgrade has been required to take up this sword of peace many times, usually at great cost to its citizens, but at no time was the city's freedom more threatened than during the Nazi bombings and subsequent occupation of World War II. As a reminder of this, four graves of more recent heroes lie near to the base of the statue. Among these are those of Tito's right-hand man in the Partisan struggle, Ive Lole Ribar, and the Marxist, Moše Pijade, one of the theoreticians that helped to give Tito an ideological framework for his reconstruction of post-war Yugoslavia.

Meštrović has another work located in the gardens nearby: his **Monument to France**, which was erected in 1930 and depicts a figure bathing. It is dedicated to the French who perished in Yugoslavia whilst fighting in the Great War. Symbolically, the statue is meant to represent the soldiers as bathing in the waters of courage. It is an altogether different monument to the Messenger of Victory, and being of a softer, more feminine nature, has never aroused the same degree of controversy. Close to this monument, behind the bouncy castle and kids' electric trucks and beneath the shade of trees is a fountain that depicts a figure wrestling heroically with a snake.

The **Kalemegdan Fortress** gets its name from a combination of two Turkish words, *kale*, which means field and *megdan*, meaning battle. The name refers to the plateau itself rather than the fortress upon it. The Turks also referred to the site as '*Fitchir-bayir*' ('hill for meditating'); the park still fulfils much the same function for many of Belgrade's citizens today. Being such an obviously strategic site, high above the surrounding plain, with clear views in all directions overlooking the confluence of two great rivers, it seems no wonder that it was occupied and defended at the first opportunity. The first military defences here were built by the Celts, later to be expanded by the Romans during their tenancy of the site. Later, in the medieval period, the fortress was rebuilt, and ramparts constructed around the lower town, by the despotic Serbian leader Stefan Lazarević who somehow managed to cling on to power here despite rapid Turkish expansion to the south. When the Turks finally arrived, the fortress fell into neglect and it was not until the arrival of the Austrians at the beginning of the 18th century that the fortress was reconstructed in its present form. Little survives of the earlier structures today, but some deep wells remain that are Roman in origin, as well as some medieval fortifications. The 60m-deep **Roman well** was rebuilt by the Austrians in the 1720s to ensure a safe water supply to the fortress. A double spiral staircase leads down 35m to the water level. It was here, at the site of the Roman well that Stefan Lazarević used to hold court in the 15th century, and, of the surviving medieval fortifications, the most impressive date from the period of his tyrannical rule. Most notable is the **Despot's gate** (Despotova kapija) named after Stefan Lazarević himself, the best-preserved of the fortifications from that period. This gate originally formed the main entrance to the upper town; now it is used as an astronomical observatory. There is also Zindan kapija, the **Prison gate** constructed a few years before the Despot's gate to provide a heavily fortified entrance to the fortress. The Prison gate consists of two round towers defended with cannons with a bridge crossing the ditch to the entrance between them. A dungeon was installed in the cellars underneath, hence the name. Just below the gate of Zindan kapija stands the **Rose Church of Our Lady**. An older church, built during the reign of Stefan Lazarević, is said to have stood on the same spot but this was razed by the Turks during their 1521 invasion. The current building was originally built as an arsenal during the 18th century but later converted into an army chapel called the Rose Church between 1867 and 1889. It was restored in 1925. Elsewhere within the fortress complex, features of interest of a later construction include Sahat-kula, the **Clocktower gate**, built in the second half of the 18th century above the south entrance to the upper town and used by the Turks as a lookout, and Leopold's gate, built in the 18th century and named after the eponymous Austrian emperor.

The plateau around the fortress was transformed into a park during the *belle époque* years at the end of the 19th century, but part of the citadel itself was put to good use in housing the Military Museum, which was established in 1878. The museum is easy to find, just look for the neat ranks of World War I and II tanks and anti-aircraft guns that fill the ditches surrounding it. Also contained within the park, to the north of the main entrance, is the **Art Pavilion 'Cvijeta Zuzorić'**. The **Belgrade Zoo** lies beyond this, spread across the park's northern slope. When Nazi Stuka dive-bombers attacked the fortress in 1941 they hit the zoo too, damaging many of the cages and allowing some of its more dangerous inmates to wander freely through the capital's ruined streets. Rebecca West, who visited before the German bombs fell, described it as being 'a charming zoo of the Whipsnade sort'.

All of the above are to be found in the medieval **Upper Town** sector of Kalemegdan but the **Lower Town**, the riverbank zone of the fortress, has a few sights of its own, although far more has been destroyed here. The **Charles VI gate** (Kapila Karla VI) was built in 1736 as a ceremonial entrance to the city and bears a coat of arms that shows a boar's head being pierced by an arrow. A late 18th-century cannon foundry stands next to the gate, later to become an army kitchen. The most prominent feature in this zone is the 15th-century **Nebojša Tower**, which stands near the river on Bulevar Vojvode Bojovića, and was originally constructed to protect the harbour with cannons. There was great resistance here during the 1521 siege of the city by the Turks: only after setting fire to the tower was the Lower Town successfully taken. Later, during Ottoman rule, it became a dungeon and torture chamber.

Returning to the Upper Town and leaving Kalemegdan Park by its southern entrance to traverse the pedestrian crossing on Pariska, you will find yourself at the very top of pedestrianised **Kneza Mihaila**. Heading south, you pass the terminus for trams numbers 19, 21, 22 and 29 on your left, fronted by a line of stalls selling all manner of souvenir porcelain; the next street running across is Kralja Petra I. Turning down this street to the left, and passing a few restaurants on the way, you reach the Royal, which is, rather surprisingly, Belgrade's oldest hotel. Just beyond here, at Gospodar Jevremova 11 is the city's only surviving mosque (at one time there were 30 in the city). The **Bayrakli Mosque**, which dates from the Turkish re-conquest of the city in 1690, and was built as a memorial to Sultan Suleyman II, has clearly seen better days. Its name means 'the flag mosque', a reference to the method in which the call to prayers was signalled in the past. Somehow, this solitary remnant of the Muslim faith gives the impression of deliberately hiding itself away in predominantly Orthodox Belgrade. With good reason perhaps; it was recently damaged during the riots that were the backlash of the anti-Serb pogrom in Kosovo of March 2004. The spirit of Orthodoxy is actually very close, just around the corner at the **Fresco Gallery** on Cara Uroša.

The mosque marks the edge of the city neighbourhood known as **Dorćol**, its name coming from the Turkish *dört yol*, meaning 'four roads'. The four roads in this case originally referred to the crossroads where Cara Dušana crosses Kralja Petra I but now the name is used to describe the whole of the quarter that stretches northwards from Skadarlija to Kalemegdan, and eastwards from Studentski Trg to the Danube riverbank. Formerly, Dorćol was host to a cosmopolitan community of Turks, Austrians, Greeks, Jews, Vlachs and Serbs. The 19th-century Jewish community occupied the area delineated by the streets of Tadeuša Košćuška, Visokog Stevana, Braće Baruh and Dunavska (one of Belgrade's first synagogues was built here, at the corner of Solunska and Jevrejska), while the neighbouring Turkish quarter of Zerek lay in the streets that surrounded the intersection of Kralja Petra and Cara Dušana – the *dört yol* crossroads itself. The first church to be established in this multi-cultural enclave was that of **Svetog Aleksandra Nevski** (St Alexander Nevsky Church) at Cara Dušana 63. The proposal for a church in Dorćol first came from Russian volunteer troops stationed in Belgrade at the end of the 19th century. It was arranged that a mobile military chapel consecrated to the Russian saint be brought to Belgrade, and half a century later, in 1928–29, a church dedicated to the same saint was constructed at this location. The church has a white marble iconostasis that contrasts nicely with its smoke-blackened interior.

Nowadays, Dorćol is a largely working-class residential area with a far more homogeneous population. Dorćol has its share of high-density housing and can seem a little down at heel in places, particularly in its northern reaches approaching the river. This is not to say that it seems threatening in any way: the area has a genuine neighbourhood feel to it and it seems that everyone who lives here is at least on nodding terms with everyone else. At its northern edge on the Danube, near the May 25 Sports Centre, there is a popular promenade that follows the river east towards the Danube quay and west to Kalemegdan Lower Town; a route which is busy in summer evenings with cyclists, courting couples, dog walkers and locals enjoying the fresh river air.

More of the area's Jewish history can be discovered at the Jewish History Museum back on Kralja Petra Street. **Kralja Petra** has a number of other sights. Heading uphill back towards Kneza Mihaila you come to a pair of fine art nouveau buildings on the right-hand side just before you reach the junction with the pedestrian street. The building at number 41 with the green-tiled façade dates from 1907 and was the house of a city merchant called Stamenković. Next door at number 39 is another fine secessionist-style building that has motif of a female face flanked by two doves above its upper balcony. This was built in the same year as its neighbour for Aron Levi, a wealthy Belgrade Jew. In great contrast, facing them, next to a *burek* take-away on the opposite side, is the 1997 Zepter building, designed by the architects Branislav Mitrović and Vasilije Milutinović, a post-modern steel-and-glass edifice that looks as if it has been slickly shoe-horned into the limited available space. It is worth going round the back of this interesting building, which houses the Zepter restaurant, to take a look at the semi-circular rear entrance that faces on to the narrow alleyway off Uzun Mirkova. Crossing Kneza Mihaila, the street plunges downhill once more, and the **National Bank of Serbia** (*Narodna banka Srbije*) is on your left at number 12. This Renaissance-inspired building was built in 1890 and it is this same branch that still serves as the National Bank's headquarters today. It is claimed that the bank was built upon the site of a Roman thermae that stood here during the 1st or 2nd century AD. Further down, on the opposite side at number 7 is the Kralja Petra Elementary School, another neo-Renaissance building constructed in 1905–06, and designed by Serbia's first woman architect, Jelisaveta Načić. Continuing down from here you arrive at the **Orthodox cathedral** (*Saborna Crkva*). The Holy Archangel Michael Church was constructed between 1837 and 1840 on the orders of Prince Miloš Obrenović, who is buried here in the crypt together with his two sons, Mihailo and Milan. The church, a mixture of classical and baroque styles, was designed by the Pančevo architect Kvarfeld, and occupies the site of an earlier church that dates back to 1728. The interior contains a finely carved iconostasis by Dimitrije Petrović and icons by Avramović. During World War II, the relics of Prince Lazar were brought here for safekeeping, away from the hands of the Ustaše who had already stolen the prince's rings from his corpse in its resting place at a monastery in the Fruška Gora. This conferred considerable importance to the cathedral as a pilgrimage centre, until 1987 when Lazar's remains were sent on a nationwide tour prior to being deposited in their final resting place at Ravanica Monastery. Prince Lazar was not the only revered Serbian to be interred here: Vuk Stefanović Karadžić, the scholar responsible for phoneticising Serbian and producing a definitive dictionary of the language is also buried in the church's graveyard, together with Dositej Obradović, another great Serbian educator and writer. There is a museum dedicated to the legacy left by these two scholars quite nearby on Gospodar Jevremova. Next door to the cathedral is the **Museum of the Serbian Orthodox Patriarchy**, and opposite is the **'?' café**. This café – a traditional Serbian *kafana* – was built in the 1820s by a man called Naum Ičko, who later sold it to Prince Miloš Obrenović. The prince made a present of it to his personal healer, Hećim Tomi, who decided to open it as a *kafana*. The property changed hands several times, as did its name, being known at first as 'Tomi's kafana', then 'Shepherd's Inn', and then 'By the Cathedral'. There were objections by the ecclesiastical authorities to this last name and so a temporary sign showing a question mark was put up, which ended up becoming its name. Setting its individual history to one side, the '?' is a rare Belgrade example of a wooden-framed, Turkish-Balkan building, as well as being a fine location for a drink or a meal (see also under *Restaurants*). To get an idea of a rather grander style of living during the early 19th century in Belgrade you could take a look at nearby **Princess Ljubica's Konak** around the corner on Sima Marković.

Returning to the pedestrian street of **Kneza Mihaila**, there are a number of fine buildings that are worth a look whilst walking south towards Terazje. The urban terrain that was later covered by the street dates back to the original Roman settlement of Singidunum, later developed during the Turkish period to become an area of houses, drinking fountains and mosques. The street itself was laid out in 1867 by Emilijan Josimović, the same city planner responsible for Kalemegdan Park, and it was immediately occupied by the great and the good of Belgrade society. In 1870, the street was given the name it still bears today. At number 56 is the **Library of the City of Belgrade**, which was formerly the Srpska Kruna hotel, built in 1869 in a Romantic style. Virtually opposite at numbers 53–55 is a slightly later, Renaissance-style building that originally served as the private home of the influential lawyer,

Marko Stojanović. In 1937, it was turned into a gallery space for the **Academy of Fine Art**. Continuing further down the street, you pass several grand buildings, all dating from the 1870s, constructed in a transitional style that lies somewhere between Renaissance and Romantic. At number 49, next to a fast food stand, you pass the headquarters of OPTOR, the coalition of opposition groups so instrumental in bringing about Milošević's downfall. The office is quiet these days but this used to be the setting-off point for demonstrations, by way of the nearby Plato café at Trg Studentski. Further down, at number 33 is the neo-Renaissance building of the **Nikola Spasić Foundation**. At the junction of Kneza Mihaila and Đure Jakšića stands the **Soldiers' Fountain** (*Delijska česma*) close to the site of an earlier Turkish fountain destroyed by the Austrians. At the next junction, where Zmaj Jovina crosses the street, the **Progress Palace** dominates the surrounding buildings. Built in 1994 by the architect Miodrag Mirković, the design is a post-modernist combination of styles from different epochs, with a rounded corner façade of reflective glass. Continuing south, you pass the French Cultural Centre, and then the 'Russian Tsar' coffee house, on your right. Opposite sits the IPS bookshop and the Press building, *Dom štampe*, with fountains leading the way down to Trg Republike. Just a little further on and you reach **'Albania' tower**, at the corner of Kneza Mihaila and Kolarčeva. This building, dating back to just before World War II, was Belgrade's first skyscraper. Somehow, it managed to avoid the attentions of the German bombers in 1941. This is the end of the pedestrianised zone and where Kneza Mihaila ends, as do the southern limits of Stari Grad, the Old City.

South of Terazije – the modern city

The sights of modern Belgrade are fewer and farther between than those of Stari Grad, but they are interesting nevertheless, especially when considering the city's more recent history. A short walk along **Terazije** from its junction with Kneza Mihaila soon brings you to the imposing and attractive façade of the **Hotel Moscow**. This building, built in art nouveau style in 1906 for the 'Russia' insurance company, is one of Belgrade's more notable landmarks, but the view across to the neon signs of Terazije, with a gaudy McDonald's concession wedged into a dull row of traffic-grimed buildings, is far less pleasing. There are some fine buildings nevertheless: at Terazije 34 is the Krsmanovića Hall built originally in 1885 as a merchant's house but used between 1918 and 1922 as the court of Aleksandar I Karađorđević and it was from here, in December 1918, that the union of Serbs, Croats and Slovenes, later to become the Kingdom of Yugoslavia, was proclaimed.

Sitting opposite the Hotel Moscow is the rather less grandiose Hotel Balkan. Walking down Prizrenska from here will soon bring you to Pijaca venac, an important terminus for the city's bus network and the prized location of a McDonald's branch. From the terrace above the bus park you can to see the chequerboard-patterned roofs of Pijaca venac, condemned by some nationalists for echoing the Croatian flag in its design. In the street behind, hidden away at Maršala Birjuzova 19, is the city's only currently active synagogue, built in 1924–25 on a piece of land donated by the Belgrade Municipality. The gate leading into it appears to be locked nearly all of the time. Steps lead up from this rather woebegone street to Obilićev venac and a whole parade of designer cafés.

South of the Hotel Moscow, Terazije morphs into traffic-crazed **Kralja Milana** (formerly called Marshal Tito, in the days when the idea of a united Yugoslavia was still a source of pride). It is along here that, more than anywhere else in the city, resonances of the former republic make themselves known: the large, state-run JAT and Putnik offices, the crowded trams clattering along the street, the faded neon Cyrillic lettering, the lacklustre shops and dusty department stores – all seem to hark back to the recent past, the 1970s perhaps. The stylish cafés and designer boutiques of Kneza Mihaila already seem another world away, as if the recently introduced free-market economy, so fêted in the streets just north of here, could not spread beyond some unseen economic fault line that ran east to west somewhere in the vicinity of the Hotel Moscow. This is purely illusory of course, but for a brief moment, walking down Kralja Milana, it can seem as if Balkan-style socialism and Marshal Tito are both alive and well. There are one or two sights: just off the street on the edge of Pionirski Park stands the **City Hall**, built in 1882 as the royal palace of the Obrenović dynasty in an Italian Renaissance style. A little further down on Adrićev venac, the **Ivo Andrić Museum** makes use of the former residence of the writer and Nobel Prize winner. There is also a monument to him at the street corner.

Kneza Miloša leads downhill off Kralja Milana to the right. It was this part of the city that took the brunt of some of the most damaging of the 1999 NATO attacks, with cruise missiles homing in on the government buildings of the Federal and Republican Ministries of Internal Affairs. The building of the Republican Ministry of Justice on nearby Nemanjina Street was also hit shortly after, and the twin towers of the Yugoslav Ministry of Defence, which stood on the corner of Kneza Miloša and Nemanjina, were bombed twice, on April 29 and May 7 of that same year. The US Embassy complex at Kneza Miloša 50 was abandoned just before these raids took place, to be lightly vandalised in the weeks that followed. The crumpled remnants of the buildings remain in place, for the time being at least: their contorted concrete and exposed girders a chilling testament to precision bombing; indeed, they look as if they have suffered from freakishly localised earthquakes. The large obelisk-like edifice in the background to the carnage is the **'Belgrade Girl'** building (*Beograd anka*), which towers above the junction of Kneza Miloša and Kralja Milana.

Returning north towards Hotel Moscow and turning sharp right onto Bulevar Kralja Aleksandra (formerly Bulevar Revolucije) **Trg Nikole Pašića** lies directly on the left. This is the youngest of the city's squares, built in 1953 along with its central fountain, and originally known as Marx and Engels Square. The Nikola Pašića monument at the square's centre is a very recent (1998) addition. The classical-style **Federal Parliament Building** pre-dates the square, building having started in 1906, with completion in 1936. In front of the main entrance stand two groups of prancing black horses. It was in front of here that many of the opposition rallies against the Milošević regime took place in October 2000.

A little further down, at the edge of Tašmajdan Park stands **St Mark's Church** (*Sveti Marko*). This Serbian-Byzantine-style church in yellow and red was built between 1931 and 1940, and occupies the site of an older church from 1835. St Mark's has been constructed as a larger-scale copy of the Gračanica Monastery in troubled Kosovo, the most hallowed religious monument of the Serbian psyche. The hall interior is quite bare, and dominated by four massive pillars supporting the roof, but the church contains a rich collection of icons from the 18th and 19th centuries, as well as the sarcophagus that contains the remains of the Serbian Emperor Dušan who died in 1355, which were moved here from the Saint Archangel's Monastery in Prizren.

On Aberdareva, directly behind the church, stands the RTS Serbian state TV headquarters. The technician's wing of this building was hit by a NATO missile on the night of April 22–23 1999, killing 16 RTS workers and wounding 18 others. What makes this even worse is that it would appear that management were fully aware that the building was going to be targeted but had decreed that any employee leaving the building during working hours, even in the event of an air raid, would be threatened with a martial court. A monument to the victims stands overlooking the site in Tašmajdan Park and asks the simple question, *Zašto?* – 'Why?' **Tašmajdan**

Park itself is a pleasant, leafy space that hosts a Honey Fair each October, when over 100 beekeepers gather to provide a wide range of different honeys and associated bee-produce from every part of Serbia. The park has another war monument that commemorates the children killed by the 1999 NATO bombings; this one was erected by one of Serbia's leading daily newspapers – *Vecernje novosti* – and expresses anger at NATO in Serbian and (misspelled) English.

Another green space nearby, just to the north of Tašajdan Park, and sandwiched between Takovska and 29 Novembra is the **Jevremovac Botanical Garden**.

Continuing down Bulevar Kralja Aleksandra, and then turning right down Beogradska, you pass close to the Nikole Tesla Museum as you cross Krunska. Beogradska continues down to **Slavija Square**, which might already have been your first experience of Belgrade if you arrived in the city by way of the JAT airport transfer bus. The uninspiring monolith of the Slavija hotel dominates the scene, and buses, taxis and trams speed dizzily around the roundabout before being catapulted centrifugally in one of seven possible directions, principally along the main arteries of Kralja Milana, Nemanjina or Bulevar JNA. There is really little reason to linger here. A better bet is to walk back a block north, to Njegoševa – a smarter, quieter street strewn with designer cafés and trendy bars along its entire length. By turning right and following this street you will soon arrive at Kalenić market, Belgrade's most interesting outdoor locale for the sale of fresh produce.

The **Church of St Sava** (*Hram Svetog Save*) is also within easy grasp from Slavija Square – just a short walk south to the Vračar neighbourhood – and the church's enormous dome can be seen from all over the city, gleaming through Belgrade's haze in all directions like a beacon. The time taken over St Sava's construction must compare to that of cathedral building in medieval times; the church remains unfinished although with the relative peace that reigns in Serbia these days there is at least an end in sight. Given the country's history over the past century, there have been very good reasons for the snail's pace of its construction. Preparations for building began as far back as 1894. Following the comparative frenzy of construction that has taken place in the post-Milošević period, it was hoped that all building work would be finished by the end of 2004. However, although the construction of the external shell has now ended, the church's interior remains incomplete. The site at Vračar was chosen as the place where the Ottoman ruler, Sinan Pasha, had the holy relics of St Sava burned in 1594, having taken them from Mileševa Monastery in Raška. The design was sought by public competition and the winning plan, by architects Bogdan Nestorović and Aleksandar Deroko, was finally approved in 1926. Construction work was seriously interrupted in 1941 by Nazi bombing, and in the immediate post-war period there were the far more pressing needs of civil reconstruction. Work was continued in 1985, only to be halted once more when Serbia became embroiled in the civil war that accompanied the break-up of Yugoslavia. Now, it seems, the work may finally be completed in the not too distant future. Unless the feat is trumped by an even more grandiose project elsewhere, St Sava's will be the world's third-largest Orthodox building. Whatever the final outcome, it is already a very impressive structure: a neo-Byzantine colossus with echoes of St Sophia in Istanbul.

Dedinje and Topčider Park

This area, south of the city centre, has smart residential enclaves, several large parks and sports clubs, as well as a few museums and galleries. **Topčider Park**, a vast green space and one of Belgraders' favourite picnic areas, was the first of the city parks to be created. It sprang up around the residence of Prince Miloš with the planting of plane trees in the 1830s. The name derives from Turkish, meaning 'valley of cannons', as it was here that the Turks set up makeshift foundries to produce the cannons used for the 1521 attack on the city. Later, the area was used for vineyards and the summer residences of the wealthy, but in 1831, after having had a *konak* built for his wife and children in town, Prince Miloš Obrenović gave instructions for the setting up of a park and settlement here. He ordered the construction of a church, a *kafana* and an army barracks, in addition to a mansion for himself that was to be designed by the same architect, Hadi-Nikola Živković, who had been responsible for his wife's residence. The building, now housing the permanent collection of the **Historical Museum of Serbia** is in Serbian-Balkan style, with some elements of central European influence. The prince stayed here only occasionally during his first reign, which ended in 1839, but this became his permanent home throughout his short, second reign that began in 1859. He died here on September 14 1860.

South of Prince Miloš Mansion, Dedinje stretches away to the east of Rackovički put, while to the west lies wooded Košutnjak Hill with its maze of walking paths. To the north, hemming Dedinje in, with yet more greenery is **Hajd Park** (pronounced in the same way as London's famous green space). Close to Hajd Park is the **Museum of the 25 May**, which houses a collection of gifts donated to Tito from heads of state around the world. It also puts on special exhibits from time to time. Just a little way up the hill from here is Tito's mausoleum, **The House of Flowers** (open 09.00–15.00, Tuesday to Sunday), the cloying name, something of a euphemism to avoid drawing too much unwanted attention to the deceased founding father of federal Yugoslavia. Nearby, **Beli Dvor** (White Court) lies hidden away atop **Dedinje Hill**, just off Užička. This Renaissance-style mansion was built in 1925 as a summerhouse for Aleksandar I Karađorđević. After World War II, President Tito took it up as his own residence, as did Slobodan Milošević later on. After her husband's involuntary trip to The Hague, Milošević's wife, Mira, demonstrated her typical determination and remained in the house until she was eventually forced to leave and live elsewhere. The property has now been handed back into the ownership of the Serbian royal family.

Much of this suburb is quite self-consciously exclusive, with luxurious mansions glimpsed behind thick, protective hedges and expensive German cars swishing the tarmac; a natural abode for foreign ambassadors, film stars, politicians and Belgrade's new money. With the anonymity desired by some of its residents, it is perhaps not surprising that the neighbourhood, while pleasant enough, is rather lacking in real character. But Dedinje also has the common touch, and plays host to the home grounds of two of Belgrade's most well-known football teams – **FC Crvena Zvezda** (Red Star) Belgrade and **FC Partizan**. The aggressive and tribalistic graffiti that decorate the exterior walls of both of these grounds injects a tougher and grittier element into what is primarily an upper middle-class neighbourhood. This is perfect if you are both wealthy *and* a football fan. The turbo-folk star Ceca still lives in the 'wedding cake' villa that her husband Arkan had built overlooking the Red Star ground (see *Sports*). Her villa is not at all difficult to spot, on the corner opposite the western gates to the stadium, although you might be approached by several burly, shaven-headed men if you spend much time hanging around her front door. There is even a bus stop here, from where you can take a number 42 back to Trg Slavija; however, it is highly unlikely that you will bump into Ceca waiting for the bus with her shopping bags here.

Northwest of Dedinje, on a site alongside the Sava River, is the development that makes up the Belgrade Fair complex. South of here, **Košutnjak Hill** (Doe Hill) is a 330ha expanse of mixed forest and open areas that is criss-crossed by numerous walking trails. It owes its name to the deer that once roamed here, as it was a royal hunting reserve until 1903 when it was opened to the public. Despite the fact that this park witnessed the murder of Prince Mihailo Obrenović in 1868, Košutnjak has become a favoured picnic spot for many of Belgrade's citizens. Horse-drawn carriages are available for hire for trips around the park, and it is worth seeking out the enormous 200-year-old plane tree that has branches so massive it require braces to keep them up. The park area contains two specialised facilities: Pionirski grad ('Pioneer's town') with its sports and recreational centre, and Filmski grad ('Film Town') with studios and buildings to service the film industry. The Košutnjak Sports and Recreational Centre lies further down the hillside with football pitches, tennis, volleyball and basketball courts, athletics tracks, and several swimming pools. There is also a ski practice slope open all year. Lying at the foot of the hill is a spring called **Hajdučka česma** that is reputed to have been favoured as a resting spot for members of the Obrenović dynasty when they went on their hunting forays; the name translates as 'Brigand's Fountain'.

New Belgrade

This part of the city, west of the Sava River, is a post-war appendage that serves as the location for Belgrade's five-star hotels, the Hyatt Regency and the Intercontinental. It is a mixture of vast, low-cost housing projects or *blok*s, and tall office buildings, with a few sports centres, embassies, shopping centres and business complexes like the Sava Centre, to complete the mix. Most of the interest is along the river itself, with numerous boats and rafts moored along the bank offering entertainment in the form of cafés, restaurants and nightclubs. The majority of the riverside life is within the vicinity of **Brankov Most**, the most northerly of the three road bridges linking New Belgrade with the old city. **Park prijateljtsva** (People's Park) extends north from this bridge, between the river and Bulevar Nikole Tesle, the main road that continues west to Zemun. The park contains the purpose-built building of the Museum of Contemporary Art. When you have finished looking at the art collection you might choose to visit one of the waterfront restaurants close by. You could have a discussion about what you have seen at the Restaurant 'Dialog' or, alternatively, have a row about it at the Restaurant 'Argument'.

The **Sava Centre** at Milentija Popvića 9 is a large entertainment and business complex next to the International hotel. In addition to its 4,000-seat main hall and 15 conference halls, there are also business offices, exhibition halls, cinemas, restaurants and a shopping mall with smart boutiques. The Sava Centre also hosts concerts by famous national and international artists. For cheaper prices than chi-chi Sava there two other options in New Belgrade. There is the open-air market along nearby Proleterske solidarnosti, and the Piramida Shopping Centre, which lies west along Bulevar Jurija Gagarina at Blok 44.

Continuing west towards Zemun you reach the **Church of St Vasilje of Ostrog** at Partizanske avijacije 21A, which is interesting on two counts: its age and its design. This is the newest Orthodox church in Belgrade, begun in 1996 and completed in 2001, and constructed by donations made by devotees of St Vasilje of Ostrog, a reputed miracle worker. It is of an unusual rounded design, with large round windows and a detached belltower.

Zemun

Continuing west along Bulevar Nikole Tesle from New Belgrade, the unprepossessing hulk of the Hotel Jugoslavia soon appears on your right. It is round about here that another sprawl of *splavovi* starts to appear along the waterfront, stretching from here all the way to the centre of Zemun.

Zemun is now a Belgrade municipality but it used to be a separate town. The town is, in fact, much older than Belgrade. With such a favourable position on the banks of the Danube, some sort of settlement existed here even in Neolithic times. Later, in the 3rd century BC, the area was settled by a Celtic tribe, the Scordisci, who named the town Taurunum. The current name probably came about with the arrival of the Slavs, with the name derived from the Slavic term for the dugouts – *zemnica* – that housed the original inhabitants. With the arrival of the Austrians in 1717 the town came under Habsburg control and it was developed as an important fortification along the border with the Ottoman Empire. The town's importance as a trade centre on the border of two conflicting empires helped to boost its standing as a cultural centre, with handicrafts and industry becoming central to the town's economy. By the start of the 20th century Zemun had become one of the most economically developed regions of Serbia. Nowadays, Zemun has something of a reputation as a mafia centre, and many of the building projects that are currently taking place there are said to be financed with money gained from various nefarious deeds. Such gangsterism is not at all apparent on the ground; indeed, if anything, Zemun has a rather staid, sleepy provincial feel to it.

The Zemun Fortress, mentioned in documents from the 9th and 10th centuries, is the oldest building in the town but most of the remains that stand today date back only to the 15th century. A far better-preserved, later structure, still standing in the centre of the fortress area is the **Millennium Tower** (*Milenijumska kula*), which was built by the Hungarians in 1896 to celebrate the 1,000th anniversary of their state. The tower, which was partially restored in 1962, is also referred to as **Sibinjanin Janko's Tower** (*Kula Sibinjanin Janka*). The Millennium Tower has a prominent vantage point at the top of Gardoš Hill, which makes it a landmark from even as far away as the Kalemegdan Fortress in Old Belgrade, although at that range you are spared the graffiti that covers much of the lower brickwork. To reach it, turn right at Trg Radičevića at the end of Glavna, Zemun's main street, go down Njegoševa then turn left at the church up Sinđelićeva and left again at Grobljanska. The tower, which is something of a hotchpotch of styles, sits in a field overlooking the Danube. These days it is looking a little neglected, covered with graffiti and surrounded by broken glass and discarded beer cans. Next door is a restaurant with an outdoor terrace. From both the tower and the restaurant there is a magnificent view over Zemun's rooftops and the Danube to Belgrade beyond. Across the road from the tower is a large and lovingly tended graveyard that is a peaceful place to wander in.

Compared with Belgade, Zemun abounds with fine old houses, mostly in the vicinity of Glavna Street. At Dubrovačka 2 is the **Sundial House**, built at the beginning of the 19th century in a mixed classical and baroque style. The famous Serbian writer Jovan Subotić spent his last years at this house. Nearby at **Petar Ičko's House** on the corner of Bežanijska and Svetosavska is a merchant's house dating from 1793 that reflects a style transitional between classicism and baroque. Along Karamatina on the way to the tower is the **House of the Karamata** family, built in 1764 for a wealthy merchant and bought in 1772 by Dimitrije Karamata whose descendants still live in it. The house has a well-preserved 18th- and 19th-century interior. On Glavna itself there is **Spirta's House** at number 9, a residence built for a Vlach family in the mid 19th century in a neo-Gothic style. It now houses the Homeland Museum of Zemun. At number 6 is a single-storey, late 18th-century dwelling in a classical style, the birthplace of Dimitrije Davidović, secretary to Prince Miloš Obrenović, diplomat, statesman, and founder of Serbian journalism.

If you are not in the mood for seeking out specific old houses, a good route to follow is to turn right off Glavna near the Central hotel, and walk down Gospodska, a pedestrian street with shops and fine old houses that leads down to the Danube. At the bottom of the street is an open-air market on Pijace Zemun in front of the church. A very pleasant riverside walk can be made from here in either direction. As in New Belgrade, Zemun has a concentration of riverside clubs and cafés along the riverside here that are quiet or closed by day, busy by night. In addition, there are many restaurants – Šaran, Skala, Sent Andreja, Alexandar, Stara Kapitanija – along Kej oslobođenja, the road that runs along the Danube waterfront: the perfect venue for a leisurely meal on a balmy summer evening.

To reach Zemun from central Belgrade take a number 84 bus. You could combine a day trip with a visit to the Museum of Contemporary Art in New Belgrade, or even base yourself here (see *Hotels*).

Ada Ciganlija

This long, flat island near the mouth of the Sava River, between the suburb of Čukarica and New Belgrade, is the preferred leisure spot of many Belgraders, especially in summer. Much of the island is covered in deciduous forest but there are extensive beaches all along its southern shoreline. Like Zemun, its name is supposed to have a Celtic origin, coming from a combination of *singa* ('island') and *lia*, a word for submerged ground. The beaches face onto an artificial lake that was created by damming both ends of the island in 1967, and which has provided water for bathing that is cleaner and warmer than the Sava River itself. In addition to swimming, the lake provides an ideal environment for a whole range of watersports including rowing, sailing and water polo, and national and international championships are frequently held here; there is also a discrete nude-bathing beach 1km upstream of the main beach area. In addition to the beaches there are other distractions in the form of open-air cafés and floating restaurants, as well as shops, picnic areas, bicycle hire, minigolf courses, and even bungee jumping. There is a marina in the Čukarica channel for boats, yachts and smaller ships. In summer, outdoor musical events are sometimes staged here.

MUSEUMS

Applied Art Museum Vuka Karadžića 18; tel: 626 494
Open Tue, Wed, Fri and Sat 10.00–17.00, Thu 12.00–20.00, Sun 10.00–14.00; closed Mon

Banjica Concentration Camp Museum Velkja Lukića-Kurjaka 33; tel: 669 690
This is on the same site as the World War II concentration camp, set up here in 1941, which saw the deaths of thousands of Yugoslav Jews and Roma.
Open Tue–Fri 10.00–16.00, Sat and Sun 10.00–14.00; closed Mon

Belgrade Fortress Museum Kalemegdan
Not to be confused with the more warlike collection of the Military Museum, this has a permanent display of models showing the development of the complex, plans and texts relating to the evolution of the fortress, and some of the tools used by the builders.
Open summer 10.00–19.00, closed Mon; winter Sun 11.00–14.00

Ethnographic Museum Studentski Trg 13; tel: 3281 888; www.etnomusej.co.yu
This well-maintained museum has a fascinating range of ethnographic artefacts from all over Serbia, Kosovo and Vojvodina with the emphasis on regional dress and village economy. The ground floor is given over mostly to costumes, the first floor to textiles, and the second floor to agriculture and traditional economy. Of particular interest are the bridal costumes formerly worn by the women in parts of Serbia like Šumadija, with their elaborate caps incorporating coins, dried flowers and peacock feathers. There is a detailed exhibit on kilim manufacture that shows all aspects of the weaving and dyeing of the cloth, as well as demonstrating the important role the monasteries had in promulgating these skills. Old photographs show the unusual sight of village men spinning, and it is interesting to note how the distaff is of great spiritual importance to

Serbs, associated as it is with many folk beliefs and customs. Elsewhere on the second floor, scattered amongst the displays, are strange gravestones with ghoulish, cartoon-like faces, like those of Bogomil tombs in Bosnia. The museum has a shop selling a range of books, craftwork and postcards, and a special exhibition area. Occasionally, musical and other cultural events are put on in the museum's large lecture hall.
Open Tue, Wed and Fri 10.00–17.00, Thu 10.00–19.00, Sat 09.00–17.00, Sun 09.00–13.00; closed on Mon. Entrance is 60din, students 30din

Fresco Gallery Cara Uroša 20; tel: 621491
This is actually a branch of the National Museum that is filled with quality replicas of some of Serbia's most important religious art. It is a good idea to familiarise yourself with the contents of this gallery first, before venturing into the Serbian backcountry to see the real thing. Although the spiritual atmosphere of a city museum cannot compare to that of a half-hidden monastery in a remote valley, at least the copies on show here can be viewed with greater ease than many of the originals, being far more conveniently positioned and better lit. Admission is free but a voluntary donation can be made as you see fit.
Open Mon, Tue, Wed, Fri and Sat 10.00–17.00, Thu 12.00–20.00, Sun 10.00–14.00

Ivo Andrić Museum Andrićev venac 8; tel: 3238 397
Located at the home of the diplomat, writer and Nobel Prize winner, born in 1892, four rooms of his former home have been converted into a museum to show the life and work of the writer.
Open Tue, Thu and Fri 11.00–17.00, Sat and Sun 08.00–14.00; closed Mon and Wed

Jewish History Museum Kralja Petra I 71a; tel: 622 634; fax: 626 674; www.jim-bg.org
As much a research centre as anything else, this museum has a fascinating display that charts the history of the Jewish community in the former Yugoslavia from first arrivals until the present day. Much of the focus is on the persecution and privations suffered by the Jewish community during World War II, and their participation in the National Liberation War. One particularly chilling panel indicates how the Jewish population was decimated (quite literally – it was reduced to a tenth of its former number) during the Holocaust.
Open Mon–Fri 08.00–15.00. Admission is free

Jovan Cvijić Museum Jelene Četković 5; tel: 3223 126
A museum set up in the former home of the internationally renowned geographer, scientist and academic, Jovan Cvijić (1865–1927).
Open Mon, Tue, Thu and Fri 09.00–18.00; closed Wed, Sat and Sun

Manak's House Gavrila Principa 5; tel: 633 335
A collection of objects, costumes and jewellery relating to the peoples of southern Serbia that was accumulated by the painter Hristofor Crinilović.
Open Tue–Sun 10.00–17.00; closed Mon. Entrance is free

Military Museum Kalemegdan Fortresss; tel: 3343 441
Here you'll find a huge collection of military hardware and associated paraphernalia from all periods of Serbian history, including an enormous range of weaponry, paintings, engravings, uniforms and flags, as well as items of specific interest like a Turkish suit of armour that dates back to the 1389 Serbian defeat at the Battle of

Kosovo. Virtually all of the labelling is in Cyrillic but the significance of much of what is on display is self-evident enough. The collection is as much a history of Serbia itself as it is a mere display of military effects: a turbulent and violent history that can be charted as a relentless succession of invasions and conflicts. Perhaps the most moving of all of the rooms is the very last one, which deals with Serbia's post-1990 conflicts and inspires the visitor to reflect on the depressingly cyclical, and seemingly unavoidable, nature of human conflict in the Balkans.
Open Tue–Sun 10.00–17.00; closed Mon

Museum of African Art Andre Nikolića 14; tel: 651 654
This museum, located in the suburb of Senjak, features the private collection of Yugoslav diplomats, Veda and Dr Zdravko Pečar. Most of the exhibits are from West Africa, with particular emphasis on masks and magical objects.
Open 10.00–18.00, Sun 10.00–14.00

Museum of Automobiles Majke Jevrosime 30; tel: 3342 625
This houses the collection of Bratislav Petković and includes about 50 historically important automobiles together with motor accessories and archives relating to the development of motor sport. The building, designed by Russian architect Valeriy Stashevsky, was constructed as the first public garage in the city centre.
Open daily 10.00–12.00 and 18.00–21.00 except Mon and holidays

Museum of the City of Belgrade Zmaj Jovina 1; tel: 638 744
The headquarters of a collection of over 130,000 artefacts. It is divided into three departments: art, archaeology and history. There is no permanent exhibition due to lack of space and exhibitions are staged elsewhere. Enquiries may be made about the whereabouts of exhibitions during normal office hours.

Museum of Contemporary Art Tel: 3115 713
This is on Ušće in New Belgrade in a parkland setting by the banks of the Danube. The museum, established in 1958, houses a large collection of Yugoslav painting and sculpture of the 20th century. The permanent exhibition is divided into three periods: 1900–18, which includes the impressionistic work of Nadežda Petrović and Richard Jakopič; 1918–41, with a wider range of styles – constructivism, expressionism, surrealism and critical realism – and featuring artists such as Petar Dobrović, Milan Konjović and Marin Tartalja, to name just a few; and 1945–present day, the era with the widest variety of styles – neo-surrealism, action painting etc – and the largest number of artists. Of special interest is the Serb and Croatian art of the 1920s and 1930s, which was clearly influenced by the Paris School, but overall it is an impressive collection and you will have to take time to pursue your own tastes and inclinations. My own recommendation is to seek out *The Frenzied Marble* by Serbia's leading surrealist Marko Ristić, and look for the scandalous but playful portrayal of lascivious monks and nuns in *Bacchanal* by Vilim Svečnjak. Modern art is bound to reflect a parallel history, and Frano Šimunović's *Column of Partisans* captures the defiant spirit of armed resistance against the Nazis perfectly. With a brooding sky, dark wintry light, and soldiers with tough, worn faces marching wearily across a snowfield, the painting just radiates cold, and engenders a mood of grim resignation. Another timely work features a wall covered in a play of symbols that surround a portrait of a pink-faced Tito. Above the portrait is a kitschy floral heart crowned by communist banners. This 1969 piece is entitled, *Comrade Tito – The White Violet – The Whole World Loves You*. It reflects a time when it was considered necessary that all art be political, although there is undoubtedly a degree of irony in its message.

As well as a permanent exhibition there is a gallery that stages the work of foreign artists in addition to occasionally putting on retrospective exhibitions of acknowledged Serbian artists. There is also a separate collection of sculptures that begins in 1900 and extends to the 1970s.

The best way to reach the museum is take a number 15, 84, 704E or 706 bus from the Pijaca venac terminus by McDonald's in the city centre. Once the bus has crossed the bridge over the Sava River, and has turned right onto Bulevar Nikole Tesle, get off at the next stop. You can walk through the park along a concreted path to reach the museum from here. The entrance facing the park, away from the river, is actually the main entrance; not the one at the side that confusingly says, 'Official entrance'. The museum is unusual in being open on Mondays. After a visit here you may be tempted to have a meal or a drink with a companion at one of the nearby river restaurants.
Open daily 10.00–17.00, except Thu 12.00–20.00 and Sun 10.00–14.00; closed Tue. Admission 80din. Tel: 3115 713

Museum of FC Crvena Zvezda Next to the home ground stadium at Ljutice Bogdana 1A; tel: 3224 412; www.fc-redstar.net/musej/musej.html
This is where you can see Red Star Belgrade's impressive collection of trophies. As well as the silverware, there are photographs and newspaper cuttings relating to the club's illustrious history.
Open Mon–Sat 10.00–14.00; closed Sun

Museum of Illegal Printing Houses Banjički venac (by the FC Red Star Museum); tel: 661 513
This is dedicated to the illegal printing by the Central Committee of the Communist Party under the German occupation during World War II.

Museum of Natural History Mali Kalemegdan 5; tel: 328 4317
Located in a former Turkish guardhouse at the fortress, on the way to the Upper Town, the museum presents its exhibits thematically and, as well as interesting displays of Serbian fauna, there is also a large collection of mineral samples and fossils on show.
Open winter Tue–Sun 10.00–17.00, closed Mon; summer daily 10.00–21.00

Museum of Science and Technology Đure Jakšićka 9; tel: 187 360
This has a collection showing Serbia's scientific and technological heritage. Occasionally exhibitions are staged at the gallery of the Serbian Academy of Arts and Sciences at Kneza Mihaila 35.
Open Mon–Fri 09.00–15.00; closed Sat and Sun

Museum of the Serbian Orthodox Church Kralja Petra Prvog 5 (next door to the Orthodox Cathedral); tel: 635 699; www.spc.yu
This collection illustrates the development of the Serbian Orthodox Church, with manuscripts, icons and a variety of religious objects.
Open Mon–Fri 08.00–14.00, Sat 08.00–12.00, Sun 11.00–13.00. Entrance is free

Museum of Vuk and Dositej Gospodar Jevremova 21; tel: 625 161
This museum is dedicated to the work of these two great scholars and national heroes. Vuk Stefanović Karadžić (1787–1864) was a self-taught linguist who devised the first Serbian dictionary and single-handedly reformed the Serbian language. Dositej Obradović (1742–1811) was a great writer, philosopher and educator. The museum is housed in the Turkish residence in which Obradović founded the first Serb high school in 1808; Vuk Karadić was one of the first pupils

NIKOLA TESLA

Nikola Tesla was born during a lightning storm at the stroke of midnight on July 10 1856. His midwife is reported to have exclaimed, 'He'll be a child of the storm', to which his mother replied, 'No, of light'. His parents were both Serb, although he was born in present-day Croatia, where he spent his early life. Tesla was educated in Karlovac, in Croatia, before going on to study electrical engineering in Graz, Austria.

In 1881, he moved to Budapest to work as chief electrician for the American Telephone Company. During his time with the company, Tesla invented a device known as the telephone repeater, a precursor to the modern wireless telephone, although he did not patent his invention until many years later.

In 1882, he moved to Paris to work as an engineer for the Continental Edison Company, where he began to develop devices that utilised rotating magnetic fields: the prototype of the induction motor. Two years later, he moved to the United States to work for the Edison Company in New York. He arrived in the country with four cents in his pocket (he had been robbed aboard ship), a book of poetry and a letter of recommendation. While working for his new employer, Edison offered Tesla US$50,000 if he could improve upon his design for DC dynamos. Tesla worked for nearly a year on this and made considerable improvements, but when he approached his boss for the money he was told, 'Tesla, you don't understand American humor.' This blow caused Tesla to resign, and to form his own company, Tesla Electric Light and Manufacturing, but this came to naught as his investors pulled out over his plan for an alternating current motor. Subsequent unemployment drove the scientist to work as a labourer for a while, in order to finance his next project.

In April 1887, Tesla began investigating what would later be called X-rays, experimenting with high voltages and vacuum tubes. He became a US citizen in 1889, and two years later established his own laboratory in Houston Street, New York, where he lit up vacuum tubes as evidence for the potential of wireless power transmission. He went on to demonstrate the first neon light tubes at the prestigious World Columbian Exposition of 1893 and, more importantly, illuminated the Exposition with electricity that used his alternating current, removing any doubt about its usefulness.

During this period, direct current was still the standard, and Edison, who was unwilling to lose patent royalties on DC current to a former employee, misused Tesla's ideas to construct the first electric chair for the state of New York in order to promote the idea that alternating currents were deadly.

Soon, Tesla was in partnership with George Westinghouse to commercialise a system of transmitting power over long distances. Together they won a contract (over Edison and General Electric) to harness the potential of Niagara Falls and generate hydro-electricity. Eventually, Edison's General Electric Company reluctantly adopted Tesla's AC system.

Tesla went on to invent numerous gadgets and devices, many of which were

here. The part of the museum dedicated to Dositej Obradović is on the ground floor, while the first floor deals with the life and work of Vuk Karadžić. Unfortunately, nearly all of the captions are in Serbian but there is a guidebook in Serbian and English available.

Open Tue–Sat 10.00–17.00, Thu 12.00–20.00, Sun 10.00–14.00; closed Mon way ahead of their time. Some, such as radio remote-control systems and electric igniters for petrol engines, are widely used today; while others, such as the 'electric laxative' demonstrated an eccentricity that was unlikely to win converts.

In 1899, Tesla moved his research to Colorado Springs where he devoted himself to experiments with high voltage and electrical transmission over distances. Here, he constructed electrical devices of Dr Frankenstein proportions, most notably his Magnifying Transmitter, a 52ft-diameter electrical coil that was capable of generating millions of volts and sending lightning arcs 130ft long. Witnesses claimed that they saw a blue glow like St Elmo's Fire emanating from the environs of the laboratory, with sparks emitting from the ground as they walked. On one occasion, a backfeeding power surge blacked out the whole of Colorado Springs.

During his time at Colorado, Tesla recorded cosmic waves emitted by interstellar clouds and red giant stars, which prompted him to announce that he was receiving extraterrestrial radio signals. But the scientific community did not share his enthusiasm and rejected Tesla's data; research into cosmic signals – radio astronomy, as it is known today – did not yet exist. Undaunted, Tesla would spend the latter part of his life trying to send signals to Mars.

In the early years of the 20th century, Tesla fell down on his luck. In 1904, the US Patents Office awarded the patent for radio to Marconi, even though this innovation was clearly based on Tesla's earlier demonstrations, and in May 1905, some of Tesla's patents expired, halting his royalty payments. In 1907, in financial crisis, he freed Westinghouse from payment on his induction motor patent for a nominal sum. Lack of funds meant that his biggest project so far, the Wardenclyffe Tower facility on Long Island, begun in 1900, had to be abandoned.

By 1916, he was living in poverty; and it was around this time that Tesla started to exhibit symptoms of obsessive-compulsive disorder: he became obsessed with the number three – *very* Serbian – and felt compelled to walk around a block three times whenever he needed to enter a building. His genius was still undiminished though, and in 1917, he set out the principles of modern military radar in the *Electrical Experimenter* journal. He even developed the concept of something he called the 'death ray', an idea he tried to get Neville Chamberlain, the British prime minister of the time, interested in. But Tesla was a gentle, altruistic soul who hated war, and even his proposed death ray, or *teleforce*, was primarily a defensive weapon, a particle beam that would supposedly protect a nation from invasion by air or sea.

By the time of his death in 1943, Tesla had more than 700 patents to his name. But that did not stop him dying half-forgotten and in debt. Despite his scientific genius, he was a naïve businessman who was frequently used and abandoned by contemporaries whose names are far better known than his today.

For a full biography read: *The Man Who Invented the Twentieth Century: Nikola Tesla, Forgotten Genius of Electricity* by Robert Lomas (Headline).

National Museum Trg Republike 1a; tel: 624 322
Founded in 1844, the National Museum possesses a priceless collection of artefacts from all periods of Serbian history – prehistoric (including findings from Lepenski Vir), Roman, Graeco-Illyrian, medieval and Ottoman – as well as an impressively wide range of classical and modern art, both Serbian and foreign, including a few

Rubens and Tintorettos, a number of 19th-century French masters – Renoir, Manet – some works by Picasso, and English artists like Sickert and Nash. The museum's greatest treasure is Miroslav's Gospel, which dating from around 1190, is the earliest example of a Cyrillic manuscript in existence. The National Museum is without doubt one of the best collections in Europe, having over 200,000 exhibits in total, but the tragedy for the visitor is that the museum is currently closed for an indefinite period while structural repairs are under way. (This is not for the first time: J A Cuddon in his 1968 *Companion Guide to Jugoslavia* remarks that during his research the museum was closed for a whole 18 months while roof repairs were carried out.) Some items from the collection may be farmed out to other museums in the city in the meantime but nothing seems very certain.

The museum is currently closed, but it is normally open Tue, Wed, Fri and Sat 10.00–17.00, Thu 12.00–20.00, Sun 10.00–14.00; closed Mon

Nikola Tesla Museum Krunska 51 (close to where Beogradska intersects it); tel: 433 886; www.tesla_museum.org
Nikola Tesla was a great Serbian physicist and inventor who almost, but not quite, became an international household name. Many say that if it were not for occasional stubbornness and a poor sense of financial management, Tesla might have ended up as famous as Edison or Einstein. Despite a lack of international recognition, he remains a Serbian national hero, and it is his face that currently decorates the 100 dinar note. You may note that Tesla bears an uncanny resemblance to the young Frank Zappa, another famous eccentric. The museum has captions in English, and a guidebook is available in Serbian and English. Some of the rooms relate to Tesla's scientific work, and have a number of hands-on displays and working models that may appeal to children. Two rooms are dedicated to the personal life of the scientist. The urn containing his ashes is housed here too. (See box, *Nikola Tesla*.)
Open Tue–Fri 10.00–12.00 and 16.00–18.00, Sat and Sun 10.00–13.00; closed Mon

Pedagogy Museum Uzun Mirkova 14 (close to Kalemegdan Park); tel: 627 538
This small museum was established in 1896 by the Association of Teachers in Serbia with a view to preserving the various school books, teaching aids and other artefacts used in elementary education over the centuries. The museum documents the Serbian history of education from the 9th century until the beginning of the 20th. There is also a reconstruction of a typical 19th-century classroom as part of its permanent exhibition. Although there are no captions or illustrative material in languages other than Serbian, it is easy enough to make sense of most of what is on view.
Open Tue–Fri 10.00–17.00, Sat and Sun 10.00–15.00; closed Mon

Prince Miloš Mansion (*Konak kneza Miloša*) Rackovički put 2 in Topčider; tel: 660 422
This houses the exhibition of the Historical Museum of Serbia. The permanent display is entitled 'Serbian Revolution 1804' and is dedicated to the 1804 uprising. The display includes documents, arms, flags and personal possessions of Prince Miloš and Karađorđe that relate to the insurrection against Turkish rule. In front of the museum grows one of the oldest and most beautiful plane trees in Europe.
Open Tue–Sun 10.00–17.00; closed Mon

Princess Ljubica's Konak (*Konak Kneginje Ljubice*) Sime Markovića 3; tel: 638 264
An early 19th-century mansion demonstrating the architecture, furniture and interior design of that period. This luxurious dwelling – or *konak* – was an inspiration of Prince Miloš Obrenović, who had the mansion designed by architect Nikola

Živković. The prince's wife and two sons moved into this Turkish-style residence in 1831, just after its completion, and lived here for the next ten years. After restoration in 1970, it was turned into a museum. The *konak* gives a good insight into the luxurious living conditions that the upper classes of the period enjoyed. There are several beautifully reconstructed rooms, all in the so-called Serbian-Turkish style that blends Ottoman spaciousness with a more formal, Western rigidity. The rooms are filled with exquisitely carved furniture collected from a number of Belgrade houses. There is also a Turkish-style *hammam* with a raised marble slab and a ceiling punctuated with cut-out stars.
Open Tue–Fri 10.00–17.00, Sat and Sun 10.00–16.00; closed Mon

PTT Museum, Majke Jevrosime 13; tel: 3210 325.
Open Mon–Fri 09.00–15.00. Free entry

Railway Museum Close to the station at Nemanjina; tel: 3610 334
This has a permanent exhibition that traces the history of Serbian railways since 1849.
Open Mon–Fri 08.00–14.00, Sat and Sun scheduled group visits only. Admission is free

Theatre Art Museum Gospodar Jevremova 19; tel: 626 630;
www.theatremuseum.org.yu
Open Mon–Fri 09.00–21.00, Sat 09.00–14.00; closed Sun. Admission is free

Tome Rosandić Memorial Museum Vasilija Gačeše 3; tel: 651 434
A museum dedicated to the work of one of Yugoslavia's greatest sculptors, Tome Rosandić (1878–1958).
Open Tue, Thu and Fri 11.00–17.00, Sat and Sun 08.00–14.00; closed Mon and Wed

Yugoslav Aeronautic Museum Belgrade Surcin Airport; tel: 601 555, ext 3582
Housed in a modernist purpose-built structure that looks like an enormous glass tyre, this collection of nearly 50 exhibits includes World War II aircraft like Spitfire, Hurricane and Messerschmidt, together with Russian MiG fighters, helicopters and gliders. There also parts of the downed American stealth fighter that Serbians are so fond of displaying.
Open summer Tue–Sun 09.00–19.00, winter 09.00–15.00; closed Mon. Entry is 300din

Yugoslav Cinematic Museum Kosovska 11; tel: 324 3250.
Open daily 15.00–23.00. Admission is free

Yugoslav History Museum Trg Nikole Pašića 11; tel: 3340 731)
A permanent display with thousands of exhibits that illustrate the history of Yugoslavia from 1918 to the present day.
Open Tue–Sun 10.00–17.00; closed Mon. Entry is free

Zemun Museum Glavna 9 (on the main street), Zemun; tel: 617 752
This display illustrates the development of Zemun, once a completely separate town from Belgrade, from prehistory through to the present day.
Open Tue–Fri 09.00–16.00, Sat and Sun 08.00–15.00; closed Mon

ART GALLERIES

Art Pavilion 'Cvijeta Zuzorić' Mali Kalemegdan 1; tel/fax: 621 585/622 281; email:
ulus@tehnicom.net; www.ulus.org.yu. *Open Tue–Sat 10.00–20.00, Sun 10.00–14.00; closed Mon*
Belgrade Culture Centre Kneza Mihaila 6; tel: 622 926. *Open daily 09.00–20.00*

Đura Jakšić House Skadarska 34; tel: 324 734. *Open daily 08.00–15.00 and 19.00–23.00*
Gallery 'Andrićev venac' Andrićev venac 12; tel: 323 8789. *Open Mon–Fri 10.00–14.00
and 17.00–20.00, Sat 10.00–15.00; closed Sun*
Gallery of Fine Arts Faculty Kneza Mihaila 53; tel: 630 635. *Open Mon–Fri 10.00–20.00,
Sat & Sun 10.00–14.00*
Gallery of the Serbian Academy of Arts and Sciences Kneza Mihaila 35; tel: 334 2400
ext 242. *Open Tue, Wed & Fri 10.00–20.00, Mon & Thu 10.00–18.00; closed Sat & Sun*
Gallery of Students' Culture Centre Kralja Milana 48; tel: 688 468. *Open Mon–Fri
11.00–19.00, Sat 11.00–15.00; closed Sun*
Gallery of the SULUJ Terazije 26/II; tel: 685 780. *Open Mon–Fri 10.00–17.00, Sat
10.00–14.00; closed Sun*
Gallery of the ULUS Kneza Mihaila 37; tel: 621 954. *Open Mon–Fri 10.00–20.00, Sat
09.00–16.00; closed Sun*
Graphic Art Gallery Obilićev venac 27; tel: 627 785. *Open Mon–Sat 10.00–14.00 and
18.00–21.00; closed Sun*
Ilija M Kolarac Foundation Studentski Trg 5; tel: 185 794. *Open daily 10.00–20.00; closed
Mon*
Petar Dobrović Gallery Kralja Petra 36; tel: 622 173. *Open Fri, Sat & Sun 10.00–17.00*
Youth Hall Gallery Makedonska 22; tel: 322 5453. *Open daily 11.00–20.00; closed Mon*

OTHER PLACES OF INTEREST

The **Belgrade Fair** complex (Beogradski Sajam, Bulevar vojvoe Misica 14; tel: 655
555) is a trade and convention centre that puts on a variety of trade shows throughout
the year. The months of February, March and October see a number of fashion
events, April is car show month and May the time of a technology fair. In October
the Belgrade Book Fair takes over (and rooms in Belgrade's cheaper hotels become
hard to find). A furniture fair follows this in November and the year ends with the,
by now traditional, New Year's Fair. For more information about events here look
at the website at www.begfair.com/indexe1.htm.

Belgrade Zoo, near the fortress at Mali Kalemegdan 8 (tel/fax: 624 526), has a
café and giftshop as well as 200 different species of fauna to look at. The zoo is open
every day from sunrise to sunset. Entrance is 100din for children, 200din for adults.

Jevremovac Botanical Garden (Botanička bašta); tel: 768 857, 767 988. The
garden is actually a unit of the University of Belgrade's Biology faculty, and was
formerly an estate owned by Prince Milan Obrenović. It was donated to the
university in 1889 on the condition that it was named after the prince's grandfather,
Jeverem, from whom he had inherited the estate. The gardens cover 5ha and house
about 250 species of tree and shrub, both native and exotic. There is also a
greenhouse, constructed in 1892, and the offices of the Institiute of Botany. It is open
between May 1 and November 1 from 09.00–19.00.

NEARBY CITY ESCAPES

Mount Avala, some 18km south of Belgrade is a popular summer day trip for many
of Belgrade's citizens. The 511m peak stands out dramatically from the flat,
agricultural terrain of the Danube and Sava valleys, and Avala serves as a natural plinth
for the **Unknown Soldier Monument** that has pride of place on top of it.

The monument, another striking work by the sculptor Ivan Meštrović, was
constructed in 1938 as a tribute to Serbian soldiers killed in World War I. Nearby is
another monument dedicated to Soviet war veterans who died in an air crash in 1964
while on their way to Belgrade to celebrate the 20th anniversary of the liberation of the
capital. At the foot of the mountain, in the village of Jajinci, is a **Memorial Garden**
that pays tribute to the 80,000 Yugoslavs executed by the Nazis during World War II.

The mountain itself is covered in a mixture of coniferous and deciduous forest, and has been under state protection since 1859. The town of Žrnov dominated the mountain top in the medieval period, serving an important role in controlling the access roads to Belgrade. Later, in the 15th century, the town was seized by the Turks who built a fortress on the summit. The most recent reminders of war are the severely damaged buildings and rubble that remain from when the 195m tower of the RTS state television network was targeted in the 1999 NATO bombing raids. Some of the black marble blocks of the Meštrović monument were also slightly damaged – chipped by flying shrapnel.

There are a few restaurants and hotels at the mountain for those who wish to stay over, although the vast majority just come here for the day, having lunch and a stroll in the woods before returning to the capital.

To reach Mt Avala from Belgrade without your own transport the best bet is to take a bus bound for Mladenovac from the main bus station. This will drop you off at the junction by the main road from where you can walk up to the summit. It is a stiff climb but you may be able to find a taxi here that could take you up, from where you could return back down from the monument on foot.

Other excursions that could be done as a day trip would be to visit **Pančevo**, **Smederevo**, or even **Novi Sad**. These will be treated separately and dealt with in subsequent chapters.

Black stork

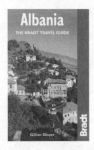

Along the Danube

Serbia's share of the Danube's 3,000km odyssey from source to sea is a mere 588km. Nevertheless, the stretch of the river that passes through Serbia is one of its most dramatic sections, transforming in a few short miles from a wide, muddy channel to the narrow defile that squeezes through the Iron Gates, where the spectacle of towering limestone cliffs on either side takes the focus off the river for once. The Đerdap Dam, the river's swansong within Serbia's boundaries, might seem prosaic, even unsightly, but it cannot be denied that the project remains nothing less than an engineering miracle and that Serbia – and Romania – would be all the poorer without it.

After leaving Serbian soil the Danube continues eastwards, circumscribing the border between Romania and Bulgaria, but even within Serbia the river is an immense physical barrier that forms a natural border between Serbia proper and the autonomous province of Vojvodina. In broader historical terms, the river has always provided the boundary between the influence of Austria, Hungary and central Europe to the north and west and that of the Near East, Byzantium and the Ottoman Empire to the south and east.

Unless you are taking part in a river cruise, travelling east along the Danube from Belgrade may not turn out to be as immediately romantic as you might have imagined. There is no public river transport to link the key towns or sites along the river these days, and so the journey must be done by road. A self-driven hire car is the simplest option but if you do not have your own transport all of the main sights can still be visited using a combination of public buses and a little ingenuity.

For those wishing to take part in a guided cruise, Putnik organise several options ranging from two-day trips to full-week excursions. See the *General Information* chapter for contact details.

SMEDEREVO СМЕДЕРЕВО
Telephone code: 026

Leaving Belgrade, the first town of significance reached by heading east along the Danube is Smederevo, a port and industrial town of about 40,000 inhabitants that is of interest to visitors because of its outstanding **fortress**. The fortress is remarkable for the sheer scale of its defences and for its state of preservation, which is impressive considering that, like many similar sites in cash-short Serbia, Smederevo Fortress has languished in cheerful neglect for centuries.

Paradoxically, this neglect is actually part of the fortress's charm. When I visited, a funfair had been set up within its grounds, boys were fishing in the moat, and young couples were taking advantage of the fortress's many hidden nooks and crannies for their afternoon trysts. It was encouraging to see that local people were making the most of the ready-built theme-park on their doorstep.

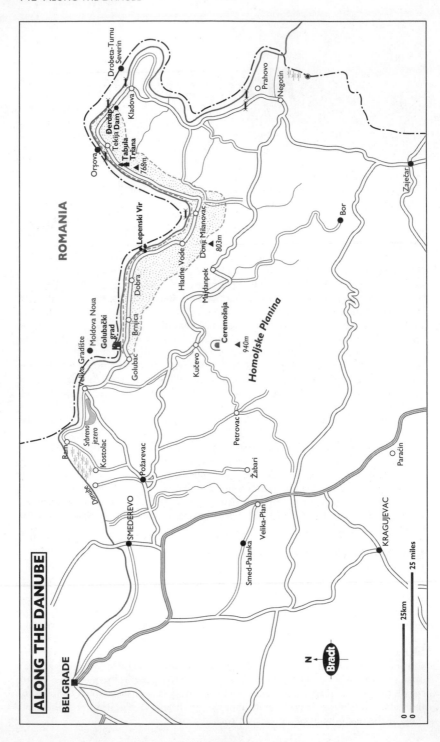

History

Smederevo began life as a Roman settlement on the route from Singidunum to Viminacium. In 1427, it became the new Serbian capital, when the Serbs were ousted from Belgrade by the Hungarians. The castle is triangular in shape, with five gates, 25 large towers, double ramparts and a moat. At one end of the complex is a smaller stronghold that consists of a palace and a citadel, which has its own moat and four bastions. On one of the bastions is the date of the building, 6938, the number of years reckoned by the Orthodox Church to have elapsed since the world was first created, which corresponds to the date 1430 in the Roman calendar. Considering that the castle was erected very quickly, within a year from 1429–30, its dimensions are hugely impressive: the walls of the keep at the north of the inner fortress are about 15ft thick, and the total distance around the perimeter is not far short of a mile.

The castle's construction was by order of Đurađ Branković, son of Vuk, who was despot at the time. The notion was to provide an impenetrable barrier to the Turkish advance that was taking place during this period. One legend states that the impoverished peasants who built the castle were obliged to provide thousands of eggs to mix with the mortar in order to firmly secure the stones, while another asserts that it was Branković's tyrannical wife, Jerina, who gave the order for the castle's construction. Either way, it is undeniable that a great deal of forced labour had to be recruited to build such an extensive and imposing structure in such a short time.

The Turks eventually arrived to subdue the fortress but it took them more than 20 years to do so. Smederevo Fortress was finally surrendered in 1459 to Sultan Mehmet I, which marked the final victory of the Ottoman Turks over Serbian territory. Immediately, the Turks made the castle the headquarters of their *pašalik* in the region and it remained in Turkish occupation, with the exception of a brief period of Austrian control, until 1805 when Karađorđe formally received its keys following his initial successes with the First National Uprising. Having survived the medieval period more or less intact, the fortress suffered considerable damage in far more recent times when an ammunition dump blew up part of it in 1941, and then later in 1944 when it was bombed by Allied forces.

Also in Smederevo is an early 15th-century monastic church that dates from around the same time as the fortress. The church is built in the style of the Morava School, in brick and stone with three apses and a central dome, and contains some 17th-century frescos that illustrate the life of Christ and the Psalms. The town's other main church, the Church of St George, is located in the central square and dates from 1854. This church, designed by the Czech architect, Jan Nevola, is built in the Romantic style and blends Serbian medieval heritage with baroque influences. The interior and the iconostasis were painted by the Russian artist, Andrea Vasilevich Bicenko.

Getting there

To reach Smederevo from Belgrade there are several buses a day from the Lasta bus station, most of which continue on to Bela Crkva. The fare is 170din. The bus station in Smederevo is close to the castle, as is the railway station, although there are no train services to Belgrade, just occasional ones to Niš and Kragujevac. There is also a frequent bus service to Vršac, via the towns of Kovin and Bela Crkva north of the Danube.

Where to stay and eat

Smederevo's close proximity to Belgrade makes it highly suitable for a day trip but should you wish to stay there is the perfectly adequate **Hotel Smederevo** in the central square at Izletnicka bb (tel: 222 511, 221 432), which has doubles for 1,400din and singles for 800din. For eating, there are a number of restaurants, cafés and bakeries situated around this same square.

THE DANUBE RIVER

After the Volga, the Danube is the second-longest river in Europe and the only major one to flow from west to east. It flows for a total of 2,850km from a source in the Black Forest Mountains in Germany to the delta on the Black Sea coast of Romania, passing through Germany, Austria, Slovakia, Hungary, Croatia, Serbia, Bulgaria and Romania along the way, and draining a basin of more than 817,000 km². The river is navigable by ocean-going vessels as far as Braila, Romania, and by river craft up to Ulm in Germany. In addition, about 60 of its 300 tributaries are also navigable, principally the Morava, Drava, Tisza, Sava and Prut, three of which flow through Serbia. Four national capitals lie along the river's route: Vienna, Bratislava, Budapest and Belgrade.

The river has always served as a crucial route between western Europe and the Black Sea. In the 3rd century AD it formed the northern boundary of the Roman Empire, and the fortresses that they built along its banks served as the main line of defence against invasion by Goths, Huns and Slavs from the north and east. Some of the Roman settlements subsequently grew to become important cities like Vienna (formerly the Roman settlement of Vindobona), Budapest (Aquincum) and Belgrade (Singidunum). One millennium later, instead of constituting a defensive line, the river actually facilitated invasion, most notably that of the Ottoman Empire's advance into central Europe.

By the 18th century, the Danube had become an important commercial link between the nations of central and eastern Europe; by the 19th century, the river linked the industrial world of the west (especially Germany) with the agricultural areas of the Balkan Peninsula, enabling a two-way flow of consumer goods and raw materials. Both the Treaty of Paris of 1856 and the Treaty of Versailles of 1919 promoted free navigation along the entire length of the river and established a European Commission responsible for supervising the river as an international waterway. A Danubian Convention was signed after World War II, which allowed just the countries that lay along the Danube itself to participate in the supervision of the river.

GOLUBAC ГОЛУБАЦ

Telephone code: 012

From Smederevo as far as Ram, where there is a campsite and a ruined 16th-century castle, the river continues to divide Vojvodina from the rest of Serbia. The Danube is wide up to this point, with low islands surfacing here and there midstream. Unfortunately there is no road following the river on this stretch and so the only way to trace the route between these two points is by boat. The road from Belgrade goes via Požarevac, the home town of Slobodan and Mira Milošević, to rejoin the Danube at Veliko Gradište, a minor resort. From here on the landscape on the opposite bank belongs to that of a different country altogether – Romania. The main road veers away from the Danube once more to join the river again just before the sleepy settlement of Golubac.

Golubac town – a village really – is quite unremarkable but takes its name from the very impressive fortress that lies just a few kilometres east. Sitting midstream in the river here, facing the town, is the large, flat island of Moldova, which belongs to Romania. Golubac makes a good stopover – there is a hotel and adequate facilities – although it can hardly be said that it is a dynamic sort of place: it is the sort of town where the locals think nothing of going shopping on their tractors.

The Danube provides a source for water supplies, irrigation and fishing but its most important role is that of allowing the movement of freight and the provision of hydro-electricity. Several countries have built dams and power plants along the length of the river, the most prominent being the Iron Gates project developed by co-operation between the former Yugoslavia and Romania, located at the end of the narrow defile of the river that forms the border between Serbia and Romania.

In recent decades the Danube's ecosystem has been sorely damaged by the increase in traffic and pollution, and much of its waters have become unfit for irrigation or drinking water as a result of this. Species such as white-tailed eagle, black stork, Dalmatian pelican and sturgeon that used to characterise the river have now become endangered. Raw sewage from the cities, agricultural run-off, industrial waste and the spillage of ship oil have all played their part in the deterioration of what was once an undeniably romantic river.

On January 31 2000, 100,000m³ of waste water contaminated with cyanide and heavy metals spilled over from a mine at Baia Mare, Romania, into the river Lupus. This deadly cargo soon passed downstream through tributaries to reach the river Somes, the Tisza and finally the Danube itself, killing hundreds of tonnes of fish and necessitating the shutting off of water pumps in Belgrade. This was not the only disaster in recent times. A year before, the NATO bombing of Yugoslavia clogged the river by destroying bridges, slowing the river's flow and altering its ecosystem; even more serious was the release of chemical spills into the river from factories bombed during the hostilities. Currently, UNEP, the European Union and the World Wide Fund for Nature (WWF) are all active in attempting to clear the river and restore it to its original state. Following the Romanian cyanide incident, The WWF has recommended a five-step recovery plan that involves the following: a clean-up of the contamination near the mine at Baia Mare; a monitoring programme along the whole length of the river; an improvement in water quality; the conservation of areas unaffected by the spill that can contribute to the re-colonisation of the river; and a river basin management plan.

Golubac Fortress lies 5km east of the town, about a 50-minute walk along the main road from the hotel. It is possible to walk the first part along a riverside walkway, but the path soon peters out and the main road soon becomes the only option. The castle is clearly visible from the town itself but as soon as you start walking it disappears around a headland and only reappears once you are almost upon it. Walking along the road you have to be aware of the steady stream of cars and articulated lorries heading for Romania that rush past at unnerving speed, although, in May, with nightingales singing in the lush vegetation above the road, and croaking frogs flopping into the water below, you can easily be lulled into believing that this part of Serbia is still a rural idyll. The impression is shattered as soon as the next rumbling truck speeds past.

The walk is well worth the effort: Golubac is the perfect fairy-tale castle, wonderfully set off by its location in the rugged landscape at the head of the Đerdap Gorge. There are nine ruined towers in all, each between 20 and 25m high. The castle's crumbling ramparts climb high up the hillside above the main road, which passes through two of the lower gateways. The extensive walls are impressively thick, with an average width of 2.8m. With a towering profile that complements the rugged geology surrounding it, Golubac is undoubtedly one of the most beautiful castles

THE RUSALIJKE OF DUBOKA

One of the most well known of the Vlach settlements in the Homolskje region of Serbia is Duboka, where in the past, local women used go into painful trances during the Whit Sunday festivities. The trances were considered to be a form of spirit possession in which prophecy and soothsaying took place. The ritual that surrounds the trances probably derives from syncretism between Slavic pagan practices and older Balkan beliefs and it was believed that, during a trance, the women became possessed by nymph-like beings. The trance was accompanied by sacred music played on bagpipes and violins: a repetitive melody that could only be played at this time of year. The women involved in this practice were known as *rusalijke* but, as Anne Kindersley reflects in her travelogue, *The Mountains of Serbia*, they were dying out even in the late 1960s. Whether or not the practice of falling into trance still occurs is highly debatable: Kindersley expresses disappointment in not having witnessed the spectacle, although she relates that the neighbouring village of Ševice was said to have a *rusalijke* of greater reliability.

along the river's length. If the aspect seen from the road is impressive enough, then the view from the river is even more splendid, especially in the golden light of an early summer's evening.

The fortress was built by the Hungarians on the same site as the Roman Castrum Columbarum, probably sometime in the second half of the 13th century, although this is uncertain as the first written record that relates to it is from 1335. Golubac was captured by the Turks in 1391 and changed ownership several times before being finally reclaimed by the Serbs in 1867. On the Romanian side of the river lie the remains of another castle, Laslovar, although this is in a far more ruinous state.

The fortress marks the beginning of the narrowing of the Danube at the Iron Gates and the western limit of the Đerdap National Park; there is a noticeboard to this effect immediately before it. There is a disused limestone quarry just before the sign and directly opposite is a roadside truckers' restaurant, which looks as if it opens only sporadically. As is the case for most ruined castles in Serbia, there is absolutely nothing in the way of interpretive material and no limits imposed on where you can wander. Although clambering among its ramparts is a tempting proposition, there are absolutely no safety barriers. The rock is quite slippery, and it is an awful long way to fall down, so be cautious and be very careful where you put your feet.

The tourist information centre is at Gorana Tosiča – Macka 1 (tel: 78 145).

Getting there

The small bus station has a smelly waiting room where you are unlikely to want to linger for long but it does provide connections along the Danube in both directions as far as Belgrade or Kladovo, as well as occasional (usually once a day) buses that go inland to places like Kučevo or Krivača. There are nine buses a day that run the 150-odd kilometres between Golubac and Belgrade, and seven heading east towards Kladovo.

Where to stay and eat

Accommodation at Golubac is simple enough: there is the two-star **Golubački Grad Hotel** (tel: 78 207, 78 552) which stands by the river to the east of the bus station and looks like a sort of rustic conference centre. The hotel's reception staff are welcoming but unfortunately the hotel operates a dual pricing tariff in which foreigners pay about 60% more than nationals. This is official, as there is a note on the wall to confirm it (in Serbian). A single room costs €23 with breakfast, €24 half board and €28 full board. Doubles are a few euros more.

Half board is probably the best deal here, as Golubac's other restaurant options are none too enticing. The food at the hotel restaurant is actually quite reasonable, apart from the annoying habit they have of microwaving the bread rolls. Other options for food and drink include **Café Ciao** opposite the hotel, the **Café Klub Kiki** Sports Bar between the hotel and the bus station, and the **Sur-Škarica** restaurant on the main street to the east of the hotel, which is where most local men congregate at night. There are a few supermarkets for provisions; the best-stocked one is next to the Golubački Grad hotel. There is a post office next to the hotel and a branch of the Vojvodina Banka opposite, but without any ATM or exchange facilities.

THE HOMOLSKJE REGION

Running parallel south of the river between Golubac and Donji Milanovac are the hills of the Homolskje range, which extend to the southeast almost as far as the industrial town of Bor. This is one of the most overlooked regions of Serbia, and home to a number of Vlach villages that still retain some of their traditional customs and crafts. Despite their relative proximity to Belgrade, the Homolskje hills are one of the least-known parts of the country, and although it is difficult to explore without your own transport, a leisurely exploration of this region would undoubtedly pay dividends. The obvious centres to use as a base are the small towns of **Kučevo** and **Majdanpek**, both of which have hotels and a reasonable range of facilities.

Kučevo

Every year at the end of May, the regional centre of **Kučevo** hosts a series of events as part of the **'Homolje Motifs'** celebrations, in which local skills such as gold-panning, Vlach cooking, spindle making, sheep milking and wool spinning are demonstrated, along with a variety of sporting competitions for local shepherds to participate in. These events are staged together with performances of folk music and dance from the Vlach community. Specific information on events can be had from the Veljko Dugošević Cultural Centre and the Kučevo Municipal Assembly and Municipal Tourist Organisation (Svetog Save 114; tel: 012 850 666; email: tokucevo@yahoo.com).

Ceremosnja, one of Serbia's most beautiful caves, first discovered in 1952, is situated close to Kučevo, 15km from the town at the foot of the Homolskje hills. This was the second cave in Serbia to open as a show cave for the public. Of Ceremosnja's 775m depth, some 431m are accessible to visitors. An underground river, the Strugarski Potok ('little river') runs through the cave. This leads to the largest underground chamber of the complex, called the Arena, with a 20m-high domed ceiling that is lined with calcite and adorned by numerous stalactites and stalagmites. From the Arena visitors pass through another chamber, called Dveri, to resurface 100m from the cave entrance after passing underground waterfalls and more highly decorated underground chambers. As is often the case with tourist cave complexes, many of the speleological features have been accorded human attributes. Visiting hours are 09.00–18.00 from April 1 to October 31, or by prior appointment in the winter months. More information can be obtained from the Kučevo Tourist Office.

Getting there

Occasional buses run from Belgrade to Kučevo and on to Majdanpek. There is a daily bus from Kučevo to Golubac on the Danube. A single daily train leaves Belgrade in the late afternoon, stopping in Kučevo on its way to Bor.

Where to stay

In Majdanpek there is the three-star **Hotel Kasina** (Svetog Save 10; tel: 030 81 338/83 461) with 37 doubles, 12 singles and eight apartments.

Kučevo has the two-star **Hotel Rudnik** (Svetog save 96; tel: 012 852 265). There is also a motel next to the Ceremosnja cave.

ĐERDAP NATIONAL PARK

The Đerdap National Park is generally better known as the Iron Gates National Park, a reference to the old Roman name, Porta Ferea, which was used to describe the narrowing of the limestone cliffs above the river Danube. The national park's western boundary begins at the fortress at Golubac and stretches as far east as the dam near Sip – a total of about 64,000ha.

Topographically speaking, the park's most noteworthy feature is the Đerdap Gorge itself, which stretches for well over 100km in a boomerang shape from Golubac to Tekija, forming the longest composite valley in Europe. Rather than a single entity, the gorge is actually a compound river valley made up of four separate gorges - Gornja klisura, Gospođin vir, Veliki and Mali kazan and Sipska klisura – each of which is separated from its neighbour by ravines. This spectacular section of the Danube abounds in superlatives: at **Gospođin vir** (*vir* means whirlpool) the waters are up to 82m deep, one of the greatest recorded depths in the world for a river channel (and now even deeper with the dam); at the canyon of Kazan, the cliffs rise up to 600m above the river, which has narrowed at this point to a mere 150m wide. The highest point within the park's boundaries is 768m-high Mt Miroc.

Of the 1,100-plus plant species found in the park, the most significant in scientific terms are those Tertiary relict species such as Turkish hazel (*Corylus columa*), walnut (*Juglans regia*) and yew (*Taxus baccata*): all survivors from before the glacial period. The yew was considered to be a holy tree by Serbs in times past, stemming from its ability to regenerate itself from a stump after felling, and a sprig of yew kept in a wallet was said to prevent money from leaving it. In addition to these ancient relict species, trees like oaks, maples, elms, limes and hornbeams are all present in great numbers and, of herbaceous plants, there is one species endemic to the Đerdap Gorge: the Đerdap tulip (*Tulipa hungarica*).

Of the larger mammals found within the park, jackal (*Canis aureus*), lynx (*Lunx lunx*) and brown bear (*Urus arctos*) are probably the most notable – and also the most elusive. With luck and determination, chamois (*Rupicarpa rupicarpa*) may be seen scrambling around on the higher rock pinnacles. Of the birds found here, raptors such as golden eagle are well represented, while other rarities like black stork also have a refuge here. During winter and on passage migration, the flooded waters of the lower Danube play host to large populations of wildfowl such as smew, pochard and goldeneye.

The park's headquarters are at Kralja Petra 1 br 14a, 19220 Donj Milanovac; tel/fax: 030 86 788, 86 877; email: npdjerdap@npdjerdap.com; www.npdjerdap.com.

Lepenski Vir

From Golubac, the river narrows markedly as it is squeezed between the limestone cliffs of the Iron Gates. The next village, Brnjica, has the Toma restaurant but little else to warrant a halt. The road continues past the minor settlement of Dobra before reaching Donji Milanovac, a small port and another possibility for an overnight stay.

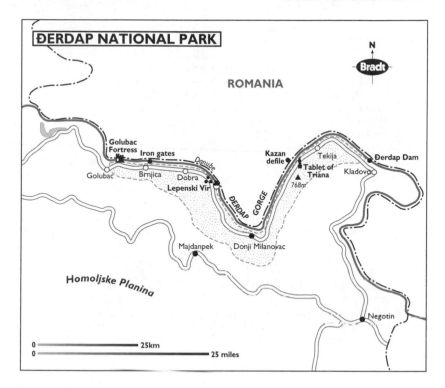

Donji Milanovac possesses nothing of note apart from a smart hotel but the real reason for stopping here is to see the site of Lepenski Vir, which sits in a recess of the riverbank just off the main road 14km northwest of the port.

The early settlement of Lepenski Vir was first uncovered in 1965 during one of the exploratory digs that preceded the building of the Đerdap Dam. The site was excavated in the following year, and in 1967 the distinctive stone sculptures that were to make the site famous were discovered. The stone sculptures, which are mostly stylised, life-size heads, are quite remarkable and appear to show human faces with the lips of fish. The carvings date back as far as about 5350BC and are the oldest Mesolithic sculptures in all of Europe.

Although nothing is certain, the heads probably represent depictions of the primitive gods that the people of Lepenski Vir worshipped. It may also have been that Lepenski Vir served as some sort of religious centre, as fish and deer bones have been found in such numbers that suggest they may have been used for sacrificial purposes. Whatever the true role of the settlement, Lepenski Vir was undoubtedly a well-chosen site: up on a raised shelf just above the Danube's waters, with plentiful fish in the river and game in the forest, although there is nothing to suggest that agricultural practice took place in any form. Altogether, some 85 huts have been discovered here: a large settlement for Mesolithic times.

In 1970, the Lepenski Vir finds were moved to higher ground 35m above the original site to avoid the flooding that took place when the Đerdap Dam was opened. By 1985, a total of 15 superimposed Mesolithic settlements had been discovered at the site, all dating from between 7000 and 4600BC.

The **Lepenski Vir Museum** at Boljetin village near Donji Milanovac (tel: 063 206 271) is under the tutelage of the National Museum in Belgrade; it is open

10.00–17.00 Tuesday–Saturday, 10.00–14.00 Sunday; closed on Mondays. The museum contains some of the tools and utensils that were uncovered during the excavations, as well as the stone heads themselves. Next to the museum is a small open-air exhibit of traditional architecture of the region with typical high-capped chimneys and arched verandas. These few houses were saved and rebuilt here after their original location, Porec Island in the Danube, was submerged when the Iron Gates Dam became operational.

Donji Milanovac

Although it is quite feasible to visit Lepenski Vir from Golubac, or from further along the Danube at Tekija, the closest place to stay to visit the site is at nearby Donji Milanovac, a new town that was completely rebuilt after its namesake disappeared under the lake following the construction of the dam. Other than serving as a base for visiting the museum and as a centre for pleasant walks in the locality, the town has little to offer apart from its comfortable hotel. The headquarters of the Đerdap National Park are in the building opposite the bus station.

Getting there

The bus station offers a reasonably frequent service in either direction to Belgrade or Kladovo, as well as occasional buses inland to Majdanpek and some neighbouring villages. If you do not have your own transport it is also possible to use these buses to reach Lepenski Vir from Donji Milanovac: catch a Belgrade-bound bus and get dropped at the turn-off for the museum; later, flag down a bus heading to Kladovo for the return journey. Be sure to check the times thoroughly first though. There is no left-luggage facility at the bus station.

Where to stay and eat

The large, comfortable, three-star **Hotel Lepenski Vir** (tel: 030 86 211, 86 210/86 122) stands on the hill just above the town. The hotel has over 200 double rooms and 70 single rooms at rates between €15 and €25 per person.

As well as the facilities at the hotel, there are a few restaurants and cafés in the town like the **Bife-Boreč** restaurant and the **Teuta** café-bar.

The Kazan Defile

From Donji Milanovac, the Danube steers north to enter the defile of Kazan, the Serbian word for cauldron. These once-rapid waters are now calmed by the presence of the dam downstream, and the water remains sluggish as the river narrows and cliffs loom high on both sides. After about 15km the river reaches its narrowest point before opening up again a few kilometres further on. If you are travelling on the river itself then you should keep a lookout for the **Tablet of Trajan** that is set into the cliff face above the water. This has been moved from its original location lower down to allow for the raised waters created by the dam.

The tablet was originally erected by the Roman Emperor Trajan in AD102 to commemorate the completion of a road along the defile that had been begun in AD28 and which had previously been abandoned as being impossible. The tablet also acknowledges Trajan's successful campaign against the Dacians. Although the road, which was cut into the bare rock, was undoubtedly an engineering miracle, no-one could accuse Trajan of false modesty. The sign reads: 'The Emperor Caesar, son of the divine Nerva, Nerva Trajan Augustus Germanicus, great pontiff, tribune for the fourth time, father of the country and consul for the fourth time, has conquered the mountain and the river and opened this road.'

Before the construction of the dam, the deep, turbulent waters of the Kazan Defile were host to enormous sturgeon of up to 900kg, whose caviar promoted a lucrative industry in Kladovo further downstream. With their migration route to the Black Sea blocked off for ever by the dam's construction, these monster fish (actually two separate species: White Sturgeon and Stellate Sturgeon) are now merely a memory.

Travelling by car or bus, the road climbs up high above the gorge before dropping down to the river again just before Tekija. The views here are magnificent, with dark, craggy rocks and the Danube's waters looming far below; the silhouettes of birds of prey soaring high overhead. Over on the Romanian side of the river, you may notice the head of a mysterious warrior figure that has been fashioned in the cliff face by the deft use of explosives. Somehow the ingenuity of this enterprise is eclipsed by its own tastelessness: nature at its most elemental, such as here, needs no such embellishment.

Tekija
The attractive sprawling village of **Tekija** is another suitable place to stop for the night. Tekija is even quieter than Golubac, but it is a pleasant enough place that offers some delightful walks in the vicinity, especially west along the river. Food and accommodation are available at the Motel Tekija, which is just up the hill, following the steps that lead up to the church, 100m or so before the bus pull-in area.

Getting there
Occasional buses and minibuses run the final 27km on towards Kladovo. Belgrade-bound buses can be flagged down at the bus pull-in.

Where to stay and eat
The one-star **Motel Tekija**, Avrama Petronijevica 12 (tel: 019 85 116) is a relative bargain, having about a dozen rooms that go for 850din per person with breakfast, 750din without. The motel has its own restaurant beneath, and the food is fine as long as you bear in mind that the majority of the items on the menu will not be available. Grilled meat and salads should present no problems. The multi-tasking man responsible for waiter/chef/concierge duties is most obliging and during my visit, as the restaurant's sole customer, I enjoyed an excellent plate of *ćevapčić* listening to Barry White's Greatest Hits and watching the UEFA cup on television. Other dining possibilities in Tekija include the **Restoran Panorama** just before the town to the west by the bridge and the **Kafana Alas**, which is on the road at the start of the village.

The Đerdap Dam
Just before reaching Kladovo, near the village of Sip, the enormous hydro-electric complex of the Đerdap Dam stretches across the river. The dam was built between 1962 and 1974 as a joint Yugoslav-Romanian venture, with contributions from other Danubian countries and the Soviet Union, at a total cost of around US$500 million. The dam's vital statistics cannot fail to impress, being 448m wide at the bottom and 1,278m at the top and rising 30m above the waters of the Danube, a river which in turn stands 35m higher than it did previously. Đerdap's annual hydro-electric capacity is a staggering 10.5 billion kilowatts. A cheap and dependable supply of energy was only part of its bounty, however: with the aid of two locks, 310m long and 34m high, the calmed waters of the resultant lake meant that ships of up to 5,000 tonnes could navigate between Belgrade and the Black Sea for the first time. The road running across the wall of the dam leads to an official border post, and forms a useful link with the nearby port of Drobeta-Turnu Severin in Romania. Although the construction of the dam undoubtedly caused ecological harm in some quarters – most famously in blocking the migration route of the river's giant sturgeon – it also created new habitat

for other species: the newly formed lakes helped provide a vast wildfowl wintering ground that had not existed before.

Karataš-Diana Roman Fort

A little beyond the dam, at the village of Karataš, lie the ruins of a Roman fortress locally referred to as 'Diana'. This fort was originally built during the reign of Trajan but it was destroyed several times over by the successive raids of Huns, Goths and Avars before being rebuilt and enlarged by Emperor Justinian in the 6th century. There is not that much to see now of what once must have been a vitally important frontier post: just extensive foundations and low, round towers built with alternating layers of stone and flat Roman bricks. Although it is not particularly rewarding in archaeological terms, the site affords good views in both directions and is probably the closest point at which you can point your camera in the direction of the Đerdap Dam without arousing unwanted interest from the police.

KLADOVO КЛАДОВО

Telephone code: 019

The riverside town of Kladovo lies 10km beyond the dam. Along with Negotin, this small town is the most important urban centre in this far-flung corner of the country, but that isn't enough to prevent Kladovo having the slightly stagnant air of a town that has seen better days. The town used to be famous for its caviar factory but, after the construction of the dam, and the subsequent calming of the waters, the famous giant sturgeon of the Iron Gates were no longer to be found and the bottom fell out of the industry. Kladovo gives the impression of being overwhelmed by what is clearly the much larger settlement of Drobeta-Turnu Severin just across the Danube. The town lies in the shadow of the extensive industrial units, cranes, gantries and docks of its Romanian neighbour and seems a little intimidated by the brash enterprise taking place there. But Kladovo is pleasant enough, if somewhat non-descript, and there are one or two things to see if you are passing through or staying here overnight.

The Roman settlement of **Diana** is just a few kilometres to the west, within sight of the Đerdap Dam at Sip, and there is a ruined **Turkish fort** on the outskirts of town in the same direction that has a plaque in Ottoman Turkish above its gateway. The fort itself is rather overgrown with long grass. There is a small **Orthodox church** in the town itself, dedicated to St George. This has a fairly crude copy of the Mileševa White Angel painted onto one of the walls, in which the androgynous features of the original have been rendered entirely feminine by a less-skilled hand. Close by is the **Iron Gates Museum of Archaeology** that has Bronze Age pottery, Roman jewellery and amphora, and copies of the Lepenski Vir heads to look at. Captions are in Serbian and English. The entrance fee is 100din and, although they receive precious few foreign visitors, the museum claims to be open daily from 10.00–22.00.

Opposite the museum is a short strip of fast food kiosks and just beyond here, at the town's western limit, Kladovo ends abruptly at a waste area where wandering brown cows lazily graze. Just to the east of here, running south from 22 Septembra, the town's high street, is Maršala Tita, a street full of open-air cafés, which is pedestrian-only during the summer months. The bus station is to be found further east on a street that runs parallel to the high street, away from the water.

Perhaps it is the close proximity of Romania but for some reason Kladovo seems to have more than its fair share of *menjačnica* exchange offices: along 22 Septembra, the town's main thoroughfare, almost every other doorway seems to be one. Also on this street at number 18 is what the National Tourist of Serbia (NTOS) list as the Kladovo Tourist Office. Unfortunately, this exists entirely for the service of people from Kladovo

THE KLADOVO TRANSPORT

Kladovo achieved notoriety during World War II as being the stumbling block for what came to be known as the Kladovo Transport. In November 1939, following the dire signals given by the Anschluss and Kristallnacht, a group of about 1,200 central European Jews set off from Bratislava by boat in an attempt to reach Palestine via the Danube and the Black Sea. At the Hungarian–Yugoslav border they were transferred midstream from the riverboat *Uranus* to three Yugoslav vessels. The refugee fleet was stopped at the Yugoslav–Romanian border near Kladovo and directed to remain in Serbia.

Aware of their plight, the Federation of Jewish Communities in Yugoslavia undertook relief efforts on behalf of the stranded refugees. They rented an additional barge to alleviate the cramped living conditions on the three boats and, in July of 1940, they opened a school in Kladovo just before the whole group was ordered to transfer to a refugee camp in Šabac in western Serbia.

Sixteen months later, in the spring of 1941, the transport was issued with 207 legal immigration certificates for Palestine, but these were restricted solely to youths between the ages of 15 and 17. The group left on March 15 1941, travelling by train through Greece, Turkey, Syria and Lebanon to reach their goal. When the Germans arrived in Yugoslavia in mid April all outside support of the transport was cut off and the thousand refugees that remained became dependant on the neighbouring Croatian Jewish community in Ruma for food and other supplies.

Soon after, both men and women from the transport were conscripted for forced labour. In July, they were relocated once more, this time to the city's fortress that had been turned into a concentration camp known as the Sava. Later that same summer, as reprisals against Partisan forces who had temporarily taken control of part of the city, the entire population of Šabac, including the Jews of the transport, was rounded up by German troops. The prisoners, who were intended to help build a concentration camp in Jarak, Croatia, were forced to run a 23km death race to the site, after first having been kept for two nights without food or water. Those who could not keep up were shot without mercy. Four days later, after the Germans decided to abandon the site, the prisoners that were still alive were marched back to Šabac.

On October 11 1941 the surviving Jewish males at the Sava camp were transferred to Zasavica, where they were killed along with 160 Roma. Four months later, the Jewish women and children from the transport were taken to the concentration camp in Sajmiste, where they were all killed in gas vans over the next few months. Only one member of the group imprisoned in Sava concentration camp lived to survive the war.

who wish to travel somewhere else, rather than as a provision for curious foreign visitors. Any requests for tourist information will be met with polite bemusement.

Internet access is available at Happy Computers, Prodavicna 2, a small street that runs west off Maršala Tita, in a building opposite Discotheque Café Bar A and next to Club Planet.

The town has an extensive walkway along the river front that makes for an interesting, if not especially scenic, evening stroll. Further along this, to the east of the

Hotel Đerdap there is a small beach where the town's young people bathe in the summer, although given the proximity of the docks at Drobeta-Turnu Severin and the river's less-than-perfect environmental record my advice would be to stay on dry land.

Getting there

The bus station has regular buses along the Danube to Belgrade; otherwise, the majority of services are to destinations in eastern Serbia: Niš via Zaječar, Bor, Leskovac and Negotin.

Where to stay

Hotel Djerdap (Dunavska bb; tel: 81 010, 81 090) is a high-rise hotel next to the Danube with over 130 comfortable rooms with cable TV, some of which afford a view over the river, the distant Đerdap Dam and the docks of Drobeta-Turnu Severin across the river. Singles are 1,700din; doubles, 2,500din.

Where to eat

The Djerdap has a cavernous restaurant typical of most large, three-star hotels. Equally good food at lower prices can be obtained at the pizzeria or grill restaurant facing the square outside. Elsewhere, there is the **Restoran Wili** next door to the museum, and a few booths opposite that offer snacks and fast food. The best bet for a leisurely meal or a pleasant drink is probably along the pedestrian stretch of Ulica Maršala Tita, where there is a choice of several cafés, a couple of patisseries, two national restaurants and yet more pizzerias. The savoury pancakes at the **Élite** pizza and pancake place along here are recommended.

NEGOTIN HEГOTИH

Telephone code: 019
Negotin lies just away from the Danube very close to the borders of both Romania and Bulgaria. It is a somewhat larger town than Kladovo and seems a little livelier, although it is still wholly provincial in character. Unlike Kladovo, the town's economic base has little to do with the Danube. The river, which is only 10km away at this point, already seems distant and of little consequence.

Negotin is the urban centre of an agricultural community, a prosperous market town that reaches its annual climax of activity during its **Autumn Fair** in September. The centre of town, a ten-minute walk from the bus station, is dominated by a large yellow baroque church and an equestrian statue overlooking a shady park with a large World War I monument. Beyond here, a handful of outdoor cafés line two busy shopping streets that lead away from the statue and church. In the opposite direction, there is a shiny new shopping mall just around the corner from a 1970s square replete with the familiar, concrete state-run hotel.

If you are staying overnight here there is little specific to see other than the **Krajina Museum** (open 08.00–18.00 Tuesday to Friday, 09.00–17.00 Saturdays, 10.00–14.00 Sundays and holidays).

Like the Homoljske range further west, Negotin lies at the centre of a region populated by a number of Vlach villages, some of which, like **Slatina**, have their own celebrations at certain times of year. It is also an important wine-producing region with some excellent and distinctive reds, even though these are not as well known as the products of other Serbian viniculture regions like Fruška Gora or Vršac.

Nearby at Prahovo and Radujevac, the Danube finally leaves Serbian territory. It was at Prahovo in the hot, drought-ridden summer of 2003 that the river's waters

GHOSTS FROM THE DEPTHS

In the summer of 2003 one of the worst droughts for many years pushed water levels of the Danube River to record lows. In eastern Serbia, the river fell to a level not seen since records began in 1888, revealing the rusting wrecks of German gunboats dating from World War II. One such ship at Prahovo, close to the Romanian and Serbian borders, had been abandoned in the water since 1944, having first been dynamited by its retreating German crew. Despite the attempts at wilful destruction by its original owners, the newly revealed boat still retained its rotating gun turret and metal holders for shells. Now, 60 years after being abandoned, it stood in just a metre of water. Not wishing to look a gift horse in the mouth, a few resourceful locals took advantage of the ship's surprise reappearance and helped themselves to still-usable electrical cable from the wreck.

The ship was just one of 130 vessels that had been scuppered by the Germans as they retreated from the advancing Soviet Black Sea fleet in 1944. Using dynamite, the Germans sank their ships in rows across the river in a last-ditch attempt to slow down the Russian fleet. Many of the ships were subsequently removed from the water when the Đerdap Dam was built but others, including a hospital ship, had remained almost forgotten until the drought exposed them anew.

dropped so low as to reveal the prows of long-forgotten German gunboats that had been rusting midstream for the past 60 years. (See box *Ghosts from the Depths*.)

Getting there

Negotin is just one hour away from Kladovo by a regular **bus service**. Other buses run to Belgrade, Zaječar, Niš, Bor, Leskovac, Donji Milanovac and nearby villages. When I visited the town in 2004 there were two separate bus terminals next door to each other, ten minutes' walk from the town centre: one was old and threadbare; the other, brand new and still smelling of paint. Each terminal served different destinations, although some places like Belgrade were served by both terminals but at different times, and so it was necessary to visit both in order to establish all of the transportation options. It is probable that the older terminal will close sometime in the near future, which will make for a less confusing situation. There is a *garderoba* at the newer terminal that charges 60din per bag.

The only **trains** that run from Negotin are to Zaječar four times a day, in addition to a local service to Prahovo on the Danube. Inconvenient train times make the bus a better option.

Where to stay and eat

Accommodation is limited to the state-run **Hotel Krajina** (Srbe Jovanovica bb; tel: 542 246) that overlooks the town's main square.

There are snack stalls opposite the church, next to the equestrian statue, and the **Inex Café**, opposite on the corner of the street that leads down to the museum, has good prices and a pleasant, outdoor location. The **Café-Pizzeria Allure** is next door to the shopping mall on the street between the equestrian statue and the Hotel Krajina. There are other cafés and bakeries along here, as well as along the street that leads to the Krajina Museum.

Central Serbia

Immediately south of Belgrade and the Danube and Sava rivers lies the region of central Serbia usually referred to as **Šumadija**, the 'wooded land'. And wooded it is in places, with dense stands of lush deciduous woodland containing species like oak, hornbeam and small-leaved lime. More generally though, this is a region of rolling farmland with small farmsteads, tidy villages, healthy-looking pigs feasting on corn husks and seemingly endless orchards of pear and plum trees. In contrast to the old-world ways of the countryside, the towns and cities of the region are, by and large, industrial.

The region is the heart of old Serbia and probably has the most homogeneously Serb population in the whole country, lacking the central European component of Hungarians, Slovaks and Croats that is found north of the Danube in Vojvodina, and the Muslim population that predominates further south in Raška and Kosovo.

The region was settled in the main during the 15th and 16th centuries by Serbs who had been driven north by their defeat at the Battle of Kosovo. When the Turks slowly started moving north to consolidate their victory some of the recent settlers feared the consequences of Ottoman rule and moved once again to Hungary or Bosnia.

Later migrations at the end of the 17th century saw the region almost completely deserted once more. The Šumadija was finally resettled in the latter years of the 18th century when some of the less prosperous and land-hungry Serbs from Vojvodina moved south of the Danube to clear patches of woodland in order to create smallholdings.

Central Serbia was at the heart of the First and Second Serbian Uprisings against Turkish rule, in 1804 and 1815 respectively. It also saw the formation of guerrilla bands during World War II and led the struggle against Nazi occupation, which brought great suffering to the region. Today, the combination of a tradition of fierce independence, coupled with a population that is almost entirely Serb has meant that central Serbia has become the natural homeland of Serbian nationalism: Tomislav Nikolić, the Radical Party's failed 2004 presidential candidate is a native of Kragujevac.

For the visitor, the main sights in this region are the monasteries, which are almost inevitably set deep in half-hidden valleys in the most sumptuous of rural surroundings. Some of these can easily be reached by public transport; others require more effort. The countryside itself is a delight, and the slow rhythm of life in the villages and small towns of the Šumadija offers a glimpse of a bygone age that has now passed much of Europe by. This is worth experiencing first hand if you get the opportunity.

The larger towns and cities of the region have perhaps less to offer, although they are mostly unavoidable as either overnight bases or transport centres. While it is certainly true that all of the urban centres of central Serbia hold great interest in historical terms, it is undeniable that in some cases their history has been so violent

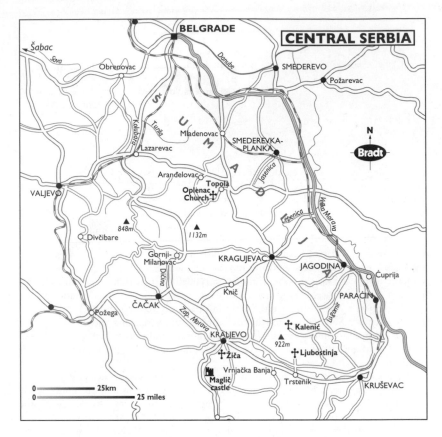

and devastating that there is little left on the ground worth seeing. Kragujevac is a case in point.

KRAGUJEVAC КРАГУЈЕВАЦ
Telephone code: 034

The city of Kragujevac, capital of the Šumadija region, has the fourth-largest urban population in Serbia with about 180,000 citizens. In contrast to the bucolic delights of the lush Šumadija countryside, Kragujevac is a modern industrial city with little to tempt the casual visitor, although its proximity to both Ljubosotinja and Kalenić monasteries make it a suitable destination for an overnight stay. Although there are few 'sights' in the city itself, those fascinated by Serbia's more recent history will find interest at the **Šumarica Memorial Park** and museum at the city's outskirts, which commemorate the dreadful events that took place here during the World War II.

History

The settlement of Kragujevac probably originates from the first half of the 15th century, in the time just before Serbia came under Turkish rule. The subsequent Turkish occupation was not continuous. Twice the town was wrested from the Turks to fall under Austrian rule, first in the 17th century, then later again in the 18th century between 1718 and 1739. Following the First Serbian Uprising in 1804, Kragujevac was liberated from Turkish rule until 1813, when the town was briefly reoccupied until the Second Serbian Uprising in 1815, after which the Turks left the town for good. Shortly after this, in 1818, Prince Miloš Oberenović made Kragujevac the capital of the new Serbian state and it retained this status until 1841. The first Serbian constitution was proclaimed here in 1835, along with the first notions of an independent electoral democracy.

By the beginning of the 20th century Kragujevac had become an important centre for socialism; the first socialist representative of the Serbian Parliament, Dr Mihailo Ilič, was elected here in 1903.

During World War I, Kragujevac was the seat of the Serbian Supreme Headquarters. In 1918, near the close of the war, a military riot took place in the barracks here, with an uprising of soldiers – mostly Slovak – rioting against Austro-Hungarian rule. The uprising was quickly crushed and 44 of the soldiers involved, all Slovak, were shot on Stanovljansko field close to the town.

After a relatively peaceful inter-war period Kragujevac was occupied by Nazi troops on April 11 1941. As a response to this, the local communist party made a decision in July of that year to form a partisan detachment and start an uprising against German rule. The limited success of the Partisans soon caused Hitler to worry about the danger of Serbian insurrection so he ordered that brutal measures be taken to stop the revolt in its tracks. As a consequence, savage reprisals were meted out by the Nazis on a scale that can only be considered genocidal. In the brief spell from October 19 to 21 1941, more than 7,000 male citizens of the town were shot by the Nazis in retaliation to the killing of German troops in an ambush. This vast number was determined by General Franz Boehme, the German military commander in Serbia, who ordered that 100 adult males be shot for every German soldier killed, and 50 for each one wounded. Three hundred of those killed were, in fact, school pupils, and another 40, their teachers. Although they supposedly selected males over 15 years of age, the Nazis also murdered boys much younger than this in order to make the numbers up.

This appalling crime against humanity is commemorated in stone at the monument park but somehow the gesture hardly seems necessary: in Kragujevac it seems as if the folk memory of the event has somehow permeated the very bricks and mortar of the place.

The city continued to suffer in more recent years when the Zastava car factory, the largest in the former Yugoslavia, was comprehensively bombed by NATO on April 9 and April 11 1999. Around 160 workers were injured in the raids, and the destruction of the factory meant that the livelihoods of 38,000 people was taken away overnight. The industrial decay had started some years earlier: the Kragujevac car industry was already in decline thanks to sanctions and economic hardships during the Milošević period; the NATO attack precipitated its total collapse.

With good reason, Kragujevac is not exactly a cheerful sort of place.

Getting there
Kragujevac, being both large and centrally situated, is well connected, with frequent bus connections to Belgrade, Novi Sad and the other main centres of central Serbia. Train connections exist but are far less frequent. The bus and train stations are close to each other, on the opposite side of the river from the city centre.

Where to stay
Rusty signs scattered around the city that point to the Hotel Sloboda should be ignored, as this establishment has long been closed.

Hotel Zelengora**** Branka Radičevića 1; tel: 336 254; fax: 336 185. This hotel, located by the church on Karađorđevića, is the best in town. It has 5 singles at €49, 19 doubles for €88 and 2 apartments at €97.50.

Hotel Stari Grad★★★ Karađorđeva 10; tel: 330 591. The Stari Grad is a smallish private hotel with 6 single rooms at €37, 13 doubles at €58 and 2 apartments for €58.

Hotel Šumarice★★★★ Desankin venac bb; tel: 336 180, 336 181; fax: 333 807. This hotel is aimed mostly at business travellers and is situated well out of the centre in Šumarica Park, so it is probably only useful to those with their own transport. The hotel has 66 singles at €48, 43 doubles at €87 and 5 apartments for €145.

Hotel Kragujevac★★ Kralja Petra I 26; tel: 335 811; fax: 331 185. This central hotel is a fairly typical, high-rise state-run concern. Reasonable rooms go for between 1,100 and 1,700din single, 2,000 and 3,000din double, depending on which floor you are on. There are also 'Lux' rooms available. Getting one of the cheaper rooms can be a bit of a battle because, as is the case in certain other state hotels, the reception staff cannot understand why you might not wish to spend as much money as possible. It does have a good central location.

Where to eat and drink

For meals there is the cheap and cheerful **Restoran Konak** at number 7, Marta 27, reached by heading left towards the river from the pedestrian street of Kralja Petra. Just beyond here, before the bridge, is a small enclave of fast food huts serving *ćevapčıĉı* and *pljeskavica*. Going in the opposite direction along Marta 27, the **Restoran Doaien** is located on the top floor of the shopping centre opposite Trg Vojvode Putnika. Continuing across Marta 27 from Kralja Petra, the **Restoran Balkan** is on the corner of Karađorđevića and Radičevića, and serves traditional Serbian food. For lighter fare, the **Time Out Caffe** next to the Kragujevac hotel has pizzas, sandwiches, snacks and drinks. Another pizzeria is the **Mamma Mia Pizzeria** at Tanaska Rajića 68, a street running parallel to and north of Kralja Aleksandra towards Šumarica Park.

There are outdoor **café–bars** all the way along the pedestrian street of Kralja Petra, along Kralja Aleksandra, the extension of Karađorđevića that leads to Šumarica Park, and also along Lole Ribera, another pedestrian street that runs north off Karađorđ evića. **La Sorafa Pizzeria** is also along here at number 7. For pancakes, **Peron Palačinkarnica** has a terrace extending in front of a marooned railcar near the Kragujevac hotel.

What to see
Šumarica Memorial Park

This large park on the city's western edge is both outdoor space and memorial. The park stands on higher ground that is a good two or three kilometres from the city centre, on the edge of the countryside with grassy meadows and haystacks.

Spread around the park are various monuments commemorating the tragic events of October 1941. These include: the *Monument of Pain and Pride* (1951) and the *Monument to Resistance and Freedom* (1961) by A Grzetić, the *Monument to the Executed School-Pupils and Teachers* (1963) by M Zivković, the *One Hundred for One Monument* (1980) by N Glid and the *Monument against Evil* (1991) by M Romo among others.

At the entrance to Šumarica Park stands the **21 October Memorial Museum**, a curious building composed of 33 towers of different heights that create the impression of a basalt rock formation or a chemical salt crystal. In the entrance hall is a piece of symbolic sculpture made from soldiers' helmets hung on a spray of rifles bayoneted into a base.

In the city centre itself, there is the **National Museum** with a small archaeological, historical and ethnographical collection in the *konak* that was the former **Palace of Prince Miloš** at Svetozara Markovića 2. In front of the Zastava offices, across the concrete bridge at the end of Marta 27, is an interesting and rather heroic **statue of a Yugoslav car worker**, a poignant sight now that the industry is on its knees in the city.

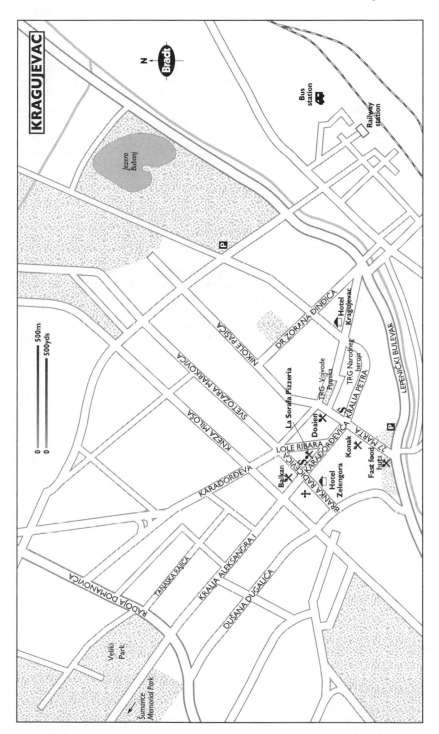

KRALJEVO КРАЉЕВО
Telephone code: 036
Like Kragujevac, Kraljevo is another industrial town that has largely been rebuilt since World War II, although its roots belong to the 19th century when it was the seat of the Obrenović dynasty. The city was badly damaged in World War II and suffered almost as much as Kragujevac in terms of the brutal Nazi reprisals that were visited upon the civilian population of the town. More recently, during the 1999 bombing campaign, several targets in and around Kraljevo were hit by NATO bombs, destroying some railway lines and a bridge. Little is left of the town's 19th-century heritage and what you see today is largely the result of socialist town planning. Kraljevo is a convenient stopover for **Žiča Monastery**, which lies just outside the town, and could also be used as a base for visiting **Studenica**, **Kalenić** and **Ljubostinja**.

There is a **tourist information centre** at Srpskih ratnika 25 (tel/fax: 311 192, 316 000) on the north side of the square. This is staffed by an extremely helpful woman who speaks excellent English and does her best to think of diversions that might interest the foreign visitor.

Getting there
Kraljevo is an important transport hub and one of Serbia's better-connected towns. There are many daily **buses** that run to Belgrade, seven of which originate in Kraljevo. Six buses a day run west to Zlatibor, and many more go east to Kragujevac and Kruševac. There is a frequent bus service south to Raška and Novi Pazar, and even far-flung destinations like Subotica and Vranje can be reached directly from the town.

Train connections are more limited, with three trains a day to Bar, three to Belgrade, three to Čačak and one to Niš, with local services going to Stalać and Lešak. Be aware that some of these leave at very inconvenient times like the early hours of the morning.

Where to stay
The **Hotel Turist** stands on the south side of the main square at Trg Srpskih ratnika 1 (tel: 22 366, 22 948). It is a bit on the shabby side but adequate enough, with single rooms going for 950din and doubles for 1,540din.

The other option is the almost new, privately run **Hotel Royal** at Karađorđeva 107 (tel: 354 004, 353 999). This smart hotel has only been in operation since 2003 and it still looks pristine. All rooms have TV and minibar, with air conditioning in the summer months. The Royal has its own restaurant and will accept VISA cards. Single rooms cost 2,000din; doubles, 3,450din; a one-person apartment, 2,800din; a double apartment, 4,200din; an apartment for three people, 4,900din.

Where to eat and drink
The **Hotel Turist** has a large dingy restaurant that is not especially inviting – the bingo hall next door seems far more animated. An alternative is to head along Oktobarskih Žrtava, the road that leads from the central square to the bus station, which has a few restaurants like the **Restoran Šumadija** and **Mirage Pizzeria**. For a drink, there is a whole string of café-bars with outside tables along Omdalinska. On the north side of Trg Srpskih ratnika, close to the tourist office, is **Boeing Pizza** at number 22. The **Pivinica Paris** next door serves very cheap draught beer.

What to see
Apart from nearby Žiča Monastery, there is little to see in the town itself. When I made enquiries at the tourist office, the helpful woman working there had to think carefully before informing me that there was 'a tank in the park' that I might wish to see. There is, but it is hardly worth a detour. Realistically, apart visiting from the

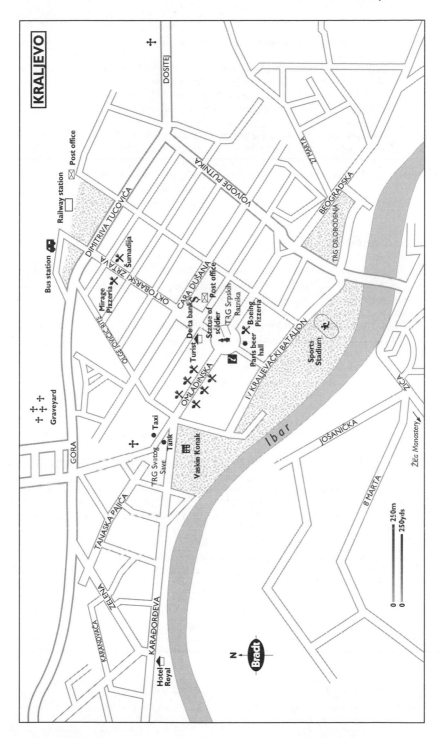

KRALJEVO

Post office

Railway station

Bus station

Graveyard

DOSITEJ

DIMITRIJA TUCOVIĆA

ĐORĐA VAJCA

OKTOBARSKIH ŽRTAVA

Šumadija

Mirage Pizzeria

CARA DUŠANA

Delta bank

VOJVODE PUTNIKA

Post office

Statue of soldier

TRG Srpskih Ratnika

Turist

Boeing Pizzeria

OMLADINSKA

Paris beer hall

17 KRALJEVAČKI BATALJON

Sports Stadium

TRG Svetog Save

Taxi

Tank

Vraski Konak

Ibar

GORA

TANASKA RAJIĆA

ZELENA

KARANDŽAĆA

KARAĐORĐEVA

Hotel Royal

27 MARTA

BEOGRADSKA

TRG OSLOBOĐENJA

JOŠANIČKA

8 MARTA

ŽIČA

Žiča Monastery

0   250m
0   250yds

N

Bradt

nearby monasteries, Kraljevo is best enjoyed by a leisurely stroll up and down the pedestrian-only street of **Omdalinska** and having a drink in one of the numerous outdoor cafés there.

The central square, **Trg Srpskih ratnika** (Square of the Serbian warrior), is actually a circle, around which most of the town's activity rotates. In the centre stands a large, sombre statue of the eponymous warrior with a gun and a banner, around which small children in battery-powered cars endlessly circulate while their parents sit on benches and chat.

Heading west along Omdalinska you soon come to the small, leafy square – Trg Sveti Save – where the aforementioned tank is parked, and which serves as a meeting point for many of the town's teenagers. The elegant, neoclassical **National Museum** stands opposite this, while the road in front serves as an unofficial taxi rank for the town. On the other side of the road is a park that houses the **Gospodar Vasin Konak**, a 19th-century residence from the time of the Obrenović dynasty.

Žiča Monastery

This is situated just outside Kraljevo, across the Reka River in one of the town's southern suburbs. It is about a 45-minute walk from the centre, or you could take a taxi or a local bus heading towards the village of Mataruška Banja; as you approach near to the monastery, you will see its three cupolas and red walls emerging through its screen of trees.

Žiča is distinctive from all other Serbian monasteries in being painted a rusty red colour, an echo of the monasteries at Mt Athos in Greece. With a single aisle, a semicircular apse and a narthex on the western side, it is a prime example of the **Raška School** and, at one time at least, was one of the grandest representatives of this style in all of Serbia. Nowadays, following an extensive repair programme that aimed to correct the damage of previous centuries, the monastery's natural ambience has been adversely affected by so much well-meant restoration: it is still grand but somehow it lacks atmosphere. Sadly, most of the original frescos have been destroyed, either by plundering Bulgarians in 1290, or by later Turks infuriated at the portrayal of the human image. All that remains of the earlier frescos are fragments around the cupola and the *Crucifixion* in the south transept. The *Dormition of the Virgin* on the west wall is later, probably 14th-century.

Despite its artistic losses, Žiča's historic pedigree is faultless and the monastery holds a special place in the affections of many Serbians. It was here that Serbia's patron saint, **St Sava**, founded the first Patriarchate on his return from his long sojourn at Mt Athos. A golden thread is said to have led him to the site, and it is this legend that gives the monastery its name (*žiča* means cord or thread).

The construction of the main church began about 1206 and it was finished around 1217. Shortly after, Žiča became the seat of the newly independent episcopacy in 1219 and the monastery became the place of coronation for Serbian kings, the first of which was Stefan, Sava's brother, subsequently referred to as Stefan Prvovenčani (the First Crowned), who reigned until 1223.

Following the damage done by marauding Bulgarians at the end of the 13th century, the monastery was reconstructed under the auspices of archbishops Jevstatije, Nikodin and Danilo II, only to be plundered several times more in later centuries under Turkish rule. The first major reconstruction was in 1562, and again in the 18th century. After the First Serbian Uprising in the early 19th century, Karađorđe constructed some new residential buildings before the monastery came under attack once more. What remains today is the result of extensive restoration works done in the period between 1925 and 1935, in addition to that carried out in more recent years.

EAST OF KRALJEVO

Halfway to Kruševac on the E-761 east of Kraljevo is the small industrial town of **Trstenik**. Just to the north of here lies the **Ljubostinja Convent**. As the monastery is only a 4km walk from the town, it makes an easy day trip from either Kraljevo or Kruševac. The frequent buses that link these two towns all stop at Trstenik. There is also the occasional train.

Ljubostinja Convent

The convent is an easy 50-minute walk from the nearby town of Trstenik, along a quiet narrow lane that leads up alongside a river, sometimes dried-up in summer. Ljubostinja is found at the end of the lane in a typical Šumadija setting of gentle, green, forested hills. The monastery buildings include a magnificent black-and-white timbered *konak*, a large number of convent buildings and a church within a walled paddock. It is still very much a working monastery and the nuns here keep busy making wine and honey when not involved with more spiritual concerns.

Externally, the church is a fine example of the Morava School, with intricately sculpted windows and doors. Inside, the frescos are something of a disappointment with only fragments surviving, the best being those in the narthex. The west wall of the north side of the door has portraits of Prince Lazar and Princess Milica, with their sons, Stefan and Vuk, on the other side.

The church was founded by Lazar's widow, Princess Milica, and was built between 1402 and 1404. An inscription in the step below the door that leads from the narthex to the naos identifies the builder, one Rade Borović. There is a secret door in the northeast corner of the narthex that leads to a narrow staircase, once used as a hideaway and place to store treasure.

Princess Milica spent her last years here in the monastery, becoming a sister along with many other noblewomen widowed by the Battle of Kosovo. Her tomb lies in the naos.

Kalenić Convent

The convent of Kalenić stands 20km or so north of Ljubostinja on a hillside of the Gledićke range deep in the Šumadija countryside. Unfortunately, Kalenić is probably the most inaccessible monastery in the whole of Serbia and almost impossible to reach by public transport – a great pity because this monastery, completed around 1415 by Bogdan, a Serbian noble, is a masterpiece of the **Morava School** and probably represents the culmination of its art.

The exterior of the church is outstanding, decorated with stripes and chequerboard patterns, and adorned with a wide array of motifs that include lions, birds, centaurs and gryphons. Intricate rosettes and minutely carved geometric designs surround all of the windows and portals. Inside, it is no less striking and the overall effect is one of grace and balance. The frescos are mostly well-preserved, having been restored during the 1950s. It should be noted how the proportions of the compositions combine with the building's dimensions; in particular, the way that the scenes in the frescos are graded with height, becoming larger as they reach up to the cupola.

The most noteworthy of the narrative frescos is without a doubt the *Marriage Feast at Cana* in the southern apse, which depicts Christ and the Virgin in the setting of a medieval Serbian wedding. The fresco is remarkable for its period detail: the Virgin appears to be speaking to Christ about the wine, while two old men in the background are happily sampling it; the groom is about to prick the finger of his bride in the part of the ancient Serbian ritual that symbolises the mixing of blood – a custom that survived until not so long ago. Other frescos include a portrait of the monastery's patron Bogdan with his wife Milica and his brother Peter on the north wall of the narthex.

To reach Kalenić with your own car, you can continue north after visiting

Ljubostinja, turning left at the village of Prevešt to reach the monastery; without private transport, getting here is going to present a problem. Buses run from Kragujevac, Kruševac and Jagodina/Svetozarevo to Oparić, a village south of Belušić, but the monastery is still 12km west of here so hitchhiking might be an option. If there is a group of you, hiring a taxi from Trstenik to do a round trip to Ljubostina and Kalenić and back is probably the easiest solution.

Vrnjačka Banja

Vrnjačka Banja, just to the west of Trstenik, is a spa resort that is held in high esteem by middle-class Serbs who are devotees of spa-tourism. A resort of this kind is probably of limited appeal to most foreign visitors but it does at least offer a wide range of facilities and comfortable places to stay for anyone touring the area. The resort is in the wooded foothills that lie beneath 1,147m Goč Mountain.

The beneficial qualities of the waters of Vrnjačka Banja have a long history that dates back to Roman times. Development of the current resort started back in 1868 and it remains one of the most popular spas in the country. There are three mineral springs at the spa – two cold and one warm: the warm spring has an average temperature of 36.5°C and is used mainly for bathing and the cold, between 14° and 25.7°C, for drinking. The spa is recommended for the treatment of diabetes, diseases of the gastrointestinal tract, pancreas, kidney and urinary tract, as well as for cardiovascular conditions.

Tourist information can be had from the **Tourist and Sports Centre**, Vrnjačka 6/2; tel: 611 105, 661 106, 661 107, 661 108; fax: 661 105, 661 108; email: tsc_vb@ptt.yu; www.vrnjackabanja.org.yu.

Where to stay

There are over 10,000 beds in the resort so you have plenty to choose from. It is very much a buyer's market and so you should be able to find something suitable in your chosen price range. Generally speaking, the pensions and two-star hotels will charge something in the order of 800–1,000din per person, the three-stars, 1,200–2,000din. Most of these hotels are geared up to providing full or half board, so to take at least your evening meal at your hotel certainly represents better value. Otherwise, there are numerous fast food and pizzeria places scattered around town.

Just a small sample of the hotels and pensions found in the resort are listed below.

Hotel Beograd Vrnjačka bb; tel/fax: 661 807
Hotel Breza★★★ Vrnjačka 26; tel: 662 140, 662 059; fax: 665 969
Hotel Fontana★★★ Cara Dušana 2; tel: 661 153, 661 154, 661 564; fax: 661 564
Hotel Orion Bulevar Srpskih ratnika bb; tel: 661 263, 664 753; fax: 661 265
Hotel Partizanska Vrnjačka 25; tel: 662 060; fax: 662 061
Hotel Poštanski Dom Banović Strahinje 8; tel: 665 922, 665 923; fax: 665 924; email: pttdom@ptt.yu; www.pttdom.co.yu
Hotel Slatina★★ Slatinski Venac 16; tel: 661 442, 665 619; fax: 661 814
Hotel Slavija★★ Svetog save 2; tel: 663 360, 663 361; fax: 662 372
Hotel Železničar★ Gavrila Prinčipa 3; tel: 661 547, 661 215; fax: 665 057
Hotel Zvezda ★★★ Save Kovačevica 7; tel: 662 201, 662 202, 662 205; fax: 662 205
Pansion Danica Jastrebačka bb; tel: 665 962
Pansion Kraljica Nemanjina 22; tel: 7773 540
Pansion Vuk★★★ Olge Jovičić 10; tel: 662 070, 662 131; fax: 662 070
Villa Sneznik Vrnačka 35; tel: 661 152; www.hotelsneznik.com
Villa San Vrnjačka bb; tel/fax: 662 150, 661 564, 661 271

KRUŠEVAC КРУШЕВАЦ

Telephone code: 037

This medium-sized town on the Zapadna Morava River, a western tributary of the Morava, is noteworthy for its fort and its well-preserved 14th-century church of the Morava School.

History

The town was founded in the 1370s and had become Prince Lazar's capital by the time of the Battle of Kosovo in 1389. It was from the fortress at Kruševac that the Serbian army under Lazar's command set off for its fateful encounter in June of that year.

Despite the Serbian defeat at the hands of the Turks it was a further 60 or so years before the Turks finally wrested the city from Serbian control, by which time the majority of the population had fled north to safety. Kruševac remained in Turkish hands for the next 400 years until it was finally liberated by the Serbs in 1833.

Tourist information can be found at Miloja Zakica 3 (tel/fax: 39 055), close to the angel monument on the main square. In theory, at least – the door was firmly locked throughout my stay.

Getting there

Kruševac lies at the southeastern corner of central Serbia. It is well connected to Belgrade by a frequent **bus** service that is more or less hourly, as well as to other destinations in southern and central Serbia. Numerous daily buses also run to the nearby resort of Vrnjačka Banja. Less regular services link the town with destinations east of the Morava River like Ćuprija, Jagodina and Niš.

An infrequent and slow **train** service runs west to Kraljevo and north to Paraćin and Smederevo.

Where to stay

Hotel Rubin Nemanjina 2; tel: 425 535. This large, state-run hotel faces out on to the town's central square. The hotel has its own restaurant and bar; currency exchange is offered in the foyer and private parking is available. The Rubin has 36 single rooms, 76 doubles and 4 apartments. Prices depend on which floor you choose: the first floor is more expensive. The tariff for a single room is 1,130–1,640din; doubles 1,880–2,980din.

Hotel Evropa Narodne armilije 2; tel: 28 331. This small hotel, tucked away just off the main square opposite a taxi rank, is altogether more modest. It has 22 doubles, 10 single rooms and 2 apartments on just 3 floors. The single rooms come with a shower and a sink but no toilet. The rooms are quite comfortable and cost a very reasonable 830din. When I stayed here, the hotel was hosting a beauty contest and leggy local girls in swimsuits were constantly parading the corridors practising their walk. This is probably not a regular event, however.

Where to eat and drink

For national dishes, the **Restaurant Župa** is just off central Trg Kosovskih Junaka, more or less opposite the Hotel Rubin, which also has a decent restaurant. The road that leads east of this square, Marka Tomića, has several cafés, pizzerias and a *postlastičarnica* with outdoor seating. Several cafés, bars and fast food take-aways can also be found along Miloja Zakija, a narrow street that runs south from the monument in the central square.

What to see

Kruševac's most important sight is undoubtedly the 14th-century **Lazar Church** that stands in the grounds of the ruined fort. To find the fort and church, walk west from the Hotel Rubin past the post office and the elegant neoclassical **Town Hall**, then turn left and head south briefly along Stevan Bisocog before taking the road that leads off to the right. This will soon bring you to the fortress park.

The church, built about 1380 and restored by Prince Miloš Obrenović in the 19th century, is a typical example of the **Morava School,** with an Orthodox cross plan, a central cupola, mixed brick and stone masonry, and elaborate, decorative carvings around the doors and windows. Although all of the original frescos have been lost, destroyed by Turkish iconoclasts, externally the church is in remarkably good condition for its age. In fact, its appearance seems almost new, the decorative red brickwork still bright and in pristine condition and the stone carvings hardly worn.

It must be said that the church may be too fussy for some tastes: with numerous arches and mouldings, rose windows, carved dragons and over-the-top tracery. Somehow, the overall effect is all a bit too much – an overstatement.

The church stands central in the park that once held **Lazar's Fortress**. Apart from some defensive walls, there is little that remains of the fort today but a noticeboard points you in the right direction if you want to work out where Prince Lazar's palace, the stables, blacksmiths and kilns used to stand.

Prince Lazar's palace is now reduced to its foundations but the **museum** that stands in the park, and which dates from 1863, is well worth investigating. Downstairs are several rooms devoted to reconstructed frescos, fragments of stoneware, illustrated manuscripts, medieval pottery and glassware, together with stone arrowheads and axes from the Neolithic period. On one wall is a medieval map showing the extent of Greater Serbia between 1371 and 1459, but pride of place must go to the glass cabinet that contains a cloak that was supposedly worn by Prince Lazar himself. The cloak – grey with yellow brocade and stylised animal motifs that seem to lie somewhere between a dog and a lion – has something of a Chinese appearance about it. Somehow, its authenticity seems doubtful. It looks more of a dressing gown than a cloak, but perhaps it was just the thing for relaxing in after a hard day on the battlefield.

Upstairs, the museum has a display of interesting modern paintings all related to the Battle of Kosovo theme. The history of the Kruševac region is represented by numerous letters and newspaper cuttings from the 19th century. There is also an ethnographical exhibit of beds, looms, clothes and tools used in homes in the region and, interestingly, a large stuffed wolf skewered on a stake. The wolf has a length of wool and a garland of chilli peppers and corn tassels hung around its neck, a bell hung from its tail. This appears to have some sort of talismanic value as old black-and-white photographs show villagers dressing up a dead wolf in the same manner in a winter ceremony. Unfortunately, all of the captioning is in Cyrillic Serbian.

Perhaps the most interesting object on display is the wooden mock-up made from sculptor Ivan Meštrović's 1912 plan for his proposed monument, *Vidovanskog Hrama*, which was intended to be built at Kosovo Polje, the site of the fateful battle. The scale of the project was truly monumental, which might go part of the way to explain why it was never even started. The design incorporates the sort of militaristic, superhuman aesthetic that Mussolini so admired. The ground plan is that of an enormous Orthodox cross, with an outer and an inner temple area divided by colonnaded walkways. At the entrances that lie at each point of the cross, ranks of lions and horses guard the steps that lead up to them. In the centre of the design is a tower composed of warrior figures stacked on each others' shoulders. Given the spectre of conflict that continues to haunt troubled Kosovo, it is probably just as well that it was never built.

The museum is open Tuesday to Saturday 08.00–18.00, and Sundays and holidays 09.00–14.00. It is closed Mondays. Entrance is 30din. When I visited, bargain vinyl hunters could purchase LP records of *Folk Music of the Kruševac Region* from the entrance shop for the princely sum of 10din.

The **town centre** itself has one or two things of note. Standing in the centre of Trg Kosovskih Junaka, the main square, is a monument of a winged angel with the dates 1389, 1882 and 1902 inscribed around it. Just off the square on the east side, around the corner from Miloja Zakica café-bar street is a very elegant stucco building that is the main building of the **University**. A small park at the end of Marka Tomića, east of Trg Kosovskih Junaka, contains an early 20th-century church built in red and yellow layers of stone. Beyond this is a small shopping centre.

Kruševac is also home to an excellent **green market**, one of the best in Serbia and at its most animated on Saturday mornings. The market site is found along the street that runs south from Hotel Rubin. There is a permanent covered area where clothes, furniture, tools and household appliances are sold, as well as a densely packed outdoor spread of stalls selling all manner of fruit, vegetables, mushrooms, fish and meat, along with locally produced dairy products like white cheese and *kajmak*. Animal lovers may baulk at some of the sights here: the bulk of chickens that change hands are still alive and clucking, and on the street outside, larks and captured songbirds are sold in tiny cages. With its colourful population of Roma vegetable vendors, and burly village women in headscarves selling eggs from buckets, there is a strong hint of the Middle Eastern bazaar here.

TOPOLA ТОПОЛА

The prime reason for visiting the small town of Topola 65km south of Belgrade is to visit the **Karađorđe Mausoleum** on the hill of **Oplenac** just outside the town. Topola served as Karađorđe's campaign headquarters during the First National Uprising and the leader's bones are still here in the church that was built for him – a curious, Byzantine-style structure dedicated to St George. The church was founded by King Peter I and consecrated in 1912. It was damaged during World War I and partly rebuilt in the 1920s; the mosaics that cover the interior were created during this period.

Because of Karađorđe's revered status as a national hero of the First Serbian Uprising, the mausoleum at Oplenac is venerated throughout Serbia and considered an important national shrine. Whether or not it holds the same appeal for foreign visitors is largely dependent on their taste for white marble and slightly gaudy mosaics. The church is on top of the hill at the south side of the town, set among pines and well-tended gardens.

Most of the walls and ceiling of the church are covered with mosaics that have been copied from frescos in Serbian monasteries. They are well executed but the colours are a tad too bright and look slightly artificial. In the south apse, Karađorđe's remains inhabit a grand coffin – also of white marble. In death at least, his humble bones have been elevated to the status of a king, as they rest next to those of King Peter I, the church's benefactor.

Downstairs in the crypt, more mosaics glint down on a series of tombs, many of which have never been occupied: the mausoleum was built for a dynasty that did not survive for as long as expected and although the tombs of King Aleksandar, murdered in Marseilles in 1934, and his mother are found here, there are many more vacant niches that will never be filled.

The other sight at Oplenac is the nearby **Historical Museum** that stands on the site of what used to be Karađorđević Castle. The Balkan-style *konak* where he used to live, and which now houses the museum, is the only extant part of this.

Tourist information is available at Kneginje Zorke 40 in Topola (tel: 811 172; fax: 811 771; email: toplenac@infosky.net; www.sotopola.org.yu).

If you wish to stay in the vicinity, there is the two-star **Hotel Oplenac** situated just below the church (tel: 811 430, 811 980; no credit cards are accepted).

The Knić area

Lying roughly halfway between Kragujevac and Kraljevo is the small country town of Knić. Although there is nothing specific to see in the town, it is central to a particularly lovely part of the Šumadija that is ideal for walking or cycling. There are also a few sights of interest close by, so Knić could serve as a suitable base for exploration.

Close to the town is the 2km-long **Gruža Lake**, a popular location for watersports and fishing while, just to the south, is the 749m peak of **Veliki vrh**, the highest point in the area.

Thirteen kilometres northwest of Knić, on a back road that meanders towards Čačak, is the small village of **Borać**, which has some ruins of an old medieval town that dates back to the time of Stefan Lazarević. The most remarkable thing here is the so-called '**hidden church**' that has three of its sides sheltered by a cliff face and its fourth concealed by a lush stand of 100-year-old lime trees. The church dates from 1350 and, true to its name, does not reveal itself until you are right at its door. The house by the gate has the key if you want to go inside. There is an interesting old graveyard nearby.

More information on local attractions can be had from the **Turistička Organizacija** office in Knić on Skupština opštine, the main street (tel: 871 115).

For accommodation in the area there is the **Motel Ravni Gaj**, a large motel with 50 beds just beyond the lake at Knić (tel: 591 140; fax: 591 011). The restaurant serves local Šumadija dishes. The **Restoran Putnik** on the main Čačak to Kragujevac road next to Lake Gruža also has rooms available (tel: 871 519). Nearby is the large and stylish **Klub Restoran Arsenijević** that serves Šumadija food in a traditional setting (tel: 871 836).

A good option would be to stay with a family in the area, which would enable you to get a closer look at the way of life here. A number of local farming households offer bed and breakfast and can be booked through Belgrade-based village tourism specialists, **Village @dventure**. Further information can be gathered from the website at: www.villageadventure.co.yu or by contacting by email at: village@ptt.yu.

VALJEVO ВАЉЕВО

Telephone code: 014

This town of 60,000 inhabitants, 100km south of Belgrade, has few specific sights but is a pleasant relaxing place to visit. The town stands on the Kolubara River surrounded by low mountain ranges with the peak of the 1,103m Divčibare about 30km to the southeast. The town had an important role in the liberation struggle in the early 19th century and some buildings remain from this period, especially in the downtown Tešnjar region of the town on the south bank of the Kolubara, where there are a number of restored 18th- and 19th-century houses and workshops. There are pleasant walks to be had along the river south of the town.

The linguist and compiler of modern Serbian language, Vuk Karadžić, was a native of the town and there is a monument to him in front of the old railway station. Supposedly, Valjevo is the place where the most grammatically perfect Serbian is spoken, although this is unrelated to the Vuk Karadžić connection.

Serbian (and Romani) language classes can be arranged with the **Amala Summer School** (tel: 014 220 224, mob: 064 177 4693; email: amal@galbeno.co.yu or office@galbeno.co.yu; www.galbeno.co.yu) that is located in the town. They also organise singing, folk dance and musical instrument workshops, as well as excursions in the locality. (For more details see *Tour Operators* in the *Practical Information* chapter.)

Valjevo has good **bus** connections with Belgrade but surprisingly few services south to Užice. Two buses a day leave for Novi Sad via Šabac, on a direct route that avoids Belgrade. The town lies on the Bar–Belgrade railway and so there are a number of relatively fast **train** connections north to Lazarevac and Belgrade and south to Užice.

The smartest **accommodation** in Valjevo is at the four-star **Hotel Grand** in the centre (Vojvode Misica 2; tel: 227 133), which has 35 rooms and five apartments. Other hotels in the town are the two-star **Hotel Beli Narcis** (Zikice Jovanića 1; tel: 221 140) with 19 doubles and 14 single rooms, and the two-star **Hotel Jabalanica** (Obrena Nikolića 18; tel: 222 367) with 50 rooms. The **Pension Bulevar** (Vuka Karađića 36; tel: 220 185/231 098) has ten rooms at just 600din per person.

The area around the market and along the riverbank has plenty of café-bars and restaurants, many of which have live music in summer. **Tourist information** on the town is available at Prote Mateje 1 (tel: 221 138; fax: 226 112; www.valjevocity.co.yu).

Eurasian griffon vulture

172

Vojvodina

HISTORY

The name Vojvodina translates as 'Duchy' or 'Dukedom', a reference to the long years in which this vast tract of land north of the Danube belonged to the Austrian Empire. The region had been inhabited since Palaeolithic times before the Romans first visited the region in the 1st century BC. By the beginning of the 2nd century AD, under the command of the emperor Trajan, most of the Banat was under Roman rule. The Romans built the town of Sirmium as their capital, choosing a site by the Danube where present-day Sremska Mitrovica is located. No fewer than four emperors were born here – Aurelianus, Probus, Gratianus and Constantius II – before the town was conquered by the Hungarians in AD441, which ended Roman rule in the region. It was subsequently destroyed by the Avars in 582.

A migration into the region began in the second half of the 4th century and continued until the end of the 9th century. The settlers were of diverse origins: Byzantines, Huns, Avars and Slavs. Magyars started to arrive in number during the 9th century and Hungarians ruled Vojvodina until the 16th century. Serbs started to settle the region from the 14th century onwards, with the result that Vojvodina's population was a relatively balanced Serbian–Hungarian mix by the early 16th century.

In 1526, following the Battle of Mohács, on the river Danube in present-day Hungary, the Ottomans took control of Vojvodina. This precipitated a massive depopulation of the region and it remained this way until the late 17th century when the Habsburg Empire successfully laid claim to the region.

Following their new territorial gains, the Austrians were intent on setting up a defensive zone between themselves and the Turks. They encouraged new migrants to settle in the region, which by now had become quite sparsely populated. Many came to take advantage of the offer, attracted by the promise of fertile farmland. Among the first to arrive were more Serbs from the south, ever fearful of a Turkish resurgence in their homeland. Within a relatively short period of time, something in the order of 40,000 Serb families took up residence here in the latter part of the 17th century. Land was not the sole attraction: the Austrians were pragmatists and allowed Serbs to freely practise their Orthodox religion, which encouraged others to follow in their steps. Soon after this migration a new Serbian Orthodox Patriarchate was established at **Sremski Karlovci** near present-day **Novi Sad**, the same town in which the Treaty of Karlowitz had been signed in 1699 to legitimise the Habsburgs' claim on the region.

Other migrants followed in the wake of the Serbs, especially those in search of land or freedom from persecution – or both. What ensued created an ethnic and cultural mix unsurpassed anywhere in Europe at the time. The Serbs were soon joined by **Hungarians, Croats, Romanians, Slovaks, Germans, Roma** and many others, even by migrants from much further away, like **Greeks** and **Macedonians** from the

173

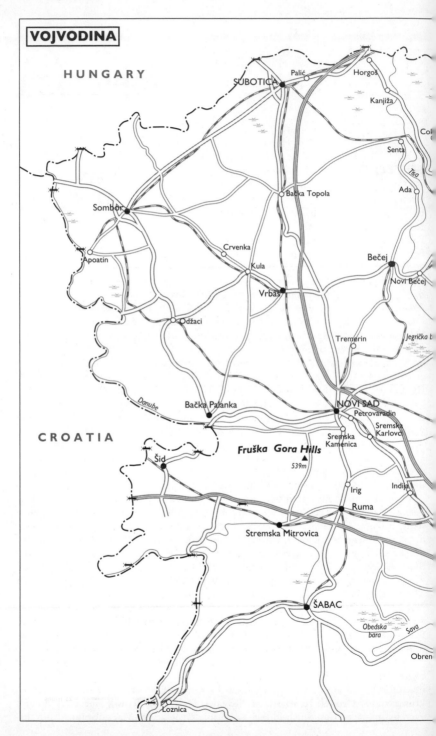

south, and **Ruthenians** from the Ukraine. This human tapestry has left its mark on the land and the same cultural diversity still exists in Vojvodina today as the descendants of the original settlers continue to speak their native language and observe the culture of their forefathers within the boundaries of modern Serbia.

With the abolition of the military frontier between 1867 and 1881, Bačka (Hungarian: Bacska) and the Banat came under Hungarian rule, while Srem was claimed by the crown of Croatia-Slavonia. The end of World War I in 1918, and the dismantling of the Austro-Hungarian Empire that followed, allowed the three Vojvodina provinces to form a union with what was then known as the Kingdom of Serbia. The Treaty of Trianon in 1920 ceded Vojvodina to Yugoslavia in 1920. After a brief occupation by Axis powers during World War II the province was restored to Yugoslavia once more and became part of Marshal Tito's new communist state. Later, in 1974, Vojvodina was given full autonomous status within the Yugoslav federation, a freedom that was subsequently rescinded by Slobodan Milošević in 1990.

It is to the credit of Yugoslavia's post-war leaders that the province's cultural diversity has been preserved and even encouraged. Following World War II, Vojvodina's children were taught in schools that allowed their native tongue to be used as well as Serbo-Croat. Such tolerance in the face of the rampant nationalism at work in other parts of the country goes some of the way to explain why Vojvodina's citizens are not always completely happy with the political machinations that take place in central government in Belgrade. The loss of the province's autonomy in 1990 did little to win hearts and minds in favour of the Milošević government, or to proselytise for the Serbian nationalist cause.

Geography

Vojvodina is comprised of three discrete geographical divisions: **Srem**, **Bačka** and **Banat**. In a region in which the land for the most part is endlessly flat, it is the province's rivers that create the geographical divisions. Srem is the region that lies south of the Danube and north of the Sava, and which extends west into northeast Croatia. Srem contains the only noteworthy hills in the province – the **Fruška Gora** range. North of here, the province is divided laterally by the Tisa River; the western portion is known as Bačka and the eastern part, which, in geographical terms at least, extends into southeast Romania, is the Banat.

BAČKA
Novi Sad НОВИ САД

Telephone code: 021

Capital of Vojvodina and, with a population of around 300,000, Serbia's second-largest city, Novi Sad is a relatively prosperous, commercial, industrial and university town on the north shore of the Danube. Long referred to as the 'Serbian Athens', Novi Sad has always been a centre of culture and learning and the atmosphere of its small but elegant city centre seems somehow a little more refined than that of the capital. Instead of looking south and east as Belgrade has historically done, Novi Sad's cultural ties are firmly to the north and west.

With a diverse and mixed population of Hungarians, Serbs, Croats and Slovaks, together with a sizeable but rather downcast Roma population, the city's cultural resonances bring to mind Budapest and Vienna rather than Belgrade or Sarajevo. As one writer has already noted, Novi Sad is the most easterly city in western Europe, and the most westerly city in eastern Europe. Famous sons – or rather, daughters – of the city include Mileva Einstein, wife of Albert (the great man himself lived here for a few years before World War I) and Monica Seles, the tennis star.

The city's most striking feature, the **Petrovaradin Fortress**, is not in Novi Sad itself but across the Danube in the separate town of Petrovaradin (which strictly speaking is in Srem but has been included here for convenience sake). Three bridges used to link the two sides of the river but all were destroyed during the hostilities of 1999. Two of these have since been replaced: one has been rebuilt, while the other is a temporary structure on pontoons. The city centre has a number of noteworthy buildings, mostly in the baroque style, together with some excellent museums and art galleries.

It is quite feasible to visit the city as a day trip from Belgrade if time is short but a longer stay here will pay dividends. Not only are there various sights in the city to enjoy, Novi Sad also serves as an excellent base for trips to other parts of Vojvodina, as well as excursions into the **Fruška Gora** hills that lie just to the south.

History

Originally known as **Petrovaradinski sanac** (Petrovaradin's trench), the city was renamed Novi Sad, 'New Plant', following a 1748 royal decree that awarded the settlement free city status. The term 'Serbian Athens' came into play during the 19th century when Novi Sad became famous as a centre of culture and learning. The city's theatre, the oldest in Serbia, was established during this period.

The original settlement had developed in tandem with the growth of the fortress at Petrovaradin across the river. This had started life as a Roman fort, with further fortifications being added in the medieval period. It was here in 1716 that the Turkish army were soundly defeated by the forces of Prince Eugene of Savoy. Most of what remains of the fortress today dates from around this time.

A large part of Novi Sad was destroyed in 1848 during a garrison revolt by Hungarian soldiers, who bombarded the city from their vantage point for a number of months. They were finally tricked into surrendering but only after they had succeeded in flattening almost two-thirds of the town. Consequently, much of what remains today dates from the latter part of the 19th century and after.

During World War II, Novi Sad was once again occupied by Hungarian troops, this time by those of the Axis persuasion, while across the Danube in Petrovaradin, Croatian Ustaša troops had control.

With the NATO attacks against Slobodan Milošcvić's rogue-state Yugoslavia in the spring of 1999, Novi Sad came once more under bombardment and went on to suffer greater casualties than the capital did in terms of human life, environmental pollution and destroyed infrastructure. The attacks came as a surreal spectacle for the city's bemused population. It was hard to understand just why they were being targeted: few of them were fans of their leader's nationalist policies and besides, Kosovo, the epicentre of the hostilities, was at the other end of the country. NATO missiles first struck the city on March 24 1999. In the days that followed, further attacks hit two of the bridges that connected Novi Sad with Petrovaradin and Sremska Kamenica south of the river. On April 5 Novi Sad's oil refinery was hit for the first time, releasing a large cloud of toxic smoke over the city. Another attack on the refinery came two days later as NATO attempted to destroy the third of the city's bridges. The oil refinery continued to be targeted and, on the night of April 16, explosions that occurred there released dangerous chemicals into the atmosphere. The third of the bridges – the Zezeljev Bridge – was finally rendered useless after the attacks of April 20. The bombing campaign continued until April 28, by which time the oil refinery had been hit once again and the city's TV transmitter, sited in the Fruška Gora to the south, had been damaged.

Getting there

Novi Sad has excellent bus and rail connections with the rest of the country. The train station (tel: 443 200) and long-distance bus station (444 021, 444 022, 444 023) sit side by side on the north side of the town about 1km from the city centre.

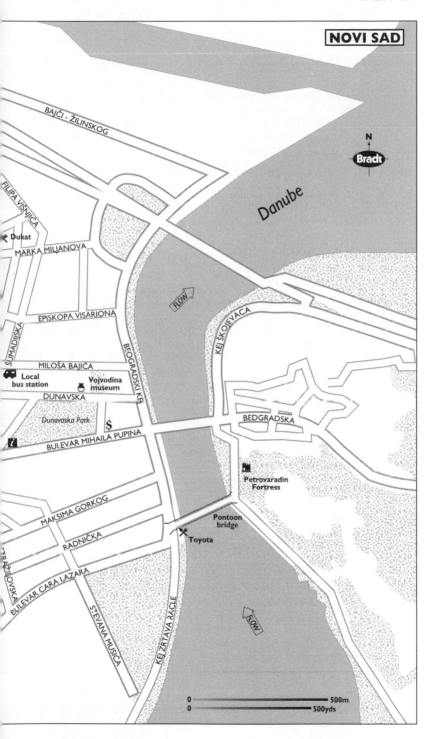

NOVI SAD

N

Danube

BAJČI - ŽILINSKOG

FILIPA VIŠNJIĆA

← Dukat

MARKA MILJANOVA

EPISKOPA VISARIONA

ŠUMADIJSKA

MILOŠA BAJIĆA

Local
bus station

Vojvodina
museum

DUNAVSKA

Dunavska Park

BULEVAR MIHAILA PUPINA

BEOGRADSKI KEJ

FLOW

KEJ ŠKOJEVACA

BEDGRADSKA

Petrovaradin
Fortress

MAKSIMA GORKOG

RADNIČKA

TRAŽILOVSKA

BULEVAR CARA LAZARA

STEVANA MUSIĆA

KEJ ZTAVA RACLE

Pontoon
bridge

Toyota

FLOW

0   500m
0   500yds

By bus

There are over 30 buses a day that link Novi Sad with Belgrade; some of these are express buses that use the motorway, while others are slower and stop more frequently along the way. Fares are between 150–250din depending on the speed of the service. The larger towns in Vojvodina like Subotica and Zrenjanin are also well-connected, with at least ten departures a day, but even more distant destinations like Niš or Novi Pazar have at least one direct daily service. The bus station has the usual facilities you would expect: restaurant, cafés, snack kiosks, *garderoba*, pay toilets, but no tourist information or currency exchange. Large Cyrillic timetables, inside and out, give full details of the services to and from Novi Sad.

By train

All of the trains that link Belgrade with Budapest and the north stop in Novi Sad and so there are relatively good rail connections too. Originating in Belgrade, two trains a day serve Budapest and Vienna, one in the morning and one late at night. Of the domestic services, 11 trains leave daily for Subotica, three run to Sombor, two to Zrenjanin and there is an overnight service to Bar on the Montenegrin coast. The trains that run to Belgrade are generally a little slower than the bus but they are also slightly cheaper. The exceptions are the international services that stop here en route to the capital.

Air and water links

Novi Sad has no airport for commercial traffic, but it is only one hour's drive from Belgrade's Surcin Airport.

Sadly, river transport linking Novi Sad and Belgrade is now a thing of the past, although the Putnik travel agency may revive a tourist service between the two cities sometime in the future.

Local bus

Closer destinations in the immediate Novi Sad area are served by the **Riblja pijaca suburban bus station** by the fish market in the city centre (tel: 527 399). This has regular services to Sremska Karlovci, Sremska Kamenica, Begeč and Veternik and other villages close to the city. There is a rather confusing timetable (in Cyrillic) and an information window at the station. It is probably best to ask about bus times rather than trust what is written.

Getting around
City bus

Most of what you will want to see in Novi Sad is close enough to visit on foot but a couple of the city bus services are useful, in particular those that link the city centre with the long-distance bus and railway stations. To reach the city centre from the bus or train station take the 11b bus that passes right to left along Bulevar Jaše Tomića in front of the stations on the opposite side of the road. The bus stop is at the corner of Bulevar Oslobođenja, the main road into the centre. To reach the long-distance bus or train station, take the 11a bus from Riblja pijaca suburban bus station. This will drop you off immediately in front of the stations, opposite the Hotel Novi Sad. The fare is 15din and you pay the driver.

Taxi

To take a taxi from the train or bus station to a central hotel should not cost much more than 100din. The following are reliable taxi firms that can be called by phone.

Dobro jutro Tel: 322 22
Dunav Tel: 451 111
Express Tel: 524 144, 522 422
Gradski Tel: 400 555
NS Plus Tel: 522 622
Pan Tel: 455 555, 455 530
Pink Tel: 653 333
SOS Tel: 450 400

Car hire
Autu-Tehna Doo Stevana Mokrnjica 1; tel: 512 343, 512 115
Avis Balzakova 29; tel: 469 655
Inex Stražilovska 3; tel: 526 666
Putnik Kralja Aleksandra 18; tel: 529 719
YU Hertz S Mokranjca 30; tel: 528 450; fax: 323 609

Tourist information
Novi Sad is fortunate in having an excellent **tourist information centre** with an efficient and dedicated staff (9 Mihajla Pupina Bulevar; tel/fax: 421 811, 421 812, 451 481; email: ticns@ptt.yu; www.novisadtourism.com and www.novisadtourism.org.yu). The helpful, English-speaking staff can provide visitors with city maps, museum information and details of current events, as well as advising on accommodation and transport. They have numerous brochures available detailing the city's museums and galleries, as well as booklets on aspects of Novi Sad's diverse ethnic make-up and history.

Local tour operators
In many ways tourism is more developed in Novi Sad than it is in Belgrade. Below are listed the main operators in the city.

Autoturist Mite Ružica 2; tel: 523 863, 451 156; email: turista@eunet.yu. This operator runs trips to the Fruška Gora monasteries and the wine cellars at Irig. They also do excursions to Sremska Karlovci and Kovilj Kulpin.
Etno Art Travel Bulevar cara Lazara 29; tel: 360 587, 466 940; email: office@etnoarttravel.co.yu; www.etnoarttravel.co.yu As their name implies, Etno Art arrange tours with an artistic dimension. They run tours around the city's churches, as well as something they call 'Bohemian Rhapsody': a 2-night tour of the old town and Petrovaradin Fortress, which includes a tour of the galleries below the fortress. They can also organise visits to Kovilj monastery and the Sremska Karlovci wine cellars. Another of their excursions is an art weekend tour that takes in most of the art galleries and museums of Novi Sad. This includes a theatre show and lunch in a national restaurant.
Magelan Corporation Zamaj Jovina 23; tel: 420 680, 423 524; email: office@magelancorp.co.yu; www.magelancorp.co.yu and www.visitnovisad.co.yu. Magelan provide a wide range of services: they run walking tours of Novi Sad and Petrovaradin Fortress (minimum 4 persons); 'Old timer' city tours (minimum 2), full- and half-day boat trips on the Danube (minimum 6–8), Fruška Gora walking and herb-gathering tours of 3–8 hours (minimum 6); mountain-bike tours of Fruška Gora that last between 2–8 hours (minimum 6); full-day visits to the Fruška Gora monasteries; full-day birdwatching/photo-safari tours of Fruška Gora with a guide (6–10 persons), and Sremski Karlovci wine and honey excursions. They can also organise longer trips that take in more of Vojvodina and Serbia (see *Practical Information* chapter).
Market Tours Bulevar Cara Lazara 55; tel: 367 612, 468 409; email: office@markettours.co.yu; www.markettours.co.yu. Market Tours organise Danube boat tours between April and October (minimum requirement: 5 persons). They can also arrange fishing

weekends (or weeks) on the Danube, as well as Fruška Gora monastery tours and Sremska Karlovci vineyard visits. They are able to provide fishing permits and rent out boats for those with an interest in fishing.

Transfer Turizam and Sport Stražilovska 1; tel: 400 066, 400 079, 521 577, 610 560; fax: 309 078; email: transns@eunet.yu; www.transfer.co.yu. This agency arranges a variety of tours around Novi Sad, the Danube, and the Petrovaradin Fortress. The minimum number of participants required is 5 for a van, and 25 for a bus. They also organise Fruška Gora monastery trips to Krušedol, Grgrteg and Hopovo that include lunch for 1,800din by minibus (groups of 5–8) or 2,200din by coach (groups of 25+).

Where to stay

As you might expect for a city of this size, there is a reasonable variety of places to stay, both state-owned and private. There are no luxurious five-star hotels in the city but there are plenty of reasonable mid-range choices. It is highly likely that more small private hotels and pensions will open up in the future.

Private hotels

Hotel Park Novosadkog sajma 35; tel: 611 711, 621 161; fax: 27 682; email: park@nspoint.net. This massive hotel is situated well away from the city centre, close to Futog Park and the site of the Novi Sad Fair and Sajmiste Sports Centre. With 7 conference halls and a congress hall, this hotel is clearly aimed at businessmen. Having about 300 rooms in total, it is unlikely that this hotel ever fills completely. The hotel was closed 'temporarily' in 2004 but will reopen in 2005 as a 4- or 5-star privately run hotel.

Pansion (or **Boardinghouse**) **Rimski** Jovana Cvijića 25; tel/fax: 443 231, 443 237, 333 587; email: rimski@eunet.yu; www.rimski.co.yu. This is a privately run hotel, first opened in 2001, that is located in a quiet street fairly close to the bus and railway stations. There are 23 rooms and 3 luxury apartments, all complete with bathroom, central heating, cable TV, telephone and minibar. The hotel has a restaurant with a no-smoking section and a conference room. Single occupancy is €48; double, €64.

Villa Una Avijatičarska 9; tel: 518 101, 310 867, 311 428; mob: 063 82 66 332; fax: 321 911. Not really a traditional hotel but a new (2002) purpose-built complex, aimed mainly at businessmen, where you can rent a private apartment with 2, 3 or 4 beds. Villa Una is situated 4km away from the city centre and 2km from the railway and bus stations, in a quiet suburb close to the Novi Sad Fair. The apartments are equipped with cable TV, kitchens, coffee-making machines, hairdryers, AC and bathrooms with tubs. Prices range between €40 and €60 per person.

Pansion (or **Boardinghouse**) **Zenit★★★** Zmaj Jovina 8; tel: 621 444; fax: 621 327; email: office@pansionzenit.co.yu; www.pansionzenit.co.yu. This cosy, well-run private hotel is right in the heart of the city centre just off Trg Slobode. Although its front entrance is through a pedestrian arcade, it has its own private parking area at the rear, reached by going along Ilije Ognjanovića by the Putnik hotel. With just 15 rooms, it tends to fill quite fast. The rooms are modern, airy and quiet although the inner-facing rooms that lack outside windows are not such a good deal. Free coffee and internet access are available around the clock. Single rooms are 4,100din; doubles, 4,700din, inner-facing rooms, 3,500din.

State-owned hotels

Hotel Vojvodina★★★ Trg Slobode 2; tel: 622 122; fax: 615 445; email: vojvodinahtl@neobee.net. This establishment, built in 1854, is the city's oldest hotel and has a very convenient central location right next to the Catholic cathedral and the City Hall. It has 37 double rooms, 21 single rooms and 2 apartments in all. There is a fountain, a small bar and a comfortable sitting area in the upstairs lobby. The cavernous restaurant downstairs, where breakfast is served, is usually empty. The rooms are light and spacious,

Above Medieval Stari Užice
fortress, Užice (LM)

Right Golubac fortress on Danube,
Đerdap National Park (LM)

Below Bee-eater, *Merops apiaster*,
Deliblatska Peščara nature reserve (LS)

Right Bicycles and Secessionist buildings, Subotica, Vojvodina (LM)

Below Art-nouveau Modern Art Gallery, Subotica, Vojvodina (LM)

and some of them look out over Trg Slobode. Single rooms cost 1,800–2,400din, depending on whether or not you choose to have a TV set and a king-size bed; double rooms are 2,600–3,200din; triples go for 3,300din; apartments, 3,600–5000din.

Hotel Putnik*** Ilije Ognjanovića 26; tel: 615 555; fax: 622 561. This is another state-run hotel just around the corner from the Hotel Vojvodina, with its own casino. 63 double rooms and 22 singles. The hotel's promotional material claims that it is 'furnished with beds suitable for sportsmen', whatever that means. Prices are slightly more expensive than the Hotel Vojvodina.

Hotel Novi Sad*** Bulevar Jaše Tomića bb; tel: 442 511; fax: 443 072; email: hupns@aspoint.net. With 78 doubles and 24 single rooms, this large, traditional hotel is very convenient for the bus and train stations but at some distance from the city centre. It has a 250-seat restaurant, conference hall, cocktail bar, discotheque and bar. Single rooms cost 2,300din; doubles, 3,200din.

Hotel Sajam*** Hajduk Veljkova 11; tel: 420 266; fax: 420 265; email: htl"sajam"@eunet.yu. The Sajam is another hotel located close to the site of the Novi Sad Fair, 2km from the city centre. It has a restaurant with a capacity of 500, parking for 300, and laundry service. Rooms on the first floor are air conditioned. 51 double rooms, 4 singles and 6 apartments. The room rate is about the same as the Hotel Putnik.

Budget

Pansion Fontana Pašićeva 27; tel: 621 760. The Fontana restaurant, close to the city centre, has a few rooms to rent above its dining area. The rooms are simply furnished but clean and pleasant. Breakfast is served in the courtyard below. Twin rooms go for 1,500din for single occupancy, 2,000din for double.

Bela Lađa Kisačka 21; tel: 616 594; email: resbelaladja@yahoo.com; www.belaladja.com. This is another friendly family restaurant with a couple of rooms to rent – probably the cheapest deal in town. The rooms are clean but rather cramped, with thin partition walls. The single, shared bathroom is on the landing. It costs €15 for single occupancy, €20 for double.

Hostels

The city's only hostel is the recently opened **Hostel Brankovo kolo** (Episkopa Visariona 3; tel: 528 263, 422 784, 622 160; email: office@hostelns.com; www.hostelns.com). This smart, modern hostel, with a good central location, has a total of 311 beds in two-, three- and four-bedded rooms. Although it is set up for large groups of young people, it also welcomes individual travellers. The facilities include: a large meeting room, dining room seating 80, garden, basketball court, two study rooms and a TV/DVD room. Internet access is available, with five PC terminals. The hostel charges €8 per person in a two bed room, €7 in a three-bed room and €6 in a four-bed room. Breakfast is available for €1.50. Unfortunately the hostel is only open in summer: from July 1 until August 25. Bookings can be made online at www.hostelns.com/onlinebooking.htm.

Other accommodation

Varadin Petrovaradinska tvrdjava 8; tel/fax: 431 122, 431 184; email: office@varadin.com. This hotel at Petrovaradin Fortress now operates as a state-owned boarding house.

Voyager Apartments Stražilovska 16; tel: 453 711, 453 712; email: voyager@neobee.net; www.voyagerns.co.yu. Well-equipped city apartments that can be rented for short or long stays for around €40 per person per night.

The **Danube Cottages Resort** Fisherman's Island at Kameničcka ada bb; tel: 466 977, 466 978; email: ribarac@eunet.yu; fax: 366 801. The resort has 42 cottages each with private bathroom. These facilities, just outside the city limits, are geared towards Serbian vacationers but might be suitable for those who desire more of a holiday atmosphere. There are 6 dining halls at the resort, together with a café, a library, conference hall and parking for 250 cars.

Also away from the centre, on the main road north, are two **motels** for those travelling by car:

Motel Jet Set Temerinski put 41; tel: 414 511; email: jetset@eunet.yu. The accommodation here consists of 8 double, 1 single and 2 triple rooms. There is a conference hall and a national restaurant with seating for 150. Rooms €30–40.

Motel Bor Temerinski put 57a; tel: 412 424, 419 215; email: bor@visitnovisad.com. The motel has 12 single, 12 double and 5 triple rooms, as well as its own restaurant. Prices are between €20–50 per person.

The satellite town of **Sremska Kamenica**, 5km away in Srem across the Danube, has a few more options for those who do not wish or need to be in the city centre.

Pansion Olimp Miloša Obilića 8; tel/fax: 463 295. With 2 single, 1 double and 2 triple room.

Pansion Kordun Moše Pijade 10a; tel: 462 860; email: kordun@neobee.net. Kordun is a small private pension that has 3 double rooms, 2 triples and 2 quadruples. There is a restaurant, a café, outdoor parking with 30 places and a lock-up garage with 5 places.

Bed and Breakfast Evangelina Branislava Bukurova 2; tel: 464 111, 463 681, 464 222; fax: 463 681; email: tehnunion@eunet.yu; www.tehnounion.co.yu. 15 double rooms and 1 single, restaurant, bar, parking with video surveillance.

Motel Ilića Ledinački put 1; tel/fax: 461 158. This is a small motel with 20 rooms that has its own restaurant and private parking for guests.

Where to eat and drink

Novi Sad is well provided with restaurants of every type. The squares and pedestrian areas around Trg Slobode, Modene and Zmaj Jovina are full of bars, cafés and pizzerias with plentiful outdoor seating in the warmer months of the year. Of the traditional restaurants, several places have *alaska čorba* on the menu, a local, paprika-rich fish soup. Paprika is used widely in Vojvodina cookery, part of the Hungarian legacy. The Vojvodina wines on offer at many of these restaurants are well worth sampling too, particularly those from the vineyards of Sremska Karlovci in Fruška Gora and those from Vršac in the east of the province.

Restaurants

Alas Daničićeva 9. This is a restaurant that specialises in fish dishes but which has all the standard grilled meat options too.

Alaska koliba Kamenička ada bb; tel: 365 683

Alla Lanterna Dunavska 27; tel: 622 022. This is a very popular pasta and pizza place at the end of the pedestrian stretch of Dunavska. Inside, there is a vaulted ceiling with wrought-iron chandeliers hanging from it. All of the walls are elaborately decorated with tiles and patterns made with pebbles that have been cemented in place. The English menu has a few vegetarian items on it, as well as a wide selection of pizzas. The pasta dishes like *spaghetti carbonara* and *arrabiatta* are also very good and reasonably priced. In winter, the tables fill quickly and you may have to wait, especially on weekend nights; in summer, the situation is generally easier as more tables are placed outside on the street. Open 08.00–midnight.

Bela Lađa Kišacka 21; tel: 616 594. A traditional restaurant that offers local dishes and a wide selection of Vojvodina wines at very reasonable prices. There is traditional music to accompany your meal most nights. On the house on the other side of the street is a plaque indicating that Einstein lived here for two years between 1903 and 1905: his wife was from Novi Sad.

Beli Lav Zmaj Jovina 28; tel: 452 788. This 4-star restaurant is considered one of the best in Novi Sad. The food is mostly Italian, with *antipasti* from 250din, pasta dishes from 300din and meat dishes starting at 500din. The fish dishes are good, but expensive. Open Mon–Fri 10.00–23.00, Sat 10.00–midnight, closed Sun.

Borsalino Vere Pavlović. A small, above-average pizzeria that is located a little off the usual tourist beat.

Bulevar Bulevar Mihaila Pupina 11. This cheap and cheerful restaurant, close to Dunav Park, is probably the best-value place to eat in town because of its student clientele. Do not expect any sort of divine culinary experience, however.

Chicken Tikka Stadium 'FC Vojvodina'. If you hanker after the UK's favourite dish you could come here and try the Vojvodina version. The restaurant is located outside Novi Sad's main football ground.

Dukat Đorđa Rakovića 12; tel: 525 190; www.dukat.co.yu. Dukat is a smart 4-star family restaurant that serves traditional dishes in an elegant setting. It has live music on some nights.

Dunavska Oaza Dunavska 25; tel: 528 028. Located on one of the city's prime pedestrian streets, this is another restaurant that specialises in fish dishes. There is a tank from which you can make your selection if you are not too squeamish about these things. Otherwise, there are plenty of standard meat items on the menu. A meal of soup, main course, salad and wine should come to about 700din.

Fontana Pašićeva 17; tel: 621 779. Fontana is a Serbian restaurant, located just off Zmaj Jovina, that has several wooden-panelled rooms inside, and a pleasant courtyard with secluded seating around a fountain outside. There is live folk music here some nights.

Gradska Kafana Sutjeska 2. This restaurant is located inside the SPENS Sports and Business Centre; the emphasis is on Serbian national cuisine.

Kuca Mala Laze Teleckog 4. A pleasant pizzeria with plenty of choices.

La Forza Katolicka porta 6; tel: 615 049. La Forza is a pizzeria run by the same family concern as Dukat. Open 08.00–23.00 daily except Sun.

Lipa 7–9 Svetozara Miletića. Located on a street that runs off Zmaj Jovina, this restaurant has a good selection of national dishes at moderate prices.

Marina Trg Mladenaca 4; tel: 424 353. This is a café-bar-restaurant by the Registry Office arch at Trg Mladenaca, which serves fairly standard Serbian and Italian fare. The pizzas are both large and tasty. There is a separate dining area with a pleasant atmosphere but this is spoiled to some extent by the loud music that emanates from the bar area.

McDonald's Trg Slobode, opposite the National Theatre.

Ognjište Dimitrija Tucovića 3; tel/fax: 450 594; email: restoran@ognjiste.net; www.ognjiste.net. Ognjište is a cosy, traditional restaurant that is decorated in a style something like a *hajduk*'s hideout, with dusty antiques, quaint wooden furniture, old lamps and all manner of curiosities hanging from the walls. This friendly restaurant, tucked away behind the football stadium, serves typical Serbian dishes at very reasonable prices. You can take a virtual tour of the premises by visiting the website above.

Plava Frajla Sutjeska 2; tel: 613 675, 622 222. This is another moderately priced restaurant in the SPENS Sports and Business Centre that specialises in Vojvodina cuisine.

Ribarsko Ostrvo (Fishing Island) Kamenička ada bb; tel: 365 683. A restaurant that not surprisingly specialises in fish dishes.

Sečuan Dunavska 16; tel: 529 693. This is a reasonable 3-star Chinese restaurant close to the bottom of the pedestrian part of Dunavska. As well as Sichuan cuisine and *dim sum*, it also serves Serbian dishes.

Surabaja Primorska 26; tel: 413 400; fax: 414 130. This is a rare thing in Serbia – an Indonesian restaurant. Surabaja is located next to the Apollo Business and Shopping Centre, close to the National Theatre. It also serves Chinese food. Open daily 09.00–midnight except Sun.

Trag Preradovićeva 2, Petrovaradin; tel: 431 989. A traditional Serbian restaurant located across the Danube in Petrovaradin.

Tvrđava Petrovaradinska tvrđva; tel: 431 122. A national restaurant situated on the terrace of Petrovaradin Fortress looking down on the Danube River. It is the view that you pay for here, although prices are reasonable enough.

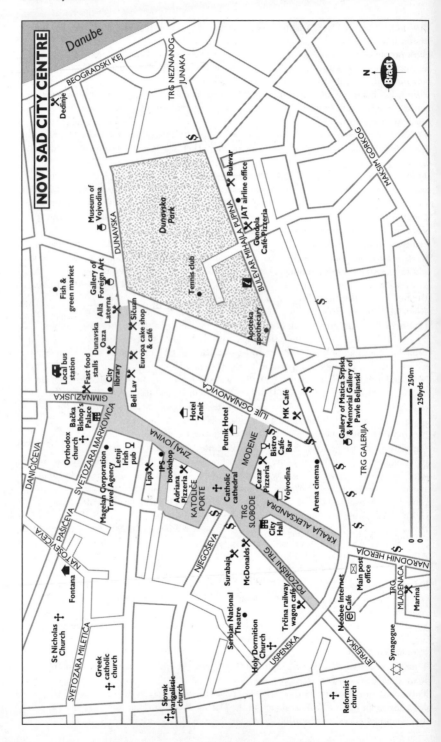

NOVI SAD CITY CENTRE

Bars, cafés, snacks and take-aways

Bistro Café Modene 4. This excellent establishment serves good coffee and draught beer in a plain, no-nonsense bar with a convivial atmosphere. The prices are perhaps the cheapest in the city centre, with cappuccino for 30din and half-litres of *točeno pivo* (draught beer) for 50din. In summer, there is also seating on a terrace outside.

Europa postlastičarnica Dunavska 6. This café-patisserie is an excellent place to stop for coffee and cakes.

Lila Café Zmaj Jovina 21; tel: 528 432. The Lila is a good choice for its superb cakes and traditional sweet dishes like *žito*. Generous portions of *torte* cost about 70din.

MK Caffe Bulevar Mihaila Pupina 5; tel: 615 700. MK is a smart café which, despite the dreaded Fashion TV, has a pleasant atmosphere and serves good coffee and juices.

Picerija Cezar Modene 2; tel: 623 538. A central pizzeria that has seating inside and out, and which sells pizza by the slice, either to eat on the premises or to take away. It also sells several varieties of *burek* and *pita*, like mushroom and potato – all excellent – as well as sandwiches.

Zepellin Beogradska kej, by the pontoon bridge. This is a curiosity more than anything: a boat that is a café, a restaurant and a Toyota car showroom! In theory, at least, you can arrange a test drive of the latest 4WD as you sip your cappuccino. Cars aside, it does offer a very good vantage point over the river, although most visitors here are probably happier watching the traffic cross the bridge.

For **fast food**, as well as the places on Modene mentioned above, there is a concentration of food kiosks on Gimnazijska at the side of the Bishop's Palace and at the Fish Market bus station.

Nightlife
Clubs

The club scene is nowhere near as big as it is in Belgrade. Check with the tourist office for what is currently hot. Below are a few suggestions:

Absolut Zmaj Jovina 10
Big Mama Zmaj Jovina 2; tel: 613 442
Foxtrot Fotoška 23, tel: 622 904
Jazz Club Đ Jakšića–Natoševićeva. A live music venue.
Scena Pozorište mladih, Ignjasa Pavlasa 4. Live music on most nights.
Trema SNP, Pozorišni trg 1; tel: 451 232

Practicalities
Airline offices

JAT Bulevar Mihaila Pupina 18; tel: 456 177

Post and telephone services

The main **post office** and **telephone centre** is on the corner of Bulevar Mihajla Pupina and Narodnih Heroja. The telephone centre is open 24 hours a day; there are also Halo payphones outside.

Banks

There is no shortage of banks and places to change money in Novi Sad. Those listed below all have ATMs for cash withdrawal.

Delta banka Bulevar Mihaila Pupina 4
Komercijalna banka Bulevar Kralja Petra 11
Novosadska banka Bulevar Mihaila Pupina 3
Vojvodanska banka Trg Slobode 7

Internet cafés
Cyber Caffe Futoška 4
Internet Caffe Bulevar Oslobođenja 63
Internet Caffe Ilije Ognojanovića
Internet Caffe 'Informatika' Bulevar Oslobođenja 100
Internet NET Studio Stražilovska 10
Neobee Net Caffe Jevrejska 1/I. this is a little hard to find, tucked away on the first floor, in an alleyway close to the synagogue. The connection is good and fast, and costs only 30din per hour.

Cinemas
Arena Bulevar Mihaila Pupina 3
Cultural Centre Katolicka porta 5
Jadran Postanska 5
Vojvodina SPENS Sports and Business Centre, Sutlejska 2

Theatres
Novi Sad Theatre – Ujvideki Szinhaz Jovana Subotica 3–5; tel: 525 552, 622 592; email: office@uvszinhaz.co.yu; www.uvszinhaz.co.yu
Portal Teatar Stevana Mokranjca 16; tel: 063 846 1880; email: portalteatar@neobee.net; www.portaltheatre.org.yu
Serbian National Theatre Pozorišni trg 1; tel: 451 452, 613 957, 20 991, 621 411; email: uprava@snp.org.yu; www.snp.org.yu
Theatre – Pozorište Mladih Ignjata Pavlasa 8; tel: 525 884, 520 543, 623 210

Shopping
Souvenirs
City Sales Gallery Zmaj Jovina 22 – Ilije Ognjanovića 4; tel: 421 651; email: citygalery@yahoo.com
Collection Novi Sad – Guernica Gundulićeva 29; tel: 528 326; fax: 457 372; email: brdesign@eunet.yu
Eko dar (Eco Gift) Zmaj Jovina 23; tel: 451 296
Ethno Art Travel Bulevar Cara Lazara 26; tel: 360 587, 365 341, 466 940
Novi Sad Kibicfenster Stražilovska 21; tel: 522 663, 522 944, 063 88 14 734; email: nsbros@eunet.yu
NS Škrinja Dunavska 18; tel: 063 412 169

Bookshops
Not surprisingly for a cultured city with a large student population there are plenty of good bookshops to be found scattered around the centre. The ones listed below stock a reasonable amount of English-language material.

IPS Bookstore 16 Zmaj Jovina; tel: 615 097. Probably has the best selection as well as having a wide choice of CDs and DVDs.
Jovan Jovanovic Zmaj Bookshop Pozorišni Trg 6; tel: 529 354; www.nolit.co.yu. Open Mon–Sat 07.30–20.00.
Stari proster Žarka Zrenjanina 18; tel: 525 365. This bookshop has a good range of books on Novi Sad and Vojvodina in English, as well as a comprehensive selection of local maps.
Stilos Vladimira Perića Valtera 2; tel: 350 371; email: stylos@eunet.yu
Vuk Karadžić 9 Zmaj Jovina; tel: 615 200
Znaje Sremska 7; tel: 624 433; email: zavodz@eunet.yu; www.zavod.co.yu

In the **SPENS** Sport and Business Centre at Sutjeska 2, there is **MB Libro** (tel: 622 134; email: librobookshop@neobee.net) and **Solaris** (tel: 624 387; email: knijgaso@eunet.yu).

What to see and do

Most of the city's sights are within a small area of the centre. The hub is spacious **Trg Slobode**, with the neo-Gothic brick-clad Roman Catholic cathedral on one side of the square and the City Hall facing it on the other. In the centre of the square stands a statue of **Svetozar Miletić**, one of the most prominent Serbian politicians of the 19th century – a 1939 creation of the seemingly ubiquitous Ivan Meštrović. The figure, in a strident, almost ranting, pose faces towards the cathedral, his back turned on the elegant **City Hall**, a neo-Renaissance, two-storey building that is contemporary with the cathedral and dates from 1895. The building is a copy of the town hall in Graz, Austria. The **Roman Catholic cathedral** (*'Katedrala'* – *Rimokatolicka zupna crkva imena marijina*) opposite was built on the site of a former 18th-century church, and has three naves and a 76m-high tower. It is not a cathedral at all – the seat of Bačka's diocese is actually further north in Subotica – but rather, a parish church dedicated to Mary. Over the years it has been its impressive size, rather than its ecclesiastical status, that has caused it to be known as the 'cathedral'. The interior is richly carved, with four altars and 20 windows designed by Czech and Hungarian stained-glass craftsmen.

The pedestrian area of the square continues along café-lined **Zmaj Jovina** to the Bačka Bishop's Palace at its eastern end and the Orthodox cathedral just beyond this. The **Bačka Bishop's Palace** (*Vladicanski dvor*) is the residential palace of the Serbian Orthodox bishop in Novi Sad. It was constructed in 1901 on the site of a former palace that dated from 1741. The building style is curiously eclectic: a mix of secessionist and Serbian Romanticism, with pseudo-Moorish plasterwork decoration on red brick. In front of the palace stands a statue of **Zmaj Jovana Jovanović**, the city's famous doctor and poet.

The **Orthodox Cathedral Church of St George** (*Sabornn crkva svetog Georgija*) lies just behind the palace. The present church was erected on the same site as an older one from 1734, which was burnt out, like so much else, by the Hungarian shelling of the city in 1848 and 1849. The restoration took place between 1860 and 1880, with a second phase of work from 1902–05, when the belltower was erected. Inside, there is a total of 33 icons on the iconostasis and two larger icons by the local painter Paja Jovanović who also designed the stained-glass windows.

Leading off from here is the pedestrian street of **Dunavska**, one of the city's most attractive thoroughfares with many 18th- and 19th-century buildings. The **City Library** (1895) is on the corner with Gimnazijska and further down, close to the junction with Ignatja Pavlasa, is the **Gallery of Foreign Art** at number 29. Beyond here, the street runs along the edge of a pleasant park with a small lake – **Dunavska Park** – a leafy escape from the city bustle.

Continuing along Dunavska past the park, you soon arrive at the busy traffic artery of Beogradski kej and the wide river Danube just beyond it, with a superb view of Petrovaradin Fortress looming high above the opposite bank of the river. The three bridges that formerly crossed the river were all destroyed during the 1999 NATO bombing raids – two have since been replaced while the third, the most southerly, is a temporary structure on pontoons. The nearest bridge, and the most direct route to the fortress, has a plaque that reads: '*Varadinski Most – original one destroyed April 1st 1999 by NATO, killing citizen of Novi Sad Oleg. M. Najov, aged 29*'. Nearby is a small statue of a man playing a tamburitza who looks uncannily like Alfred Hitchcock. It is not the film maker, however, but a memorial to a local musician: '*Janko Balaž 1925–1988*'.

Returning to the Orthodox cathedral, and walking northwest along Pašićeva, you come to the entrance of the grounds of the church of St Nicholas located in a quiet, shady corner between Pašićeva and Đurejakšića streets. The small **St Nicholas Church** (Nikolejevska crkva) is the oldest Orthodox church in Novi Sad, mentioned in official records from 1739 as the endowment of the Bogadanović family, wealthy merchants in the city at that time. The church served as both a Serbian and a Greek Orthodox place of worship for many years. It was damaged in the 1849 bombardment of the city, and again in 1862, after which it was renovated at the expense of benefactors Jovan and Marija Trandafil. The church, unusually, has a small gold-plated onion dome in the style of a Russian Orthodox church. This was probably a symbolic response to the generous donations it received from the Russian Church after being damaged in the 1862 uprising. Mileva and Albert Einstein's sons were christened here in 1913.

There are many more churches dotted around Novi Sad, which is to be expected given the multi-ethnic make-up of the city. Scattered around the city centre are the places of worship of a broad range of denominations: as well as Orthodox and Roman Catholic there are Greek-Catholic, Reformist, Pentecostal, Adventist, Slovak-Evangelistic, Baptist and Methodist. There is also a synagogue – before World War II Novi Sad had a sizeable Jewish population.

The **synagogue** is on Jevrejska ('Jew Street') at number 9, with other important buildings previously owned by the Jewish community flanking it on both sides. The whole complex, all constructed using the same light-yellowish brick, was built in 1909, designed by the architect Lipot Baumhorn (1860–1932). The synagogue – a three-nave basilica, smaller but similar in design to that in Szeged, Hungary – was the fifth to be built on exactly the same spot. It has stained-glass windows throughout and a large rose window facing the street, along with golden letters in Hebrew that spell out the invitation: 'This is the house of worship for all nations'. The building came through World War II relatively unscathed, serving at the end of the war as a collective centre for Jews deported to the concentration camps. Services were revived in 1945 but ten years later nearly all of Novi Sad's surviving Jewish community migrated to Israel, leaving the building largely redundant as a place of worship. In 1991 the synagogue was handed over to the city for a period of 25 years. It is now a regular concert venue for both classical music and jazz. The building next door at number 7, formerly a Jewish school, currently serves as a ballet school.

Walking back along Jevrejska from the synagogue, the city's main post office dominates the corner with Bulevar Mihajla Pupina. Immediately behind this is the small wedge-shaped square of Trg Mladenaca ('Newlyweds Square') by the Registry Office, with a curious Baroque-looking arch in the centre, purpose-built for wedding- photo opportunities. Crossing the road back towards Trg Slobode you cannot fail to miss the vast concrete structure of the **Serbian National Theatre** at Pozorisni Trg (Theatre Square). The building is large – very large (ground area: 20,000m²) – and seems rather out of scale with its surroundings, having more the appearance of a university campus building or a conference centre rather than a theatre. There are three stages inside, the largest of which seats 700.

Museums and galleries

The city has a number of excellent galleries and museums, which, in most cases, are efficiently organised and well-run. The tourist office can advise on specific interests but a brief overview is detailed below. Note that winter opening hours (from November to March) may be more restrictive than those given. Check before visit.

Collection of Rajko Mamuzić Vase Stajić 1; tel: 520 467

This collection represents the work of post-World War II Serbian/Yugoslav painters. It was presented to the city of Novi Sad as a gift in 1972.
Open 09.00–17.00; closed Mon and Tue

Gallery of Matica Srpska Trg Galerija 1; tel: 421 455; email: galmats@eunet.yu
This collection was founded by Matica Srpska in Budapest in 1826 and opened to the public in 1847. In 1864 the gallery was transferred to Novi Sad and it was placed in its current building in 1958. The gallery, one of the best collections of paintings in the country, represents Serbian artists working in Vojvodina from the 17th to the 20th century.

The collection is spread throughout 19 rooms, and laid out in chronological order. The ground floor is given over to copies of frescos taken from various Fruška Gora monasteries. The works on the first floor are mostly by 18th-century artists, and are largely of a religious nature and by unknown artists. In the rooms representing the 19th century, the work of Pavle Simić (1818–76) and Đura Jakšić (1832–78) features heavily but there are also some fine, very human portraits by Pavel Burković (1772–1830) and by Nikola Alexsić (1811–73), whose women all seem to wear a provocative expression that lies somewhere between conspiratorial and sexually precocious. Displayed among the works from the early 20th century are the rather sinister self-portraits of Stefan Meksić (1876–1923). In one of these, a worried-looking man is portrayed smoking a cigar and drinking wine while a violin-playing skeleton leers at him from over his shoulder: clearly the work of an artist preoccupied with his own mortality. Other artists from this period, like Šerban, have work that displays a riot of impressionistic colour – like Van Gogh on acid – while experimental artists like Sava Šumanović (1896–1942), who was killed by Croatian Ustaše during World War II, have works like *Sailor with Pipe* (1920–21) and *Two Nudes* (1930) that display both structuralist and cubist influences.
Open Tue, Wed, Thu and Sat, 10.00–18.00, Fri 12.00–20.00, closed Sun and Mon. Entrance, 50din

Institute for the Protection of Nature in Serbia Radnička 20a; tel: 421 143, 421 144; email: zzpsns@eunet.yu
The Institute has a collection of over 60,000 items from various fields of study: geology, palaeontology, botany, ornithology etc. Among an extensive display of animal skeletons, stuffed birds, dioramas and fossils the most impressive item is the skull and tusks of a woolly mammoth from the Pleistocene period.
Open 08.00–19.00

Museum of Vojvodina Dunavska 35–7; tel: 420 566; email: musejvojvodine@nscable.net
This large, rambling, but excellent museum is housed in two buildings next door to each other opposite Dunavska Park. The museum at number 35 deals in the archaeology, earlier history and ethnology of the province, from Palaeolithic origins right up to the *belle époque* period of the late 19th century. At number 37 next door, the focus is on more recent history – from the first half of the 20th century up until the end of World War II. There is much to see here, especially in the sections on archaeology and early history, but the museum's greatest treasure is undoubtedly that of a beautifully preserved Roman helmet fashioned from pure gold.
Open Tue–Fri 09.00–19.00, Sat and Sun 09.00–14.00; closed Mon

The Museum of Foreign Art 29 Dunavska; tel: 451 239
The work on show here is the legacy of Dr Branko Ilić and includes artworks from the Renaissance right up to the 20th century. Most of the collection comes from the central European region.
Open 10.00–16.00; closed Mon

The Novi Sad City Museum Petrovaradin Tvrđava 4; tel: 433 145, 433 613; email: muzgns@eunet.yu
The standard display on show here concerns the cultural history of the city, with a selection of fine and applied art from the mid 18th to the mid 20th century that includes paintings, religious icons, musical instruments and furniture. There are also curiosities like the remains of an enormous wooden boat, probably of Celtic origin, that was dredged from the bottom of the Danube (a similar one can be found in the museum at Sremska Mitrovica). With some advance notice, the museum staff can organise tours of the fortress's underground galleries. Tours take place between 10.00–17.00, but not on Mondays.
Open 09.00–17.00 daily

Pavle Beljanski Memorial Gallery Trg Galerija 2; tel: 528 185; email: szpb_pr@ns.sbb.co.yu
This gallery, first opened to the public in 1961, is composed entirely of the work of Serbian artists from the first half of the 20th century. The collection of paintings, sculpture and tapestries was bequeathed to the city by Pavle Beljanski, a prominent Novi Sad lawyer and diplomat.
Open Wed, Fri, Sat and Sun 10.00–18.00, Thu 13.00–21.00; closed Mon and Tue

Petrovaradin Fortress

This impressive fortress has often been referred to as the 'Gibraltar of the Danube'. Petrovaradin started life as a Roman fortress and various additions were made through the medieval period. That which exists today, however, dates almost entirely from the early 18th century, when the fortress was comprehensively enlarged and fortified by the Austrians after their successful defeat of the Turkish army in 1692. The notion was to build on this success and construct an invincible barrier that would prevent further Turkish expansion into central Europe. The French military architect Sebastian Vauban was enrolled and the massive project was begun.

Although the Turks returned for a final battle in 1717, the fortress was already a white elephant by the time the fortifications were complete. By now, any serious threat of attack had almost completely vanished; not only had the Turks become far less of a threat as the 18th century progressed but the nature of warfare had changed so much that the fortress was rendered redundant. The enormous expenditure that had been made in terms of cash, materials and manpower was, in hindsight, a profligate waste of resources.

It was not a complete waste of time, however; the fortress's extensive **underground galleries** have been put to good use as dungeons from time to time, playing host to some very distinguished prisoners. Karađorđe was imprisoned at Petrovaradin during the First Serbian Uprising at the start of the 19th century and Marshal Tito himself spent a brief time in custody here when he was a young NCO in the Austrian army getting himself into trouble as a firebrand socialist. Other guests to the fortress, coming as distinguished foreign visitors rather than prisoners, include the Ethiopian emperor, Haile Selassie, and the young Prince Charles.

The construction of the tunnels was a massive task that took an enormous toll in terms of human life. The convicts forced to labour on its construction called it the 'Castle of Death' with good reason, as many thousands perished during the excavation of the underground galleries. It took a total of 88 years to build; work began in 1692 and was not completed until 1780.

There are 18km of galleries in all, at four different levels beneath the fortress. The original idea was that, if the fortress was attacked, then up to 30,000 men could hide underground and cover the surrounding area by firing their muskets through the 18,000 loopholes that had been installed. Very few people knew the layout of the tunnels in their entirety. Officers would be familiar with just their own small section of the tunnel complex and numerous devices were installed to fool or trap the enemy if they were smart enough to find their way into part of the tunnel system.

Today, only one kilometre of the tunnel complex is open but even this is still highly impressive. As well as a tourist attraction, the tunnels have found modern usage as an ideal location for horror films – if you take a tour you may notice remnants of fake cobwebs here and there.

Above ground, there are other things to see. Many of the original buildings have been converted for alternative usage: the **City Museum** (see above) is housed in buildings that originally served as a barracks and an arsenal; the Historical Archive of Novi Sad is housed in another block of barracks, and the long terrace of barracks that look out over the Danube have been converted into the (currently closed) Hotel Varadin and a variety of art studios. Between the Hotel Varadin and the Historical Archive is a small street of craft shops. The seating area immediately below the clocktower – **Ludwig's Bastion** – and the terrace of the adjoining restaurant both offer excellent views over the Danube River and Novi Sad beyond. You may notice that the hands on the **clocktower** are the wrong way round, with the minute hand replacing the hour hand and vice versa. The reason for this is that it is said to make them easier to see at a distance. For many years, a clock tax was imposed by the Austrians, which was applicable to any household able to view the clocktower from their home. Under Habsburg rule, the privilege of knowing the correct time did not come free.

Festivals and events

Novi Sad is host to numerous cultural events throughout the year. A list of what is on each month can be found at the Visit Vojvodina website: www.visitvojvodina.com. Regular annual events include the **International Agricultural Fair** (tel: 525 155; email: info@nsfair.coyu for information) and the **Sterijino Pozorje** drama festival that takes place at the end of May and the beginning of June (information from Sterijino Pozorje, Zmal Jovina 22; tel: 451 273; email: sterija@eunet.yu; www.pozorje.org.yu). **Zmajeve Decije Igre** is a festival for children that has been run annually since 1958 (information: Zmajeve deje igre, Zmaj Jovina 26/II; tel: 613 648; email: nspop@eunet.yu; www.zmajevedecjeigre.org.yu). The **Novi Sad Cultural Centre** (Katolicka porta 2; tel: 528 972; email: kcns@eunet.yu; www.kcns.org.yu) organise a number of annual events: the **Novi Sad Old Gold Jazz Festival**, the **Digital Arts Festival**, the **Euro NS Film Festival** and the **International Festival of Alternative and New Theatre**.

The event that has attracted the most attention in recent years is undoubtedly the **EXIT Music Festival**, staged at Petrovaradin Fortress in early July, which now attracts up to 50,000 festival-goers annually. EXIT is currently said to be the largest music festival in southeast Europe. Whether or not this is true is uncertain, but it cannot be denied that EXIT has been very influential in recent years; even Belgrade has followed suit by putting on the similar but smaller ECHO Festival a couple of weeks earlier.

During the EXIT Festival, the fortress area is given over entirely for musical performances and around 20 stages of varying sizes are erected to take advantage of the spectacular setting and impressive acoustics. Despite an emphasis on electronics, some of the smaller stages concentrate on music that is not so obviously 'urban'; these include a Balkan Fusion stage, a Jamaican Reggae stage, a Progressive stage, a 'Deep, Down and Dirty' stage, a Jazz and Blues stage and even an Extreme Sports stage for those in need of an adrenalin fix. Daily performances start around 19.00 and finish late.

For accommodation, the festival campsite provides free camping and puts on a few low-profile musical events of its own – so do not expect an undisturbed night's sleep.

An alternative would be to stay at the Novi Sad hostel, or try and book a hotel room, but it would be wise to do this well in advance.

Prices are very reasonable for what you get: an all-inclusive four-day ticket costs 2,850din (or 2,450din when bought in advance); a two-day ticket, 1,790din (1,590din in advance); a single-day ticket, 1,100din (950din in advance).

Ticket outlets in Serbia include the National Theatre office in Novi Sad, and IPS, Bilet Servis or Mamut Store in Belgrade. Tickets can also be purchased in the UK from Avant Garde Travel, 3 Betterton Street, Covent Garden, London WC2H 9BH; email: info@avantgardetravel.com; telephone booking: +44 (0)20 7836 1414. They can either sell you just the tickets or arrange an inclusive package deal.

In the last few years EXIT has attracted (mostly British) international names like Massive Attack, Roni Size, Iggy Pop, Asian Dub Foundation, Cypress Hill, as well as home-grown stars from the Serbian scene like Darkwood Dub, the Orthodox Celts and Boris Kovać and his Laadaba Orchestra. Further information about the festival and line-up may be found at: EXIT, Pozorišni trg 1; tel: 420 735; email: office@exitfest.org; www.exitfest.org.

Around Novi Sad
Sremski Karlovci Сремски Карловци

This small historic town, 11km southeast of Novi Sad on the banks of the Danube, is one of the most attractive in all Serbia. The tree-shaded central square, Trg Branka Radičevića, named after the Romantic poet Branko Radičević, a native of the town, has a 1770 marble fountain with four lion figures as its centrepiece. Surrounding this is an array of buildings from the 18th and early 19th centuries: a neoclassical **town hall** built between 1806 and 1811, a baroque Orthodox **cathedral** constructed between 1758 and 1762, with a 19th-century façade, and a considerable number of 18th-century houses. The cathedral has a splendid carved iconostasis by Teodor Kračun and Jakov Orfelin, with icons by other renowned 18th-century Serbian artists. Several of the wall paintings are by Paja Jovanović.

Another building of note is the **high school**, which as an institution in the town dates from 1791. The current building is a striking combination of traditional Serbian and secessionist styles. The neo-Byzantine Patriarchate nearby is now home to the town's **museum**, which provides an archaeological, historical and ethnographical account of the town and surrounding area, in addition to having a gallery of work by local artists from the 18th century to the present.

The **Upper church** in the northern part of the town was originally founded at the end of the 15th century as a nunnery, a property of the monastery at Hilandar in Greece. It was rebuilt in 1737. The **Lower church** south of the main square dates from the first quarter of the 18th century and has a very old and beautiful plane tree in its churchyard.

Historically, the most important building is the so-called **Peace Chapel**, which stands on a hill at the south end of the town. This curious, circular building commemorates the signing of the Treaty of Karlowitz in 1699 that brought peace between the Turks and the Austrians in the region. The current chapel was built in 1817 and mimics the shape of a Turkish military tent with four entrances to enable all of the participating parties to enter the room at the same time, thus putting them on equal terms. The chapel's windows are said to be patterned on the Union Jack flag – a nod of recognition to Britain, which was a co-signatory of the treaty.

The **tourist office** on the main square at Branka Radičevića 7 (tel: 882 127; fax: 881 026; email: info@karlovci.org.yu) is very helpful and well-resourced, with plenty of information about the history of the town as well as more general detail about the Fruška Gora area. They sell a detailed map of the town for 120din.

The **Hotel Boem** (tel: 881 038; fax: 27 124; email: hboem@eunet.yu) opposite the cathedral at Trg Branka Radičevića 5 can provide accommodation for 800din per person per night. For dining, there is the **Kućerak i Sremu** restaurant by the High school and the **Netirn** (tel: 881 987) at Stražilovska 20. Fish meals may be had at **Riblji Restoran Dunav** (tel: 881 666) or **Restoran Sremski Kutak** (tel: 882 343) both on Dunavska, the road that leads under the railway line to reach the river Danube. There is also a bakery that sells good *burek* just around the corner from the Hotel Boem, and a few simple restaurants and a bank on the strip where the bus stops near the main road.

To reach Sremski Karlovci from Novi Sad take bus number 61 or 62 from the bus station at the fish market. Buses leave more or less half-hourly between 06.00 and 21.00.

Fruška Gora National Park

By any standards this modest range of hills, 80km long and clearly visible to the south from Novi Sad, is not especially high – or spectacular – but it provides welcome relief from what is otherwise the occasionally monotonous, flat terrain of Vojvodina.

The highest point of Fruška Gora ('Holly Mountain') at **Crveni Cot** is a mere 539m above sea level, but what makes this range a delight is its lush, forested slopes filled with wildlife, a plethora of hiking trails, and the monasteries tucked away half-hidden in the folds of the hills, mostly on the southern side of the range. On the same warmer slopes, woodland gives way to agriculture at the lower reaches, and sunflowers, orchards and grapevines take advantage of the sunshine and adequate rainfall. Some of Serbia's better wines hail from the vineyards of this area. Above 300m, the hills are almost entirely covered by forest: this is the densest concentration of small-leaved lime (linden) in Europe.

The whole area has been a national park since 1960, and covers an area of 22,460ha. Animal life includes deer, lynx, marten and wild boar, although you would be very lucky to see any of these on a casual visit. The birdlife is prodigious and the hills and valleys are said to have over 700 species of medicinal herb (see *General Information* chapter).

The best gateway to the park is by way of the historic town Sremski Karlovci, which, as well as having the park management office, is worth a visit in its own right.

If you want to stay in the area, rather than travel the short distance from Novi Sad, there are a few possibilities. The best idea is probably to stay in Sremski Karlovci, which lies just outside the national park, but if you would like to be a little closer there is the **Restaurant Brankov Čardak** (tel: 882 521) at **Stražilovo**, 4km from Sremski Karlovci, inside the national park in the Fruška Gora foothills. The restaurant has six two-bed bungalows to rent that are equipped with bathroom, TV, refrigerators and heating during the winter. The restaurant serves grilled meat, fish and game dishes.

Another option would be to stay at **Iriški venac**, a cluster of buildings around a crossroads in the eastern end of the range 500m above sea level. Here there is the **Motel Vojvodina** (tel: 463 008), which has an attached restaurant offering Vojvodina dishes like venison and a good selection of wines. The motel has 12 rooms with 30 beds in the attic space above the restaurant. Another restaurant, the **Restoran Venac** (tel: 463 023) is located right by the crossroads. This also serves game and venison dishes at lunchtimes but it is closed at night. A visitor centre and museum are currently under construction at Iriški venac and should be able to provide local information when they are completed. For the time being, tourist information at Sremski Karlovci has the most information on the park and the surrounding area.

Monasteries of Fruška Gora

In the period between the 16th and 18th centuries a total of 35 monasteries were built in these hills. Today, just 17 remain, tucked away along the length of the range. Some, like Besanovac, Kuvezdin and Sisatovac are just ruins these days. Others, like Đipsa, Rakovac, Grgteg, Jazak, Hopovo and Velika Remeta, which have suffered similar heavy damage, have been completely or partially restored, although nothing can realistically be done to faithfully restore the frescos that formerly graced Krušedol, Vrdnik, Mala Remeta, Petkovica and Pribina Glava monasteries.

The monasteries were founded during the period of wars and migrations caused by Turkish occupation further south. They became vital communities that ensured that Serbian identity and Orthodox religion would survive through difficult times. They also became places of pilgrimage, filled with sacred art and the relics of Serbian saints that attracted both pilgrims and patrons alike.

It would take a real enthusiast to visit all of the monasteries, and it is probably best to concentrate on just two or three in order to avoid 'monastery fatigue', a temporary psychological state that is even more common in central Serbia than it is here. The monasteries of Fruška Gora are not as old as those further south belonging to the Raška and Morava schools, nor are their frescos as well–preserved or impressive. If you are short of time and have to make a decision between the two, it would be better to see just those in central and southern Serbia. Nevertheless, a day or two spent visiting monasteries in Fruška Gora is a delightful way to see the best of the Vojvodina countryside. If you decide to visit just one or two, then Novi Hopovo, Krušedol and Vrdnik are the ones probably most worthy of your time.

Some of the more outstanding monasteries of Fruška Gora are detailed below.

Krušedol, which lies 8km east of the small town of Irig, was founded in the late 15th century by Đurađ Branković, who ruled Serbia for about ten years before becoming an archbishop. It has been destroyed and reconstructed on several occasions since. Most of its frescos are from the mid 18th century although a few 16th-century remnants remain. The church, which also contains the remains of many members of the Branković family, as well as King Milan Obrenović (died 1901), was used as a prison by the Ustaše during World War II; many Partisans were tortured and murdered here. This is probably the most visited monastery in the Fruška Gora range.

Grgeteg, further west, was built between 1465 and 1485. The monastery was deserted before the great migration but was renovated by Bishop Isaija Đakovic in 1708. It has been restored again in recent years. Grgeteg has an icon of Mother Trojerućica that is a copy of the famous icon from Hilander Monastery at Mt Athos, Greece.

Novo Hopovo, built in 1576, is located 7km from Irig, next to the main road that leads to Novi Sad. The church shows a Byzantine influence in its design, rather like those of the Morava School, and has an elegant 12-sided dome that is encircled by colonettes. Inside, there is the famous fresco of *The Massacre of the Children at Vitlejem* by the painter Teodor Kracun. The monastery was badly damaged during World War II, its iconostasis torn down and religious treasures stolen.

Velika Remeta, close to Sremski Karlovci in the eastern part of Fruška Gora, was built, entirely of bricks, during the 16th century. There is some evidence to suggest that the monastery already existed in 1509. The belltower, built 1733–35, is one of the tallest in the region at nearly 40m high. Most of its frescos were destroyed during the last war.

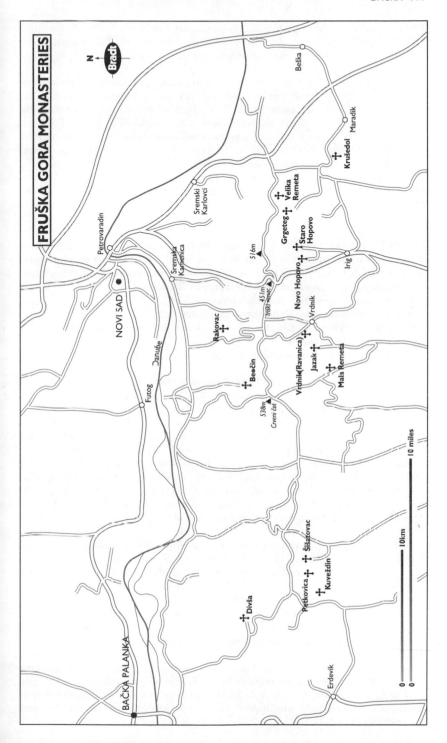

FRUŠKA GORA MONASTERIES

Mala Remeta, founded by Dragutin Nemanjić, lies 2km west of Jazak. Monks from Žiča Monastery came here to live at the end of the 17th century. The original church was destroyed by the Turks and the present one dates from 1759.

Vrdnik (Ravanica) lies close to Vrdnik, a former mining settlement. The date of its founding is unknown but it is mentioned in documents from 1589. Monks from the monastery of Ravanica in eastern Serbia arrived here in 1697, bringing with them the relics of Prince Lazar. Lazar remained here until World War II when he was temporarily moved (with German assistance) to Belgrade to prevent his remains falling into disrespectful Ustaša hands. (See box *Prince Lazar's Remains* in *General Information* chapter.) The current church dates from 1811.

Jazak lies 2km north of the village of the same name. It probably dates from the first half of the 16th century. The relics of King Uroš Nejaki were kept here from 1705 to 1942.

Visiting Fruška Gora National Park and the monasteries
With your own transport you can meander around the Fruška Gora to your heart's content. Without a car, it is much easier to take one of the tours provided by agencies such as Magelan Corporation, Market Tours or Transfer Turizm in Novi Sad, or Belgrade Sightseeing or Jolly Travel in Belgrade.

Public transport into the Fruška Gora is sparse and rather inadequate. Although pleasant forays into the hills can be made from Sremski Karlovci, visiting the monasteries themselves entails an awful lot of walking and backtracking. However, it is just about possible. A suggested itinerary is outlined below.

A day's walk in the Fruška Gora using public transport
From Novi Sad's long-distance bus station take a bus heading for Šabac or Sremska Mitrovica and ask to be let off at Iriški venac. There are several buses leaving in the morning, fewer in the afternoon. Get off at the crossroads at the top of the hill, by the Venac restaurant, then follow the woodland track that leads east through the picnic area behind the restaurant. Following the red and white triangles marked on the trees will lead you to the Hotel Venac, a rather forlorn-looking building that is currently closed. Attached to one of the trees in front of the hotel is a small sign in Cyrillic that points to a downhill track and says something to the effect of: *Manastir Novo Hopovo – 1 hour*. The narrow track leads down through dense woodland, fragrant with lime blossom and alive with the sound of birds and insects in summer.

After about 45 minutes you will come to an open area where there is another track leading sharply off to the left. Ignore this for the time being – you will return this way later. Just ahead, is a motor-able dirt track that bends sharply around a fishing pond. Take the right-hand fork of this, which will lead you across meadows to **Novo Hopovo** Monastery, another ten minutes' walk away.

After visiting the monastery, return to the fork by the pond. From here, take the track back in the direction you originally came from and fork right through a meadow. Very soon, you should see a metal sign nailed to a tree that points up to the right and indicates Stari Hopovo 2.2km away. This track climbs up steeply through woodland at first, then starts to level off as it passes an isolated house with a vineyard. Soon it meets a wider track at a junction by another house and garden. Turn left. This track leads past meadows, fields and orchards, with open views of the valley below. If you are here at the right time of year you can help yourself to delicious plums from the trees that skirt the track.

Stari Hopovo Monastery is soon reached, situated in a sloping meadow beneath pine woodland – a lovely peaceful spot. A few dedicated monks are hard at work restoring it but at the moment the church is still in quite a ruinous state. From Stari Hopovo, you can continue along the track a little more until you reach a small shrine by a stream and a wooden footbridge. There is a water pipe inside the shrine and the water from it seems to be fine to drink: a good place to top up canteens. The track continues north then east along a route known as the Fruška Gora Transversal. It eventually leads to **Grgeteg** Monastery by a meandering route that climbs back up to the ridge of the hill. This is still a long way distant however – a good 10km further on. Unless you have limitless time and energy it is better to return the way you came, as far as the house at the T-junction by the track from Novo Hopovo. Instead of turning right to retrace your previous steps, continue straight in a southerly direction. The track leads slowly down, passing fields of sunflowers, vines and maize. Eventually it will lead you to the small town of **Irig**. The bus station is at the bottom end of the town, next to a road sign that points towards **Krušedol** Monastery 7km away. From here you can get a bus to take you back to Novi Sad – they run throughout the afternoon until early evening. There is also a direct bus to Belgrade at 16.15. According to the bus station timetable, a local bus runs to Krušedol at 13.15 – another possibility if you have made an early start – but unfortunately there is no bus back to Irig after this one, so you would have to return on foot.

Sombor СОМБОР

Telephone code: 025

The medium-sized town of Sombor lies in the northwest part of Bačka close to both the Croatian and Hungarian borders. Sombor is a pleasant, leafy sort of place with an attractive central square and a leisurely pace of life. Like Subotica, it has a large Hungarian population and most signs and notices in the town are written in two languages. The town is especially attractive in autumn when the leaves turn yellow and cover the streets in drifts.

Leaving the **bus station**, a sign points you along a tree-lined road towards the centre. Walking for ten minutes in this direction, you arrive at a quiet leafy park and a twin-towered church to the right. The central square with its large, pink-painted **Town Hall** is just one block further on. The square is surrounded by attractive buildings on all sides: the Town Hall in baroque style is dated 1862. Opposite the Town Hall is the **Town Museum** with a permanent gallery devoted to the work of Milan Konjević, a well-known local artist. Adjacent to the Town Hall is an outdoor market area that is overlooked by a wall-mounted sundial with an inscription in Hungarian painted beneath it. Alongside the museum, a pedestrian street in yellow brick leads down to Trg republike and the ugly but adequate two-star **Hotel Sloboda**, the only place to stay in town (tel: 025 24 666, 469 620; with 70 double rooms and four singles).

Sombor's most notable church is that dedicated to **St George**, which is in the baroque-rococo style and has a very ornate iconostasis with two rows of columns decorated with gilded vines and flowers. The oldest building in town is of Turkish origin, a large *konak* that was formerly the summer residence of the Belgrade pasha.

One thing that you may notice in Sombor, and also in Subotica, is the large number of bicycles in the town. It seems that everyone rides them here, both young and old. It makes sense topographically speaking – northern Bačka is as flat as *palačinke* and the residential areas of low-rise Vojvodina towns like Sombor are usually quite spread out. It is, in part, the bicycles that help to reinforce the impression of unhurried calm in the town. Watching the cyclists making slow, shaky progress across the cobbled square, with bulging bags of tomatoes and onions slung from the handlebars, can have a slightly soporific effect, rather like watching a tank of tropical fish.

To reach Sombor by **bus**, you can take one of the 12 daily buses that come from Belgrade (and Novi Sad) along the motorway, or one of ten slower buses. There are ten buses a day that leave for Subotica, as well as a morning service to Zagreb at 07.45 and a bus to Baja in Hungary at 08.30. The bus station has a *garderoba* where you can leave bags for 40din an item.

Tourist information is at Trg Cara Lazara 1 (tel: 468 141).

Subotica СУБОТИЦА
Telephone code: 024

Travelling from Hungary, and particularly from Szeged, with its colourful secessionist buildings, Subotica does not come as too much of a surprise; if anything it seems more of a continuation of that which has gone before. The border does not seem to count for much here and you do not suddenly plunge into a Serbia that is culturally at odds with anything you have seen further north. There is good reason for this: like the rest of Vojvodina, Subotica has spent far longer under Hungarian control than it has as part of Serbia but, unlike most of the other large towns in the province, it has always had a majority Hungarian population as well. It remains very much a Hungarian town, even today. To complicate matters further, that which is not Hungarian in the town is just as likely to be Croatian as it is Serbian, although this ethnic variation is nowhere near as obvious.

Subotica, the second most populous centre in Vojvodina after Novi Sad, is Serbia's most Hungarian town by a long chalk. Signs on the street are dual-language, and many local newspapers, radio stations and television channels use the Hungarian language rather than Serbian. The Magyar influence even extends to the food, with paprika and *gulaš* featuring heavily on many menus.

For the visitor, the novelty of all this depends on which direction they are heading. Travelling from the south, it can come as a pleasurable jolt that Serbia suddenly seems a long way distant, that Turkish influences are nowhere to be seen, and that the hegemony of the Orthodox Church has suddenly faded away. Coming from the north, it may just seem like more of the same. Either way, the gaudy elegance of middle European secessionist architecture is a dominant feature of the townscape. Love it or hate it, it is the architecture of the town that is Subotica's greatest draw.

History
The town was first recorded as a settlement in the 16th century but the majority of the town's buildings date from around the turn of the 20th century when the taste for architecture in the bold, secessionist style was at its peak. The resort of Palić, on the shores of the nearby lake, was developed around the same time, closely followed by the inauguration of a tram service to ferry citizens to and from the new resort.

Getting there
Subotica lies on the Belgrade–Novi Sad–Budapest railway line and so has good connections both north and south. Two express trains run direct to Budapest daily from Subotica's **railway station**; they originate in Belgrade and arrive in Subotica around three hours later, one in the middle of the night and the other at midday. Two more trains go to Szeged in Hungary, one in the morning and the other in the early afternoon. From Szeged, there are connecting services to Budapest by train or bus (the express trains from Belgrade do not travel via Szeged). Three further train services link Subotica with the capital and Novi Sad, but these do not

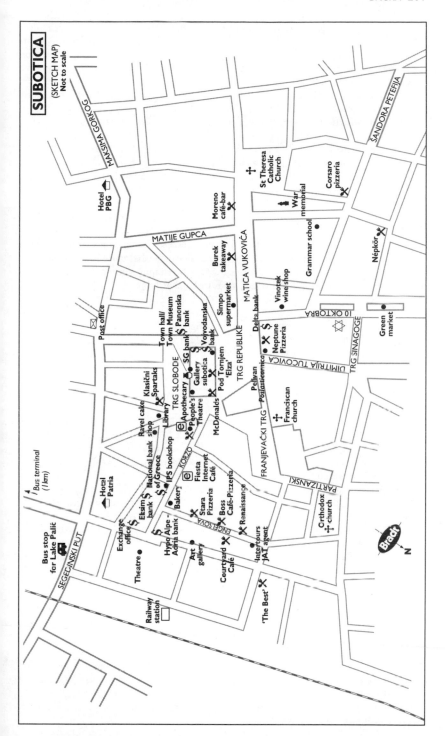

SUBOTICA
(SKETCH MAP)
Not to scale

continue over the Hungarian border. Daily train services from Subotica serve other destinations in Vojvodina: four to Sombor, three to Kanjiža, two to Senta and two to Kikinda.

A very useful train for travelling on to Hungary is the local two-carriage morning service that leaves Subotica at 08.40 and arrives in Szeged about 1¾ hours later, stopping at Palić and the border at Horgoš along the way – a bargain at just 137din. Another train leaves in the early afternoon.

The railway station is conveniently situated in the town centre near to the Likovni Susret gallery.

The **bus station** is located a little further out of town, about 1km along the main Novi Sad–Belgrade road. It can be reached by taking a number 1 bus from the town centre; the fare is 10din. There are more than 20 buses a day to Belgrade, 20 to Novi Sad, five to Senta, five to Niš and three to Kikinda. A daily bus leaves every evening for Sarajevo in Bosnia-Herzegovina.

Getting around

All of Subotica's main sights are within the fairly compact town centre. Two local bus services are useful: the number 1 bus that runs along the Belgrade road to and from the bus station, and the number 6 service that can be caught at the corner of Maksima Gorkog and Trg Lazara Nešića, which goes to Lake Palić.

Tourist information

There is a very helpful tourist information office on Korzo opposite the pedestrian passageway. Staff speak English and can provide maps of the town and information on sights of interest in both Subotica and Lake Palić. They also have several English-language publications for sale on the region.

Where to stay and eat

Hotel Patria★★★ Đure Đakovića bb; tel: 554 500; fax: 551 762; email: info@patria-su.com; www.patria-su.com. This hotel is conveniently central and perfectly comfortable. It has 41 single rooms, 103 twin-bed rooms, 54 rooms with double beds and 7 apartments. Facilities include a bar and café, a 250-seat restaurant and a congress hall. There is an exchange office and a travel agency in the lobby. Single rooms cost 1,500din, doubles 2,500din and triples 3,300din. Apartments go for 3,800–6,300din. Tax is 50din.

Hotel PBG★★★ Harambašićeva 21; tel/fax: 554 175, 556 542. The PBG is a small privately run hotel, built in 2001, in the south part of the town, just 5 minutes from the centre. It has a restaurant, a conference room and reserved parking. All rooms are equipped with TV sets and minibar. There are 66 beds in total. Single rooms are 1,800din, doubles 3,100din and apartments, 6,900din.

Malcon Stipana Kopilovića 15; tel: 553 510; fax: 546 568. This is basically a restaurant that has a few rooms to rent. Malcon is located 1.5km from the centre, on the main Belgrade road just beyond the bus station. To reach it, take a number 1 bus and get off at the next stop after the bus station, outside the 'Pionir' factory. The restaurant is down Stipana Kopilovića opposite, at the first corner. Beds cost 750din per person without breakfast. There are no en-suite rooms.

Subotica has a few restaurants in the centre that specialise in local dishes, as well as several pizzerias and numerous outdoor café-bars.

Restoran Pod Tornjem 'Elza' Trg slobode 1; tel: 557 800. This 2-star place is upstairs inside the Town Hall building, just around the corner from McDonald's. It serves excellent Hungarian-influenced food at very reasonable prices. Although it is quite smart, a full meal with wine should only cost between 500–700din. The service is attentive and there is musical entertainment most nights.

Restoran Klasični Spartaks Trg slobode 6; tel: 555 676. This is another 2-star traditional restaurant on the main square by the Town Hall. Looking at the photographs in the window it would appear that this is the place that gets booked for most of the town's larger social events.

Népkör Žarkar Zrenjanina 11; tel: 555 480. A spacious 3-star Hungarian restaurant that is located in a quiet street close to the market.

Neptune Caffe-Pizzeria Dimitrija Tucovića 2; tel: 554 522. Neptune has an outdoor terrace on the square in summer and a basement inside for use in cooler weather. They do a broad range of pizzas, soups, pancakes, desserts and even breakfasts. The menus are in 3 languages: Hungarian, Serbian and English.

Engelsova, just around the corner from the tourist office, is a narrow pedestrian street of elegant frontages that is almost entirely given over to cafés, bars and restaurants, a very popular place on warm summer evenings. Good places along here to eat, or to just have a drink, are: **Stara Pizzeria**, **Caffe Boss** at number 7 (tel: 551 675) – which stretches along both sides of the street and has a good range of pizzas, salads, pasta dishes and draught beer – and the restaurant **Renaissance**.

Another area rich in café-bars is along **Korzo** towards the Town Hall. Facing the Town Hall the imposing neoclassical **People's Theatre** has a large seating area outside. Inside, there is an internet café (60din per hour) in the foyer area and further seating for customers.

A good choice of ice-cream flavours is available at the **Pelivan** *poslastičarnica* on Trg republike, and there is an excellent **bakery** on the corner of Korzo and Engelsova.

For musical entertainment, the **Brick and Steel** bar (Borisa Kidrica 10; tel: 525 141; www.brickandsteel.co.yu) stages performances by jazz and contemporary artists. Ask at the tourist office about other venues in the town.

What to see

The art nouveau **Town Hall**, built in 1903, is easily the town's most impressive building even if it is not to everybody's taste. With fancy gables and towers, patterned brickwork and gaudy colours, it is an architectural mishmash of styles that could be said to verge on the tasteless. The rhythm of its design might be described as heavily syncopated – frenetic even – but what it lacks in harmony it makes up for with sheer cheerfulness. As well as the town's administrative offices, the building houses several banks, restaurants, gift shops and the municipal museum. There is even a branch of McDonald's, a singular location for a fast food chain that prides itself on the uniformity of its product.

The **Town Museum** (tel: 555 128) is entered through a side door of the Town Hall on Ulica Strosmajerova. As well as a large pottery section it has a large ethnographic collection from the Subotica region, with plenty of local costumes and musical instruments as well as oddments like beekeeping equipment and an enormous 1831 wine press. All captions are in three languages: Hungarian, Cyrillic Serbian and Croatian. The museum is open from 10.00–16.00 Tuesday, Wednesday and Friday, 10.00–18.00 Thursday, 10.00–14.00 Saturday; closed Sunday and Monday.

It is possible to take a tour up to the **clocktower** from the museum. Departures are at 12.00 and 13.00. You are supposed to have a minimum group of five persons but they seem to be quite flexible and were good enough to take me on my own. Admission to the watchtower is 30din, or 20din if you are one of an organised group. It is a steep climb but from the top you are rewarded with a marvellous view over the town and surrounding countryside. Telescopes are provided for a closer look at the world below.

Another good thing about taking a clocktower tour is that you get to take a peek inside the everyday working part of the Town Hall where Subotica's citizens go about their business, filling in forms, queuing outside offices and so on. This would seem perfectly normal were it not for the elaborate interior decoration found throughout: it seems as if every surface has been stencilled with a variety of naïve floral patterns in pastel shades, rather like the designs on a Slovakian chest of drawers. For the bureaucrats of Subotica Town Hall it must be like working inside an architectural chocolate box.

Facing the Town Hall are the six tall pillars of the neoclassical **People's Theatre** (*Narodno Pozorište*, or *Népszínház* in Hungarian), dating from 1854 and the oldest theatre in the country. The rest of this central zone is contemporary with the Town Hall and several other examples of the art nouveau/secessionist style can be seen along the pedestrian street of **Korzo**, such as the building that now houses the **Continental Bank**, which has heart shapes around the windows and *trompe l'oeil* shutters on the upper floor.

Behind the Town Hall, in the park that merges into Trg republike, is a large art nouveau **fountain** in an electric shade of cobalt blue, which is especially striking when illuminated at night. Not for the first time in the town, it seems as if the hand of the Catalan maverick, Gaudí, has been at work here.

There are more secessionist buildings nearby at the northern end of Dimitrija Tucovića but the most important remaining edifice in this style is the imposing synagogue that stands alone close to the town's market area.

The **synagogue** was one of the first art nouveau buildings to be constructed in Subotica, designed by Dezso Jakab and Marcell Komor who were responsible for several other buildings in the town. The temple has a large green hexagonal dome, with curved gables and large rose windows that are crowned by smaller ones with Star of David brickwork. Now that virtually all of Subotica's Jewish community have gone – either killed during World War II or as migrants to Israel – the building is rarely used and it is starting to look a little run-down.

Almost opposite the synagogue is the town's **marketplace**, which in autumn is full of local produce like peppers and mushrooms. You can buy garlic by the kilo here, live trout in buckets, enormous plastic bags of pre-shredded cabbage and paprika in industrial quantities (Horgoš, the epicentre of European paprika production, is just a few kilometres up the road).

The twin-towered **Catholic cathedral** of St Theresa of Avila is nearby. The cathedral was built in two separate stages at the end of the 18th century and was the tallest building in the town before the construction of the Town Hall. In the churchyard is an interesting statue of God the Father and Jesus atop a pillar with a radiant sunburst above. Beneath them is the Virgin Mary surrounded by a group of four angels.

Directly opposite the cathedral stands a social-realistic **memorial** by Toma Roksandic, erected in the 1950s and dedicated to 'the victims of Fascism'. On one side is a panel of naked men locked in combat; on the other, simply the dates 1941–1945.

Near the railway station is perhaps the best example of art nouveau architecture in the town, the **Likovni susret** (Artistic Encounters) gallery. Once again, it seems like it came straight from the sketch pad of Gaudí but it is, in fact, the work of one Ferenc Raichle. Originally designed as a dwelling house, it later found new life as a gallery of contemporary art. Opening hours are supposed to be Tuesday to Friday 07.00–19.00, Monday 07.00–13.00, Saturday 09.00–13.00; closed Sundays. Unfortunately when I last visited, in the summer of 2004, the entrance was heavily encased in scaffolding, suggesting that the building was about to undergo extensive and lengthy renovation. Hopefully it will reopen at some stage in the future as the interior is supposed to be as striking as its stunning façade.

Lake Palić

Palić started life as a spa in the mid 19th century. By the turn of the 20th century it had become a popular health resort and vacation spot for the wealthier citizens of the region. During this period a number of flamboyant art nouveau public buildings were erected, most notably the **Water Tower** and the Grand Terrace on the lake.

Palić has a picturesque location and makes for a pleasant outing from Subotica. It may strike some people as a bit of a theme park but, in fairness, this is exactly what it was designed to be.

If you decide to spend some time here there is a variety of things to do at the lake. There are beaches for swimming, tennis courts, bikes for hire and a zoo. Both boating and fishing are permitted on the lake. Alternatively, there are plenty of waterside cafés to watch the world go by from.

Tourist information on Lake Palić can be had from the Palić-Ludaš office at Park Narodnih heroja 9; tel: 753 121; fax: 753 474; email: jp.plaic@tippnet.co.yu; www.palic.co.yu.

A number 6 bus from Subotica will bring you here, as will one of the local trains that run twice a day between Subotica, Horgoš and Szeged in Hungary. The main bus stop for the lake is by the Water Tower, which you really cannot miss as it resembles a giant ice-cream cone by the roadside; from here, walk along a shady avenue of trees to reach the lake. Emerging from the arch at the end of the avenue you arrive at an attractive fountain just before the lake promenade. Walking left leads to the Hotel Prezident, while turning right will take you past an art nouveau house that looks as if it has been transported from Disneyworld, and then to the four-star fish restaurant, Riblja Čarda. There is lots of artsy statuary to look at along the way.

There is no shortage of places **to stay** or **eat** at the resort. Below are just a few suggestions.

Hotel Prezident★★★★ Lovranska bb; tel: 622 662; fax: 622 607; www.prezident-su.com. This recently built hotel, 50m from the water and next to a park, is probably the best choice at Lake Palić. It has its own bar and restaurant, a guarded car park, conference room, terrace and garden, as well as a Turkish bath and a Jacuzzi. All rooms come equipped with TV, minibar and phone. With 16 double rooms, 32 singles and 4 suites, singles rooms cost 3,150din, doubles are 5,600din and suites 7,900din.

Hotel Park I Jezero★★★★ Park Nardonih heroja 9; tel: 753 112: www.elittepalic.co.yu

'Kod Janje' apartments Kanjiški put 42; tel: 754 421, 754 879. Private suites to rent with living room, kitchen, terrace and cable TV.

Two of the best four-star **restaurants** in Palić are run by the Elitte Palic company that also owns the Park Hotel: **Restoran Riblja Čarda** (tel: 755 040) and **Restoran Mala Gostiona** (tel: 753 447).

More basic places can be found on the main road to Horgoš, near to where the bus stops: **Caffe-pizzeria Don Corleone** at Horgoški put 65 (tel: 753 324) and **Picerija PUB** at Horgoški bb (tel: 753 103).

Lake Ludaš

This nature reserve is close to Lake Palić, just a few kilometres further east along the Horgoš–Szeged road. It has been listed as a wetland of international importance since 1977 and, because of its importance for waterfowl, is one of three protected Ramsar sites in Serbia. In 1994 Ludaš was given the status of a Special Nature Reserve.

A total of 214 bird species have been recorded at the lake and over 40 are regular nesters. Typical species include: squacco heron (*Ardeola ralloides*), bearded tit (*Panurus biarmicus*), marsh harrier (*Circus aeruginous*), bittern (*Botaurus stellaris*), white stork (*Ciconia ciconia*), black-necked grebe (*Podiceps nigricollis*), purple heron (*Ardea purpurea*), and little bittern (*Ixobrychus minutus*). It also serves as an important feeding station for passage migrants.

In addition to being a haven for water birds the lake is home to other scarce creatures like pond terrapin (*Emys orbicularis*), a decreasing and endangered species in Serbia.

The reserve is managed by the **Palić-Ludaš** public enterprise in collaboration with the Belgrade-based Institute for Protection of Nature in Serbia and the Ministry of the Environment.

Fantast Castle

This is a hotel and tourist complex to the south of Subotica in the eastern part of Bačka; a popular overnight stop for organised tours of the region. 'Fantast' is located on the Bačka Topola–Bečej road, 14km west of Bečej. The complex includes the castle (now a hotel), a horse stud, a chapel and a parkland area. The 'castle', which is really more of a folly than anything else, was built at the beginning of the 20th century by Bogdan Dunđerski, a local landowner and the richest man in Vojvodina at the time. The building, which is in a mixture of neoclassical, baroque and romance styles, has four towers, the largest of which resembles that of a medieval castle, hence the name. Tours of the castle are available on request, horseriding lessons may be had at the stud and there are tennis courts for the use of guests.

Contact details for the hotel are: **Hotel Fantast** Bačko toploski put bb, 21200 Bečej; tel: 813 531; fax: 815 200. There are 17 double rooms, two suites and one triple room, a 90-seat restaurant, café and conference room.

THE BANAT
Kikinda КИКИНДА

Telephone code: 0230

If you are arriving from Romania, Kikinda may be the first Serbian town that you come across. It is a pleasant enough place to spend your first or last night in the country although, in truth, it is probably not worth making a special detour for.

Archaeological evidence points towards the Kikinda region being settled back in the Bronze and Iron ages. At the site of Gradište at nearby Iđoš artefacts from the Neolithic age have also been discovered. Today the town's industry revolves around the manufacture of tiles – it is home to the country's largest tile factory – and signs around the town proudly proclaim, 'Kikinda – Tile capital'.

Tourist information may be had from the town hall at Trg srpskih dobrovoljaca 12 (tel: 26 300).

Getting there

The town is somewhat out on a limb, deep in the Banat, and its best connections with the rest of Serbia are through Zrenjanin to the south. Sixteen buses a day go to Belgrade and 13 daily buses leave for Novi Sad, ten via Novi Bečej and three via Zrenjanin. Four daily buses run to Subotica, three to Zrenjanin and two to Bečej. There is also a daily bus to and from Senta, which has bus links with Szeged in Hungary. The bus from Senta leaves for Kikinda at 14.15 making a connection possible if you take one of the morning buses from Szeged. Be aware that there are no currency exchange facilities at Senta bus station, and that the Hungarian bus does not usually stop at the border long enough to change money.

Kikinda also has a railway station on the edge of the town, which has a service to and from Subotica twice a day. Another train – a single carriage – runs across the Romanian border to Jimbolia twice a day at 06.00 and 15.20, arriving at 07.18 and 16.38 respectively. In Jimbolia, there are connections with these trains that continue on to Timiďoara. The journey takes less than 20 minutes but bear in mind that Romania runs on Eastern European Time (EET), an hour later than Serbia, which is in the Central European Time (CET) zone. All customs and passport checks are performed on the station premises before boarding. This is very much a local smugglers' train and you may see a little surreptitious greasing of palms taking place but, as a tourist, you should experience no difficulties whatsoever.

Where to stay and eat
The only hotel in town is the comfortable, four-star **Hotel Narvik** at Trg srpskih dobrovoljaca 2a (tel: 23 910, 23 306), a five-minute walk from the bus station and just a block away from the main central square. The hotel has nearly 100 spacious rooms with cable television and minibar but no air conditioning. There is a large national restaurant, a cocktail bar, solarium and sauna. Largish rooms cost 2,350din for single occupancy, 3,600din for double.

Kikinda has a wealth of café-bars but a dearth of restaurants. The main square, Srpski dobrovoljaca, has café-bars all the way around it. The streets that lead onto the square have more cafés, as well as a number of ice-cream parlours and bakeries. There are a couple of pizzerias along the south side of the square, to the west of the Town Hall. **Tins Pizza-Palačincarnica** close to the Town Hall has basic pizzas, pancakes and pasta. Further on, across the next junction, is a large bakery with an outdoor seating area, before coming to the **Conti Pizzeria** at Svetosavska 21 (tel: 34 443) that has a reasonable selection of pizzas and pancakes. Just across the road are a few fast food huts and the curiously named **Angrohit supermarket** if you get stuck. The only national restaurant in town seems to be the one attached to the Hotel Narvik: **Lala's Room**.

Practicalities
There are three banks in the town centre that have VISA-friendly ATMs: the **Vojvoďanska banka** and the **Central banka** on the main square, and the **Delta banka** that is on the road south off the main square, parallel to and west of the road that has the Hotel Narvik. The **post office** lies at the end of the shady café street that runs south from the square between the two churches.

What to see
All of Kikinda's sights are in the central square of **Srpski dobrovoljaca**. The most arresting is the pastel pink, 1835 **Town Hall**, which is built in classical style with ornate stucco work. Along the square to the west is the **Orthodox Church of the Archangels Michael and Gabriel**, which has a sundial on its southern wall. Across the square from the church is the **National Museum** that has a skeleton of a mammoth among its exhibits.

Zrenjanin ЭРЕЊАНИН
Telephone code: 023
This, the largest town in the Banat, is too close to Novi Sad to really warrant an overnight stay; despite its considerable size, it has little in the way of attractions when compared with the Vojvodina capital. That having been said, there are a few things to see here if you wish to break your journey for a few hours.

The central square of **Trg Slobode** is quite attractive, with some ornate lamp-posts and a large neo-baroque **Town Hall**. The building dates from 1887 and is painted in two pastel shades of avocado green. It was undergoing extensive restoration when I visited in 2004. Leading off Trg Slobode is **Kralja Aleksandra**, a pedestrian street thoroughfare that has several restaurants and cafés, a Putnik travel agency and a branch of Delta banka with an ATM that accepts MasterCard and Maestro. A good café along here is the **Plus Plus** Café at number 29, although it does insist on showing Fashion TV.

The **bus station** is on the edge of the town, a 20-minute walk or a 15din bus ride from the town centre. Local buses run past the bus station and along Bulevar Beogradski towards the centre; you get off at the turn-off to the town centre where there is a large mural of horses on a gable end. This road, 29 Novembra, leads directly to Trg Slobode and the town centre.

If you want to stay over, there is the three-star **Hotel Vojvodina** at the corner of Trg Slobode (tel: 023 612 33), which has 40 rooms that cost 1,600din for a single, and 2,600din for a double.

Tourist information may be found at Koce Kolara 68 (tel: 523 160, 523 260).

Just to the north of Zrenjanin is the spa of **Banja Rusanda-Melenci** that offers a variety of therapies alongside facilities for sports training. Further information may be found at www.melenci.co.yu.

Čarska Bara

The Stari-Begej-Čarska Bara complex is situated to the southwest of Zrenjanin, close to the village of Ečka, and an appealing destination for anyone interested in wildlife. This 1,767ha reserve, designated as one of just three Ramsar Convention sites in Serbia, is actually a complex of various wetland ecosystems that include lakes, swamps, meadows and forest. With 250 recorded species (140 breeding, the rest migrants) and the largest marsh harrier population in Serbia, the reserve is of special importance to wetland birds. It also provides a valuable habitat for marsh flora and a variety of fish species like carp, pike and perch.

Currently, Čarska Bara is mostly used for scientific research, school visits and recreational pursuits like sports fishing, which is permitted in certain areas of the complex. Interest in birdwatching is still at a fairly low level in Serbia but it is on the increase. A visit to the reserve is a feature of the birdwatching and photographic safari packages run by Magelan Corporation (see *Novi Sad* section). They also run one-day trips from Belgrade.

If you would like to visit independently, accommodation can be found at **Hotel Sibila** at the Ribnjak Ečka fish farm in nearby Lukino Selo (tel: 884 020, 885 131; email: ecka@beotel.yu) who can also organise birding boat tours of the reserve, as well as photo safaris, horseriding and excursions in horse-drawn carriages. The hotel has 48 beds in total, and a restaurant. Singles are €15; doubles, €26. Meals can be provided: €2 for breakfast, €10 for lunch, €9 for dinner. Further accommodation is available in Ečka at the 16-room **Hotel Kastel**, Novosadska 7; tel: 881 013.

Vršac ВРШАЦ

Telephone code for Vršac and Bela Crkva: 013

The medium-sized town of Vršac lies out on a limb in the southeast Banat and is not a place you would pass through unless you were heading for Timiďoara in Romania. This is a pity as it has a fair amount to offer and is worth considering as an excursion in its own right. Although there are adequate places to stay, it is possible to visit the town as a lengthy day trip from Belgrade.

Two things make Vršac stand out from other towns of the Banat. Firstly, there is a welcome break in the interminably flat relief that characterises the rest of the region. Vršac stands on the edge of a hilly border region known as the **Vršačke planine** that rises above the Pannonian Plain in a way that seems quite dramatic after having made the mental adjustment to big skies and long horizons. The southern slopes of the

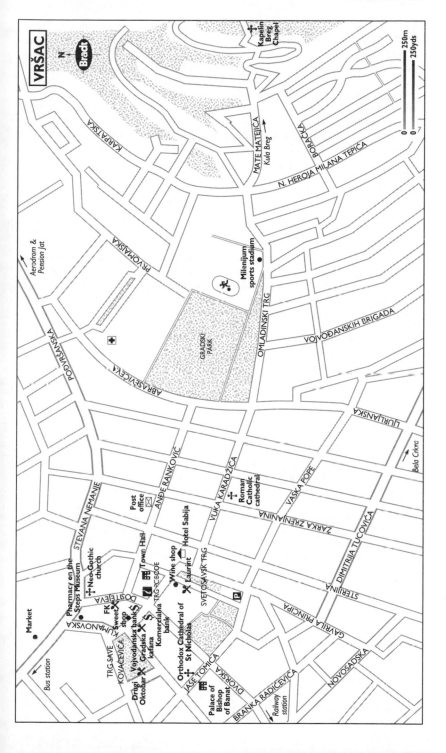

Vršac hills are put to good use, being home to vineyards that produce a quite distinctive red wine that locals are proud of.

The town's other distinguishing feature is its abundance of architecture from the Habsburg period, with an interesting mix of 18th-century classical buildings alongside others that betray a more wayward neo-Gothic influence.

Vršac has its own aerodrome that is not used for commercial flights but by the JAT flight school that has its base here. The track at the aerodrome has also played host to the Serbia and Montenegro Motorcycle Grand Prix. With the recent construction of the state-of-the-art Millennium Sports Centre to the east of the town centre, Vršac is poised to play a role as one of the hosts of the 2005 European Basketball Championships.

Getting there

Nearly 30 **buses** run every day between Belgrade and Vršac; ten run to Novi Sad and three leave for Niš via Bela Crkva and Smederevo. There are more limited services to Vatin and Markovac, villages which lie close to the Romanian border. Six daily buses run to nearby Bela Crka, and there is a single early-morning service to Kikinda. The bus station is a flat, 20-minute walk northwest from the town centre along Miloša Obilića.

Train services are less frequent. There are four trains a day between Vršac and Pančevo Glavna, which take between 1¼ and 1½ hours. One train leaves Vršac for Belgrade every morning at 08.00; the return journey from Belgrade leaves in the late afternoon. The journey takes about 2½ hours. The railway station is a 20-minute walk southwest of the town centre.

Where to stay and eat

The three-star **Hotel Srbija** at Svetosavski Trg 12 (tel: 815 545), just east of the main central square, has over 60 rooms on six floors and should always have space. Single rooms range from 1,100 to 2,000din, doubles 2,000–3,000din, depending on the size of bed and which floor it is on. There are also quite expensive luxury rooms which the reception staff may try and book you into unless you insist otherwise.

The other option is to bed down with the pilots at the **Pansion JAT**, Podvrsanaka 146 (tel: 823 033). This has 21 doubles and 34 singles and is not exclusively for the use of JAT staff. The trouble is that it does not have a terribly convenient location as it is out of town next to the aerodrome.

For dining, the **Hotel Srbija** has its own bunker-like restaurant. Otherwise, there are a couple of other choices for food. The **Restoran FK** next to the Vojvođanska banka at Dositejeva 4 (tel: 815 642) is friendly and welcoming and has a reasonable selection of soups, salads and grilled meats at low prices. Up at the west end of Trg Save Kovačevića, behind the cross and the fountain, is the **Restoran Drugi Oktobar** in an ugly modern building at Stevana Nemanje 26 (tel: 821 425). For fast food, there are plenty of take-aways along Vuka Karadića between the twin-spired Catholic cathedral and Gradski Park.

For drinks, the central square of Trg Save Kovačevića is lined with cafés on both sides and has plenty of outdoor seating in summer. The **Gradska Kafana** on the corner at Trg Save Kovačevića 4 is a very pleasant place from which to watch the world go by. Immediately opposite is **Slatka Kuća**, a large old-fashioned sweet shop with a bewildering selection of sweets and chocolates to choose from. Closer to the Hotel Srbija is the well-shaded **Caffe Laurint** by the small park at Svetosavsk Trg.

Practicalities

There is a **tourist information centre** at Trg Pobede 1 (tel: 822 554) at the side of the Town Hall building. Unfortunately, they are unable to offer any help or advice in English but may be able to come up with a town map.

For cash, there is a handy ATM at the **Komercialna banka** by the drinking fountain in Trg Save Kovačevića. The **Vojvođanska banka** in the attractive round building at the bottom of the square also has an ATM. There is an **internet café** next door to the Komercialna banka.

Vršac is well known for its distinctive red wine. A good selection of these can be found at **Vršački Vinogradi**, Svetosavski trg 1, opposite Hotel Srbija next to the small park, or you could visit the vineyard itself that is just out of town on the Bela Crkva road.

What to see

Vršac is a town whose Habsburg heritage is only too apparent. While there are a few specific sights well worth seeking out, much of the charm of the town lies in its domestic architecture as, unusual for Serbia, there are whole streets that have changed little in 200 years. One such street is **Jase Tomića**, which runs east–west across Dvorska, the high street at the bottom end of Trg Save Kovačevića. There is an impressive row of period houses in the Vojvodina style running along here, in particular numbers 30/30a next to Dom Omladine, and the bright yellow residence a little further along that is dated 1608. This same street is also the location for the **Palace of the Bishop of Banat**, a large pink baroque building that dates originally from 1759 but which was later rebuilt. Inside the palace, the **Chapel of Holy Archangels Michael and Gabriel** has some fine icons by Nikola Nesković.

On the other side of the street is the **Orthodox Cathedral of St Nicholas**, built 1783–85, with an iconostasis originally painted by Pavle Đurković but which has had most of its panels clumsily restored since.

Nearby, just to the north of Trg Pobede and on the corner of Kumanovska and Stefan Nemanje, is the **Pharmacy on the Steps Museum** (Apoteka na stepenikama Musej) with the entrance on steps above the street as the name implies. Unfortunately to visit this museum you have to time your visit carefully as, according to the notice on the door, it is open only on Sundays from 10.00–13.00 and 15.00–19.00. Just around the corner, where Dositejeva meets Stefan Nemanje, is a rather curious **neo-Gothic church** with red and yellow brickwork, a cupola and a tower inlaid with ceramic images of saints.

East of Trg Pobede, the imposing chocolate-coloured **Town Hall**, built in 1757, is a mixture of both classical and Gothic styles. Continuing east along Vuka Karadžića you come to the twin spires of the neo-Gothic **Roman Catholic cathedral** that was constructed between 1860 and 1863 and later rebuilt. The **town museum**, which is close by, more or less parallel to the Roman Catholic Cathedral on Anđe Ranković, has an interesting ethnographic exhibit and an art collection that has a special selection dedicated to the painter Paja Jovanović who was born here.

Also worth seeking out in town is the 18th-century building known as the **Two Pistols Inn** where Karađorđe is said to have lodged and the **Old Magistrates Court**, another neo-Gothic building built in 1860.

Kula breg

Clearly visible from anywhere in town is **Kula breg**, a 15th-century defensive tower that surveys the plains from its 400m vantage point on a round volcanic hill immediately above Vršac. Although close scrutiny does not reveal very much more about the site, it is as good a destination as any for a walk outside the town.

The best approach on foot is to head east from the Hotel Srbija along Vuka Karadžića past the Catholic cathedral and continue up the wide, gently sloping road that passes through Gradski Park. Fairly soon, you will pass the spanking new **Millennium Sports Complex** on your left. Just beyond here you come to a four-way junction. Take the narrow road that is the second from the right – the least likely looking candidate. This leads up to a series of steep steps that pass through a smart new housing development and eventually reaches a small white chapel, **Kapelin breg**, which although clearly visible from the town below seems to disappear into the trees as you get increasingly close. Just above here is the main road and, on the other side of it, a meadow with a noticeboard, picnic tables and small amphitheatre. The larger church of **Sveti Teodor**, also visible from the town, is just off the road to the left down a track. There is a car park area to the left of the road and a rustic café-restaurant with a garden next to it.

To reach the tower from here you have two options. The first is to follow the main road for a couple of kilometres. The road bends anticlockwise around the hillside and eventually you will see a sign and a drinks hut from where there is a steep path that leads uphill to the tower and the radio mast. The other option is to follow the track that leads into the woods from the car park restaurant. When you come to a parting of the ways take the right fork. This brings you to a wide track that more or less follows the contour line of the hill in a clockwise direction. There are a few rocky outcrops from which to admire the view before the path ventures into thick woodland that is very fragrant with blossom in summer. The track eventually circles the hill and brings you out at the main road at the drinks hut where the path leads up to the tower. Realistically, there is probably not much difference in the actual distance for either approach but it is certainly more pleasant walking through woodland on a hot day than it is to follow tarmac.

There is not much to see once you arrive at the tower, apart from the view of the Pannonian Plain, the town and the aerodrome. There are some rough foundations at the base of the *kula* but little else other than the inaccessible tower itself. Nevertheless, the view is excellent, and the tower has quite a foreboding presence about it, which adds to the atmosphere. The walk from the town should take an hour or so, depending on how often you stop for breath.

If you are driving to Kula breg, the road to take is the one towards Bela Crkva and then turn left off this up the hill along the road that is signposted: *Turistički put Breg*.

Bela Crkva

The pretty town of Bela Crkva ('White Church'), 35km south of Vršac, is tucked away in a pocket of Serbia that is surrounded on three sides by Romania. It is a fairly pristine place, without much industry and set in fairly flat but pleasant countryside. The river Nera, which more or less defines the frontier, is close by, as are several small lakes and the Danube–Tisa–Danube Canal. So much water has inevitably meant that the town has been dubbed the 'Venice of Vojvodina' but this is overstating the case somewhat.

Like Vršac, Bela Crkva has a number of baroque façades in its centre, but the town is most renowned for its **Flower Carnival** that takes place each summer.

The town has an interesting history. After centuries of invasion and occupation of the area by groups as diverse as Avars, Slavs, Hungarians, Turks and Bulgarians, Bela Crkva was established in 1717 by Count Claudius Florimund of Marcia. The town became heavily colonised by German settlers in the 18th century, who developed different trades and industries, in particular viniculture. The first grapes were harvested in 1733 and by 1816 wine traders from as far away as Vienna were visiting the town to buy its produce. Serbs, Romanians and others later joined the earlier migrants but the town remained predominantly German until 1945.

After World War I and the subsequent break-up of the Austro-Hungarian Empire, Bela Crkva found itself right on the border of the new entity of the Kingdom of Serbs, Croatians and Slovenes. Consequently, much of its economic power was lost as roads were cut and markets were denied. Following the next war, and the bitterness that ensued after years of Nazi occupation, virtually all of the Germans left the town for good.

Today, the town promotes its fresh air, fishing and bathing. There is a **beach** in town that has swimming facilities such as showers and changing cabins, and undeveloped beaches can be found at some of the nearby lakes. There is also a **town museum**, dating from 1877, that has paintings by 19th-century local artists and a small archaeological collection.

For accommodation, the **Vacation Complex Jezero** at Beogradska bb (tel: 851 152) by the town lake has five bungalows with 55 beds in total; each room or apartment has its own entrance, terrace and bathroom. The complex has its own restaurant with terrace. Nearby in a park at Kozaračka bb (tel: 851 094) is the **Hotel Turist** with its own restaurant and sports facilities. Singles are 840din, doubles 1,120din, apartments 1,260din. There is also a campsite.

As well as the 100-year-old Flower Carnival that takes place in late June there is also a catfish-catching competition held each summer. More information may be had from the **Tourist Organisation of Bela Crkva**, J Popovica bb, 26340 Bela Crkva; tel: 851 091, 064 1324 758; email: toobc@ptt.yu; www.belacrkva.co.yu.

Deliblatska Peščara

This unique area that forms a northwest to southeast arc between Bela Crkva and Belgrade is an area of remnant sand dunes left over from the draining of the Pannonian Sea. Much of the area has been afforested as a means of preventing land erosion and the unique habitat provided by this has created a suitable environment for a variety of species of animal and plant. Of the nearly 30,000ha covering the area, roughly 2,000ha are protected as reserve. On the remaining land, hunting is popular, with the majority of hunters coming from Italy, Germany and France. The most famous predator here, however, is the wolf. Wolves used to be considered vermin here and numerous attempts were made to eradicate them throughout the 19th century. By 1912, the wolf population was almost completely wiped out but the Deliblato wolves managed to increase their numbers slightly through the 20th century, despite continued persecution.

The whole area is excellent for birdwatching, and is home to rare species like imperial eagle (*Aquila heliaca*), corncrake (*Crex crex*) and saker falcon (*Falco cherrug*). The Novi Sad-based travel agency Magelan Corporation offer one-day birdwatching tours of Deliblato Peščara that start from Belgrade. If you are driving your own vehicle, you should head for the villages of Dolovo, Mramorak, Deliblato and Šušara that lie between Pančevo and Bela Crkva.

Pančevo ПАНЧЕВО
Telephone code: 013

Pančevo, an industrial town of around 100,000, lies close to Belgrade on the river Tamiš, a tributary of the Danube. Although the town existed as an important centre of Serbian culture during the Turkish occupation, Pančevo expanded during the early 18th century when it received migrations of Serbs from Romania and German colonists from the Upper Rhine region. The modern town has grown up around its post-World War II petrochemical industry.

On the night of April 15 1999, NATO attacked the city, bombing the HIP chemical complex that produced petrochemicals and fertilisers. Fires and explosions at the factories caused huge quantities of toxic chlorine compounds to be released into the air and river, and large tracts of land were polluted with oil derivatives, mercury, ammonia and acids. The effects of this widespread ecological catastrophe are still being felt in the area and the Pančevo district remains one of most ecologically damaged regions in all Serbia.

Despite its troubled recent history, Pančevo has a quiet, relaxed town centre with a number of attractive 19th-century buildings, which makes a good half-day trip from the capital. Interesting walks may be had down by the Tamiš River and there are some pleasant places to eat and drink down at the waterfront.

Pančevo can be easily reached from Belgrade by taking one of the **trains** that run more or less hourly from Karađorđev Park station near St Sava's Church. As well as Belgrade services, Pančevo Glavna station has four trains a day to Vršac and two to Zrenjanin and Kikinda. Fairly regular **buses** run to Belgrade, Vršac and Zrenjanin, although some of the Belgrade buses go only as far as the Dunav bus station in the north of the city by Dunavska bridge. The railway station and the bus station are some distance from each other in the town. The railway station is a 20-minute walk south of the city centre, while the bus station is more central, to the east of the river. Next to the main railway station of Pančevo Glavna is a large open-air market, known locally as the **Chinese Market**, which has a lot of cheap smuggled goods from Romania on sale.

There is just one place to stay in Pančevo: **Hotel Tamiš** (Mose Pijade bb; tel: 342 622, 345 840), with 58 double rooms, 54 singles and four apartments. Singles are 1,030din, doubles 1,720din. For food, there is the **Citadela restaurant** (tel: 515 286) close to the Byzantine-style church on Dimitrija Tucovića, the main street that leads from the railway station to the centre. Down by the Tamiš River is an old **railway carriage** that serves both as a **café-bar** and unofficial railway museum. There are a couple of restaurants by the river down here: **Kakadu**, on a boat on the river, and also the **Kafana Stari Tamiš**.

Information on events in the town can be had from the **Tourist Organisation of Pančevo**, Sokače 2 (tel: 351 366).

Kovačica

This small but sprawling town lies directly north of Pančevo. Kovačica is well known for two things: its majority **Slovak population** and its tradition of **naïve painting**.

The town is quite spread out with long, tree-lined avenues radiating off a central park with a church; not really that different from many others in Vojvodina. The Slovak influence is not that pronounced but can be seen in the houses, some of which have small plaques that record the householder's name on the gable, along with the date of construction. There are more blond-haired children than usual too, as you might expect, and a few older women riding around on bicycles who still wear the traditional Slovak embroidered apron over their black voluminous skirts.

The Slovakians first came to the area 200 years ago as soldiers of the Austrian army on the front line against the Ottomans. In return for their services to the Habsburgs they were given land to farm. The Slovaks in Kovačica today speak a language that has changed little in the two centuries they have been in the area, and which is barely understood by modern Slovaks in Bratislava.

The tradition of naïve painting started in 1939 when two locals, Martin Paluška and Ján Sokol began to paint. The tradition developed in the 1950s when Paluška, Sokol and a few others formed a painting club and more Slovaks from Kovačica, Padina and the surrounding area took up paintbrushes to try and represent the rural environment they lived in. The first exhibition took place in 1952 on the occasion of the 150th anniversary of the Slovaks' arrival in Kovačica; three years later the first gallery of naïve art was opened.

A large and varied collection of the work of the Kovačica artists can be seen at the **Galerija naivne utmetnosti** (tel: 661 157; email: office@artkovacica.co.yu; www.artkovacica.co.yu) the state-run gallery in the town. Naïve art is not to everybody's taste but there is a striking amount of variety in the work on display and many of the painters on display here have instantly recognisable styles. The themes, of course, are all rural, but even these cover a wide a range of subject matter.

Next door to the state gallery is the private **Gallery Babka** (tel: 661 631; fax: 661 522; email: babka@eunet.yu; www.yu.co.yu/babka) with a more limited range. They have reproductions and small cameos for sale as well as full-size paintings. In the same group of buildings are the workshops of several practising artists. One that is well worth visiting and which welcomes visitors is that belonging to **Zuzana Holúbeková** at Jánošiková 92 (tel: 661 929; mob: 063 8191 884; email: jonovska@panet.co.yu) whose more recent work has quite a marked erotic quality about it.

Buses run from Belgrade's BAC bus station to Kovačica several times a day. The journey takes just over an hour and costs 100din. More frequent services run to Pančevo and Zrenjanin. The infrequent trains that run to Zrenjanin from Belgrade also stop in Kovačica. To reach the art galleries and workshops from the bus stop on the main road, turn right past the park and church and walk for five minutes; they are on the right-hand side of the road beyond a few shops and cafés.

SREM
Sremska Karlovci and Fruška Gora both belong to Srem but have been dealt with previously in the Bačka section – *Around Novi Sad*.

Sremska Mitrovica СРЕМСКА МИТРОВИЦА
Telephone code: 022
This town in western Srem, which lies just off the main Zagreb–Belgrade highway, has a long history of settlement that goes back 7,000 years. The earliest colonists here were Illyrians, later followed by Celtic settlers, but the greatest undertaking was undoubtedly made by the Romans who built **Sirmium** on the same site as the modern town, close to the banks of the Sava River. Sirmium was an extensive settlement that was far more than a mere garrison, having all of the usual trademarks of Roman sophistication: baths, mosaic floors, public sewage systems, a hippodrome and palaces. Much of what the Romans left still lies under the streets of the modern town, awaiting the will and the finance necessary to excavate. However, there are a couple of places in town where the foundations have been cleared enough to appreciate the scale and sophistication of Sirmium without needing to have a trained archaeologist's eye. The town's museums also have plenty of interest, with some fine pieces of Roman sculpture.

Getting there
There are 21 **buses** a day from Novi Sad and 11 from Belgrade. Four daily buses also run from nearby Ruma. Being close to both the Croatian and Bosnian borders there are also international connections: five buses run from Banja Luka in the Republka Srpska entity of Bosnia Herzegovina, and two more from Brčko.

Sremska Mitrovica is on the main Ljubljana–Zagreb–Belgrade train line and so all through **trains** stop here at the town's rather grim railway station.

The train and bus stations stand side by side, a 20-minute walk from the town centre. A war memorial in the form of an obelisk with the communist red star stands in the road between the two stations – a rare sight in modern Serbia.

Where to stay and eat
Sremska Mitrovica is an easy day trip from either Novi Sad or Belgrade but there are two options if you want to stay over. The two-star **Hotel Sirmium** in the centre of town at Boska Palkovljvica Pinkija 6 (tel: 226 333) is close to everything that you

might wish to see. The foundations of a Roman palace are just outside the entrance and the Museum Srem is immediately opposite, facing the park. Single rooms are around the 1,000din mark; doubles, 1,800din. The other choice, and in the same price range, is the two-star **Hotel Srem**, Sutjeska bb (tel: 221 828, 225 700).

Beyond what the hotel restaurants have to offer, dining choices are rather limited. **Restaurant Srem** (tel: 216 974) at Masarikova 4, just behind the park, serves national cuisine. The **XL Caffe Pizzeria** at 18 Trg Ćine Milekića (tel: 221 360) has a good range of pizzas, sweet and savoury pancakes, milkshakes, beers and soft drinks, and is open late into the night. The **Caffe Aureus** in the park by the museum is a nice shady spot for a drink in warm weather.

What to see

Although there are no specific buildings to point out, Sremska Mitrovica has an interesting mix of building styles and to wander down through its streets to the river is a pleasant experience. Among the weather-worn 18th- and 19th-century façades are a surprising number of old-fashioned shops that seem to have changed little since Tito's time.

Remains of the extensive **Roman town** of Sirmium are clearly visible in the few places around the town where excavation has already taken place. The best are found near the river along the main road running south from the Hotel Sirmium, at a fork in the road a few hundred metres past the Orthodox church. In the triangle of land formed by the junction are the excavated remains of what would have been one of the **trade quarters** of the Roman town. There is also evidence of a high street that would have been one of the main traffic routes connecting the river Sava with the town's forum. Fragments of the pedestrian zone are quite clear, especially the public sewer with its arched brick roof that still remains in places. In the south part of the site some remains of the city wall can be seen.

Continuing down the road from here you soon arrive at the river. There is a large new pedestrian suspension bridge arching across to the south bank of the Sava, and a river promenade to follow in either direction should you so wish. The road to the right of the Roman site leads to a small white church with a few cafés clustered around it.

The other major Roman excavation in the town is just behind the Hotel Sirmium. This probably represents some of the remains of an **emperor's palace** and most probably belonged to Constantine's son. It is likely that more of the palace will be revealed in the future, when the excavations over the road outside the Srem Museum are completed. So far, a beautiful marble head of Diana has been discovered here, giving further evidence that the palace was the property of a powerful and influential figure. The Diana head should be on display in the museum by 2005. Further evidence that a palace existed here is supported by findings around the town that reveal traces of a large hippodrome. If this were the palace of someone as important as an emperor's son then it would have been positioned right next to the hippodrome; so far, all of the evidence seems to point towards this.

The **Museum of Srem** (*Musej Srema*) is divided into two sites. Opposite the Hotel Sirmium, in the large building facing the park, is the part of the museum that displays the ethnographic and art collection. This is currently open only in the mornings and work is disrupted to some extent by the excavations taking place outside. This situation will probably have changed by 2005. The other site is an 18th-century nobleman's house, virtually opposite the church at Trg Sveti Stefana 15 (tel: 223 245). This branch deals with the palaeontology and archaeology of the region. Downstairs in the courtyard is an impressive array of Roman finds from Sirmium:

statues, columns and intricately carved coffins. Most impressive of all is the blackened skeleton of an enormous wooden canoe-like boat that was dredged from the mud of the Sava River some years ago, and is similar to the one in the collection at Petrovaradin Fortress in Novi Sad. Upstairs, there is a reconstruction of a Celtic house and a Roman tent, various pottery finds and some mammoth and giant elk bones. All of the labels are in Serbian although there is a limited amount of interpretive material in English downstairs. The collection is open for visitors 09.00–15.00 weekdays, 09.00–13.00 Saturdays. Both museums are closed on Mondays.

The **church** opposite the museum is also worth a quick look. It has a finely detailed iconostasis and stained-glass windows that feature Lazar, Stefan Nemanja and other members of the Nemanjić dynasty.

Obedska Bara bird sanctuary

This, the third of Vojvodina's Ramsar Convention wetland sites in Vojvodina, consists of an area of marsh and floodplain on the north bank of the Sava River 65km west of Belgrade, close to the town of Šabac. The reserve lies inside an old oxbow lake with open water areas, extensive reed-beds and wet meadows.

Over 200 bird species have been recorded here. Black stork breeds here and white-tailed and lesser-spotted eagle (*Aquila pomarina*) have both been seen. Typical birds present here include great white egret, spoonbill (*Platalea leucorodia*) and little bittern. There is also a heronry of 250-plus birds.

The sanctuary is reached from the main Belgrade–Zagreb E-70 motorway by taking the Pećinci village exit and continuing south to the village of Obrež at the oxbow lake. Accommodation is available at the **Obedska Bara Hotel** in Obrež village (tel: 022 886 22).

Zasavica Special Nature Reserve

The Zasavica reserve is situated in the small enclave of Srem that lies immediately south of the Sava River close to Sremska Mitrovica. It consists of around 2,000 hectares of protected wetland that is made up of meadows, canals, creeks and the Zasavica River itself. The area was first put under protection in 1997 on the recommendation of the Institute for the Protection of Nature in Serbia.

Zasavica has over 200 plant species including many water lilies (*Nymphaea alba* and *Nuphar luteum*) and some rare relict species that are included in Serbia's *Red Data Book*. The reserve is also host to around 120 bird species, 80 of which breed, as well as a number of rare reptiles and amphibians, and elusive aquatic mammals like otters. Fishing is permitted in specific locations of the reserve, and carp, pike and golden carp are all present in its waters.

Information and guides are provided by the managing authority, Pokret Gorana, based at Svetog Save 19, Sremska Mitrovica (tel: 214 300; fax: 226 089; email: zasavica@zasavica.org.yu; www.zasavica.org.yu).

The Sremska Mitrovica tourist agency Anitours (Vuka Karadžića 8; tel: 226 089) can also help provide tourist information as well as organise accommodation and tours.

Clocktower at Petrovaradin Fortress,
Novi Sad

West and Southwest Serbia

The gently rolling countryside of central Serbia becomes increasingly dramatic as you venture west or south from Kraljevo. From Čačak west, the main road follows the course of the Ovčar River, a tributary of the Morava, a region of small monasteries hidden away in the valleys of forested hills. Beyond here lies Užice, an interesting industrial town with an important place in modern Yugoslav history. Further west, close to the Bosnian border, is the Zlatibor region, an upland farming area with Kraljeve Vode (Partizanska Vode), a resort popular with Serbian holidaymakers, at its centre. Although west Serbia is not a distinct region in any political sense of the word, it does have a character all of its own, which seems to echo the dark green mountains of Bosnia that lie beyond.

Heading south from Kraljevo along the river Ibar, the predominantly Muslim region of Raška is soon reached: a poor, but starkly beautiful region that historically has served as a buffer zone between Orthodox Serbia and Muslim Bosnia.

The **highlights** in this southwestern part of the country are undoubtedly the monasteries of Studenica, Sopoćani and Mileševa, all tucked away in gorgeous lush valleys; Novi Pazar with its Turkish bazaar atmosphere and ancient churches that lie just outside the town; the majestically bleak highlands of the Pešter plateau that rises to the west of Novi Pazar; and the small villages of the Zlatibor region – Mokra Gora with its fascinating switchback railway and Sirigojno with its open-air folk museum. Winter sports enthusiasts will also find plenty to amuse themselves with in the ski resort of Kopaonik.

UŽICE УЖИЦЕ
Telephone code: 031
History

Although nothing is immediately apparent from its appearance, this city, formerly known as Titovo Užice, holds a unique place in modern Serbian and Yugoslav history. It was here, in the autumn of 1941, that the Užice Republic was declared: a free Partisan state that lasted a mere 67 days until the town was surrendered to the Germans after a heroic defence. For the brief time that the republic lasted, Užice became the headquarters of the war effort and the strategic centre from which Tito planned his Partisan operations.

Although it was a short-lived liberation, a provisional government was set up in the town, and presses put to work to print propaganda and newspapers. The eventual evacuation and defeat, when it came, was quite dreadful, with horrifying losses as the German army took back the town with its 10,000-strong strike force. This was to be one of the Partisans' worst defeats. With such overwhelming odds, it was inevitable that Užice would sooner or later fall back into Nazi control; nevertheless, the town

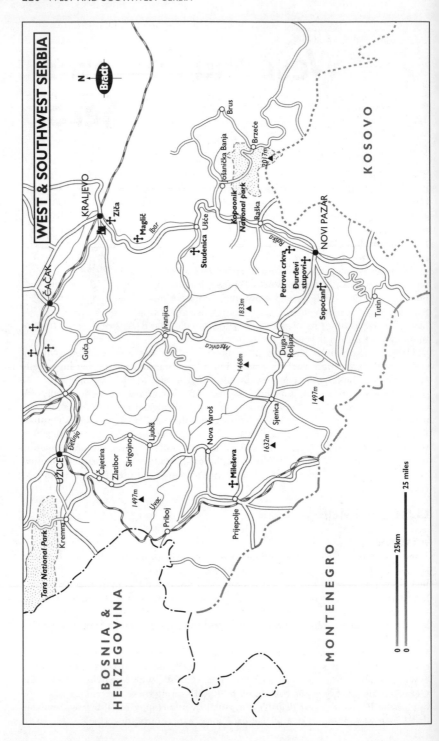

was defended almost to the last man. As a result of this, Tito felt obliged to tender his resignation as Partisan leader; it was, of course, rejected outright. Following the appalling losses at Užice, the Partisans made a desperate withdrawal across the Zlatibor Planina, a march made in the depths of winter in which they suffered further casualties.

The city was renamed Titovo Užice in 1946 in honour of the Partisan leader and kept the name until 1992, when both the prefix, and the large statue of Josip Broz Tito that stood in the central square, were removed once and for all.

Today, the city is a reasonably attractive sort of place, set deep in the valley of the Đetinja River, a tributary of the Zapadna Morava, at an altitude of 411m, surrounded by lush, dark green hills. With blocks of public housing climbing up the hillsides, Užice has a prosperous, if somewhat utilitarian, air about it. The city has grown quite rapidly since World War II and today has a population approaching 60,000 that are mainly employed in the chemical industry and copper and aluminium processing. The city centre is testament to the occasional successes of modern urban planning and, although it is quite compact, it has a light and airy feel, despite the plentiful presence of concrete high-rises, the most notable of which is the concrete skyrocket of the Zlatibor hotel.

Coming from the west, Užice's most notable landmark is clearly visible before the modern town opens up to view in the valley below: high on a bluff above the river, the ruins of a medieval fortress look down over the town, with steep stone walls and terraces like an Inca ruin. This fortress gives evidence to a strategic importance that has existed since Roman times.

The city may have Celtic origins but the first mention of the town comes from a document in the archives of Dubrovnik from 1329, when a trade colony was developed here. It was conquered by the Turks in the middle of the 15th century, and by the 17th century had become an important craft and cultural centre. Užice became a military base at the time of the wars between Austria and Turkey in the late 17th and early 18th century and played a crucial role in the First Serbian Uprising. In 1805, the town was liberated from the Turks by Serbian insurrectionists only to fall under Ottoman rule once again in 1813. In 1862, the Turks finally left after another siege and a great fire that virtually destroyed the town. The city was finally connected to Belgrade by railway in 1912. With the exception of the fortress and some churches, most of what can be seen today is post-World War I. The German bombardment of 1941 was not quite the last word in the military action that Užice would witness: in the hostilities of 1999, the city post office was hit by a NATO bomb, killing and injuring a number of civilians and putting 18,000 phone lines out use. The reasons for this seemingly pointless attack remain unclear.

Getting there

Užice's rail and train stations stand side by side on the south side of the river, just five minutes' walk from the city centre. The bus station is clean and modern with more than adequate facilities; the railway station is a little less plush. There are plenty of buses to Belgrade that go via Čačak and Gorni Milanovac, a journey that takes about three hours. Four buses a day run to Novi Sad, two of which are direct via Valjevo, two via Belgrade. There are 20 buses a day that run a shuttle service to nearby Čačak, while several buses also run to points further east like Kraljevo, Kruševac and Kragujevac, as well as to local destinations in western Serbia.

The city is on the Bar–Belgrade train line and so there are plenty of services in either direction, stopping at Priboj and Prijepolje (for Mileševa Monastery) going south, and Valjevo and Lazarevac, heading north to Belgrade.

There is a small airport nearby but currently this does not handle commercial flights.

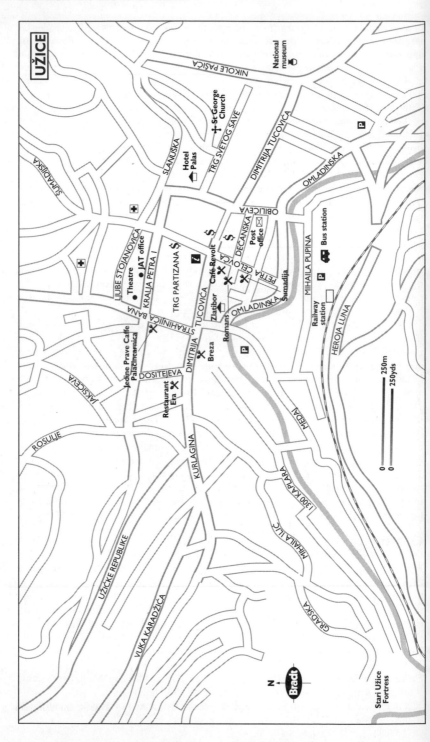

Tourist information and local tour operators

For information about travel, hotels and excursions, the charming staff at the **tourist office** at Trg partizana 10 (tel: 513 485, 514 761) are extremely accommodating and go out of their way to help. They have little printed material available in English but can advise on accommodation, transport and city sightseeing. For booking services, a local travel agency can be found at **Raketaturs**, Dimitrija Tucovića 64 (tel: 512 588, 512 864). For booking or confirming flights, there is a **JAT** office at Ljube Stojanovića 5 (tel: 513 870, 513 664).

Most of the **banks** are clustered around Trg partizana and Dimitrija Tucovića; the Delta bank has an ATM, otherwise there are plenty of exchange offices in the same area.

Where to stay

Hotel Zlatibor Dimitrija Tucovića 48; tel: 29 183, 24 467. You cannot fail to notice this 3-star monstrosity in the centre of town, dominating the square south of Trg partizana. The Zlatibor is an object lesson in hotel decline; no doubt it was quite grand once but standards (and maintenance) have slipped to the extent that it now looks distinctly threadbare. The lift – which you are grateful for if you have been booked into a room in one of the upper storeys – is highly erratic, seemingly with a mind of its own. The carpets range from threadbare to completely worn out, and the eccentric and numerous light fittings, standard to all of the rooms, have clearly seen better days – I counted 13 in my room, 7 of which worked. To make matters worse, the glue that holds up the heavy-duty wallpaper has seemingly lost its battle with gravity and the paper is peeling off like tree bark in places. Downstairs, the vast reception area offers plenty of space to stretch your legs while you are waiting for the lift to arrive but the circular bar only seems to be functional if you bring your own drinks along. The adjoining restaurant resembles a glazed car park. On a more positive note, the rooms are clean, the staff are quite friendly, and the view from the upper floors really is good. There are 280 beds here and so it is unlikely that the Zlatibor ever has been, or ever will be, fully booked. Singles cost 1,045din (or €15); doubles 1,800din (€25).

Hotel Palas Trg Svetog Save 3; tel: 512 752. This 2-star hotel is also in the city centre and is a better bet if you prefer something a little more intimate. While not exactly a palace, the rooms with bathrooms are clean and simple, and reasonably spacious. Double-glazing cuts down on street noise. Generally good value, with singles at 930din and doubles at 1,700din.

Hotel Turist 1300 kaplara bb; tel: 24 509. At the time of writing, this hotel by the river was undergoing extensive refurbishment. It will eventually be reopened under private ownership, either in 2005 or 2006, but for the time being the ground-floor area appears to have found a new lease of life as a gym.

Where to eat and drink

Era Dimitrija Tucovića 142; tel: 518 645. This is a traditional restaurant with occasional music where you can try out the *kajmak* that the city is reputedly famous for. The restaurant is closed all day on Sun.

Breza Dimitrija Tucovića 157; tel: 514 751. This is a more basic place just across the road from the Era restaurant. It is open 07.00–22.00, but closed on Sun.

Šumadija Petra Ćelovića 22; tel: 514 785. Another traditional restaurant that serves regional specialities, located on a quiet street running south from Dimitrija Tucovića. On the next corner, heading north back to the square, is the basement café-bar **Revolt**.

Romansa Dečanska 21; tel: 512 157, 514 095. On the other side of the square from the front entrance of the Hotel Zlatibor. Next door is the **Café Grand**.

For snacks, there are a couple of *burek* places like **Blue Moon Burek** on Slanuška behind Trg Svetog Save.

There are several pizza and pancake places scattered around the centre. A good bet for sweet and savoury pancakes and ice-creams is **Jedina Prave Caffe Palaćinkarnica** at Strahinjica Bana 17 (tel: 519 700), which is along the street that runs parallel to Trg partizana on its west side.

What to see

The author Brian W Aldiss, writing in 1966, describes Užice as having the appearance of a frontier town so swarming with wild people that 'it was almost impossible to drive a car down the main street' and where 'every sturdy Serbian dame was accompanied by a child, a lamb, or a porker'. Aldiss found Užice to be a place where 'men sat alone, clutching sharp knives and devouring hunks of meat and bread off bare tables'. He concludes stating that, 'the morals of Titovo Užice are reputed to be low; one has only to see the place to believe the rumour' before confessing that he did not have enough time at his disposal to spend the night there. Alas, things have changed somewhat since then: these days, Serbian dames are far more slender and Užice's men use more genteel cutlery to eat their pizza as they sit quietly with their girlfriends. However, despite the humdrum trappings of modern provincial life, there are still a few things worth seeing in the city.

Stari Užice Fortress

This medieval fortress perches on a rock just to the west of the city above the river, probably on the same site as an earlier Roman *castrum*. It is first mentioned historically in 1373, during the reign of Nikole Altomanović, but little is known of the detail of its subsequent demise. Despite a complete lack of interpretive material, it is well worth a visit for the view at least – east across the modern city, and west over the green valley of the Đetinja River and on to the hills of the Zlatibor range. Although the fortress remains undiscovered and unexploited by the Serbian tourist industry it has not been overlooked by local youths, and the presence of extensive graffiti – both crude *četnik* ciphers and less politically motivated scrawl – has had an undesirable effect on what might otherwise be a numinous atmosphere.

To reach the fortress, walk along the river west from the centre – it does not matter which side you choose, as there are plenty of footbridges. You will soon reach a small hydro-electric plant and a waterfall. Steps lead up to the right to reach the iron bridge that crosses the river here, actually a decommissioned railway crossing. It is possible to follow the old railway line, west along the valley through tunnels and over more bridges; this has some potential for a rewarding mountain-bike route, although as it stands, the bridge crossings would be extremely hazardous on two wheels until some sort of protective barrier was put in place. Hiking is a possibility too: with a number of paths leading off temptingly in several directions, there is undoubtedly great walking potential to be explored in the hills around the city.

Returning to the iron bridge, steps lead up a narrow path through woodland. This soon reaches a road higher up where you turn right past some houses, then sharp left at the next junction along Gradska, which leads straight up to the fortress. The fortress, which clings to the steep summit, has unprotected precipitous drops on all sides, so care is required.

Partisan Square

If this guide had been written a dozen or so years earlier I would be advising you to visit the giant statue of an austere, great-coated Tito in this, the city's central square. Unfortunately, in 1992 the statue was removed along with the city's old name, to leave a large, empty space where it formerly stood. Although it is easy to understand why Užice, and Serbia in general, wants to shed painful memories of the recent past, it seems a pity that there is nothing whatsoever to remind us of the heroic struggle that took place here in 1941 – another case of praiseworthy and valiant babies being thrown out with communist bath water. Now Trg partizana appears to be too large for a city of such modest size, and lacks any real focal point. In summer, its eastern flank is lined by outdoor cafés, which takes up some of the space, but still the square seems a little forlorn, as if haunted by the ghost of the ousted statue.

National Museum
Dimitrija Tucovića 18; tel: 521 360, 520 657

The museum, formerly known as the Museum of the 1941 Insurrection, occupies the same building that was the headquarters of Tito's Popular Army of Liberation in the autumn of 1941. It contains a number of exhibits from the war effort during this period, together with displays from later, communist times. A small tank is parked outside the entrance. The opening times given are what it says on the door but the last time I visited it was inexplicably closed.

Open daily 09.00–17.00, Sat 09.00–14.00; closed Mon

Jokanovića House
Slanuška 10a; tel: 513 035

This typical 19th-century house is preserved as an ethnological and cultural monument with a permanent exhibition. It stands close to the grey-washed **Church of St George** (1844) that occupies the same cobbled square that is a popular hangout of the city's student population. Užice's other noteworthy church is that of the white-washed **Church of St Marko** (1829) with its rustic wooden clocktower.

ČAČAK ЧАЧАК
Telephone code for Čačak and Guča: 032

Halfway between Kraljevo and Užice, the large industrial town of Čačak on the Zapada Morava River has little to offer the casual visitor other than a gateway to Guča, an ordinary provincial town for 51 weeks of the year but a quite extraordinary place during the annual **Dragačevo Trumpet Festival** that takes place there each summer.

The town played a prominent role in the anti-Milošević protests of October 2000 when the outspoken mayor of the town, Velimir 'Velja' Ilić, organised an enormous convoy of over 10,000 protesters from Čačak to Belgrade, personally leading them through numerous police road blocks on the morning of October 5. The Čačak convoy was as much carnival as it was protest group and included 50 buses and 1,000 cars in its ranks to transport the protestors. Ilić also took the precaution of taking a bulldozer with him, to assist in negotiating the blockades. On arrival in Belgrade, the machine was used to smash a way into the entrance of the Serbian RTS television building. Later, after spearheading the storming of the Parliament building, Mayor Ilić's supporters were heard singing: 'We are the Čačak boys, bulldozers are our toys'. The image stuck in people's minds and as a result of Čačak's central role in the countrywide protest the mayor soon became better known by his new nickname, 'Bulldozer' Ilić.

Despite the laudable anti-Milošević pedigree, Čačak was quite badly damaged by the 1999 NATO bombing campaign, in particular the 'Sloboda' factory, which despite producing vacuum cleaners and other home appliances was identified as a military target.

Today, the town is a dull, modern place of about 100,000 with little to see other than the **Church of Christ's Assumption** in the town centre. The **tourist office** at Trg ustana 4 (tel: 342 360; fax: 225 069; email: toc@ptt.yu) may be able to provide further suggestions.

There are three hotels and an adequate selection of restaurants in town if you want to stay but it is probably advisable to press on to either Užice or Kraljevo. The accommodation options consist of the three-star **Hotel President** on Bulevar Oslobođenja (tel: 371 401, 371 417), the two-star **Hotel Beograd** at Gradsko šetalište 20 (tel: 224 593) and the one-star **Hotel Morava,** Vuka Karađića 2 (tel: 227 022). Twenty buses a day connect with Belgrade; many more go to Kraljevo, Užice, Gorni Milanovac and Kragujevac.

GUČA ГУЧА

Guča is a small market town 18km south of Čačak that lies at the foot of the Krstac hills. In recent years this anonymous little town has become famous for the annual **Dragačevo Trumpet Festival** that takes place in early August. Since the first festival was organised in 1961 the festival has grown beyond anyone's imagination. Attendance is now said to be over 300,000, which may be an exaggeration but it is certainly big – very big – and any hope of finding somewhere to stay during the festival should be abandoned unless prior arrangements have been made. (See box *The Dragačevo Trumpet Festival.*)

The rest of the year, accommodation can be found at the three-star **Hotel Zlatne Truba** on Trg Slobode, the main square in town (tel: 854 459), and at the privately run **Hotel President**, with 49 rooms and 1km from the centre on Bulevar Oslobođ enja bb (tel: 371 401; fax: 371 417). Across the street from the Hotel Zlatne Truba is **Dom Kultur** (Culture house) where live concerts are put on during the festival. Turning right at Dom Kultur there is the famous **Statue of the Trumpet Player** that celebrates the festival at the next corner. Turning left here brings you to the square where most of the tent restaurants are and where most of the off-stage live music takes place during the event. The brass competition itself is held in a football field at the edge of town.

If you want to visit the festival, it is probably best to book transport and accommodation in advance. One option is to book through the www.guca.co.yu website which offers transportation Belgrade–Guča–Belgrade for €20 return, and four nights' accommodation, including breakfast, in a private home in the town for €140. Transportation and accommodation are slightly discounted at €150 per person when booked together. This should be booked well in advance as places are limited. Their website has a message board for past and prospective Guča visitors and some excellent photo galleries that really bring home the noise and mayhem of the event.

Another good-value festival package is offered by a Slovenian organisation on www.veslilca.net, which offers accommodation in Guča town centre and return transport to Ljubljana for €139. Bookings for the August festival have to be made by mid June.

The other option is just to arrive with a tent, find a pitch somewhere and just hope for the best; as anyone who has attended will tell you, sleeping is a fairly low priority at the festival.

Guča may have the lion's share but it does not have a complete monopoly on musical events in the area. In late July, a flute-playing festival takes place in the village of Prislonica, just to the north of Čačak. The **'Oj Moravo' Flute-player Assembly** is an annual gathering in which folk music is performed on the *frula*, an indigenous Serbian form of the flute. Like Guča, this is essentially a competitive event, and the best *frula* player is chosen from competing entrants. As well as music, there are other traditional activities such as folk dancing and poetry readings. Information about the event can be had by contacting the Čačak Tourist Office (tel: 342 360, 225 069; email: toc@ptt.yu).

THE DRAGAČEVO TRUMPET FESTIVAL

Better known simply as 'Guča', this extraordinary annual event is now approaching its 45th year. Over the past ten years it has grown to become an enormous national spectacle, which is now televised and shown on Serbian TV, but it has far more modest origins.

Trumpets were first introduced into Serbian life by Prince Miloš Obrenović, who ordered the formation of the first military band in 1831. It was probably the presence of a large amount of decommissioned military brassware that led to the trumpet (along with other brass-band instruments like flugelhorn, tuba and baritone) being adopted as the musical instrument of choice for all sorts of social occasions: births, baptisms, weddings, *slava* days and church festivals. Many musicians in south and central Serbia, Roma especially, took to playing the trumpet as a result; they had their advantages over more traditional instruments, being harder-wearing, easier to keep in tune and, most important, they were much louder.

The first Dragačevo Assembly of Trumpet Players was held in 1961 (Dragačevo is simply the district to which the town of Guča belongs) in the yard of the Church of St Michael and St Gabriel in the town. It remained a small, almost clandestine, celebration for a number of years, a reflection of the political atmosphere at the time, which did not always approve of celebrations that did not directly involve the state.

Over the past ten years the Guča festivities have grown enormously, and are now attended by trumpet players, brass bands and folk song and dance groups from around the world. Some old hands say that the festival has become over-commercialised (there is much sponsorship these days by Serbian beer companies) and over-attended by those more interested in the riotous party atmosphere than the music itself. In 2002, it was estimated that over 300,000 attended during the three days of the festival. In 2004, 500,000 were expected, and the festival was extended by another day to become a four-day event.

Past stars of the festival include Milan Mladenović, Ekrem Sajdić, Elvis Ajdinović, Fejat Sejdic and Zoran Sejdic. The greatest star of all, and multiple winner of the *Zlatne Truba* 'Golden Trumpet' award, is the Roma trumpet player, Boban Marković from Vladičin han in southern Serbia (an area rich in brass bands and exemplary musicians), who was so good they had to ban him in order to give the rest of the competition a chance. Now his son Marko is proving to be equally talented. As none less than trumpet maestro Miles Davis himself remarked when he visited the festival, 'I didn't know you could play trumpet that way.'

Monasteries of the Ovčar-Kablar Gorge

Leaving Čačak in a westerly direction along the E-761 towards Požega and Užice, the road runs alongside the picturesque Ovčar-Kablar Gorge. The area is something of a playground for the nearby industrial centres and the river Morava is lined with fishing lodges along much of the way. Hidden away high above the river in dense woodland is a succession of **17th-century monastery churches**. The monasteries are for the most part small and remote, dating from a time when monks were compelled to hide themselves away from the Turks as much as possible. The ten that lie along the gorge are deemed in some quarters, somewhat fancifully, to constitute a Serbian equivalent of Mt Athos. They nearly all require a detour and although interesting enough and in lovely surroundings, they are probably not worth devoting too much time to if you are planning to visit, or have already seen, the cream of Serbian monasteries like Studenica, Sopoćani or Manasija.

Probably the most accessible is **Vavedenje Monastery**, close to the main road only 8km from Čačak, which dates from 1452 and has a painted doorway from the early 19th century. The **Church of the Annunciation** at **Blagoveštenje Monastery** lies above the village of **Ovčar Banja**. The church was built in 1602 and, as well as a fine iconostasis, houses several important manuscripts in its library, the most notable being a Holy Gospel from 1552. **The Holy Trinity Monastery** (*Manastir Svete Trojice*) on the opposite bank, originates from 1694, although there are vestiges of 13th-century design in its construction. The church contains two icons dated 1635: *Christ with the Apostles* and the *Mother of God with the Prophets*. The **Sretenje Monastery** is close by – at least, as the crow flies – situated on the southwest slope of Mt Ovčar at a height of 800m above sea level. The monastery is home to an 18th-century Russian icon: *Mother of God with the Child*. The monastic library was burned down during World War II but a handful of 16th-century documents and Bibles were saved. **St Nicholas's Monastery** (*Manastir Nikolje*) on the river's north bank has been destroyed several times in its turbulent history but still retains some interesting frescos.

The rest of the monasteries are of more recent date but have all been built on the site of older monastic foundations. Close to the peak of Mt Kablar is a small church, dedicated to St Sava, built close to a mineral spring that is said by locals to cure eye problems.

SOUTH ALONG THE IBAR VALLEY

Leaving Kraljevo, the road south follows the river Ibar towards Raška, Novi Pazar and the territory of the Sandžak. It is a beautiful drive, with densely forested green hills on either side of the valley. The river, fast flowing even at Kraljevo, becomes increasingly turbulent further upstream, shadowed by the main road. Steep, wooded slopes rise on both sides of the narrow valley but, here and there, tiny, garden-sized plots of agriculture appear where there is just enough flat land to cultivate a few crops.

Two spa resorts lie just off this road: **Mataruška Banja** to the east, about 12km from Kraljevo, and **Bogutovačka Banja** 10km further on, a couple of kilometres west of the village of Bogutovac on the main road. Both have hotels with the usual spa facilities. Further information on these may be had from the helpful Kraljevo tourist office.

After about 20km or so, the medieval castle of **Maglić** appears to the left, high on a bluff above a bend in the river. Maglić Castle was constructed by a 14th-century archbishop who wished to protect himself from marauding factions. You can only assume, given the castle's forbidding and impregnable appearance, that he was entirely successful in his venture. Like many of Serbia's abandoned castles, Maglić probably looks more impressive from a distance – and especially from below, where it maintains a sense of scale and dominance over the surrounding landscape. Buses will stop here, should you wish to get off and explore; there is a footbridge a little further on beyond the bus stop, which you can use to cross the river before clambering up to the ruins.

The road continues a further 25km south to the small town of **Ušće** at the confluence of the Ibar and Studenica rivers, where there is the turn-off to Studenica Monastery. Although there is a large sign near Kraljevo announcing that the monastery is 55km further on, and another just 20km short of it, there is no sign at the actual turn-off when coming from the north. The road to take is the one immediately before the town, to the north of the river. The road to Studenica climbs up steeply through pine forest, snaking its way through a series of tight bends. The monastery is reached about 12km from the junction, although it will probably seem further than this by the time you get there.

Studenica Monastery

Deliberately remote, the monastery of Studenica sits in splendidly mountainous surroundings, high above the river that bears the same name, and even higher above the Raška valley, a dozen kilometres to the east. Originally established by Stefan Nemanja at the end of the 12th century, this is undoubtedly one of the country's greatest monasteries and one of the holiest places in the Serbian national psyche.

The monastery consists of three churches within an oval walled complex (originally there were nine). The largest of these, and central to the complex, is that of the **Church of Our Lady** (*Sveti Bogorodica*), completed in 1191. This church, the prototype of the Raška School, takes its influence from both Romanesque and Byzantine sources. The exterior is of polished marble, unique in Serbian medieval architecture, with elaborately sculptured leaves, figures and mythological beasts in the Romanesque style decorating the windows and doorways.

Inside, the effect of the smooth marble is marred by a clumsily executed exonarthex, added by Radoslav, one of the later rulers of the Nemanjić dynasty, who saw fit to add this maladroit extension around 1230. Entrance to the interior is made through the exonarthex. Inside, the iconostasis, with its unusually cheerful-looking representations of Jesus, Mary and God, dates from the 16th century. The marble tomb of Stefan Nemanja is situated in a chapel to the right of the exonarthex beneath a fresco that shows him holding a model of the church and being presented to Christ and the Virgin. It was at Studenica that Stefan Nemanja abdicated before his retirement to Mt Athos in Greece. His body was returned here after his death. His feast day is May 24 and there is a pilgrimage here every year to celebrate the event. Stefan's son, Stefan Prvovenčani, is entombed here too, and his body lies in the exonarthex in an elaborate 19th-century walnut casket inlaid with designs in mother-of-pearl and ivory.

Most of the original frescos, completed in 1209, and probably the work of a single artist, were repainted in 1569. They are divided into an upper part that has a gilded background, a middle part with a yellow background and a lower part, with blue background. The work reflects a development in the Serbian tradition in which there is an increased emphasis on the human form, its physical strength and its definition of character. Exceptions to the 16th-century repainting are part of the *Annunciation* and the *Crucifixion*, which adorns the west wall and shows the figure of Christ flanked by St John and the Virgin. The colours used here – blues, maroon and gold – are particularly deep and rich.

Next door, and tiny in comparison, is the **King's Church** (*Kraljeva Crkva*), built by King Milutin in 1314. The frescos here are very well-preserved and represent some of the greatest religious art in the country, painted in the period when Serbian fresco art was at its peak. The north wall has the fresco of the *Birth of the Virgin*, which shows how Serbian artists had gone beyond mere symbolism by this date to become increasingly interested in portraying realism and technique. To the left of the Virgin child, a woman holds a tray of surgical instruments while the figure of Destiny fans the newborn child; in the foreground, a woman is portrayed testing the temperature of the water with the back of her hand.

The third remaining church is the 13th-century **Church of St Nicholas** (*Sveti Nikola*), which has a few surviving frescos of interest.

It should not be forgotten that Studenica is no mere museum but a thriving, working community that, while welcoming visitors, is not in the least dependent on them for its existence. For the monks here, the monastery is both a religious retreat and a workplace where spiritual contemplation is mixed with more mundane tasks like chopping wood and growing vegetables. Visitors are steady and frequent but rarely overwhelm the tranquillity of the place. Rather than just visit as a day trip, it is also possible to stay for longer and absorb the peaceful atmosphere here. The adjoining **hotel** has accommodation in segregated three-, four- or six-bed dormitories and charges just €5 per person per night. For food, there is a fairly basic restaurant near the entrance to the complex by the road.

Practicalities
The best way to reach Studenica if you do not have your own car is by bus from Ušće. These are relatively infrequent: according to the bus timetable displayed in the town there are buses serving the monastery at 07.00, 11.45, 14.30, 19.30 and 22.15. As always, it is always best to ask around and confirm that the times stated reflect more than just wishful thinking. Presumably, the same bus returns to Ušće from the monastery after a short break there. Once again, it is wise to check first – it is a long walk back to Ušće; at least it is downhill.

Getting to Ušće from either Kraljevo or Novi Pazar should present no problems, as passing buses can be flagged down on the main road. There are also buses to Kraljevo that originate from the town.

Ušće has several basic places to eat but nowhere to stay in the town itself. The nearest option, other than at the monastery, is the **Motel Fontana** on the main road about 1km south of the town. There is another motel a few kilometres back in the Kraljevo direction but this appeared to be closed when I last passed by.

Towards Kopaonik
South of Ušće, the road south enters the historic territory of the *Sandžak*. Ten kilometres after leaving Ušće, at the village of **Biljanovac**, a road leads off to the left bound for the high pasture and ski runs of **Kopaonik**. This is Serbia's prime ski- resort area and, for some winter holidaymakers, all they get to know of the country. This is a pity because, although the region has undeniable natural beauty, the resort itself has the ambience you might expect from a popular winter sports destination. It is perfectly possible to visit in summer of course, thus avoiding both the ski-season crowds and the often unpleasant mugginess of the lower altitudes, but even then it may be difficult to ignore exactly where you are: a slightly brash, purpose-built ski resort.

Package-holiday companies invariably provide coach transport for the long transfer between Belgrade's Surcin Airport and Kopaonik, which takes anything from five to six hours. Of late, more and more operators are taking advantage of the recently reopened airport at Niš, which effectively halves the transfer time.

Driving your own car, the best way to come is to turn off the Kraljevo–Novi Pazar road at Biljanovac and head towards the small town of **Jošanička Banja**, with its Turkish *hammam* and constant source of warm spring water, 10km along this route. Just beyond the town is a road to the right that leads to the **Monastery of Gradac**, founded in the late 13th century by Helen, the wife of King Uroš I, and mother of kings Dragutin and Milutin. The church is in a style that combines Gothic and Byzantine elements, and has some resonance with Studenica in that it would appear that its craftsmen had some familiarity with the religious architecture of western Europe. The frescos within – a *Crucifixion* on the west wall, a *Dormition of the Virgin* on the north wall, and scenes from the life of the Virgin in the narthex – are all badly damaged.

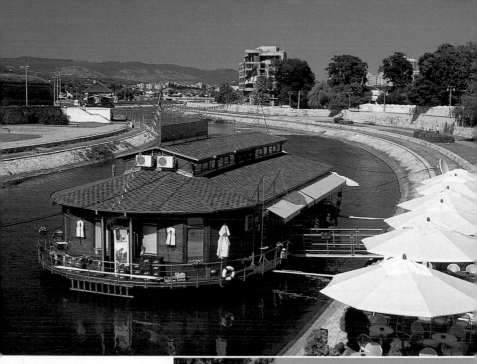

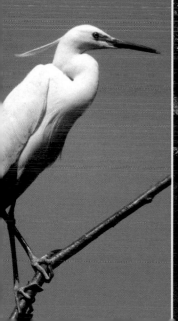

Above Café-boat on River Nišava, Niš (LM)
Right Worker statue at Zastava car plant, Kragujevac, central Serbia (LM)
Below Little egret, *Egretta garzetta*, Stari Begej – Čarska Bara nature reserve (LS)

Above Town centre in early evening, Prizren, Kosovo (LM)
Below right Studenica Monastery, southwest Serbia (LM)
Below left Sinan Pasha Mosque, Prizren, Kosovo (LM)

From Jošanička Banja the road winds up through spectacular mountain scenery to the resort at Kopaonik, and then on to **Brzeće**, an alternative base in the region, some distance beyond.

By public bus – not an easy option unless you find direct transport to and from Belgrade – you must travel beyond the junction at Bilanovac and on to Raška to find a connecting service. Be prepared to spend the night in Raška as buses to the resort are infrequent.

KOPAONIK NATIONAL PARK
Geography

Kopaonik was declared a national park in 1981. It is not a single peak but a flattish plateau-like massif called Suvo Rudište with several peaks rising above the 1,700m level of the plateau. The national park is spread over 12,000ha, the boundaries of which are defined by natural phenomena: the valleys of the Ibar to the west, Jošanica to the north, the Rasina and Gornija Toplica to the east, while its southern slopes blend into the northern reaches of Kosovo above Leposavić. The highest of the peaks is **Pančićev vrh** at 2,017m.

The area's main features were formed by massive earth movements some 70 million years ago, the deep clefts formed creating a path for the flow of andesite-basalt that was responsible for the rich mineral deposits in the area. The mineral wealth associated with this rock form – iron, copper, lead and silver – is found in abundance throughout the massif. Consequently, the area became an important mining centre and this was the mainstay of the local economy before tourism was developed in the area. The name Kopaonik is derived from this practice (*kopati* means 'to dig').

Because of an altitude that is in excess of 1,600m, the Kopaonik area has a sub-alpine climate, tempered to some extent by its southerly latitude and its plateau shape. The relative flatness of the massif means that clouds tend not to sit on the mountain for long and so, without this cloud cover, Kapaonik is exposed to the sun for extended periods in winter, making it warmer than might be expected. Nevertheless, snow cover remains for an average of 159 days a year from November through to May, providing a long and relatively stable ski season. On average, Kopaonik enjoys 200 sunny days a year, with most rainfall coming in summer in July and August.

Natural history

The flora of Kopaonik is particularly rich, with numerous species of trees, ferns, mosses and herbaceous plants. The foothills have forests of oak, Turkey oak, hornbeam and common pear, which give way to beech forest higher up as far as 1,500m. Above the belt of beech forest is a zone of spruce forest, now much depleted after heavy deforestation in the past. At the highest elevations, above 1,800m, mountain juniper (*Junipeus nana*) finds a foothold due to the species' tolerance of extreme cold. Now pasture has replaced the high alpine forest in many places. Mountain cattle-rearing was formerly important here, with the animals spending the warmer months grazing on the high meadows. Now this activity is starting to die out and many of the meadows are being cultivated.

The evergreen zone holds a number of rare bird species that include red crossbill as well as a species of grasshopper that is more usually found in Siberia. Larger animals like wolves, hares and foxes survive here despite reduced numbers, but bear, lynx, deer and wildcat have all disappeared in recent years.

Skiing at Kopaonik

The Kopaonik Ski Centre provides a total 44km of ski paths. There are 22 chairlifts and drags. The resort is at an altitude of 1,770m and the highest station reaches 2,017m. There are four nursery slopes. Of the main slopes, 12 are designated 'easy' runs; five, medium, while two are considered difficult. The longest ski run is 3.5km and the maximum vertical rise is 521m. As well as the vertical ski runs, there are also around 20km of cross-country tracks.

Where to stay and eat

Both UK-based Balkan Holidays and the Serbian operator Putnik organise ski holidays in the Kopaonik area (see *Practical Information* chapter). If you come on an organised tour here your accommodation will, of course, already be provided. If you decide to visit independently then you can expect a wide selection from which to choose. Below is just a small sample of the hotels available at the resort.

Grand★★★★ Tel: 036 71 037. This is the most luxurious hotel in Kopaonik, having an indoor swimming pool, Jacuzzi, sauna, indoor tennis court and fitness centre.
Putnik Club A★★★★ Tel: 036 71 613. A very central hotel, built in a traditional style, just 100m or so from the ski lifts. The hotel has two restaurants, a bar, tavern, gym and an indoor swimming pool with sauna.
Putnik★★★ Tel: 036 71 224, 71 030, 71 038. The Hotel Putnik is situated just 200m from the 'Sunny Valley' ski lift, with two restaurants, a shop and a large sun terrace.
Srebrnac★★ Tel: 036 71 025. A 'B' category hotel near the ski lifts.
Jugobanka★★ Tel: 036 71 062, 71 040
Olga Dedijer★★★ Tel: 036 710 33

There are also a number of categorised apartment complexes with rooms to rent.

Apartment Complex Investbanka★★★★ Tel: 036 713 01
Apartment Complex JAT★★★★ Tel: 036 710 12

At **Brzeće** nearby:

Hotel Junior★★ Tel: 037 833 193
Apartment Complex Kopaonik★★★ Tel: 037 833 130
Apartment Complex Ragione Tel: 037 827 707

The resort is well served by restaurants and bars. The following are just a few of the options.

Café-gallery **Trezor** Tel: 063 605 108
Etno Club Tel: 063 8199 735
Restaurant **Kopanički Vajat** Tel: 036 717 82
Pizzeria **Koala** Tel: 036 719 77
Pizzeria/snack bar **Red Bull** Tel: 036 719 77, ext1653
Restaurant **Zvrk** Tel: 036 719 77, ext1632

THE RAŠKA REGION

Continuing along the main road south of Ušće, the first town of any size is **Raška**, 18km beyond the Kopaonik turn-off. Raška is a spread-out, sizeable place, with a reasonable amount of industry stretching along the roadside. There is not that much to see in the town and little to be gained by breaking your journey here unless you need to change buses. All buses stop here and a main road branches off with the railway to follow the river Ibar into Kosovo by way of the troubled town of Kosovska Mitrovica.

Beyond Raška, the road follows the river that takes its name from the town until, after a further 20km, the region's capital, Novi Pazar, is reached.

History of the region

Sandžak was the Turkish term used to describe its administrative provinces and this predominantly Muslim corner of southwest Serbia (and northeast Montenegro) sometimes uses this term as an alternative to Raška. The region, which remained a buffer zone between Serbia and Montenegro until late in the 19th century, was the last part of Serbia to be liberated from Turkish rule, remaining as part of the Ottoman Empire until 1912 and the First Balkan War when it was overrun by Serbian and Montenegrin troops. At the end of World War I, Raška was included into the newly created Kingdom of Serbs, Croats and Slovenians.

Following the establishment of Serbian and Montenegrin regional governments in the region, many of Raška's Muslims migrated to Turkey with the encouragement of both the newly established kingdom and Turkey itself. This migration continued even into the years that followed World War II, with deals continuing to be struck between communist Yugoslavia and the Turkish government. The reasons for this unexpected co-operation were twofold: from the Yugoslav position, there were doubts about the loyalty of its Muslim citizens and it was happy to let them go; from Turkey's point of view, it was an ideal opportunity to help populate vast uninhabited areas of Anatolia. It is estimated that over a million inhabitants of modern-day Turkey are actually of Raška origin – more than the current population of both the Serbian and Montenegrin Raška today.

Muslims have continued to leave since the last agreement between Yugoslavia and Turkey was signed in 1954, mostly to western Europe or Bosnia-Herzegovina, and mainly driven by economic hardship. The current trend for an exodus of the Serbian Orthodox population is actually something of an anomaly, a phenomenon that has occurred largely in the wake of the Kosovo crisis.

In topographical terms, Raška, which straddles both sides of the Serbian–Montenegrin border, is largely a remote region of forest, mountains and few decent roads. It is the rearing of livestock that is the main economy here, rather than the fruit-growing and arable farming that is the mainstay further north, although as might be expected in a mainly Muslim province, pigs are conspicuous by their absence.

Raška is noticeably poorer than the rest of western and central Serbia and, according to many of its inhabitants, largely neglected by central government. The figures bear this out: the GDP of predominantly Muslim Novi Pazar is 53% of the Serbian average, and in Sjenica, which is 85% Muslim, it is even lower at 41%; in nearby towns that have a Serbian Orthodox majority, GDP is higher; 87% in the case of Raška town. The poverty, the politics and the ethnic imbalance mean that some parallels can be drawn with the situation in Kosovo, except that here the large Muslim population is not of Albanian origin but ethnic Slavs who converted to Islam in the distant past. Thankfully, the ethnic violence that has torn Kosovo apart in recent years has had no equivalent here.

NOVI PAZAR НОВИ ПАЗАР

Telephone code: 020

Sitting among low hills where the river Raška has its confluence with the Ljudska, is the large town of Novi Pazar ('New Bazaar'), capital of the region. Almost immediately upon arrival you notice how different it seems from similar-sized towns to the north like Kraljevo or Čačak. Other than in Kosovo, Novi Pazar is the town with the most pronounced Muslim atmosphere in the country: instead of church domes, it is minarets that stab the skyline, and rather than the relaxed and carefree mixing of the sexes that takes place throughout most of Serbia, men and women seem to live more separate existences here. Almost everywhere you look there are coffee houses full of huddled groups of men drinking small glasses of *čaj* or *turska kava*, talking and playing backgammon in a haze of cigarette fug. Even without the existence of mosques and old Ottoman buildings, such characteristics give evidence that this is still very much a Turkish town and, despite the worst excesses of 1970s Yugoslav town planning, modernisation has failed to destroy the distinctly Muslim character of Novi Pazar.

Although Novi Pazar has some of the appearance and atmosphere of Kosovo, its Muslim population is comprised, not of Albanians, but of Serbs who converted to Islam centuries ago. These proselytised Serbians are now commonly referred to by the rest of the population as Bosniaks, Muslims, or even 'Turks', which in this context might be considered a pejorative term. Whether it is a product of religion, culture or development – or all three – the atmosphere here is markedly different from the rest of the country. The steady Orthodox migration away from the Novi Pazar region that has taken place over the past ten years, talked-up by fears of cultural domination and Kosovo-type repression, has contributed to the Muslim character of the town in many ways. It is not just the visible backdrop of mosques, tea houses and narrow bazaar streets that define this character, but also in the way people carry out their daily life: in Novi Pazar, the evening *korso* is dominated by groups of strolling young men, few restaurants openly sell alcohol, and many woman cover themselves up in the Islamic manner.

There seems to be a slightly conspiratorial air about the place, as if trouble is expected on the horizon. Given the sad realities of nearby Kosovo, this is, perhaps, reasonable enough, but up to now the town and province has managed to avoid the spiteful conflict that has blighted its neighbour.

In some ways this is one of the most interesting towns in the country, which makes it all the more mysterious why there is such an utter absence of information about the place. It can almost seem like a conspiracy: Novi Pazar has no tourist office; there are no town maps available; and there is precious little mention of the town in any of the tourist literature that does exist. The reason for all of this, alas, is most probably political. There is a palpable nervousness about what might happen in Novi Pazar in the future. Having had its religious institutions secularised, and its town centre ripped apart by Yugoslav town planners in the 1960s and '70s, Novi Pazar seems keen to return to its Turkish roots in the post-Milošević period. The Islamic character of the town is becoming increasingly more pronounced as the cultural mix has changed in favour of the Muslim community. Until a couple of decades ago, Novi Pazar was a town with a fairly even Orthodox–Muslim mix. Nowadays, its population is something like 75–80% Muslim, an imbalance caused partly by the higher birth rate of the Muslims and partly by the recent migration of many Orthodox Serbs away from the region. Naturally, this demographic shift continues to alarm those Orthodox Serbs that remain. Fears of Kosovo-style divisions and a general resentment and distrust of central government in Belgrade have done little to allay such fears.

It is undeniable that the Raška region, and Novi Pazar in particular, has suffered long years of neglect, with a distinct lack of investment in its industry, services and infrastructure. Unemployment is much higher here than elsewhere in the country, the roads are even worse than usual, and the statistics show that public health in the region is well below the national average. It is no wonder then that a certain degree of resentment is in the air.

This is not paint a bleak picture: Novi Pazar is *not* a place of extremist sentiment – it is nothing like Saudi Arabia, or Pakistan, or even Egypt – but its Islamic character, which was suppressed and diluted as part of the former Yugoslavia, continues to strengthen with time. True to its Ottoman roots, the town today feels more like Turkey than anywhere else in Serbia; indeed, it is closer to old Turkish traditions than a lot of Turkish Mediterranean towns that have embraced mass tourism in recent years.

Until recently, the town was probably most famous for its textile industry, particularly for the manufacture of denim jeans, which it churned out in great quantity and in a variety of guises and fashion labels, genuine and otherwise. Cheap imports, mostly from China, have put an end to this and the town's unemployment figures have soared.

Getting there

Novi Pazar is well connected by bus to most parts of Serbia. Over 20 buses a day run to Belgrade, one to Podgorica (in Montenegro), two to Novi Sad, four to Niš, five to Kragujevac, seven to Kraljevo, ten to Sjenica, over 20 to Raška and a couple to Baćica on the Pester plateau. Occasional services also run to Sarejevo, Skopje and Istanbul. There is a large noticeboard at the bus station listing all the departure times. The trouble is, some of the listed services do not exist at all, or the bus concerned may run at times completely different from those stated. It is best to ask and clarify what the bus times are well in advance of when you want to travel. There is an office at the bus station that proclaims itself 'Informacije' but do not set too much store by this. When I pointed out some of the incorrect times on the departures board to the grumpy men on duty there, they were so unimpressed that they completely ignored me.

Novi Pazar has no rail service, nor airport.

Practicalities

For money, the **Eksimbanka** and **National Bank of Greece** have branches on Stevana Nemanje, the road that leads to the centre from the bus station. The former has an ATM, as does the **Raiffessen Bank** that is found in the walkway of the large concrete block on the right-hand side of the Stevana Nemanje as you head into town. Just before this is the **Enter Internet Café** that has a reasonably fast connection. There is also Internet Club **The Best** opposite the bus station. There is a post office on 28 November. For everyday items, there is the **Pazarka Shopping Centre**, a large supermarket close to the central square.

There is no **tourist information** office in the town. A tourist agency that can help with local travel arrangements and organise tours is **Ecco Travel** at 28 November number 54 (tel: 23 832, 311 575; mob: 063 855 4754, 880 9775; email: taecco@verat.net). They speak English and German.

Where to stay

Hotel Tadz * ** Rifata Burdzevica 79; tel/fax: 311 904, 316 838; email: hoteltadz@ptt.yu. By far the best hotel in town, this gleaming new private hotel is only five years old and offers modern comforts in plain, well-appointed rooms. It is situated near the river just a few minutes' walk west of the centre. The hotel has its own private parking area; you drive right through the building to reach it – quite literally. The Tadz has 45 beds in total. Single rooms are €36; doubles €57, or €41 with single occupancy; apartments €86.

Vrbak Hotel * ** Maršala Tita bb; tel: 24 844; fax: 25 548. This very odd state-run hotel is hard to miss in the town centre. The hotel's design is a weird hybrid of neo-oriental and 1970s space-station design. Rooms on three levels surround the central atrium that houses the reception desk. There are some nice design touches here and there: lozenge-shaped windows, fancy wrought-iron work and stained-glass windows. In less cluttered surroundings, the Vrbak might appear impressive but here, in the centre of an old Turkish town, it just looks a bit silly. Nevertheless, I am sure the architects must have won a prize for their work; for originality at least. Singles are 1,200din, doubles 2,200din, doubles with extra bed 3,400din.

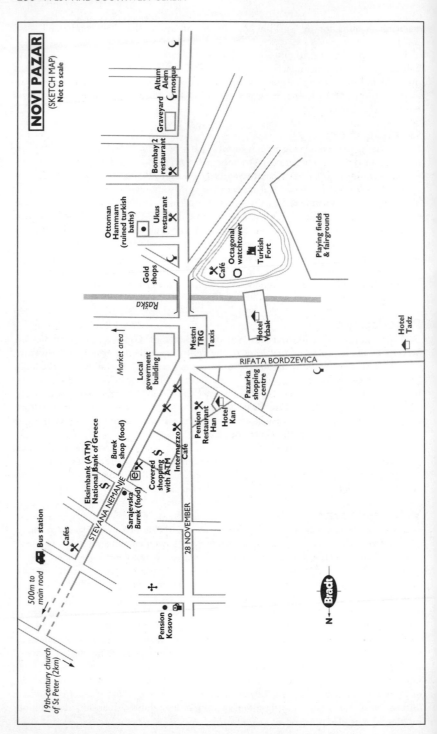

Hotel Kan★★★ (or **Cannes**, depending on the sign) Rifata Burdzevica 10; tel: 25 250. This is another private hotel, located right in the town centre next to the Pension Han with modern en-suite rooms with minibar and TV. The rooms are clean but rather cramped and with thin walls; a little overpriced for what they offer. Single rooms cost €20, doubles €25.
Pension Han★, which is located virtually next door to the Hotel Kan, has basic rooms to rent above its cavernous restaurant. The building was originally an 18th-century travellers' *han*. It has been modernised a little since then ... but not much.
Pension Kosovo★ R. Halilovića 32; tel: 23 833/24 892. At the top of 28 November, just to the right of the garage. This also offers basic accommodation above a restaurant-bar for around 800din per person.

Where to eat and drink

For dining, all of the hotels have their own restaurants but none of them is really anything special. The Hotel Kan has a cosy basement restaurant with paintings on the wall and fish in tanks (but not for eating). The fish look a little crowded, rather like the rooms upstairs. Although there are one or two pizzerias dotted about, the best bet really is to eat in the bazaar area where there are numerous *ćevapčíći* places that offer good food at very affordable prices. The **Ukus** restaurant on the road leading up to the Alem Ateh mosque is particularly good, with a choice of salads and sweets as well as *ćevapčíći* and other grilled meats. For international fast food you may wish to check out **Mr Donald's** café on 28 November with its cheeky – and probably litigious – 'M' logo.

Elsewhere, there are *mlećni* restaurants all around town, and especially near the centre along 28 November and Stevana Nemanje streets. *Mlećni* refers to milk, rather like milk bars, an indication that these places do not serve alcohol. If you want a beer or something stronger then you could try the slightly insalubrious café below the Pension Han, or one of the trendy café-bars with darkened windows and booming music up near the bus station. For Turkish coffee or *ćaj*, there are numerous options in the bazaar, along 28 November, or up near the bus station where I counted something like eight in a row. However, these places do tend to be male preserves and female visitors will probably feel uncomfortable if not unwelcome; better to use one of the more upmarket café-bars that are also quite plentiful. The **Intermezzo** café on 28 November does good cappuccino if you need a break from *turkska kava*. For cakes, snacks, and especially for *burek*, there are numerous possibilities all around town.

What to see

Part of the pleasure of being in Novi Pazar is to simply absorb its vaguely exotic atmosphere. The evocative sound of the *muezzin* – the call for prayer five times a day – that emanates from the mosques is a reminder that Turkey and the Middle East are not so very far away. The smells are redolent of the East too, with the ever-present, sweet-and-sour aroma of roasting coffee beans and grilling *ćevapčíći* managing to overpower the stench of exhaust fumes even in the heart of the town centre. Unfortunately, if you arrive by public transport the first smell that will greet you at the bus station will probably be stale urine from the neglected toilet facilities there, so make a swift exit, turn left at the traffic lights and a ten-minute walk will bring you to the town centre.

The central square of **Mestni Trg** is little more than a large car park but it lies close to most of the town's major sights and all of the important modern and bazaar streets emanate from this one central hub. With one or two exceptions, everything worth seeing in Novi Pazar is no more than a ten-minute walk from here.

The old **Turkish quarter** lies east over the bridge from here, beyond the **Turkish Fort** that looks down over the central square, the grubby river and the dubious architecture of the Hotel Vrdnk. The fortress, which dates from the 15th century, was formerly the seat of the Turkish *sanjak* in the region, and is home to a pleasant park these days. It was originally built to a triangular plan probably on the order of Iša-Bey Išaković, the town's founder. New buildings and reinforcements were added later, between the end of the 17th century and the middle of the 19th. Some of the original ramparts remain, together with an octagonal watchtower, but otherwise there is little to see. Nevertheless, its benches offer cool shade on a hot summer's day, and there is a good view from the terrace of the park's outdoor café.

Heading south over the bridge from the square, a narrow road leads through the old bazaar area to the early 16th-century mosque of **Altum Alem**, the most important Turkish building in the town. Access to the mosque can be gained through the courtyard at number 79, which houses several Ottoman-period graves and the entrance to an Islamic school. Altum Alem, built by the master builder Abdul Gani, is of a square plan, with a dome and a spacious porch covered with cupolas that are not typical for the region. There is a wooden gallery and a colourful *mihrab* within.

The road that leads to the mosque is lined with small restaurants that specialise in *ćevapčići*; coffee houses, butchers' shops and small bakeries selling *burek*; closer to the bridge is a small enclave of shops that specialise in gold jewellery. Nearby is a ruined **hammam** – Turkish bath – that probably dates from the 1460s and which was endowed to the town by its founder Iša-Bey Išakovć. It is a symmetrical structure with facilities for simultaneous bathing by men and women.

The only thing that spoils the enjoyment of wandering these bazaar streets is the constant stream of exhaust-belching traffic that keeps you on your toes. The Serbian tradition of parking on any available piece of pavement is taken to its extreme here, constantly forcing pedestrians out into the narrow streets into the path of taxis and minibuses.

Back across the bridge to the north there is an outdoor market area along the river, opposite the bazaar area. Most of the items on sale are household utensils and cheap clothing, especially the cut-price jeans for which the town used to be famous. On the square itself, you will probably see men with suitcases selling duty-free cigarettes, together with makeshift stalls selling Islamic texts, Korans and stylised scenes of the *Kaaba* in Mecca.

On the north side of Mestni Trg is an old **Ottoman han** dating from the 17th century, part of which currently serves as a restaurant and a guesthouse. This is comprised of a group of four buildings facing onto a common courtyard. In the past, the upper floor would have been reserved for the accommodation of passing traders (it still is), while other parts would have housed the cattle and animal stock that the visitors brought with them. In contrast to this, on the opposite side of the square, is the **Hotel Vrbak**, one of the most unusual hotels in the country. It is hardly beautiful but the Hotel Vrbak cannot fail to impress, and gives weight to the theory that however much communist-period architects were under instruction to produce cheap, utilitarian housing for the proletariat, they were given completely free rein when it came to the design of hotels; that is, as long they stuck to a vaguely futuristic concept. The Vrbak is a prime example of this: a whacky architectural conceit that was taken seriously by a planning committee and immortalised in concrete. The building consists of two hexagons joined together on two sides, with an extension reaching south across the lacklustre river channel that passes unglamorously through the town. Inside, the cavernous atrium has a vaguely retro-Ottoman feel to it. The Balkan commentator, Misha Glenny, who passed through this way in the early 1990s, describes the building as drab, depressing and shoddy, and remarks that it is 'a prince among such hotels'. It is almost exquisitely ugly, and fits in perfectly with the brutal modernisation that the rest of the town centre underwent in the 1970s.

Still, it is not without interest: for aficionados of the old Eastern-bloc aesthetic, the Hotel Vrbak is a real gem.

AROUND NOVI PAZAR

Novi Pazar's other sights of interest lie just outside the town and belong to the Orthodox rather than the Islamic or communist traditions. Studenica Monastery is also well within range for a day trip from the town.

Church of St Peter (*Petrova*)

This wonderfully atmospheric church lies at the base of a grassy hill, about 3km south of the town centre. To reach it, walk back past the bus station, turn left at the main road, continue straight over the junction and you will soon see it just above the road to the left. You may notice, walking this way out of town, that this northern part of Novi Pazar is still predominantly Serbian Orthodox. The tell-tale signs are all there: Cyrillic rather than Latin signs on shops and houses; Orthodox death notices pinned to doors; crates of Jelen Pivo beer bottles stacked outside cafés.

The small church of St Peter is the oldest in the country, dating from the 8th or 9th century – the only pre-Nemanjić church in existence anywhere in the country – and was the seat of the Orthodox See of Raška for a period of almost 900 years. It was here that Stefan Nemanja held the council that outlawed the Bogomil heresy in Serbia.

The church is circular in plan with a central cupola and three radial apses. It is built in a style that shows the influence of an earlier Byzantine tradition, and which probably arrived in Serbia via the Adriatic. It is highly likely that the church was constructed on a site that was sacred to earlier settlers in the region as, in 1958, the 5th-century grave of an Illyrian prince was discovered beneath the floor here, along with a number of accompanying burial items like jewellery, masks and ceramics in the Greek tradition that are now in the keeping of the National Museum in Belgrade.

The interior is dark, and consists of a single, circular nave surrounded by the tombs of a number of Serbian princes. In the apse to the right, steps lead down to a sunken font where St Sava is purported to have been baptised. Such frescos that survive are severely chipped and in poor condition but their use of unusual colours – red and black – lends considerably to the mysterious atmosphere that this small church possesses. Outside the church is an evocative cemetery of heavily weathered old gravestones stained yellow and gold with lichens.

If the church is locked, the woman in the house next door has a key, although there may also be a friendly young priest in attendance who will show you around. He does not speak English but is highly enthusiastic in his efforts to communicate. A donation to the church collection box is appreciated.

Đurđevi Stupovi (St George's Pillars)

A few kilometres to the west of Novi Pazar, the monastic church of Đurđevi Stupovi occupies a wistful, windswept site, high on a hill above the town. This 12th-century church was originally created by Stefan Nemanja and contains some weather-beaten frescos, most notably one of St George on a galloping steed. Some of the other frescos have long been removed to the National Museum in Belgrade for protection and the site has recently been restored with a large expanse of plate glass to keep out the elements, which, although providing protection, does little for its general aesthetic appeal.

Đurđevi Stupovi is visible from St Peter's Church and can be reached from there by walking up the grassy track that leads west up the hill. After a while the track becomes indistinct but at long as you keep heading in the same direction you will eventually reach the church. There is said to be another track that leads from the town somewhere off the Sopoćani road but I could not locate this.

Sopoćani Monastery

This is undoubtedly the most important sight in the region. The monastery lies about 16km west of the town, along a wild and lonely road that penetrates deep into the Raška heartland. The best way to reach it if you do not have your own transport is to take a taxi from Mestni Trg, Novi Pazar's central square. The cost should be about €15 or 1,000din both ways, including an hour's stop at the monastery. If you just wish to be deposited there it should be something more like €10 or 700din one-way. There are no buses.

The road, which is quite pot-holed in places, heads west from Novi Pazar along a beautiful valley filled with pine forest. About halfway to the monastery, you reach the ruins of **Ras**, which now just consists of a lot of foundations and low walls. It is probably not really worth stopping here, as there is not much to see on the ground, but you could negotiate a brief stopover with your taxi driver should you wish to do so.

Ras was the ancient capital of the Nemanjić kings, and dates from the 9th century. It became the capital of the early Serbian kingdom of **Raška**, a name that most Orthodox Serbs prefer to use for the region that is otherwise referred to as the Sandžak. The city was severely damaged in the 12th century in clashes between the Serbs and the Byzantines but remained the capital until 1314. As Novi Pazar developed as the new regional centre, Ras dwindled in importance. Nowadays, it would take a trained archaeological eye to make much sense of the little that remains. If you want to stay there is accommodation nearby at the **Motel Ras** (tel: 22 014).

Sopoćani Monastery lies beyond, higher up and close to the source of the Raška River that gushes from a spring in the rock. Founded in the middle of the 13th century by King Uroš I, the monastery of Sopoćani is one of the finest examples of the Raška School. It was severely damaged in 1689 and completely abandoned at the end of the 17th century, allowing it to fall into ruin. Considering that the monastery stood as a roofless ruin for the best part of two centuries, it is quite remarkable that so many fine frescos have survived. Many have managed to evade the worst effects of the elements during Sopoćani's long period of neglect and the renovated monastery is home to some of the greatest religious art in Europe and, many would agree, the highest achievement of all Serbian art. An English-language booklet is on sale at the monastery, as well as candles, icons and postcards of the frescos. It may be a good idea to buy a few of these as photography of the church's interior is not permitted.

The centrepiece of the complex is the **Church of the Holy Trinity**, built in an adapted Romanesque style with narthex, naos, semicircular apse and cupola. In the 14th century, the emperor Dušan added an exonarthex, which collapsed some years afterwards leaving just the belfry standing. Surrounding the church, monastery buildings of the same period – a refectory, kitchens, monks' cells and a water fountain – all now lie in ruins.

The frescos in the narthex date from 1270 and depict subjects new to Serbian iconography at the time, like the *Last Judgement* and the *Legend of St Joseph*. As well as praising God, the frescos here celebrate and elevate the grandeur of the Nemanjic dynasty: Queen Anne, the mother of Uroš, is depicted almost as reverentially as a Virgin figure would be, and on the east wall, the council of Stefan Nemanja is portrayed as an equal alongside the seven ecumenical councils. Details from the life of Stefan Nemanja portray him as a monk at Mt Athos, and the subsequent movement of his body to the monastery of Studenica.

The greatest works, however, are in the naos. *The Dormition of the Virgin* on the west wall shows Christ holding a baby in swaddling clothes, with the Apostles standing alongside in a carefully composed group. The figures portrayed are very human, demonstrating great dignity and calm; the colours used are bright but subtle

– green, maroon and gold – and the overall effect created is one of emotional but serene resignation. The north wall has the *Birth of Christ*, the *Descent into Limbo* and the *Transfiguration*; the west, the *Crucifixion, Presentation at the Temple* and *Christ among the Learned Men*. All of these were executed a little earlier than the narthex paintings, the creation of master painters from Constantinople at work around 1265. They show a brilliance and visionary quality that can only be compared to some of the creations of the Italian Renaissance that followed. Impending Turkish rule would see to it that Serbian art would not be able to develop beyond this early inspirational blossoming.

There is accommodation next door to the monastery at the **Hotel Sopoćani** (tel: 24 892, 23 883) should you wish to spend more time here. Apart from the obvious benefit of having more time to study the frescos, it would be a wonderfully restful experience to spend the night, or even a few days, here. Sopoćani, like all Serbian monasteries, is located in extraordinarily beautiful surroundings and the potential for quiet walks in the surrounding hills must be endless.

WEST OF NOVI PAZAR

Heading south, Novi Pazar is pretty much the end of the road before Montenegro or Kosovo is reached. If you do wish to visit Kosovo, this is one way to do it (see *Kosovo* chapter for details). If you want to visit Montenegro there are plenty of buses that run to Rožaje, from where you can pick up connections to points beyond.

Heading west towards Nova Varoš and Prijepolje, the road climbs up high from the Raška valley to skirt the edge of the **Pešter plateau**, a very isolated sheep- and cattle-raising area that borders Montenegro. With your own transport, this would be a fascinating region to explore with plenty of time at your disposal and a full fuel tank. It is one of the remotest parts of the country, without many towns to speak of, and consists mostly of open moorland and endless swathes of gently undulating pasture.

Without a car, the best you can do is to take the bus through Sjenica to Nova Varoš and Prijeplolje. There is a daily through bus from Novi Pazar that leaves in the morning, contrary to what it says on the bus station departures board.

Leaving Novi Pazar, there is a steep climb up to the hilltop village of Duga Poljana, which has some shops and a restaurant but no hotel. From here you travel across a high, bare plateau. There are a few fields here and there but mostly it is cattle country that brings to mind the more upland parts of Northumberland or the North York Moors. It is a lonely but spectacular landscape, with a rambling farmstead standing in isolation by the road every few kilometres. The clear, upland air, the gently undulating terrain and the lack of trees make it possible to see for miles in any direction. Just before the town of **Sjenica** is reached, a sign by the roadside proclaims the altitude to be 1,509m above sea level.

SJENICA CJEHИЦA

Telephone code: 020

Sjenica lies in a natural bowl, high on the plateau, surrounded by pine forest and bleak pasture. Even in summer, it is easy to understand why it is considered to be the coldest town in Serbia. With the exception of Tutin that lies further south, close to the Montenegrin border, this has the highest Muslim population of all the towns in the Raška region. Life is tough here, eking out an existence in a hostile landscape but the locals seem to do well enough, given their circumstances. There is little specific to see here but the town stands in the middle of magnificent landscape and so there is the temptation of using Sjenica as a base for walks in the surrounding countryside.

The town itself seems surprisingly large because of its rather rambling nature: space is not at a premium up here on the plateau. Nor is there any clear-cut demarcation made between where the town stops and the countryside begins – cows are led around on ropes to graze on any available plot of waste land. There a few nods made to Sjenica's urban status: a leafy, central square with a large new mosque; a national-style restaurant next door to the tiny bus station and a few basic pizzerias nearby.

The town's only hotel, the two-star **Hotel Bor** (Milanovana Jovanović bb; tel: 71 242) is set in some pine woodland just off the road, a couple of kilometres east, back towards Novi Pazar. Some signs refer to the hotel as the Hotel Borici but it is one and the same place. Reasonable rooms are available for 800din, single; 1,200din, double. The hotel restaurant is good too – friendly and inexpensive – but be aware that much of what appears on the menu will not be available. Better to let the waiter tell you what the cook is willing to prepare. It would appear that the hotel is the setting for many an amorous escapade, judging by the way the walls and wooden fittings of the rooms have been carved with the initials of a succession of loving couples – one man's graffiti is another man's romantic gesture.

There are infrequent buses that leave Sjenica for Prijepolje, Novi Pazar, Belgrade and Kragujevac daily, but it is best to seek confirmation of the departure times first if you intend catching any of these. Quite amazingly, there is also a direct bus to Istanbul, which stops in Sjenica on its way from Sarajevo.

After Sjenica the road climbs even more through pine forest and pasture to reach Nova Varoš after a further 37km. There is another road shown on maps that links Sjenica directly with Prijepolje but it is in poor condition and virtually all vehicles heading for that town make a detour through Nova Varoš.

NOVA VAROŠ НОВА ВАРОШ

Nova Varoš is a medium-sized alpine town sprawling up and along both sides of the valley. There is a noticeably larger Serbian Orthodox population here than further east and, unusual for this part of Serbia, the domes of Orthodox churches are as visible in the town as are minarets. After travelling through the Pešter plateau, Nova Varoš may strike you as quite urbane and sophisticated but unless you have a particular reason for being here it is probably best to push on south to Prijepolje and Mileševa Monastery. Should you need them, there are a couple of accommodation options: the **Hotel Panorama** Babica Brdo (tel: 033 61 772; fax: 033 61 203; www.hotel-panorama.co.yu) on top of the hill, a couple of kilometres short of the town, and the **Motel** at the central bus station.

Zlatar Mountain

Mt Zlatar (highest point, 1,927m) lies close to the town of Nova Varoš. There is a resort here, surrounded by spruce and birch forest and meadows that are carpeted with wild flowers in late spring. Lying at some considerable altitude, the climate is halfway between Mediterranean and Alpine but generally it is sunny. The resort offers skiing in winter along with summer recreations such as tennis and swimming. Fishing and sailing may be done at nearby lakes while the whole area is perfect for energetic walking in summer.

Information about the Nova Varoš–Zlatar area may be had from **Turistička organizacija 'Zlatar'** at Karađorđeva 36, 31320 Nova Varoš; tel/fax: 033 62 621; email: tozlatar@verat.net; www.novavaros.org.yu.

For details about the resort itself contact Zlatar, Babica brdo bb, 31320 Nova Varoš (tel: 033 61 880; fax: 033 61 481) or look at their singing and dancing (but Cyrillic only) website at www.zlatar.co.yu.

Uvac-Mileševka Griffon Vulture Sanctuary

For birdwatchers, the Griffon Vulture Sanctuary at the Uvac-Mileševka Dam is close at hand. The sanctuary consists of several limestone gorges surrounded by forest and the pasture which supplies the birds with their food supply, mostly dead calves. Thanks to careful management, numbers have increased in recent years from just ten nesting pairs to several hundred. In 1999, there was considerable concern for the fate of the vultures when a NATO plane crashed into the Mileševka Canyon close to the nest sites – griffon vultures are prone to abandoning their nests when disturbed – but they seem to have survived this annoyance.

A road leads down to the dam wall from Nova Varoš by way of the village of Komarani. You will need to arrive early in the morning if you want to see them sitting on their nests and their roost ledges, as the birds take to the thermals after about 09.00. The vultures range over an incredibly large territory searching for the carrion that they feed on and you may be lucky enough to see one along the Sjenica–Nova Varoš road as I did.

PRIJEPOLJE ПРИЈЕПОЉЕ

Prijepolje lies 27km southwest of Nova Varoš on the main train line that links Bar on the Montenegrin coast with Belgrade. The town itself has little to see but it serves as a convenient base from which to visit the Mileševa Monastery. Because the town is well connected by train, and to a lesser extent by bus, it is not really necessary to spend the night here but there is the three-star **Hotel Mileševa** Novovaroska bb (tel: 033 21 078, 21 076) should you want to stay.

The railway station stands next to the small bus station at the southern end of town. Five trains a day run north to Belgrade via Užice and Valjevo, and the same number south to Montenegro via Bijelo Polje and Podgorica. Buses are less numerous and serve mostly local destinations. The railway station has one restaurant upstairs and another outside by the car park but it's a bit of a gloomy place for a lengthy wait. Unfortunately, there is no left-luggage facility whatsoever, which is a nuisance if you are just passing through the town to take a look at Mileševa Monastery. The best thing to do, if you wish to visit Mileševa, is to take a taxi from the railway station and have it wait for you while you look around the monastery. This way, you can take your bag with you. The return trip to the monastery, including a reasonable wait, should cost no more than €5.

Mileševa Monastery

The monastery lies 6km up a valley to the east of Prijepolje, on the southern slopes of Mt Zlatar. As soon as you arrive at the monastery you cannot fail but notice the large Serbian Orthodox flags flying on poles outside the entrance – as much a political gesture as anything else in this predominantly Muslim part of the country. Further along the valley, the dramatic-looking ruins of a medieval castle are visible on a crag in the distance, most probably the stronghold of a long-deceased Bosnian king, although local legend tells of it being built at the whim of a rich woman who did not know what to do with her wealth.

There is not much to see of the monastery buildings themselves; quite clearly, Mileševa is poor and in decline. However, a few monks hang on and will be pleased to show you round, although you will be lucky to find anyone who speaks English, or anything written in English at the monastery shop.

Mileševa was founded by the grandson of Stefan Nemanja, Vladislav, in about 1234. It was originally planned as his mausoleum but the monastery was to gain greater fame when it became the final resting place of Vladislav's uncle, St Sava. Soon after his death, a cult developed around St Sava's relics, one which was observed by both Orthodox Christians and Muslims alike. This alarmed the Turkish authorities to the extent that they had the saint's remains taken to Vračar in present-day Belgrade, where they were burned. A legend tells that his body rose from the flames and hovered in the sky above. The spot chosen for the burning has subsequently become the site for the construction of Belgrade's enormous St Sava's Church.

The main body of the church consists of one single space, since the wall that separated narthex and nave collapsed many centuries ago. Since the collapse, the church is usually described by what may be termed its 'blue' and 'gold' parts, the predominant colours used in the frescos. The frescos were executed around the same time as the church was built and were the work of three men, Dimitrije, Đorđe and Teodor, who were most probably native Serbs. The most familiar of these frescos decorates the south wall of the nave: the *Angel of the Resurrection* – better known simply as the *White Angel* – a cool, rather androgynous, figure that casts his eyes serenely down on the observer in a slightly superior, almost haughty manner. This famous iconic image oozes mystical power and has, in recent years, been adopted by the United Nations as an emblem, having earlier been projected across the Atlantic as part of a pioneering UK–USA satellite link-up. The image has been much copied but, like the smile on the *Mona Lisa*, the enigmatic quality of the original has been hard to replicate. Just above the *White Angel*, and hard to see in the gloom, is a serene representation of the *Virgin of the Annunciation* scene next to a *Deposition* that shows Christ being lovingly tended to by Mary Magdalen and the Virgin.

ZLATIBOR ЗЛАТИБОР

Zlatibor is the name given to a mountain range and a region rather than to a particular place, although the tourist centre of **Partizanska Vode** at the heart of the region is often referred to simply as 'Zlatibor'. Roughly speaking, Zlatibor corresponds to the area west of Užice that extends as far as the Bosnia-Herzegovina border, and to the south almost to Nova Varoš. It is a region of high mountains, pine forest and alpine meadows, with little in the way of large settlements other than the market town of -- **Dajetina** that serves as a sort of lower town to the resort. For an upland region it is surprisingly well connected: the E-761 leads east from Užice through the sprawling community of Kremna to the Bosnia-Herzegovina border and Višegrad just beyond – an important route that links Belgrade with Sarajevo – while the main Bar–Belgrade railway passes through, linking the south of the region, **Priboj**, with the north, **Užice**, after a brief excursion into the territory of Republika Srpska in Bosnia-Herzegovina.

Being only four hours from Belgrade by road, Zlatibor is a firm favourite with domestic tourists: many come to Partizanska Vode in winter to ski, or in summer to walk and escape the big-city heat. The spectacular '**Šargan Eight**' railway line that runs from **Mokra Gora** is also immensely popular, as is the Village Museum complex at **Sirogojno**.

For the foreign visitor, perhaps the best way to enjoy the region is to explore the possibilities for **village tourism** and base yourself in one of the villages such as **Kremna** and **Gostilje**, which offer accommodation and board with local families – a great way to experience rural life and to enjoy delicious home-produced fare that is far superior to anything you could buy in a restaurant.

Geography of the Zlatibor region

Zlatibor gets its name from a combination of *zlato*, meaning gold, and *bor*, pine. The whole area is a vast rolling plateau that is geographically defined by the territory between the rivers Sušica and Uvac, the eastern slopes of Mt Tara and the western slopes of Murtenica. The average altitude of the Zlatibor region is around 1,000m above sea level. As its name suggests, the region is characterised by large expanses of coniferous forest comprised of pine, fir and spruce, together with upland meadows and pasture. The highest mountain in the region is Tornik at 1,496m. In the northern, limestone, part of the region the only river is the Sušica, whose name means 'dry', a reference to its periodic disappearance during the summer months. Accompanying the limestone are the expected geological features like caves and springs: Zlatibor abounds in speleological phenomena and a total of 98 caves and 44 pits have been identified in the region. The greatest of these is 1,691m-long **Stopić's Cave** (*Stopića pećina*) that lies off the Sirogojno–Užice road, 30km from Užice. The cave boasts a 30m wide, 18m high, entrance and the deepest rimstone pool in Serbia. In contrast to the limestone, the main rock type, away from the northern and eastern fringes of the plateau, is green serpentine and this forms the largest serpentine massif in Serbia.

Zlatibor enjoys a sunny, sub-alpine climate but, with about 100 snowy days a year, there is an abundant supply of snow for skiing between November and March. The region is equally popular in the summer months, especially in July and August, and Serbians come here in large numbers to walk, relax and breathe the cool mountain air.

Zlatibor (Kraljeve Vode)
Telephone code: 031
The tradition of tourism at Zlatibor began early in the 19th century when Prince Miloš Obrenović chose to spend his summers on the mountain. Following the arrival of King Aleksandar Obrenović in 1893, the small settlement of Kulaševac soon became known by its new name of Kraljeve Vode (King's water). In response to the honour, the king built the fountain that still stands in the town centre on which is engraved: *Kralj Aleksandar I, 20 avgusta 1893.*

At the beginning of the 20th century, the town had just a few private summerhouses owned by wealthy Užice residents but, after 1927, when the first bus line was opened from Užice, the construction of new houses, restaurants and hotels soon began in earnest. After World War II the name changed again to Partizanska Vode (Partisan's water) to reflect Yugoslavia's new political direction. Most maps and signs still use this name today although it has now officially reverted to its old name of Kraljeve Vode.

Getting there
Buses run frequently to and from Belgrade, Užice and more local destinations. There is also a Zlatibor stop on the Bar–Belgrade railway but this is some way out of town.

Where to stay
There is a wide range of accommodation to choose from, with hotels of all classes, as well as simpler pensions and apartment complexes that are generally more amenable to longer stays.

Hotel Jugopetrol★★★★ Kamalj bb; tel: 841 467; fax: 841 493
Hotel Palisad★★★★ Tel: 841 151; fax: 841 147. This one is owned by an ex-basketball star.
Hotel Zelenkada★★★★ Gajevi 1; tel: 841 051, 831 131: fax: 841 051
Apartment Complex Kraljevi konaci★★★★ Tel: 841 230
Hotel Dunav★★★ Tel: 841 126; fax: 841 183
Hotel Zlatibor★★★ Naselje Đurkovac 26; tel: 841 021; fax: 841 812
Hotel Olimp Naselje Sloboda bb; tel: 842 555; fax: 841 953; email: hotelolimp@ptt.yu
Hotel Lovac Tel: 841 165
Hotel Ratko Mitrovic Kraljeve vode bb; tel: 841 369; fax: 841 491
Special Institute Zlatibor-Đigota Tel: 841 141, 841 180; fax: 841 182. You do not have to participate in their weight-loss programme if you want to stay here.

Away from the resort in the neighbouring town of **Čajetina**, there is the **Motel Inex**★★ (Zlatiborska 18; tel: 841 021; fax: 834 017), while in the village of **Ljubiš** there is the **Pansion Ljubiš**★★★ (tel: 801 113).

Where to eat

There are numerous places in the town centre for food and drink. As many of the hotels provide full board to their guests most places just offer drinks and snacks, but there are a few pizzerias dotted around town. Most of the cafés have comfortable outdoor seating that allows patrons to soak up the ultra-violet while they sip their cappuccinos.

What to see

Zlatibor-Partizanska Vode is pleasant enough but, unless you are a sociologist interested in studying the Serbs at play, there are probably better choices in the region. It is very much a purpose-built resort and consequently it lacks any real character. The pine forest that reaches almost as far to the town is attractive but the extent of ongoing building development is such that you need to walk a long way from the town centre in order to get a sense of undisturbed nature. Nevertheless, if you are content to spend your days strolling around town, eating heartily and lounging in one of the town's numerous outdoor cafés then you will be content enough. Partizanska Vode would also be a suitable base for day trips into the hinterland if you had your own transport, as the well-developed infrastructure here guarantees that you will be well catered for in terms of accommodation and food.

The centre of the town is very compact, with a dense concentration of souvenir shops, cafés and restaurants close to the bus park. Close by, next to the King's Fountain, is a small artificial lake surrounded by pines that is used for bathing and sunbathing in summer and for skating in winter. For a swim in wilder surroundings, there is an artificial beach called **Kod komša** 7 km away, where the natural course of a stream has been interrupted and enclosed with stones. Do not expect the water to be warm. Meanwhile, in the town itself, an Olympic-size, open-air swimming pool is under construction. The **Đigota Institute** also has a heated indoor swimming pool that is open year-round to its guests.

Tourist information can be gleaned from the **Tourist Office of Cajetina-Zlatibor**, Naselje Jezero bb; tel: 841 646; fax: 841 244.

Internet access can be had at the **Net Walker Internet Café**.

Activities

Zlatibor developed as a ski centre in the period between the wars. There are three ski lifts in operation and a choice of slopes that vary in level of difficulty. There is also a track for cross-country skiing. The beginners' slopes are at **Obudovica**, just to the west of the town centre, with those at the **Tornik Sports Centre** at nearby **Ribnica** more suitable for experienced skiers. More information on skiing at Zlatibor can be had from www.skijanje.co.yu. The town also has numerous walking paths in the vicinity and that, together with skiing in the winter, is one of its greatest draws, but health tourism is important here too and many Serbs come for treatment. The clear, pure air of Zlatibor has given it a reputation for healing a variety of heart and respiratory complaints as well as for disorders of the thyroid; indeed, there is a clinic dedicated solely to thyroid problems at the crisply titled **Special Institute for the Prevention and Treatment of Thyroid Gland Disorders and the Rehabilitation of Patients**. Another therapy that the town specialises in is weight loss following a course of treatment called the Đigota program. The town is also a popular choice for basketball and football teams preparing for tournaments, and for summer sports camps in tennis and swimming.

There are a number of **festivals** held in the town: at the end of July, Zlatibor hosts a trumpet festival; at the end of August, an international film festival, known as MEFEST is held; and at the end of February, the town plays host to a hunters' gathering called the 'Wolf Chase' in which oxen are roasted, lectures on hunting are given and moving targets ranging from clay pigeons to real wolves are shot at by trigger-happy macho types – needless to say, it is probably not to everyone's taste.

VILLAGES IN THE ZLATIBOR REGION
Sirogojno

The **Open Air Village Museum** (tel: 802 291; email: office@sirogojno.org.yu) was set up here in 1979 by the Yugoslav Republic Institute for the Protection of Cultural Monuments with the idea of recreating a typical 19th-century Zlatibor homestead. The buildings were collected from all over the region, dismantled and then reconstructed here on this hillside site. There are examples of all the components you would expect in a 19th-century homestead: a house, a cottage – specially built for married members of the family and just used for sleeping – a guesthouse, dairy, granary, forge and animal compounds. The buildings are complete with furniture and fittings, and display artefacts typical of the economy and period; they are also used to stage demonstrations of traditional village skills from time to time.

The museum is set out in the same way as a typical homestead, positioned on a sunny slope with the highest point reserved for the living quarters, with stables, pigsties, sheep pens and vegetable plots a little lower down. All of the buildings are covered with a steeply pitched shingle roof, a safeguard against the considerable winter snow that this region receives.

Even without the interest of the museum, Sirogojno is an attractive place, high on a hillside with lovely views across the valley. A small, pristine 19th-century white church stands close to the museum site. At the museum entrance are various craft stalls selling high quality hand-knitted woollens, wooden craft items and mountain dairy produce like cheese and *kajmak*. The hand-made jumpers, designed by Dobrila Vasiljević-Smiljanić, and knitted by Zlatibor women for the past 30 years, are world famous; they are not cheap but they still offer exceptional value for money when bought at the source here. The museum itself has an excellent gift shop that sells a wide range of textiles, basketry, dried herbs, home-produced jams and cheeses, as well as a staggering (quite literally, if you drink too much) range of herb-flavoured fruit *rakija*s.

Sirogojno can be reached by occasional buses from Užice.

Gostilje

This village, just to the south of Sirogojno, is one of several that offer local accommodation as part of a Village @dventure package. The surroundings are idyllic and perfect for walking, while the village itself is very peaceful, with expansive views of the valley and the limestone outcrops that stand proud of the forest west of here. There is a waterfall close to the village that can be easily reached by a short walk. Heading down from the car park by the bridge, you pass a watermill and a flat meadow that doubles as a football pitch. A path leads down to the waterfall just beyond a very basic, but beautifully situated, campsite. Apart from the stunning scenery, the village's only other diversion is a fish farm full of thrashing trout.

The village of **Ljubiš**, another 7km south, has accommodation at the **Pension Ljubiš** (tel: 801 113).

Mokra Gora

This small village close to the Bosnia-Herzegovina border is where you embark on the spectacular **Šargan Eight Railway** (Šarganska Osmica). The railway is so called

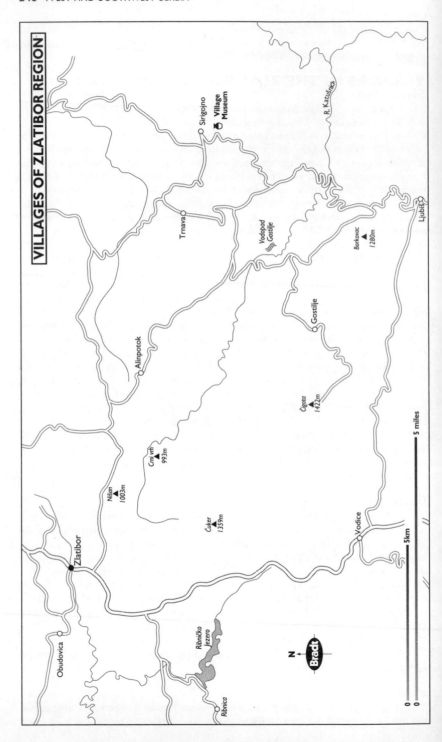

THE 'ŠARGAN EIGHT' RAILWAY

In a former life, the short stretch of convoluted track that is now called the 'Šargan Eight' used to be just one small section of the narrow-gauge line that connected Belgrade with the Bosnian capital, Sarejevo. The train was a lifeline for many communities that had previously been poorly connected and, until its closure in 1974, the Ćira train used to link the isolated villages in this part of western Serbia with the outside world.

The difficult, mountainous terrain of western Serbia ensured that it was a spectacular journey through steep cuttings and rocky gorges. Some sections were more problematic than others, however; in particular, the short section between Mokra Gora and Šargan-Vitasi. Although the horizontal distance between these two stations was a mere 3.5km, the height difference between them was a daunting 300m. Clearly, no ordinary train could cope with an incline this steep. The engineers came up with an ingenious solution to the problem and designed a loop in the shape of a number eight to connect the two stations. The loop – soon to be known as the Šargan Eight – was about 13.5km long and included 22 tunnels and ten bridges and viaducts along its length.

After 50 years of successful service, the Ćira line was declared to be unprofitable and the decision was made to close it down; the last train ran on February 28 1974. A quarter of a century passed by until fresh ideas of reopening the railway started to emerge, this time as a tourist route. During 1997 and 1998, villagers from around Mokra Gora organised voluntary work brigades to make the course of the old railway passable once more. The route was finally cleared during the months of the NATO bombing in 1999, with the additional help of the Serbian army. Narrow 760mm-gauge track was laid along an 8km length of the line, a committee was formed to take charge of the railway's revitalisation, and the professional assistance of the Želnid Railway Museum was sought. The emphasis was on authenticity: stations at Mokra Gora, Jatare and Šargan were reconstructed exactly as they had been in 1925 when the line was first opened. Two museum trains – Škoda and Elza – were overhauled and put into service, and authentic wooden passenger coaches were repaired and refurbished. Since its inauguration as a tourist line, the Šargan Eight has become a rare success story in troubled times. It has even captured the interest of film maker, Emir Kustarica, who used the railway as the setting for his last movie and built a film-set village on a hill above Mokra Gora. Now, there are plans afoot to eventually continue the line on to Višegrad in Bosnia-Herzegovina.

because of the extreme curvature of the tracks and the shape they make when seen from below. The track changes direction to such an extent that it is difficult to work out which direction you are travelling in after you have been on board for a while. (See box: The 'Šargan Eight' Railway.)

Approaching Mokra Gora, you may notice the outline of a traditional-looking village set high on a small plateau above the village. This is the set constructed by Emir Kustarica for his 2004 film release, Život Je Čudo (Life is a Miracle).

Mokra Gora is a small, pleasant village but the real reason for visiting is to take a ride on its unique railway. The Šargan Eight Railway, with its charming wooden carriages and sensational views, is a wonderful excursion and certainly not just one for rail buffs. The train leaves Mokra Gora station for Šargan-Vitasi twice a day between

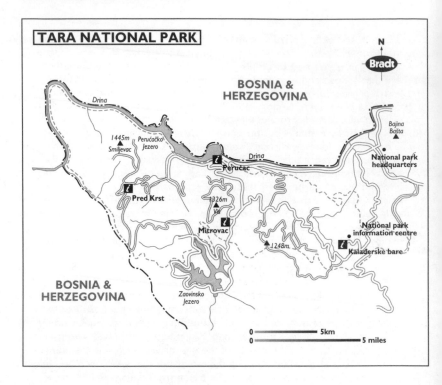

April and September at 10.30 and 14.00, taking about 40 minutes to cover the short distance downhill. It returns to Mokra Gora after a 15-minute break and takes an hour for the uphill return journey. A return ticket costs 400din for an adult, 200din for a child. The 14.00 departure is the one generally reserved for group excursions, so there is a slim chance that this one may be full if you have not pre-booked.

It is possible to hire the whole train for a bespoke trip, which costs between 40,000 and 100,000din, depending on the time of day or night and whether or not you wish to charter a steam engine.

Mokra Gora village is connected to Kremna and Užice by public bus. Further information and reservations on the railway can be made by contacting Đoko Topalović, Stanica Užice; tel/fax: 513 564; mob: 064 810 6429.

Where to stay

Mokra Gora railway station has its own **hotel** and **restaurant** right on the platform. Singles are 700din for bed and breakfast, 1,060din for half board, 1,410din for full board – slightly less per person for double occupancy.

Kremna

Kremna is a rather spread-out village that lies on the main E-761 road to Bosnia-Herzegovina, just to the south of the **Tara National Park**. As well as being at the heart of a beautiful area for walking, Kremna could provide a good base for visits to Mokra Gora and the Tara National Park. The village has a range of accommodation that can be booked as part of a village tourism package with Village @dventure Tours. If you are just passing through, rooms may be available at the house above the roadside restaurant at the entrance to the village. Buses run to the village from Užice.

TARA NATIONAL PARK

The Tara National Park lies just to the north of Kremna, in the panhandle circumscribed by the bend of the river Drina that extends northwest into Bosnia-Herzegovina. Tara, which includes both the Tara and Zvezda mountain ranges, was declared a national park in 1981. The park covers an area of about 22,000ha that lie between 250 and 1,500m above sea level. The park is almost entirely comprised of high mountains and deep gorges, three-quarters of which are covered by forest, together with the caves and springs typical of a karst landscape. Tara is home to a rare endemic tree species, the Pančić spruce, that is now confined to just a small area of the park and under state protection. Several species of rare and threatened birds and mammals like golden eagle and brown bear are present within the park's boundaries.

Three roads lead into the park: one from Bajina Bašta directly by way of the Bajina Bašta–Kaluđerske Bare road; a second from Bajina Bašta along the Perućac–Mitrovac road; and another from Kremna on the road that leads to Kaluđerske Bare. The road that continues through to Bosnia-Herzegovina at Kamenica does not constitute an official border crossing point.

Fairly basic facilities that can be found within the park are at Kaluđerske Bare, where there is a hotel complex, and at Mitrovac, which has a children's recreational centre and some catering facilities. The Drina Gorge that separates Serbia from Bosnia-Herzegovina is also an integral part of the park and can be toured by boat. Various water-based activities are offered along the river here.

The main management office is in nearby Bajina Bašta. Information about the park can be had from its headquarters at Tara National Park, Milenka Toalovica 3, 31250 Bajina Bašta; tel: 851 445, 853 644; email: nptara@ptt.yu; www.tara.org.yu.

Đurđevi Stupovi

East and Southeast Serbia

The region of the Homolskje Mountains that run parallel to and south of the Danube River has been dealt with in the *Along the Danube* chapter. This chapter covers the area south of the Homolskje range and east of the Morava River, as well as the whole of the Niš hinterland as far as the borders with Bulgaria, Macedonia and Kosovo. In many ways, this is one of the least-known parts of Serbia. Many travel through it – along the E-75 motorway that splits at Niš to lead east to Sofia and Bulgaria, and south to Macedonia and Greece – but few stop to see what the region has to offer. This is a pity, as there is plenty of interest in some of the towns of the region, and some fine countryside if you travel a short distance away from the motorway in either direction.

The **highlights** of the region are undoubtedly the monasteries of Manasija and Ravanica, hidden away in the hills just east of the E-75 motorway, and the city of Niš with its historic sites – the Turkish Fortress, the Skull Tower, and the Roman site at Mediana. Another interesting Roman site in the region is at Gamzigrad, close to Zaječar. Niš is also a good centre for outdoor pursuits: the Sokobanja region to the north of the city and the nearby Suva Planina (Dry Mountain) range both offer excellent hiking and cycling possibilities.

ZAJEČAR

Telephone code: 019

An hour south of Negotin, and only 11km from the Bulgarian border, Zaječar is the cultural and geographic centre of the Timočka Krajina region. With a population of about 40,000 inhabitants, it is a quiet, self-contained sort of place: a middle-sized town without many specific sights of its own but a pleasant enough stop for the night, having some very reasonable hotel options.

Probably the best reason for being here is to visit the Roman ruins of Gamzigrad that lie 12km west of the town, but even without this intention there is a good museum and a few Turkish buildings to see, as well as the pleasure of simply absorbing the atmosphere of a relaxed provincial town. Foreign visitors are quite rare here and local people are warmly accommodating as a result. Admittedly, the same could be said for quite a lot of Serbia.

The centre of Zaječar is dominated by the tall edifice of the Hotel Srbije, which forms a centrepiece to the main square below, Trg Nikola Pašić, which is named after the founder and former leader of the Radical Party who was born in this town. The square is a light, airy place with a few outdoor cafés along its western edge, with popcorn sellers and toy electric cars for children. On the square's northern side is the building that houses the town museum, unavoidably conspicuous with its bright-orange paintwork. The street running left from the museum leads down to an

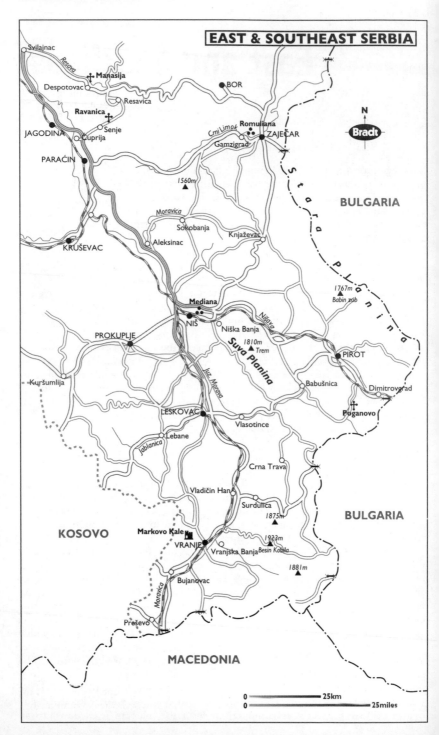

interesting outdoor market area and the bus and train terminals. Despite rampant modernisation, Zaječar still has a few traditional *konaks* scattered around the town. One that can be visited is **Rudul Beg's Konak**, a 19th-century Turkish house museum located at the end of Ulica Ljube Nešića, the main street that leads north from the main square. The *konak* was built for a local Turkish ruler between 1843 and 1856 and, as well as having period furniture and rooms laid out in the style of the period, there is a permanent exhibition dedicated to 'old Zaječar'. The museum is closed weekends but open Monday–Friday 07.00–15.00, and holidays 09.00–13.00. Further down this street at number 39 is another *konak* that operates as a *kafana* – **Kafana Hajduk Veljkov Konak** – a place full of old-fashioned character, and a good choice for a meal or just a drink.

The **National Museum** has an interesting collection of archaeological, ethnological and historical exhibits from the region, with particular emphasis on the Roman site at nearby Gamzigrad. It is open Tuesday–Friday 07.00–18.00, Saturdays and Mondays 07.00–15.00, holidays from 09.00–13.00; closed on Sundays.

In late May and early June, the town hosts the **'Golden Hands of Zaječar'** festival, a series of events celebrating the food and culture of the region. Information on events can be had from the **Municipal Tourist Organisation** (tel: 421 521).

Getting there

Zaječar has seven buses a day that run to Belgrade, and the same number to Bor, should you wish to go there. The 11 or so daily buses running west to Boljevac can drop you at the turning for the Gamzigrad ruins. The village of the same name is also served by six buses a day, although Gamzigrad village is some way short of the site itself.

Train connections are slower and less frequent. The only direct train to Belgrade leaves in the middle of the night and takes six hours. There are four trains a day leaving for Niš, four to Bor and four to Negotin, although the same journey by bus is invariably quicker.

Where to stay

For its size, Zaječar has a surprising number of accommodation options. A good choice is the **Hotel Konj** at Vojvode Mišića (tel: 27 004). This privately owned two-star hotel is found down an alley opposite Hotel Srbije and the main square. The immediate surroundings look a little grotty but the hotel itself is clean and efficiently run. To find it, go down the alleyway that lies opposite the Hotel Srbije, following the sign that points to the Rivendell Irish pub; the hotel lies just beyond here. Comfortable, modern rooms are available at 1,380din (or €20) for a single, 2,100din for a double, and 2,550din for a triple. A 'French bed' can be had for 2,100din and an apartment for 2,850–3,500din. There is a small bar area, and original oil paintings in the dining area. A choice, other than the usual ham and eggs, is offered for breakfast. The reception staff are welcoming and speak good English.

The town's biggest and most obvious hotel is the state-owned, three-star **Hotel Srbije** on Trg Nikola Pašića (tel: 432 546). Rooms cost 1,030din for a single and 1,570din for a double. The hotel has a large restaurant, which, on Sundays at least, seems to play host to large noisy wedding parties and their accompanying brass bands.

Another option is the three-star **Hotel Grinka M** at Prote Mateje 15 (tel: 423 330). This hotel, a white villa with wrought-iron balconies, is another privatised venture found down a quiet side street a little way from the centre. It is signposted from the main square. Bear in mind that a two-star private hotel is likely to have better, and more modern, facilities than a state-run three-star hotel. A final option in town is the two-star **Hotel Salas** (Salas bb; tel: 69 200, 69 842) where the accommodation consists mostly of apartments, with just four singles and a solitary double.

Where to eat

Apart from the hotel restaurants, most of the restaurants in the town seem to be pizzerias. There are several around the centre like **Bombay Pizza** on Dimitri Popovića, and **Pizza-In** close to the Hotel Srbije. For snacks, the **Novi Ukus** bakery is on the corner of Bojković Ljiljan and Dimitri Popovića. For more traditional fare, the choice is limited: there is the **Kafana Valentino**, also on Dimitri Popovića, and the **Kafana Hajduk Veljkov Konak** at Ljube Nešića 39 (tel: 424 254). This last choice is situated in an old Turkish *konak* with a wooden ceiling and chairs made out of barrels, and is rather like Zaječar's own version of the '?' café in Belgrade. Wrought-iron work with a *hajduk* theme decorates the walls and, as well as a communal area, there are secluded cubicles available for dining parties. Prices are very reasonable, although it is unlikely that everything on the menu will be available. As well as food, it is also a good place to try out some of the wines from the area. Zaječarska pivo – the local beer sold here – is pretty tasty too, and has a pleasant nutty flavour.

Practicalities

Internet access is available at **Verat.net** upstairs in the Tržni Centar that faces onto Trg Nikola Pašića; the fast connection here costs only 30din per hour. A branch of **Jugobank** with an ATM is next door. The **post office** is along the next street heading towards the bus station from here, facing the other entrance to the Tržni Centar. There is a good **outdoor market** selling local fruit, vegetables and dairy produce next to the bus station.

Gamzigrad (Felix Romuliana)

The 3rd- and 4th-century ruins of the Roman fortress of Felix Romuliana at Gamzigrad are located a dozen kilometres west of Zaječar. Although the site was already well known, archaeologists digging here in 1984 unearthed the remains of an imperial palace within the ramparts of the fortress, finding especially fine mosaics, a vestibule, atria, marble floors, public baths and city gates.

All of the evidence suggests that the palace at Romuliana was first built as the residence of Roman Imperator Galerius Valerius Maximillian. It appears to have been suddenly and mysteriously abandoned by its original creators, and then subsequently rebuilt by Justinian in Byzantine times, having been occupied and reinforced by Slavic tribes in the interim period. The site was eventually abandoned altogether and totally forgotten for a thousand years before its rediscovery in the 19th century.

Although most of what remains is extensive foundations and grassed-over mounds, it is still possible to get a good idea of its original plan from the ramparts. The ramparts, which originally had six towers on either side, form a trapezium measuring 300m by 230m. This, in turn is reinforced by an inner defensive system of 20 cylindrical towers with four gates. Some of the remaining pillars are in very good condition, as is some of the fine mosaic work found on the pavement. Part of the vestibule to the bath is intact, and consists of an octagonal chamber with a large room over the hypocaust and a larger room with an apse. The vestibule dates from the later Constantinian period but the mosaics, which show beasts fighting each other, and a hunter with his dog, are undoubtedly earlier, probably 3rd-century.

ĆUPRIJA ЩУПРИЈА

Telephone code: 035

Ćuprija is a small but sprawling town just off the E-75 motorway on the Morava River. The only real point in coming here is to use it as a base for visiting the nearby Ravanica Monastery.

Many of the buses that go north and south along the motorway do not stop here, although they may stop at Jagodina, the next town north. There are some direct buses to and from Belgrade however, about 12 a day, in addition to four daily services from Kruševac and six from Niš. There is also supposed to be a daily service to Svilajnac via Despotovac that leaves in the early afternoon. This could be a useful way of getting to Manasija but confirm the time (and the very existence of the service!) carefully at the bus station first.

The bus station is at the edge of town next to the *autoput*. It was undergoing radical renovation when I last used it but work should be completed by the time you read this. To reach the centre of Ćuprija from the bus station, turn left (ie: in the *opposite* direction to the motorway) and follow the road into town. A 15-minute walk will bring you to a square and a T-junction – this is Cara Lazara, the town's high street. The **Hotel Ravno** (Cara Lazara 2; tel: 471 314), the only place to stay in town, is hard to find. It is hidden away up an alleyway behind the square. Walk left from the square, turn left at the travel agents and the hotel entrance is in front of you. Despite its hiding away from the public gaze, the hotel is reasonable enough; the staff here are friendly and the rooms are adequate. It is good value too, at only 600din for a single, and 1,100din for a double. There is a restaurant attached to the hotel and a few other places to eat in town. The **Canzone Pizzeria** on Cara Lazara does reasonable pizzas and the **Caffe Mozaik** on the square near the hotel can rustle up pancakes as well as drinks.

To reach **Senje**, the village close to Ravanica Monastery, there is supposed to be a local bus that picks up along Cara Lazara before heading out to the village. There probably is, but I waited fruitlessly for 45 minutes before giving up on the idea. No-one I asked seemed to know how frequently they ran. There are plenty of buses along Cara Lazara that link Ćuprija with the nearby towns of Jagodina and Paraćin should you wish to visit these.

A more reliable way to visit the monastery is to take a taxi from the town centre or, better still, from outside the bus station. The price to Ravanica should be around 300din; if you add on a reasonable amount of waiting time at the monastery, and the fare back to Ćuprija, it will be something like 700din. The monastery lies to the east up a valley, about 10km from Ćuprija and a couple of kilometres beyond the attractive village of Senje.

Ravanica Monastery

This fine fortified monastery of the Morava School, the first to be built in this style, dates from around 1376. It was founded by Prince Lazar, whose body was brought here after his death at the Battle of Kosovo in 1389. It remains here today but only after having travelled a great deal around the Balkans in the interim period (see box, *Prince Lazar's Remains*). Lazar's well-travelled relics finally returned here in 1989, the 600th anniversary of his demise.

Ravanica lies just beyond the village of Senje, surrounded by green meadows beside a forested hillside. The monastery buildings are completely surrounded by a continuous fortified wall that previously had ramparts and towers like those of Manasija to the north. The church, with five cupolas, is built to a cruciform plan with apses on the north and south arms as well as on the more usual east. Alternate layers of brick and stone have been used for the walls and these are decorated with ornate bas-reliefs around the windows, doorways and cupolas.

The church was attacked several times by the Turks who destroyed most of the original frescos. The narthex of the church is a later 18th-century addition, dating from a time when extensive restoration took place. The benefactor responsible for this work, the abbot Stefan, is portrayed on the west wall.

PRINCE LAZAR'S REMAINS

It remains uncertain whether Prince Lazar was killed during battle, or shortly after, in the hands of the Turks, who probably would have beheaded him. Whatever the cause of his death, his dead body would soon become an object of pilgrimage for many Serbs, who through the coming centuries would attribute great spiritual significance to his mortal remains.

At first, his body was interred at Ravanica Monastery, where it became the centre of a cult that drew pilgrims from all over Serbia. When the Ravanica monks were forced to flee from their monastery in 1690, they took the bones with them, settling first at Szentendre near Budapest, then at a monastery in Srem called Sremska Ravanica. Rebecca West, during her pre-war travels in Serbia, tells of shaking the prince's hand whilst he was interred here. Lazar remained here until 1942, when he was moved, with German help, to Belgrade after Croatian Ustaše had stolen golden rings from his corpse. During his Belgrade years in the Patriarchate, Lazar once again became the focus for pilgrimage, especially on June 28, St Vitus' Day – *Vidovan* – the date of the battle that brought his end. Lazar's body remained in Belgrade until 1987 when, as a precursor to the forthcoming 600th anniversary of the Battle of Kosovo, his well-travelled remains were taken on yet another tour of Serbian and Bosnian monasteries. With the festivities over, Lazar was returned once more to Ravanica, where he now receives visitors every Sunday, and where a plastic canopy prevents visitors from actually making physical contact *à la* Rebecca West. It is no exaggeration to say that Prince Lazar must have travelled a far greater distance in death than most of his contemporaries ever managed while they were alive. Hopefully, after 600 restless years of motion, his weary bones can remain at Ravanica for eternity now.

The older frescos in the nave are in poor condition, partly because of Turkish mutilation and partly because of badly prepared plaster that faded the colours prematurely. The figure of Lazar with his wife Milica and their two sons adorns the wall opposite the southern apse but this fresco is quite badly damaged. Better is the *Cycle of Miracles* on the south wall and the *Entry into Jerusalem* around the southern apse.

Manasija Monastery

This Morava School monastery in the Resava valley is so heavily fortified that it resembles a Byzantine castle. In all, there are 11 towers stretched along the high defensive walls. The fortifications were not just for dramatic effect; when this monastery was being constructed by Lazar's son Stefan in the early years of the 15th century (probably between 1408 and 1418) it was perfectly clear that it was only a matter of time before the Turks would move north to consolidate their earlier victory at Kosovo Polje. In the end it took them another half-century before they did this but there could have been no doubt in Stefan's mind that their fate was already sealed.

In the first half of the 15th century, under the patronage of Stefan Lazarević, Manasija became a haven for writers and artists from provinces that had already fallen under Turkish subjugation. Had the Turks not interrupted these artistic endeavours, it may also have become the focal point for the Serbian equivalent of the Italian Renaissance.

In many ways Manasija represents the final statement of a Serbian golden age that ended with the advent of almost half a millennium of Turkish domination.

The church within the walls is of marble, simple enough on the outside but decorated inside by frescos that represent the pinnacle of the Morava School of painting. Many of the original frescos have been destroyed but of those that remain, the *Warrior Saints* on the north wall and the *Parable of the Wedding Feast* on the north apse are among the finest of their genre. It is thought that these frescos are either the work of Greek masters or of local artists that had been trained in Salonica. Although the frescos are partly ruined, it is easy to see that they represent the culmination of an artistic movement that had been developing and improving for decades. The colours used are bright and vivid, and the figures represented in the paintings seem cultured and worldly, fully engaged in the celebration of life.

DESPOTOVAC ДЕСПОТОВАЦ

This small town is the best place to aim for if you are visiting Manasija and want to spend the night in the vicinity of the monastery. It is a pleasant place in the middle of some beautiful countryside and so the lack of sophisticated facilities and night-time entertainment is hardly a hardship. Accommodation is available at the **Hotel Resava**, about 1km east of the bus station just past the junction for Manasija. The hotel has a restaurant but there are also a few grill restaurants and a pizzeria in the vicinity of the bus station.

Tourist information in Despotovac may be found at Mose Pijade 2—4; tel: 611 110, 611 117, 633 007; fax: 611 008.

Four direct buses run daily to Despotovac from Belgrade via Svilajnac at the entrance to the Resava valley, and there is also an early-morning bus that originates in Svilajnac and travels on through to Ćuprija. Bus timetables are rarely carved in stone, so enquire at the bus station for the exact times of this service.

Manasija Monastery is an easy walk from the town. From the town centre walk towards the Hotel Resava and turn left along the road that crosses the river. After the bridge, the road curves around to the right in the direction of the river and leads to the gates of the monastery.

Resavska Cave

This impressive cave system is found 20km to the east of Despotovac. The total length of the galleries extends for 2,850m, although the tourist path itself is only 800m long. The system consists of three levels connected by artificial tunnels. Parts of the upper and middle galleries may be visited, while an underground stream flows through the lowest gallery making it out of bounds for visitors. All of the galleries are rich in stalactites and stalagmites, and the rock itself is quite variable in colour. The underground temperature hovers around 14°C; humidity is 75–80%.

Resavska can be visited between 08.00 and 18.30 in summer (from April 1 to October 31) and from 10.00 to 17.00 in winter (November 1 to March 31). There is a guide service and tours of the cave last around 40 minutes.

NIŠ НИШ

Telephone code: 018

Niš, with an estimated population of around 250,000, is Serbia's third-largest city. Some even insist that it has overtaken Novi Sad as the country's second-largest conurbation in recent years, although no-one seems very sure of this. Whatever the city's status, few seem to have a good word to say for the place. Authors of long-defunct guidebooks to the former Yugoslavia talk of a large 'dull and dirty town' and an air of 'grey, grim abandonment'. Even Serbian nationals are downbeat about the city, but when you take the conversation a little further you invariably find out that you are receiving second- or third-hand information. It usually turns out that the person reinforcing this negative image has never actually been there but they have 'heard that it is not very nice' and that the city is still an industrial wasteland.

There is a little truth in all of this, but not much. In industrial terms, Niš has certainly seen better days: its manufacturing base has largely been decimated over the past 15 years, thanks to economic sanctions, poor planning and NATO bombing. This has left a large, skilled workforce in search of alternative employment. It is not the prettiest of places either; then again, neither is Belgrade.

Like Belgrade, Niš seems to make the most of what it does have – the Turkish fort by the river has been developed into a pleasant park, and some of the original buildings have been converted to galleries and smart café-restaurants; the main shopping street, Ovrenovićeva, like its counterpart Knez Mihaila in the capital, has been pedestrianised to become the route for a crowded *korso* every evening; the number-one tourist 'attraction' of the grisly Ćele Kula (the Skull Tower) has been protected from the elements and – unusual for Serbia – is actively promoted as a tourist site.

As well as a few interesting historical sites, the city has quite a lot else to offer: a number of good but inexpensive restaurants, a relaxed atmosphere, some reasonable places to stay and a nearby spa resort. It is also serves as a good base for hiking trips into the nearby hills. Ignore the rumours – Niš is really quite nice!

History

The history of the city goes back to well before Roman times. Discoveries at Bubanj and Humska čuka, close to the city, suggest that the area was populated in the Neolithic and Bronze Age periods. The Celtic inhabitants of the region named the river that ran through it, Navissos, and a variation on this the name was adopted by the Romans who eventually colonised the region.

As **Naissus**, Niš became an important city of the Roman Empire, and the emperor, Constantine the Great, was born here around AD274–280. Constantine was appointed emperor in AD307 and in 313 he issued the Milan Edict in which Christianity, previously persecuted, was given equal status with all the other religions of the Roman Empire. He went on to move the seat of the emperor east to Constantinople and by doing this lay the foundations for the new Byzantine Empire. During this period, Niš became an important economic and artistic centre. Constantine returned to the city periodically, spending time at his summer residence of Mediana, the remains of which can still be seen just outside the city on the road to Niška Banja. Records testify that Constantine passed several more laws while he was resident here in Naissus – in 315, 319, 324 and 334.

The city was destroyed by Atilla in 441, and later again by further Hun attacks in 448 and by Barbarians in 480. It was rebuilt in the 6th century by the Byzantine Emperor Justinian only to be destroyed once more in 615 by marauding Avars. Around about 987, the town was taken under the control of the Bulgarian Emperor Simeon. Byzantium later regained control over Niš and the surrounding area in the early part of the 11th century but in 1072 the town was raided once more by Hungarians.

Slavs had been in the region since the 6th century but were a fairly disparate group until the organisational skills of the Nemanjić dynasty came to bear. Stefan Nemanja incorporated Niš as part of Serbia in 1183 with the intention of making it his capital. The city did not remain under Serbian control for long; in 1196 Stefan Nemanja was defeated by the Greek, Isak Angelos, and the city did not return to Serbian hands until 1241. The city slowly recovered and rebuilt itself under the leadership of the

Nemanjić dynasty. After the years of uncertainty that followed the defeat at the Battle of Kosovo in 1389, the Turks finally wrested the city in 1448 and their rule lasted right up until 1877, apart from one brief period of Austrian rule.

As elsewhere in Serbia, there were revolts against Ottoman rule from time to time, most notably at the beginning of the 19th century, during the First Serbian Uprising. These were brutally put down by the Turks. One particular incident of this kind in 1809, at the Battle of Čegar Hill, led to the construction of the city's famous Ćele Kula (Skull Tower) as a deterrent to would-be insurrectionists.

On January 11 1878, Prince Milan Obrenović entered the gates of the fortress after a long and exhausting battle. After more than 400 years of Turkish rule, Niš was finally back in Serbian hands.

Niš became the Serbian wartime capital for a brief period during World War I, from July 1914 until October 1915, when it was occupied by the Bulgarian army until the end of the war.

During World War II, the city suffered as much as, if not more than, most other Serbian towns. The Nazis built the concentration camp Crveni Krst in 1941 as an internment centre for the Jews, Roma and others they considered undesirable, and adopted Bubanj Hill just outside the town as the setting for many of their mass killings. Over 10,000 citizens were shot here during the war.

The most recent loss of life in the city as a result of armed conflict is depressingly fresh in the city's memory. Niš was targeted quite extensively during the 1999 NATO air campaign. Bombs destroyed the airport, a tobacco factory and part of the industrial zone, as well as misfires that destroyed civilian property. The worst 'misfire' was a missile that hit an ambulance by accident killing several civilians and injuring dozens more.

Getting there and around

Niš is easily reached from all directions. The main E-75 *autoput* bypasses the city en route for Macedonia and Bulgaria. Numerous daily **buses** link Niš with Belgrade, over 20 run south to Leskovac, the same number go southwest to Kuršumlija and 17 head southeast to Pirot. Four daily buses run as far as the Bulgarian border at Dimitrograd. Two buses cross the border into Bulgaria and on to Sofia, and a total of eight leave daily for Skopje in Macedonia. The bus station is just around the corner from the fortress, beyond the market area to the left of the Istanbul gate. If you arrive here, go out through the turnstiles, turn left past the market and then right over the bridge opposite Istanbul gate to reach central Trg Kralja Mihaila.

Niš is also on an international **train** line, although these are not as frequent or as reliable as the buses. As well as going to Belgrade and Novi Sad to the north, there are train services east to Sofia and Istanbul, and south to Skopje, which continue to Thessaloniki and Athens in Greece. The bus stop opposite the station provides a service to the city centre.

The city's **airport**, now known as 'Constantine the Great' Airport, was reopened in the autumn of 2003, having been put out of action during the 1999 NATO air war. It has just a few scheduled flights at present – a twice-weekly service to Belgrade – and a handful of charter flights, but it will probably expand its services in the future. It is also hoped that Niš will become the destination for more charter flights as companies running ski packages to Kopaonik look to cut down the lengthy transfer times to that resort. Airport buses meet all flights to provide a service to the city.

The city centre is small enough to walk around but a useful **local bus** service is the number 24 that runs along Voždova passing Ćele Kula and Mediana on its way to Niška Banja. Another useful route is that between the railway station and the centre of the city. On all routes the flat fare is 30din, paid to the driver, or 25din from

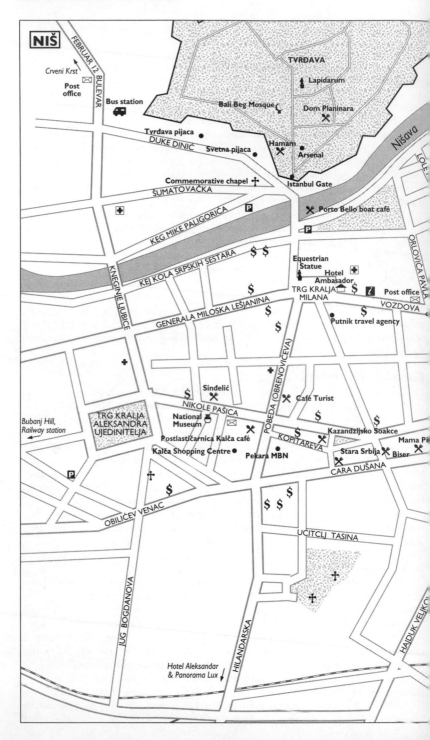

NIŠ

FEBRUAR 12 BULEVAR

Crveni Krst

Post office

Bus station

TVRĐAVA

Lapidarum

Bali Beg Mosque

Dom Planinara

Tvrđava pijaca

DUKE DINIĆ

Svetna pijaca

Hamam

Arsenal

Nišava

LOLE

Commemorative chapel

Istanbul Gate

ŠUMATOVAČKA

Porto Bello boat café

KEG MIKE PALIGORICA

ORLOVIČA PAVLA

KEJ KOLA SRPSKIH SESTARA

$ $

Equestrian Statue

Hotel Ambasador

TRG KRALJA MILANA

$

Post office

VOZDOVA

GENERALA MILOSKA LEŠJANINA

$

$

Putnik travel agency

$

KNEGINJE LJUBICE

Bubanj Hill, Railway station

TRG KRALJA ALEKSANDRA UJEDINITELJA

Sinđelić

POBEDA (OBRENOVIĆEVA)

Café Turist

$

NIKOLE PAŠICA

National Museum

$

Kazandzijsko Soakce

$

Mama Pi

Postlastičarnica Kalča café

Kalča Shopping Centre

Pekara MBN

KOPITAREVA

Stara Srbija

Biser

CARA DUŠANA

$

OBILIĆEV VENAC

$ $

UCITCLJ TASINA

JUG BOGDANOVA

HILANDARSKA

HAJDUK VELIKO

Hotel Aleksandar & Panorama Lux

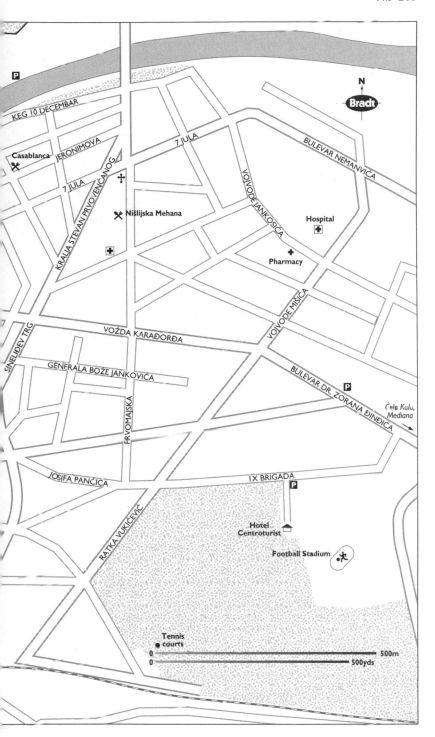

a Niš–ekspres stand. A one-day ticket can be bought at a Niš–ekspres stand for 75din, or on the bus for 80din. **Taxis** in Niš are easily found, although they may seem a little more expensive than Belgrade when used for short rides. Flag-fall is around 50din and the cost per kilometre 30–40din.

Tourist information

There is a very helpful tourist office close to the Hotel Ambassador at Voždova 7 (tel/fax: 523 118; email: tonis@tourist-nis.org.yu; www.tourist-nis.org.yu). They sell maps and booklets and can help with information on accommodation and sightseeing in the city.

Local tour operators

ACE Cycling and Mountaineering Centre B Krsmanovic 51/8; tel: 064 247 6311, 199 3124; fax: 472 87: email: info@ace-adventurecentre.com; www.ace-adventure.com. They organise a variety of tours in the southeast Serbian region. They specialise in hiking and cycling weekends in the Niš region but can custom design a tour according to specific requirements. ACE (Artists, Constructors, Engineers!), run by two cycling brothers, pride themselves on providing comfortable accommodation and gourmet meals as part of their package. All tours are guided. The hiking – or cycling – involved in the tours can be tailored to personal levels of fitness ranging from easy to challenging. Their weekend tours tend to be in the Sokobanja, Suva Planina or Stara Planina areas that are fairly close to Niš but they will happily design a tour around any desired location. They also run week-long escorted tours to Bulgaria, Austria, Italy and Greece.
Putnik have an office on Voždova opposite the Hotel Ambassador.

Other practicalities

There are several **banks with ATMs** throughout the city: Société Generale on Voždova, Komercialna banka and Nacionalna banka on Nikole Pašića, and Jubanka on Pobeda. There are numerous **exchange offices** along Pobeda. The **post office** on Voždova offers internet access for 60din per hour. Opposite the post office on the corner of Voždova and Orlovića Pavla is the **JAT airline office**.

Where to stay

Two of Niš's central hotels – the Hotel Park and the Hotel Niš – were closed in 2004, meaning that there was a bit less competition for the other state-run hotels in town, the Ambassador and the Centroturist. If they can find the right investors, the Park and Niš may be renovated and reopened sometime in the future, although it is probably more likely that they won't be. To fill the void, there are a few, new privately owned hotels opening up in the city. Unfortunately, these are all a long way from the city centre and not ideally located if you do not have your own transport.

Hotel Ambasador★★★ Trg Kralja Milana; tel: 525 511. The Ambassador is the multi-storey building that towers over the city's most central square. With 106 double rooms, 8 apartments and 31 singles spread over 8 floors, there is plenty of space here and it is unlikely to ever get completely full. Some of the rooms can get very hot during the daytime in summer. The hotel is perfectly adequate but seems a bit overpriced for what it offers. The location, however, could not be better. A buffet breakfast is included in the price, which is a pleasant change from the usual grease-and-egg scenario. Single rooms are 2,200din, doubles 3,300din.
Hotel Centroturist★★★ IX Brigade 10; tel: 22 468, 22 477. This hotel is in a quiet location next to the FC Radnički football stadium in Čair park … well, quiet as long as there isn't a match! Breakfast is served in the restaurant next door. There are just 30 twin rooms at 1,700din per person.

Hotel Aleksandar★★★ Njegoševo bb; tel: 562 333, 065 20 20 222; email: hotelaleksandar@medianis.net; www hotelaleksandar.com. Located high on a hillside above the city, this private hotel makes up for its awkward location with fine views – fine if you have a car. With 7 apartments, 2 single rooms and 13 double rooms, each with TV and minibar. The spacious rooms are scrupulously clean and nicely decorated with modern abstract paintings. Wireless internet connection is available. The hotel has a restaurant with a terrace and a snack bar. Prices start around €45 per person.

Hotel Panorama Lux★★★ Svetolika Rankovića bb; tel: 360 680, 063 433 783, 063 406 004. This is the city's best hotel, located quite close to the Hotel Aleksandar and having the same advantages and drawbacks. The en-suite rooms come with satellite TV, minibar and individually controlled AC. The restaurant is able to cater for vegetarian and diabetic diets. There is an aperitif bar and 24-hour room service and money exchange. Visa and MasterCard are both accepted. Prices are around €50 per person.

Hotel Lion★★ Kneževačka 28a; tel: 570 010. This hotel (pronounced *Lee-on*) is located to the east of the city centre on the north side of the Nišava River.

Outside the city are a couple of motels that might be worth considering if you have a car: the **Motel Nais★★★** on the autoput just before the city turn-off (tel: 601 066) and the **Motel Mediana** (tel: 530 010) halfway between Ćele Kula and Mediana on Bulevar Svetog Cara Konstantina.

Where to eat and drink
Restaurants

Hamam Located to the left of the entrance to the fort in what used to be a Turkish bath house. The interior has been renovated and makes for an interesting dining location, although, on a hot summer's night, it is probably more enjoyable to eat outside on the terrace. The restaurant serves excellent food at moderate prices. Try *pilać ražnića* – chicken kebabs wrapped in bacon. A good meal with wine should cost 700–1,000din.

Sinđelić Nikole Pašića 25. This restaurant, located in a *konak* close to the city centre, specialises in Serbian national dishes. The building formerly belonged to a Niš merchant. It was completely reconstructed in 1981.

Casablanca Jeronimova 26; tel: 523 353. The emphasis here is on international dishes, with a few vegetarian choices. A full meal will cost 700–1,000din.

Biser Koste Stamenkovica 1; tel: 48 205. Serbian cooking in a traditional restaurant that has a few tables out on the pavement. Biser has good food, friendly English-speaking staff and low prices.

Mama Pizza Cara Dušana 43. This is considered to be the best pizza restaurant in the city, as it has an authentic wood oven for cooking. There is an outside courtyard area where you can sit. Open Mon–Sat 09.00–midnight, Sun 14.00–23.00.

Nišlijska Mehana Prvomajska. This is a national restaurant that comes recommended by many. It is said to have the best *ćevapčić* in the city. There is live music every night.

Ribli Restoran Zlatni Kotlić; tel: 22 514. One of the city's few fish restaurants.

Kazandzijsko Soakce Kopitareva 31. This is a typical *kafana* on a street full of cafés and bars. The menu is fairly limited, with the usual choice of grilled meats and salads at low prices. The helpings are huge, easily enough for two.

Stara Srbija Located at the corner of Cara Dušana and Trg republike, this old-fashioned place, close to Kopitareva, has good national food at very moderate prices. There is an outside terrace and a dark, rather musty dining room inside. Beware of liberties being taken in 'rounding up' the bill, as the waiters do not seem to be very good at arithmetic here.

Amerikanac This restaurant is located south of the city, up the hillside on Kovanlučka, and is highly rated by locals who all seem to know where it is. The owner spent some time in the United States in his youth, hence the name.

Cafés, bars and snackbars

There are far too many cafés in the city to make many specific recommendations. The café-per-capita ratio here seems even higher than elsewhere in the country, but there tends to be concentrations of café-bars in certain locations around the city.

At Tvrđarva, the Turkish fortress, there are several upmarket places close to the entrance gate. Across the river, around Trg Oslobođenja, are a few more, and the pedestrian street of Pobede has trendy cafés with outdoor tables and cushioned seating all the way along it. Other café-bar enclaves include Kopitareva (Coppersmith's Street), a narrow pedestrian street that runs off the top of Pobede by the Kalča Centre, and also along IX Brigade next to the park. A newly emerging area for cafés, very popular with Niš's younger population, is the park opposite Pariske Komune in the east of the city. Many of these places put on live music during the warmer months of the year, usually a singer and a keyboard player who perform anything from Latin jazz to Beatles covers – or both.

What follows are just a few suggestions.

Dom Planinara (Mountaineers Club) At Tvrđava. A no-nonsense sort of place with tables spread out beneath the trees at the fortress. There is nothing fancy here, just good *kava turska* and bottles of Jelen beer for 50din. To find it, walk through the entrance into the fortress, turn right up some steps after you have passed the Turkish arsenal-art gallery and the public toilets. The café is under the trees ahead. Watch out for mosquitoes after dusk.

Porto Bello The café-boat moored on the Nišava River by the bridge that leads to the fortress. A nice atmosphere even if the drinks are a little overpriced. There is sometimes a large TV screen set up here for special football matches. The same screen goes on to show Fashion TV when the match is over, which gives you some idea of the mixed clientele that frequent this place.

Postlastičarnica Kalča Pobede bb kupola; tel: 548 345. This smart café-pastry shop is next to the **Kalća shopping centre**, and faces out onto Nikole Pašića and Pobede. It is relatively expensive but has superb cakes and a wide range of coffees to choose from. There is a fan-cooled terrace outside and an air-conditioned saloon inside.

Pekara MBN Kopitareva 23. This is an excellent central bakery, with outside tables where you can eat your purchase. There is a wide range of *burek* and *pitta* to choose from and prices are very cheap. The corn bread with cheese and spinach is recommended.

Olimpys Next door to Pekara MBN. A good fast food place with its own outdoor seating area that does *gyros*, *čevapčiĉi*, *pljeskavica* etc.

Café Turist Pobede. This is nothing to do with tourists but a sit-down ice-cream place with a tempting variety of flavours.

What to see and do
Niš Fortress (Tvrđava)

The fortifications that exist today date only as far back as the beginning of the 18th century, but the Turkish fortress that survives was built on the same site as earlier fortifications of Roman, Byzantine and medieval origin. The fortress extends over an area of 22ha, with 2,100m of wall 8m high that has an average thickness of 3m. Outside the walls is a moat, the northern part of which still survives. Of the original gates, the southern **Istanbul Gate** (*Stambol kapija*), the main entrance today, and the western, Belgrade Gate, are the best preserved. The *hammam* by the Istanbul Gate, which is now a restaurant, dates from the 15th century and is the oldest Turkish building in the city. Water would have been brought to the bath from the Nišava River by means of underground wooden pipes.

Just beyond the smart cafés that extend along the walls to the left of Istanbul Gate, is a curious monument that looks like an extended lipstick and which is dedicated to

Milan Obrenović and the liberation from Turkish rule. A little further on, standing alone at the centre of the fortress area, is the early 16th-century **Mosque of Bali Beg**, now an art gallery. A library once stood next to the mosque but only a ruin remains today. Close to Bali Beg's Mosque is the **Lapidarium**, a small display of Roman gravestones and sculpture found within the fortress area and gathered together here. The **arsenal** to the right of the Istanbul Gate, which dates from 1857, is now an art pavilion while the adjoining guards' rooms have found new usage as a souvenir shop. On the northern side of the fortress are the remains of a Roman building with some mosaics.

The whole of the fortress area is a popular venue for the citizens of Niš, especially on warm summer evenings when the city's more youthful element congregates at its bars and cafés. The Tvrđava complex also serves as a park area where joggers, cyclists and young families with toddlers all make the most of the shade and greenery. It is possible to climb up on the walls to get a better look over the city and the Nišava River – just climb up the steps immediately to the right of the Istanbul gate on the inside of the fortress. Unfortunately, the broken glass and smell of urine does not encourage you to linger for long up here and you are better off enjoying the prospect at an outdoor table of one of the cafés below.

Ćele Kula – the Skull Tower
Bulevar Braće Taskovića bb; tel: 322 228
This grotesque memorial was erected by the Turks as an example to others of the folly of opposition to their rule. Its construction followed the Battle of Čegar in 1809 at the time of the First Serbian Uprising when the Serbian General Stevan Sinđelić – 'The Falcon of Čegar' – fearing an ignominious defeat, famously blew up himself and his outnumbered troops, along with a large number of Turks, by igniting a gunpowder store. It is estimated that about 3,000 Serbian soldiers were killed in the explosion, along with at least double the number of their Turkish counterparts.

The tower was the Turkish response to this defiant yet suicidal act. On the order of the Turkish Pasha Hurshid, the Turkish commander at the time, Serbian skulls were gathered from the battlefield and skinned before being mounted in rows on a specially built tower 3m high.

Originally there were 952 skulls embedded in the tower and past visitors to the monument have written of its eerie quality. In 1833, the French poet Alphonse de Lamartine stopped in front of the tower and recorded what he saw in his book, *Journey to the East*. He commented that:

> The skulls, bleached by the sun and rain ... completely covered the victory monument. Some of the skulls still had hair on them which fluttered in the wind like leaves on trees...

He went on to write:

> My eyes and my heart greeted the remains of those brave men whose cut off heads made the corner stone of the independence of their homeland. May the Serbs keep the monument! It will always teach their children the value of the independence of a people, showing them the real price their fathers had to pay for it.

Now only 58 skulls remain, the rest taken for a proper burial or presumably prised out by souvenir hunters in the interim period. In 1892, a chapel was built around the depleted column and, rather than fulfilling its original purpose as a totem of deterrence, it was reinvented as a monument to the spirit of Serbian courage.

Another tower exists on **Čegar Hill** outside the city at the site where the battle took place. It was erected on the 50th anniversary of the liberation of Niš from the Turks on June 1 1927. In 1938, this was supplemented by a bronze bust of the Serbian hero Stevan Sinđelić. To visit the skull tower take a number 24 bus from the stop opposite the Ambassador hotel. The tower is within a small chapel in a park. Just before this is a ticket office where someone will sell you an entrance ticket and unlock the door for you. Admission is 40din.

Open Nov 1–Mar 31 09.00–16.00, Apr 1–Oct 31 07.30–19.30

Pobeda

This is the main café-lined pedestrian street, otherwise known as Obrenovićeva, that runs from Trg Kralja Mihaila south past the Kalča shopping centre to Cara Dušana. There are several wealthy merchants' houses along its course, like that of Andon Andonović at number 41 built in 1930.

National Museum of Niš

Nikole Pašića 59; tel: 22 532
This was built in 1894 as a bank and was used for this purpose for 70 years until it became a museum in 1963. It houses an archaeological exhibition with a range of sculpture from Roman times.

Open daily 09.00–16.00

Mediana

Emperor Constantine the Great, who was born in Niš, is said to have returned a few times in his life. At Mediana, alongside the Niš–Niška Banja road, a luxurious villa was built at his command in the early 4th century. What remains today are the foundations of several buildings spread over an area of 40ha: a villa, a baptistery, baths, lesser villas and a granary. There are also some well-preserved floor mosaics that have been roofed to protect them from the elements.

There is evidence of a street that ran in an east–west direction, connecting the various buildings. The central area was taken up by the palace, nymphaeum and baths, while to the west was the granary and to the north, a building with octagonal and circular rooms. Domestic buildings lay to the south of the complex.

The **museum** on the site (tel: 322 228; open 09.00–16.00) has mosaics and an exhibition of various Roman artefacts found on the site.

Mediana is to the left of the main road that runs past Ćele Kula to Niška Banja. It is about halfway to the spa, opposite an area of factories belonging to Niš's now-decaying electronics industry. The ranks of disused bus shelters in front of the factories, no longer needed by a shrunken workforce, tell the tale of a dying industry.

Crveni krst (Red Cross) Camp Museum

12 Februar Bulevar bb; tel: 25 678
The camp was first built as an army depot in 1930 but was adopted by the Germans during World War II as a transit camp for Roma, Jews, Partisans and Communists who were thrown in here prior to torture and/or execution or their deportation to death camps. It is a grey, sombre place that seems full of ghosts, as well it might. Despite hopeless odds, a desperate escape bid was made on February 12 1942 when a breakout was attempted by scaling the walls. At least 50 prisoners were machine-gunned down immediately, while another 100 managed to escape to freedom.

The main building on the right shows the conditions under which the prisoners had to live – on concrete floors with straw for bedding. The solitary confinement cells in the attic are perhaps the most chilling. On the walls are numerous photos of the inmates taken in happier times, their smiling, handsome faces blissfully unaware of the fate that was to befall them, making them all the more poignant. Another photograph shows the leering face of the camp commander, Komandant Schulz, nicknamed 'Stick' because of his taste for beating inmates to death with his cudgel. All the captioning is in Cyrillic but this hardly detracts from the sheer existential horror of the place.

There is also a room that has paintings done by children from a local school, which graphically depicts the scenes of horror in the camp – attempts on the wire, beatings, rapes, torture – in the earnest, unflinching manner of children whose imagination has been painfully awakened.

The perimeter walls, the barbed wire and the watchtowers are all still in place. Visiting the camp is hardly a fun day out but it is a sombre reminder of the dangers of totalitarianism and the horrors of war, not that any citizen of Niš should need reminding, given the city's turbulent history.

To reach *Crvni krst* walk past the bus station on 12 Februar and keep going until you reach the Kafana 'Dve Lipe'. Turn right here across an area of waste land to enter through the camp gates. Tickets are sold at the gatehouse to the left of the entrance. *Open daily 09.00–16.00*

The city's ghoulish memories do not end at *Ćele Kula* and *Crveni krst*. Southwest of the city, on top of Bubanj Hill, stands the **Bubanj Monument**. This monument, which resembles three giant clenched fists, commemorates the death of over 10,000 Niš inhabitants who were shot up here on the hill during World War II. The monument, the work of sculptor Ivan Sabolić, was erected in 1963 and symbolises the popular resistance to Nazi oppression.

In the same spirit, but much more recent, is the **Commemorative Chapel** (built in 2000) in the park by the main entrance to the fortress, which was constructed in memory of the civilians killed during the NATO bombardment of 1999.

The market area

Just like a medieval city, the market area in Niš is clustered around the fortress, which is probably exactly where it was during Ottoman times.

To the left of Istanbul Gate, heading towards the bus station, is a small outdoor market, **svetna pijaca**, which sells mostly clothes and household items. A little further on is the much larger **Tvrđava pijaca**, a vast indoor market with row upon row of stalls selling fresh vegetables, fruit, meat and fish. Around the entrance to these markets, and along the congested roadway of Đuke dinić that links them, are dozens more vendors selling all manner of things: mushrooms, plums in buckets, sprigs of herbs and dried flowers. Most of the vendors are old, black-clad, country women or Roma of either sex, too marginalised by poverty and the limited goods they have for sale to afford a pitch inside. Also along the same street are several Chinese supermarkets – each one an Aladdin's cave of cheap imported goods. There is a sizeable Chinese community in Niš.

Walking in the opposite direction from the fortress gate, east along Jadranska next to the river, you come to an area known as **auto pijaca**. This market has grown up around an area of car workshops and has every conceivable spare part and car-related accessory that you can think of. As with the green market, the pavement leading up to it has become an informal extension of the sales area, with dozens of hopefuls trying to sell spare parts, tools and oddments like second-hand windscreen wipers. If you are looking for a spare gearbox for your old Yugo, this is the place to come.

Festivals and events in Niš

During July each year, an **International Choir Competition** is held at various locations in the city. This is followed, in August, by the **Niš Film Festival.**

Nišomnia is a three-day music festival held in August. The festival was inaugurated in 2002, and for the past three years has taken place in mid August around three stages in the fortress complex. Nišomnia (motto: 'Stay awake') is in the same vein as Novi Sad's EXIT or Belgrade's ECHO festival, with a mixture of live acts and DJ stages. Although it is not yet as big as either of these, each year it is attracting an increasingly large audience. The 2004 line-up included the Wailers, the Stereo MCs and Serbia's own Darkwood Dub.

Nišomnia visitors can find dormitory accommodation at the Student Centre of the Technical Faculty at Gradsko polje behind the fortress for €10–15 per night, including all meals. Alternatively, you could use one of the hotels in the city or Niška banja if you prefer more privacy. Accommodation at the Student Centre needs to be reserved in advance through the **Niš Tourist Information Office** at 7 Voždova, 18000 Niš (tel: 523 188; fax: 523 188; email: torg-nis@bankerinter.net; www.tourist-nis.org.yu). Cheap food is also available at the Student Centre at Gradsko polje, and a full meal can be had for around €2.50.

Information on line-up and tickets can be obtained from the Nišomnia office at Skupština grada Niša, 7 jula 2 (tel: 512 172; fax: 513 277; email: info@nisomania.org.yu; www.nisomnia.org.yu). Tickets represent excellent value, especially when compared with the cost of music festivals in western Europe. It costs around €20 for the full three days (€16 for advance sale) and about €10 for a single-day ticket (€8 in advance). Online ticket purchases may be made through www.biletservis.co.yu or by emailing haphouse@eunet.yu.

NORTH OF NIŠ
Sokobanja

Sokobanja ('Hawk's bath') is a pleasant resort town to the north of Niš, close to the mountains of Ozren (1,117m) and Rtanj (1,568m) on the banks of the Moravica River. The town lies roughly halfway along the main Aleksinac–Knajževac road.

Sokobanja's thermal springs have been known since Roman times. The Turks continued the tradition and built a *hammam* here and the town remains a popular destination for Serbian holidaymakers. Sokobanja has the distinct advantage of being close to excellent walking country and so a stay here does not necessarily have to mean days of languid inactivity, although that is perfectly feasible too should you so wish.

The town itself is quite pleasant, with more character than most spa resorts, even if it is more or less completely given over to domestic tourism. There is a genuine Turkish *hammam* that you can visit in the town (currently undergoing restoration) and some fine walks in the nearby hills. One suggestion is to walk up past the Hotel Banjica along the stream to **Sokograd**, a ruined medieval city on a pinnacle with superb views.

There are plenty of places to stay in the town, most of which offer full board. There are a number of large, state-owned hotels like the Hotels Moravica, Sunce and Zdravljak, as well as more recently opened private pensions that tend to be smaller and intimate, and generally cheaper.

Hotel Moravica charges 1,300din for a single room, 2,300din for a double, 3,450din for a triple room.
Hotel Sunce charges 1,190din for a single room, 1,980din for a double, and 2,970din, triple.
Hotel Zdravljak charges 1,650–1,980din for a single, 2,560–3,080din for a double, 3,840–4,620din, triple.

Of the pensions, both **Pension Restaurant Aleksandar** and **Pension Splendid** offer good value.

All of the hotels and pensions have their own restaurants and provide full board should you require it. Other places to eat in the town include **Kafe Pizzeria Hram**, on the high street, and the **Cave Restaurant**, just off the trail that leads to Sokograd, which is situated underneath a rocky overhang, and has a water-powered rotisserie for roasting lamb. The **Milošev Konak** is an attractive place for a drink, although it no longer has a functioning restaurant.

Information on local walks, accommodation and events in the town can be had from the helpful **tourist information centre** on the main street (tel: 833 988, 063 8154 200).

EAST OF NIŠ
Niška Banja

Niška Banja is a health resort built around a natural hot mineral spring on a hillside 10km east of the city. The mildly radioactive waters here are said to help rheumatic and cardiovascular complaints. Naturally, it was the spa-loving Romans who first discovered the spring here. Following the Ottoman colonisation the Turks built *hammams* here to take advantage of the natural source. The water here is used for bathing, drinking and steam inhalation. Mud packs are also prepared, using a combination of the water from the spring and peat. There are eight indoor swimming pools filled with naturally heated water, as well as special treatment rooms for specific complaints. Scattered around the resort are pools and channels of warm spring water where you can soak your feet to your heart's content. Bear in mind that the water is slightly radioactive and so it is wise not to do this endlessly.

Above the complex are steps that lead up into the fragrant woods beyond – a nice place for a leisurely walk and an escape from the noise and heat of the city in summer.

Niška Banja could serve as an alternative place to stay if all of the hotels in Niš turn out to be full (unlikely) or if you just prefer somewhere quieter. There are two state-run hotels to stay in, the **Hotel Ozren★★★** (tel: 542 008) and **Hotel Partizan★★★** (tel: 542 803) both on the main drag. A third hotel, the **Hotel Srbija**, is closed to visitors for the time being. A large communal restaurant serves both of the main hotels, which are more used to guests taking full or half board, rather than just bed and breakfast. Other options for eating are the **Beli Dvor**, **Toplica** and the **Raj**. Snacks, pancakes and sandwiches are served at **Caffe Pedoni**. Tourist information is at the **Pošta**, just above the Hotel Srbija and bus terminus.

Beyond Niška Banja the road east follows the Nišava River to reach the **Sićevačka Gorge**. The two-lane E-80 is often busy and congested here, especially with trucks, as this is the main road that leads to Sofia, Istanbul and the Middle East beyond. All road freight coming from or going in that direction needs to take this route. Just as in Ottoman times there is still a major trade of goods between eastern Europe and the Near East, but these days the caravans consist mostly of Turkish heavy goods vehicles.

The sheer cliffs of the Sićevačko Gorge rise high above the road to the south here, with the occasional bird of prey circling high above the rumbling procession of trucks.

The small village of **Sićevo** stands high above the road to the north. It is worth driving up here if you have your own car, as the view over the gorge from the village is stunning. Sićevo is a wine-growing centre, and there are vineyards stretching up the hillside all around the village. The vines, the rustic quietness and the stone houses of the village, all give the impression that you have momentarily been transported to Provence. Next to the village car park is the building of the local wine-growers' cooperative, and across from this is the household of the Vidanović family who will be happy to sell you the fruit of their vines. They have red and white wines made from their own grapes, as well as *šljivovica*, *vinjak* and other spirits that they sell straight from the barrel for around 200din per litre.

PIROT ПИРОТ

Telephone code: 010

Pirot lies 70km east of Niš, about 1½ to 2 hours by bus, depending on the traffic. This sleepy town on the Nišava River has little for sightseers but it still has some repute as a centre for *ćilim* (Turkish: kilim) weaving (see box, *The Ćilim Weavers of Pirot*). These days the town is in decline. Its economy is centred upon the rubber industry, and factories at the edge of town still produce rubber goods like Wellington boots and tractor tyres. Pirot's other industry used to be the mass production of textiles (factory-made carpets, not *ćilims*) but that has completely collapsed in recent years.

The town is actually older than you might think. It was marked on Roman maps from the 2nd century AD as Mutatio Tures. Later on, Greeks would call the town Pirgos, which the Serbs changed to Pirot in the 14th century.

Pirot can be reached by train or bus by direct services from Belgrade, and 11 buses a day run to and from Niš. The small **central bus station** (tel: 332 548) is at the north side of the town. Walk away from this and past a market area to reach a bridge that crosses the Nišava River. There are nice shady walks along the river if you follow the bank to the left here. In summer, local children swim from some of the river beaches. Continuing across the bridge, you soon come to the town's central square, **Srpskih vladara**, with the **Hotel Pirot** and the **Italy Nightclub** next door. Pirot's central square backs onto a run-down shopping precinct that resembles the sort of shabby 1960s development that you sometimes see in towns of the English Midlands. Turning right at the main street here leads back to the river and the site of the **Kale**, a Turkish fort of Byzantine origin that has quite well-preserved remains. Occasional theatrical and musical performances take place here in the summer months. There is a bus stop and a ticket kiosk outside the *kale* where all buses to and from the town will stop.

Another place of interest in the town is the **Ponišavlje Museum** at Nikole Pašića 49 (tel: 313 850, 313 851), which is located in one of the town's few remaining *konak*s. If you would like to find out more about Pirot's *ćilim* tradition, you could try contacting Slavica Jovanović, a *ćilim* maker and representative of the Weaver's Association in the town. Her contact details are: Slavica Jovanović, Udruženje za očuvanje i razvoj tkanja pirotskog Đidima, Predraga boškovića 3/10 Pirot; tel: 332 373; email: slavica@tigar.com.

There are just two hotels in Pirot. In the centre of town, at Srpskih vladara, is the three-star **Hotel Pirot** (tel: 313 455, 312 493) with a total of 88 rooms, where singles cost 1,050din, doubles are 1,700din and triples 2,400din. A little further out at Nikole Pašića 213 is the much smaller **Hotel Tigar** (tel: 311 212, 311 213). Both hotels have their own restaurant, otherwise there are a few fast food places by the bridge like the **Čevapnička Šeki**. The **Caffeteria Davolo** and **Italy Nightclub** are both reasonable places for drinks.

From Pirot, the E-80 continues to the Bulgarian border along a narrow canyon where the road and railway line are squeezed in next to each other. Just beyond Dimitrograd lies the frontier with Bulgaria. This is a wild region and one that requires private transport to explore properly. For the intrepid, there is the **Monastery of Poganovo** to visit at the end of a lonely mountain road southwest of Dimitrograd. The monastery, which has some well-preserved frescos, was built at the end of the 14th century by the Serbian nobleman Dejanović.

SOUTH OF NIŠ

The E-75 dual-carriageway degrades into a two-lane road just south of the city. It continues through a wide flat plain to reach Leskovac, 40km south. **Leskovac** used to be known as the 'Serbian Manchester' because it used to have a thriving cotton industry, which, as with its northern England counterpart, is now much in decline. Leskovac is probably better known these days for its spicy grilled meat dishes – many towns throughout the country have restaurants that claim to serve genuine Leskovačka dishes.

West of here, 32km away, are the remains of the fortified 6th-century Byzantine town of **Caračin Grad**. Some think that Caračin Grad may have been Justinian's capital in this part of the Balkans. Whatever the truth of this, the extent of the remains suggests that it was certainly a very important centre; the fact that a 20km aqueduct was built to supply the town with water reinforces this. It is thought that the settlement was relatively short-lived and most likely was abandoned by the beginning of the 7th century, probably as a result of Slav attacks.

Outside the town's walls, which still have the remnants of towers and five remaining gates, are the remains of a basilica and some baths. Well-preserved portions of mosaic flooring survive in the narthex and nave of the basilica. The entrance to the town is through the south gate, from where a wide street leads past the foundations of a cruciform church that was most probably a private chapel. On the other side of the street is another basilica with three aisles. The town's *forum* is 50m further on, a large circular space, around which are the remains of public buildings and another large basilica. The *acropolis*, at the highest point of the town, is enclosed within a second set of ramparts. On the left of this is the cathedral, a large basilica with a baptistery, and on the right is the Bishop's Palace. At some distance away to the east is another basilica that has a large crypt beneath it where important clerics and local dignitaries would have been buried.

Unfortunately, there is no easy way to reach the site without your own car. If you have transport, you should drive first to Lebane, southwest of Leskovac along the Priština road. From here, you take a right turn and follow the road to the village of Prekopčelica. The ruins lie 8km beyond the village, on a hillside a 15-minute walk from the main road.

Continuing south from Leskovac, the valley narrows dramatically as the road enters the canyon of the Grdelička klasura alongside the Južna Morava River and the railway line. The small town of **Vladičin han** is reached 43km from Leskovac. It is probably not worth stopping in the town as there is nothing really to see. However, it is worth noting that you are in the heart of brass-band country and that musical traditions are particularly strong here. All of the villages in this region have their own brass bands, mostly Roma – some have several – and the players around here are considered to be among the best in the country. The much-fêted Guča champion, Boban Marković, hails from Vladičin han.

After Vladičin han the valley widens once more and, after a further 25km, the largish town of Vranje is reached.

VRANJE ВРАЊЕ

Telephone code: 017

Although Vranje is an unremarkable agricultural centre and army garrison today, it was an important town in Ottoman times. There is still enough evidence of this – a Turkish quarter with a small Ottoman bridge, a *hammam*, a *paša*'s residence – to make an overnight stay here worthwhile. There is also **Markova Kula**, an atmospheric medieval fortress high above the town, a few kilometres to the north, which serves as an excellent focus for country walks in spectacular countryside.

THE ČILIM WEAVERS OF PIROT

The carpet-making tradition in the southeast Serbian town of Pirot goes back at least seven centuries, a skill first introduced by the Turks and one that was continued after their eventual departure. Part of the reason for the carpet-weaving tradition to establish itself here, rather than anywhere else, is the surrounding countryside. To the east of Pirot, and reaching up to the Bulgarian frontier, is a region of parched craggy hills and arid mountains where villagers eke out a living by rearing sheep. Having a ready source of raw material so close to hand helped to maintain the tradition in the town. Nowadays, many of the mountain villages are severely depopulated, with only the older villagers remaining – sheep-farming with its hard life and low profits is something that rural youth does not wish to pursue – and this has had its effect on wool production in the region.

Čilim production is a cottage industry, done solely by women, with the carpets being made on looms that are kept in the weavers' homes. The carpets are woven, not knotted – exactly the same technique used to make kilims in Turkey and central Asia – and because of this flat weave they are reversible, unlike a knotted carpet. Čilims can be made in any size required and are used for a variety of purposes: as floor covering, wall hangings, throws for furniture, even for cushion covers and bags.

Čilim manufacture in Pirot is not quite yet in its death throes but it has declined steeply in recent years. As recently as 1965, there were up to 1,800 townswomen involved in čilim production, now there are only 15 who still weave. Those few who keep up the tradition would like to encourage others to train in the art but learning the necessary skills is time-consuming (on average, training to a reasonable standard, at four hours a day, three days a week, takes around six months). There are currently two state-run workshops in Pirot but they are a little run-down and only function periodically. There is vague talk of setting up a čilim museum, something that Pirot's women weavers would dearly love to see, but without government funding it is unlikely that this will become a reality in the near future.

Čilim-weaving is hard work: to produce about one-quarter of a metre of carpet takes about a month, working part-time. Traditionally, only natural dyes were used, although chemical dyes are easier and are sometimes used these days, instantly recognisable for their brighter, more garish colours. The designs of the carpets utilise a range of fairly standardised motifs, many of which reflect their Turkish origin and incorporate Islamic patterns like that of a stylised mihrab (originally used in prayer rugs) and the universal 'Tree of Life' design. With the development of čilim-weaving in Orthodox Serbia, these historic patterns have become Christianised, with the inclusion of Orthodox symbols like fish and incense-holder motifs into the pattern. Certainly, the (Orthodox Serb) women who weave these carpets today are blissfully unaware of any remaining Islamic elements in their work.

Getting there and around

Vranje is well served by buses from Leskovac and Niš to the north, although few of the buses that serve Skopje stop here. Four buses a day leave for Surdulica, east of Vladičin han. The **bus station** is at the south end of town, and it is a fairly stiff, uphill walk to the centre and Hotel Vranje. During my visit a large proportion of the town's streets had been ripped up to make way for new pipes and road resurfacing; hopefully you will find the town in less of a state of disarray than I did.

Vranje is on the main Belgrade–Niš–Skopje railway line and there is a limited number of daily services north and south. The **railway station** is even further from the centre than the bus station, on the far side of the *autoput*, close to the Južna Morava River. A taxi is definitely recommended if you are arriving or leaving by train.

Taxis can be found outside both stations and in the town centre close to Trg Maršala Tita. Buses to the nearby spa of Vranjska Banja can be caught at the stop next to the taxi rank.

Where to stay and eat

Hotel Vranje★★★ Trg Republike 4; tel: 22 366, 21 776. This large hotel is the only one in the town centre. It has a helpful staff and clean, spacious rooms with TV and phone. There is an attached restaurant and terrace bar. With 68 rooms in total, singles cost 2,000din and doubles 3,000din.

Hotel Pržar★★★ Pranžska bb; tel: 23 900. This small hotel, just outside of Vranje, is about to pass into private ownership. Located on a hill to the north of the town, it is really too far out of town to consider staying here unless you have a car. There are 9 single and 9 double rooms in all.

Apart from pizza and take-away fast food, there are limited dining options in Vranje. Close to the Hotel Vranje, on the same square, is the **Kafana Bašta**, a traditional sort of place, and also the **Vranski Merak Restoran**, virtually next door to the hotel. The **Pizzeria Roma** is at the bottom of the pedestrian café-bar street that leads down from Gradski Park to Kralja Stefana Prvovenčanog. There are plenty of cafés with outdoor terraces in this small enclave, and some fast food places by the park. One of the cheapest and least pretentious cafés in this area is the small burger and beer place immediately in front of the museum that does good *pljeskavica*. There are a handful of smart café-bars along the northern side of the park, although some of them like **Intermezzo** tend to play music at deafening levels of volume. Further downhill, clustered around the central square of Trg Maršala Tita, are a few simple grill restaurants like **Rostilj Cap-Cap** and **Rostilj Bum**. Just off Trg Maršala Tita, on the corner of Beogradska and 29 Novembra, is **Kafe Kašana**, next to the town's main taxi stand, which although it mostly functions as a café also serves reasonable pizza. A good bakery, the **Simco Lux,** can be found on the upper part of this street between Trg Maršala Tita and Trg Republike.

What to see and do
National Museum
Pionirski 1

The museum is in a *konak* built in 1765 by the *paša* Rajif Beg Džinić. It is an elegant airy building on two floors, which now houses a small ethnographic collection of costumes and period furniture alongside a few pre-historic finds from the region. Entrance is 30din.
Open Tue–Sat 09.00–15.00; closed Sun and Mon

The large pink house next door to the museum is another *konak* that is contemporaneous with the *paša*'s residence. This was where his harem used to reside. Formerly, there would have been a 'bridge' connecting the two dwellings so that all movement between the two houses went unseen by the town's population.

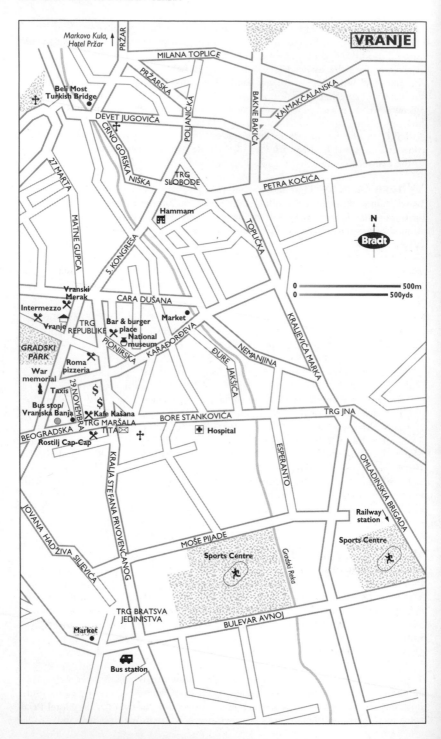

The hammam, Roma quarter and Turkish bridge

The *hammam* is reached by walking north along 5 Kongresa from Trg Republike, then crossing the bridge across the river. The building is on the first corner to the right. The brick-built *hammam* originates from around 1690 and has three hexagonal domes. It has been restored and partly modernised but no longer serves its original purpose. Continuing up here, you soon reach Trg Slobode, the heart of the **Roma quarter** of the town. Poljanička, the street that leads north off the square, is pure Roma, with women in long dresses sitting on their haunches smoking, violin music blaring from cassette players, and groups of burly men in singlets playing cards on the pavement. You may notice that most of the houses are built according to Roma tastes, opening straight onto the street, with external steps leading down from the upper floors. It is an intimate scene: poor but with a satisfied, self-contained air, a completely different atmosphere from a few hundred metres away where life is lived much more behind closed doors. There is no problem walking through the area as long as you don't appear to take too much interest in what you see. Roma, understandably, do not take kindly to outsiders nosing in on their affairs. Stopping to take photographs uninvited is probably ill-advised too.

At the top of Poljanička, turning left along Devet Jugovića will bring you to **Beli most**, the Turkish bridge. The bridge is nice enough but it is hardly Mostar – just a small footbridge over the town's river, which here is barely a trickling stream. Some of the stone blocks are damaged but the inscription plaque in the Arabic script of Ottoman Turkish is in good condition. The bridge, dating from 1844, is known locally as *most ljubavi* – 'lovers' bridge' – because of a story that tells of a Muslim girl and an Orthodox boy who became lovers. The girl's father was incensed by their liaison and shot at the pair of them while they were crossing the bridge, the single bullet killing his daughter, much to his distress. This seems to be an almost universal folk tale: one that relates to forbidden love between those belonging to opposite sides of a divided community. If the story is true, the irate father would have to have been pretty quick off the mark as the bridge is tiny and takes mere seconds to cross.

Just back along the riverbank from the east side of the bridge is a tiny chapel that has a belltower that is a simple structure of wooden logs. Take the road running alongside this to return to Devet Jugovica and the top of Poljanička.

From here, you can continue uphill along Pržar, a road that eventually leads to the ruined fortress of Markova Kula. The streets are steep in this part of town and the houses are a mixture of old and new. The older houses all have red pantile roofs and white-washed walls with enormous stacks of firewood piled against them. Many have their own wells. Although this is still effectively a northern suburb of Vranje the sense of rural tranquillity here is quite palpable. The garden plots are full of plum trees and small stands of maize. The only sounds are children's laughter, a distant radio playing folk tunes and sporadic hammering from one of the new building plots – a delightful place to live if you can put up with a stiff uphill walk back from the town centre every day.

Markova Kula

The ruined fortress of Markova Kula was originally built by the Serbs in medieval times. After the Ottoman invasion of the mid 15th century, it was taken by the Turks who expanded and fortified it further. It is said to have later become a *hajduk*'s stronghold, although the evidence for this is uncertain.

Markovo Kula is reached by following Pržar out of town to the north. The road continues climbing and winds around several spurs of the valley, offering an ever-improving view of Vranje and the plain of the Južna Morava River far below. After a few kilometres, there is a signposted turn-off to the right to reach the Hotel Przar. The traffic on the road towards the fortress is almost entirely that of heavily loaded lumber trucks coming downhill with brakes screaming, laboriously negotiating the sharp bends down into Vranje.

The fortress is located high above a bend in the road, six or seven kilometres from Vranje. The remains of Markovo Kula sit precipitously astride a steep ridge. A track leads off the road and swings around to the right to reach the ruins. There is not much to see of the fortress today, just some fortified walls and unidentifiable foundations, but the views south to Vranje and north and west to Kosovo are wholly magnificent.

To reach the fortress you can walk if you are feeling energetic – it is quite a steep climb all the way. An alternative is to take a taxi one-way and then walk the 7km back to town. This offers the best of both worlds as it is downhill all the way. A taxi taken from Beogradska in the town centre to Markova Kula should cost around 300din one-way, perhaps 500din if you get them to wait for you to bring you back.

South of Vranje

From Vranje, it is less than 40km to the Macedonian border. The only towns south of here, Bujanovac and Preševo, have sizeable Albanian minorities and the region has been the scene of sporadic disturbances over the past few years, with Albanian KLA-inspired factions being caught up in small-scale conflict with the Serbian army. The situation appears to have settled for the time being but the British FCO continues to advise against travel to this border area. Of course, if you are just driving through along the E-75 then there is absolutely nothing to worry about.

The main point to bear in mind is that there is really not that much to see in the Bujanovac-Preševo area anyway; your time would probably be better spent elsewhere in the country. If you do decide to explore this far southern region, first check the current British FCO recommendations at www.fco.gov.uk.

Kosovo

Kosovo – *Kosova* if you are Albanian, *Kosovo-Metohija* if you are a Serb – even the name is a political issue. This troubled province remains at the heart of Serbian thinking and is a place of great spiritual importance for many Orthodox Serbs. Kosovo has been part of Serbia for more than 800 years and represents an important part of the Serbian cultural inheritance as it is the location for many of the most important churches and monasteries of the Serbian Orthodox Church. The name *Metoh* means 'church land' and Serbs are very particular about adding the *Metohija* suffix to Kosovo, perhaps to remind themselves of their spiritual claim on the province. The short history below is a brief account of what has befallen the province over the past 600 years.

HISTORY

In early medieval times, the region now known as Kosovo was inhabited mostly by Serbs but after Prince Lazar's defeat at the Battle of Kosovo Polje in 1389, close to present-day Priština, much of the Serbian population moved north to escape from Turkish subjugation. This created a vacuum and the territory abandoned by the fleeing Serbs was taken up by land-hungry Muslim settlers of both Turkish and Albanian origin. Neighbouring Albania became an independent state after the Second Balkan War in 1913 and the neglected backwater of Kosovo came under Serbian control once more as the Serbian-dominated Kingdom of Serbs, Croats and Slovenes emerged.

During World War II, many Kosovars and Albanians fought against the Partisans in the hope that the Nazi invasion of Yugoslavia would help bring about a post-war pan-Albanian state, although, no doubt, an equal number fought on the Partisan side too. Tito's 1945 victory kept Kosovo as part of Serbia within the new Yugoslav Socialist Federal state. Meanwhile, neighbouring Albania became an isolationist and deeply suspicious Stalinist state under Enver Hoxha. Because of a deep mistrust of any nationalist agendas that might threaten the new socialist state, the Albanian language and even Albanian customs were declared illegal in Kosovo.

The 'Albanian question' became more of an issue as the 20th century progressed. At the beginning of the century, Albanians made up only one-third of the province's population but by the 1960s it had become two-thirds. This dramatic change of Kosovo's ethnic make-up was brought about by two factors: the much higher birth rate of the Albanians, with families of six children being considered pretty average, coupled with the gradual departure of ethnic Serbs from the province. Even before the 1999 crisis and the mass exodus that followed, Serbs were leaving Kosovo in droves. It is estimated that about 60,000 Serbs left Kosovo during the 1970s, a time of reasonable stability. At the time of writing, the percentage of ethnic Albanians that make up Kosovo's current population must be something like 85–90%.

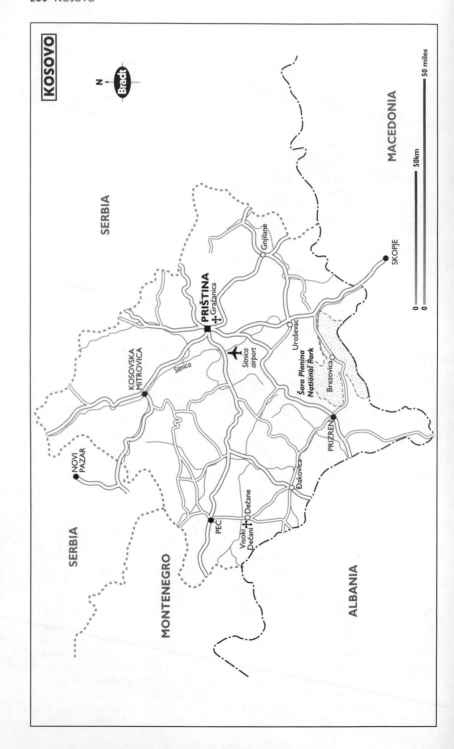

Serious rioting in the province in 1968 forced Tito to change his policy and make some reforms, of which the recognition of Albanian and Turkish as official languages was probably the most vital. He gave Kosovo a greater degree of autonomy and increased financial support to what was, without doubt, the most neglected corner of socialist Yugoslavia. This was probably too little, too late, though. Unemployment remained extremely high compared with prosperous states like Slovenia and Croatia, and a lot of the money coming into the province went on ill-conceived schemes like building Priština skyscrapers, which had little bearing on the lives of Kosovo's poor.

Despite the reforms it was still the case that, by and large, the Serbs that lived here were better off in terms of jobs and positions of power, while the Albanians had to contend with unprofitable farming, mining and manual labour, or seek employment abroad. Many did, and left in droves to work as migrant labourers in the West. It is not because of a successful education system that so many middle-aged Kosovars are able to speak German today.

In 1981, student protests soon turned to widespread riots that gave voice to long-held resentments. Very soon, nine were dead and hundreds were injured as demonstrators confronted the Yugoslav authorities. The Yugoslav army were sent in, resulting in hundreds of protestors being arrested and given long prison sentences on charges of sedition.

In 1988, it was the Kosovo Serbs' turn to protest. They felt that now it was they who were being discriminated against by a newly empowered Albanian majority. With a long-repressed majority finally finding their feet (the Albanians) and the former elite sensing that they had become the new victims (the Serbs), the necessary conditions were in place for all-out conflict. As had happened elsewhere in the unforgiving political climate of the Balkans, a violent cycle of revenge and counter-revenge was slowly starting to gather momentum. The Kosovo situation had been tense for years but the state-sanctioned repression of the Yugoslav federation had usually kept a lid on it. When the former Yugoslavia started to break up in the early 1990s many eyes focused on Kosovo and predicted, not unreasonably, that this would be the next flashpoint.

It is a matter of opinion as to how great the effect of Slobodan Milošević was on the war in Kosovo. Milošević came to power in 1987 and gained popular support with his promise that he would put an end to the violence against the Serbs in the province. In 1990, rather than give in to Albanian calls for greater autonomy, he abolished the autonomous status of the province, which caused further resentment among the Kosovar Albanians. Shortly after, the regional parliament in Priština declared full independence from Serbia for Kosovo, a futile gesture perhaps, but one which led to further repression of Kosovo's Albanians by Milošević's forces.

By the mid 1990s, the Kosovo Liberation Army (KLA) started to emerge as a force dedicated to fighting for an independent Kosovo (and a Greater Albania). In the eyes of many Kosovar Albanians the KLA were 'freedom fighters' but they were viewed as straightforward terrorists by the Serbian government. In January 1998, the KLA began a series of attacks on Kosovan Serbs in the province. Milošević responded by sending in troops to quash the unrest.

By the summer of 1998, the violence had escalated to a full-scale civil war, with hundreds dead and hundreds of thousands more displaced as refugees. The United States, the Organisation for Security and Co-operation in Europe (OSCE) and NATO decided that it was time to intervene. A NATO-brokered ceasefire in October 1998 saw a large contingent of OSCE peace monitors move into Kosovo. The ceasefire broke down in December 1998, which led to many more deaths on both sides. Most notorious was the massacre in the village of Racak in which 45 Albanian villagers were killed in a supposed anti-KLA operation.

In February 1999, Serbia and the KLA representatives went to the negotiating table in Rambouillet, France. Here, the United States threatened air strikes against Serbia if Milošević continued to reject a NATO plan that wanted to station international troops in Kosovo to enforce a peace agreement.

The talks broke down on March 19, when both the Serbs and the KLA rejected the terms of the agreement. The US had assumed that the KLA would sign and the Serbs would walk away, which would have paved the way for NATO air strikes on Serbia. But the KLA refused to sign unless the agreement promised them complete independence and not simply self-rule. Finally, on March 18, after heavy pressure by US Secretary of State Madeline Albright, the KLA signed while the Serbs continued to refuse because they objected to what they considered a NATO occupation.

After the withdrawal of OSCE monitors from Kosovo, the NATO bombing campaign began on March 24 1999, an action still considered in some quarters to be of dubious legality. As well as the air attacks on Serbia, NATO flew 38,000 combat missions over Kosovo. Serbia claims that these caused the deaths of between 1,200 and 5,700 civilians, although NATO acknowledges 1,500 at most. Many Kosovar Albanians fled the continuing inter-ethnic conflict to become refugees in Albania and Macedonia. On April 7 1999, Serbia closed its borders to prevent ethnic Albanians from leaving but after protests from the West reopened them a few days later. More than 800,000 Kosovar Albanians are estimated to have left Kosovo at this time, mostly to refugee camps in Albania.

In July 1999, when the Serbian armed forces were finally ousted from Kosovo, some 40,000 NATO-organised KFOR troops were sent in as peacekeepers. Ethnic Albanians started to return to the province from their refugee camps over the border, and embittered by what had gone on before, many felt urged to take revenge on what remained of the Serbian population. Between July 1999, when KFOR troops first entered Kosovo, and November 1999, more than 80 Serbian churches were destroyed in the province. The aftermath of the war saw a reduction in Kosovo's Serbian population by at least 75%, along with other non-Albanian minorities like Roma and Gorani who suffered similar persecution. Even with KFOR protection, which cannot be guaranteed, it is almost impossible for them to return in the current climate.

The most recent serious violence in the province was in March 2004, when a story circulated that told of Albanian boys being pursued by Serbs with dogs, driving them into a river where three of them drowned. This prompted a sudden outbreak of inter-ethnic violence in the province, especially in Kosovska Mitrovica, the only remaining town with a sizeable Serbian population. Serbian property was attacked across the province and Serbian churches and monasteries burned and looted. In response, mosques were attacked in Serbia, with those in Belgrade and Niš being gutted by fire. This story was later proven to be wrong, the fabrication of the surviving boy of an accidental drowning.

GEOGRAPHY

Geographically, Kosovo is a high flat plateau that is framed by mountain ranges along its borders with Serbia, Montenegro, Macedonia and Albania. The mountains to the south, the Šara Planina range, that form a border with Albania, have the highest summits in the country, up to 2,748m. At the other end of the province, the Kopaonik massif of southern Serbia delineates Kosovo's northern boundary, while the Mokra Planina in the northwest forms a natural barrier between Kosovo and the Montenegrin Sandžak.

Because of the lack of investment there was never much in the way of manufacturing industry here, although mining has always been important around Kosovo Mitrovica. Most of the province is given over to farming: arable in the flat central plain, with endless fields of wheat, maize and sunflowers; pastoral in the more mountainous areas, with milk cows grazing at the lower margins and herds of sheep and goats on the poorer land higher up.

VISITING KOSOVO

For the time being, Kosovo remains part of Serbia, and because of this, and because of all of the historical antecedents that connect the province with the Serbs and their culture, I feel that I should include it in this book. The current FCO recommendation is to advise caution but it has relaxed its earlier warning against 'any unnecessary travel to the province'.

Currently the province remains under the interim administration of the United Nations and it is difficult to predict what the future will hold. It is equally difficult to say how risky independent travel is in the province. It can be relatively stable for long periods, as it was in the period up to the riots of March 2004, but violence can flare up in an instant and with little provocation. If you decide to go – and that decision is entirely up to you – then there are certain precautions that you need to take.

Good advice would be to:

- Keep a low profile
- Carry identification at all times
- Do what you are told by KFOR soldiers
- Keep away from any demonstrations or inter-ethnic confrontation
- Do not speak Serbian, unless you are in a Serbian enclave
- Do not wander away from marked paths and tracks in the countryside
- Listen to what people have to say but keep your own counsel

Foreign nationals travelling in Kosovo are assumed to be either UNMIK (United Nations Mission in Kosovo) staff or aid workers, or possibly journalists – tourists are unheard of. Besides, the notion of being a tourist in an infamous trouble spot has something of an unpleasant voyeuristic ring to it.

This chapter does not attempt to provide a comprehensive travel guide to the province, just a brief overview. I will concentrate on the places that have (or used to have) the most significant sites and those places which hold the most importance in terms of Kosovan history: Priština, Gračanica, Prizren, Dečani and Peć. Ten years ago there would have been much to see, now sadly little remains that is not destroyed or dangerously off limits. The real tragedy, of course, is what has befallen the people of the province – to be born in a land where your ethnicity means everything.

TRAVELLING TO KOSOVO

As long as you enter Kosovo from Serbia, travelling either directly from Delgrade or from somewhere nearer like Novi Pazar, you may cross back into Serbia. If you enter Kosovo from the south, by way of Macedonia or Albania, then you must exit via Macedonia, Albania or Montenegro as the Serbia–Kosovo border is not recognised as an official crossing point by the Serbian government and the lack of an official Serbian entry stamp in your passport will cause problems.

The currency used throughout Kosovo is the euro; Serbian dinars are only accepted in Serbian enclaves and are useless elsewhere. US dollars and British pounds can be changed easily enough at exchange offices. There is an increasing number of ATMs in Priština and larger towns like Prizren although it is still best to carry a reasonable supply of euros in cash and not to leave it to chance.

Kosovo still retains the same international dialling code as Serbia: +381. Most mobile phone numbers begin with 044, rather than 063 or 064. The cost of a call to anywhere outside of Kosovo is about the same as Serbia.

PRIŠTINA (Albanian: PRISHTINË)

Telephone code: 038

Priština is a strange place: a dense cluster of futuristic high-rises in search of a city centre; a place that sometimes seems to be all front and no substance. The high-rises come courtesy of the misguided 1970s and '80s investment in the province, a sop to the Albanian majority who felt – correctly – that they were being left behind the rest of the country. The new, ultra-modern city centre of enormous banks, glitzy hotels and wide roads became a white elephant almost overnight, a useless bit of window-dressing that benefited no-one other than the contractors who built it.

The tradition of throwing money at the city has not stopped. Post-war Priština is awash with ambitious building projects, its streets lined with the fancy offices of international aid agencies and the parked 4WDs of expense-account development workers. It is all rather soulless, as if the downtown area of a medium-sized American city has been dumped wholesale in the city centre and left to decay. The buildings do not seem to fit with the people walking the pavements beneath them. The scale is wrong and, if the tacit effect of this token modernism is to suggest that this is a wealthy, go-ahead sort of place, then nothing could be further from the truth. No-one seems very much at home here; it is as if the city's population had gone away en masse only to come back and find a brand-new city thrust upon them, one they had not yet managed to find their way around.

There are elements of an older, more traditional way of life here and there: the cluster of mosques near the museum; the *burek* shops and the crowded street markets where the ripe fruits of the countryside brighten up the grey of the city. There are surreal touches too: roads renamed after US presidents – Rruga Bill Klinton – and the saintly ethnic-Albanian, Mother Theresa – Rruga Nëne Teresë (in Kosovo, Bill Clinton is considered almost as saintly as the Calcutta hospice founder); a hotel that has a copy of New York's Statue of Liberty standing on its roof; a huge museum that, despite expensive-looking laminated boards describing the prehistory of the province in detail, has virtually nothing left to display. Driving standards around the city are pretty surreal too, especially when it comes to parking.

Getting there and around

Priština's smart new **bus station** is at the western end of the city some way from the centre along Rr Bill Klinton. There are numerous services all over Kosovo and the people who work here are generally very helpful. International services run frequently to Skopje in Macedonia and at least daily to Tirana in Albania.

The **railway station** offers only one service at present, west across to Peć (Peja) – a picturesque journey but much slower than the bus.

The **airport** has direct flights to the United Kingdom with British Airways. Prices are in the order of £200–250 return when booked in the UK. There are also flights to Tirana and several cities in western Europe but there are none to anywhere in Serbia.

Taxis are useful in Priština, partly because of the distances involved in crossing what is quite a sprawling city but also because of the difficulty in finding places. Most street names have been changed recently from Serbian to Albanian names, and many are not named at all, which leads to problems of orientation. Taxi drivers, along with the majority of Priština's citizens, tend to orientate themselves by means of well-known landmarks rather than street names. Prices are very reasonable, many people speak a limited amount of English and most are scrupulously honest. A ride across town from the bus station to Velania should cost between €3–4 or €15–20 to the airport. There is a taxi barrier outside the bus station that drivers have to pay €1 to pass through but you can get out just before this.

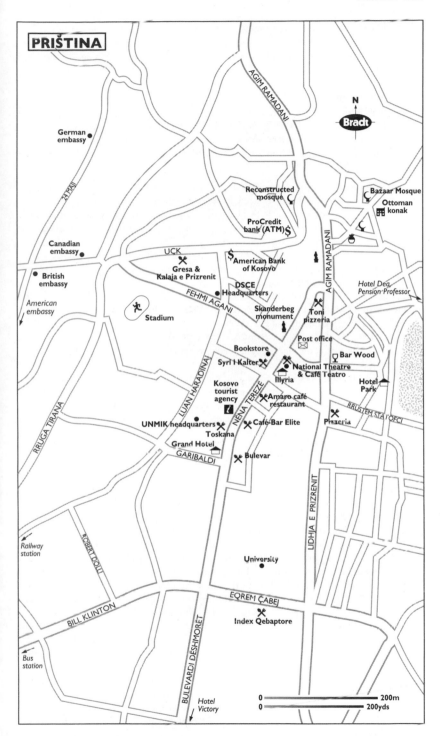

PRIŠTINA

German
embassy

Canadian
embassy

British
embassy

American
embassy

24 MAJ

UCK

FEHMI AGANI

LUAN HARADINA

RRUGA TIRANA

ROBERT DOLLI

BILL KLINTON

BULEVARDI DESHMORET

Railway
station

Bus
station

AGIM RAMADANI

AGIM RAMADANI

N

Bradt

Reconstructed
mosque

ProCredit
bank (ATM)

American Bank
of Kosovo

Gresa &
Kalaja e Prizrenit

DSCE
Headquarters

Skanderbeg
monument

Stadium

Bookstore

Syrl I Kalter

Kosovo
tourist
agency

UNMIK headquarters

Toskana

Grand Hotel

GARIBALDI

NENA TEREZE

Illyria

Amaro café
restaurant

Café-Bar Elite

Bulevar

Bazaar Mosque

Ottoman
konak

Hotel Dea,
Pension Professor

Toni
pizzeria

Post office

Bar Wood

National Theatre
& Café Teatro

Hotel
Park

RRUSTEM STATOFCI

Pizzeria

LIDHJA E PRIZRENIT

University

EQREM ÇABEJ

Index Qebaptore

Hotel
Victory

0   200m
0   200yds

As already mentioned, most streets have been renamed fairly recently. What used to be Vidovdanska is now Rruga ('street') Nëne Teresë – Mother Theresa Street; Ramiz Sadikij has become Rr Lidhja e Prizrenit, and Kralja Petra Prvog Oslobodioca, Rr Bill Klinton.

Where to stay

The presence of so many aid workers and UNMIK staff in the city has sent prices rocketing. The natives of Priština are used to foreigners being on hefty salaries and expense accounts and so prices are sometimes higher than you might think. This applies mostly to the cost of hotels though, food and transport costs are little different from southern Serbia.

Grand Hotel Rr Nëna Terezë; tel: 500 123, 20 211; fax: 548 138. The Grand, with over 300 rooms, is the largest and most centrally located hotel in the city, close to the offices of UNMIK. The grand has a vast lobby that has a bar, shops and currency exchange office. Next door is an equally large restaurant. The hotel is popular with businessmen and representatives of the media. Rooms cost €60 single, €90 double.

Iliria Hotel Rr Nëna Terezë; tel: 24 400 reception, 528 205 office. This is the other main hotel in the centre on the same street as the Grand Hotel, right next to the National Theatre. €30 for single rooms, €50 for doubles.

Hotel Dea Tel: 533 820; mob: 44 114 443; fax: 516 772. This modern small hotel with 29 rooms is high on a hill above the city in the smart Velania district. Clean spacious rooms with cable TV cost €50 for a single and €60 double.

Hotel Park Rr Sharrit 16; tel: 526 946, 24 454; fax: 26 887. A small private hotel located by Gradski Park, just east of the city centre. Friendly reception and clean modern rooms at €40 single, €50 double

Guest House Bujtinë Velania Velania 4/34; mob: 44 167 455. This guesthouse in the Velania district, just around the corner from President Rugova'a residence and close to the Hotel Dea, is much better known to taxi drivers as **Guest House Professor**. This is by far the best deal in town. The 'professor' is a friendly, helpful man who does his best to make his guests feel welcome. Most rooms have satellite TV, and there is a kitchen for the use of guests. It is very popular with groups of young visitors to Priština and as a consequence fills up fast. It is best to book ahead. €13 single, €18 double

Where to eat

There are plenty of options in the city, especially for Western food as Priština's restaurants try their best to attract the lucrative ex-pat trade. **Toni Pizzeria** is centrally located on the corner of Nëna Terezë and Lidhja e Prizrenit, just around the corner from the National Theatre, and is probably better known as **Spaghetti Toni's**. It is an unpretentious pizza and pasta place popular with journalists and International Community workers. There is another good **pizzeria** nearby on Lidhja e Prizrenit. On Nëne Terezë, close to the Iliria Hotel are **Amaro** café-restaurant and **Café–Bar Elite**. Closer to the Grand Hotel, by the square, is the **Toskana** restaurant. All of these serve standard Kosovan dishes and good *ćevapi*. The city's smarter restaurants tend to be further away from the city centre. Two recommended ones are **Rio** on Rruga për Gërmi (tel: 44 209 169, 199 870) that specialises in fish dishes, and **Pëllumbi** on Rruga për Fushovë (tel: 548 713, mob: 44 238 400) which is popular with diplomats and UNMIK top brass.

A relaxing place for a drink in the city centre away from the noisy traffic is at **Bar Wood** on Lidhja e Prizrenit, just up the road from Toni Pizzeria. This is a simple but spacious bar with tables inside a sort of mock wood-cabin structure. There are a couple of fast food places just outside. *Burek* shops can be found all over the city. A good choice for coffee and cakes is **Bulevar** opposite the Grand Hotel, as is **Syri i Kalter** opposite the Iliria Hotel.

What to see

The city does not offer very much in the way of sights beyond those of a city rebuilding itself after war. The **Kosovo Museum** has an interesting display on Kosovo prehistory but, as the management will painstakingly point out to you, the vast majority of their exhibits are currently in Belgrade, and the Priština museum is trying to get them back. A total of 677 archaeological pieces were loaned to Belgrade as part of a travelling exhibition, 'The Archaeological Treasures of Kosova', in January 1999, in addition to 571 ethnological pieces that went to various other Serbian museums. Another 13 boxes of ethnological artefacts were looted from the museum at the end of the war in June 1999. Entrance to the museum is €1.

Close to the museum are two 15th-century mosques: the Sultan Mehmet Fatih Mosque and the Bazaar Mosque.

The large **Sultan Mehmet Fatih Mosque** dates from 1461. The blue and white windows of the mosque are embellished with calligraphy in Arabic script. There is a large garden to the front of the mosque that is the location for an old Turkish fountain in need of repair. The **Bazaar Mosque** is an altogether smaller building that dates from 1440. The interior has a women's gallery with wooden paintings and there is quite elaborate floral decoration around the dome. There is a large garden next to the mosque with a kiosk that sells Islamic literature. Close to the mosque are several traditional men-only tea houses that make this quarter of the city seem very Turkish in character.

For a more modern perspective of the city, it is worth taking a look at the **UNMIK headquarters** behind the Grand Hotel. This concrete monstrosity belonged to the JNA (Yugoslav army) central command prior to 1999 and, as such, was a secretive and much-feared operational centre, especially during the late 1980s and early 1990s.

Ten kilometres south of the city is the small Serbian enclave of **Gračanica**. It is little more than a village but has a remarkable Orthodox monastery that holds an important place in Serbian history. The Serbian population that remain here are extremely vulnerable, surrounded as they are by hostile neighbours. Many Serbs have left in recent years but a small community still hangs on doggedly. The enclave is currently under heavy KFOR protection and, unless you have personal contacts there, it is unwise to make any attempt to visit it.

Gračanica Monastery

The tall, gracious church at Gračanica was built between 1313 and 1321 by King Milutin alongside a monastery that no longer exists. The church is a fine example of the Central School of Serbian architecture – perhaps the finest – and is a graceful structure of brick and stone with four cupolas and a dome raised in pyramid form above arched gables. The brick is utilised in herringbone and cross-stitch patterns against the pale pink-coloured stone and the overall effect is that of a complex but meticulously balanced geometry. It is Gračanica that was the inspiration for the larger 20th-century St Mark's Church in Belgrade.

Inside the church, the walls are almost entirely covered with frescos. The best of these are in the narthex and are contemporaneous with the original construction: portraits of King Milutin and his fourth wife Simonida, a Nemanjić family tree and the *Last Judgement*. The frescos in the naos are later and included the *Dormition of the Virgin*, scenes from the life of Christ and various saints.

PRIZREN

Telephone code: 029

Prizren lies about an hour and a half by bus from Priština, at the foot of the misty Šara Planina range that form the border with nearby Macedonia and Albania. The contrast with the capital is striking: where Priština is a brash and modern city for the most part, the first impression of Prizren is that of a peaceful, rural backwater spread along a river and clinging to the hills above. With a closely packed mixture of mosques with tall minarets, Orthodox churches, traditional houses up a hillside and Turkish footbridges across the river, it must have been very beautiful at one time. It still is, if you view the town with unfocused eyes, squinting to ignore the remains of roofless houses high up the hill and the fire-blacked walls of the KFOR-guarded churches. The sound of a KFOR helicopter constantly circling above the town reinforces the war-zone atmosphere.

Rather like Mostar in Bosnia-Herzegovina, it is the incontestable beauty of the place that makes the signs of recent devastation seem all the more poignant. In comparison with Priština, which has always appeared fairly chaotic even in peacetime, the signs of the recent inter-ethnic conflict here are uncomfortably tangible.

History

Like so many modern towns in the Balkans, the site that is now Prizren was first settled by the Romans. They called their new settlement Theranda and the town became an important crossroads under Byzantine rule. It was annexed to Serbia by Stefan Prvovenčani in the late 12th century and became the seat of the Nemanjić kings during the 13th and 14th centuries. Prizren became prosperous during this period and three important churches were constructed at this time: the **Church of Bogdorica Ljeviška** (Our Lady Falling Asleep) built by King Milutin in the early 14th century; the **Monastery of the Holy Archangels**, 3km outside the town, built by Dušan in the mid 14th century (and where he is buried); and the **Church of Sveti Spas** (The Saviour) whose ruin sits above the town, built in 1348 also by Dušan.

In order to defend the town, King Dušan constructed the **Kaljaja Fortress** on a hill above the river but, despite these defences, Prizren eventually fell to the Turks in 1455 and they remained here until the Serbs finally regained control in 1912.

Under Ottoman rule, Prizren became a Turkish town par excellence and it still retains much of this heritage today, with several mosques, a large *hammam* and a 15th–16th-century **Ottoman bridge** all being preserved. The most important and finest mosque, the **Sinan Paša Mosque**, dates from 1615 and has recently been restored along with the Ottoman bridge that it stands near. The 16th-century **Gazi-Mehmed Pašin Hammam** is now an art gallery. Unusual for Kosovo, Turkish remains as one of the main languages of the town, which is surprising for somewhere that is just 20km from the Albanian border. Many people in the town claim Turkish descent rather than Albanian.

Prizren's version of Islam is not necessarily an orthodox one. The town is well-known for its dervishes who practise the *zirka*, a ceremony that involves chanting, dancing and psychological release, which is intended to bring the participant into direct union with God. One location where Prizren's dervishes continue to meet and practise the *zirka* is the **Tekké of Sheh Osman** that stands in a side street behind the Hotel Theranda, built during the Ottoman period and restored in 1982.

Prizren is easily reached by **bus** from Priština, and there are regular services to Đakova, Peć and Skopje from the bus station, a 20-minute walk from the centre at the western end of town. Travel agents around the bus station can help book buses for more far-away destinations like Sarajevo or Istanbul. Minibuses parked around the bus station run to local villages and also provide a cross-border service to Tirana in Albania.

For **accommodation**, there are a few reasonable choices. In the town centre near the Ottoman bridge the old state-run **Hotel Theranda** (tel: 22 292; fax: 42 505) is adequate and has rooms for €15 single, €25 for a double. Opposite is the more comfortable and privately owned **Hotel Tirana** with rooms for €30. Closer to the bus station on Rr William Walker, the main road leading out of town, is the **Hotel Prizren** (tel: 32 434; fax: 41 552) where the rate is €20 for a single and €25 for a double. Nearby on Rr William Walker opposite the junction with Rr Jesut Gervalla is the **Hotel Residence**, which describes itself as a 'Business and comfort Hotel'. Rooms here cost €35 for a single room and €60 for a double. German but not English is spoken here.

There are numerous places to eat in the centre around the Sinan Paša Mosque and the Ottoman bridge, some of which do very good Turkish-style food. Recommended is the **Liridona Turkish Restaurant** (tel: 44 139 782), by the river behind the Hotel Tirana, and the **Besimi Family Restaurant** (tel: 33 668), next to the Sinan Paša Mosque, but most of the others are equally good.

Prizren has an excellent **weekly market** on Wednesdays that spills over from its designated location to fill many of the surrounding streets. It attracts villagers from all around the region and has all of the usual rural produce you would expect, along with other items that reveal the distinct tastes and needs of Albanian (and Turkish) culture: small hand drums and stringed musical instruments painted with the Albanian eagle, Albanian music cassettes, posters of Mecca, Muslim women's baggy trousers, hand-painted cribs, the white felt skull caps of the Gheg Albanians, wedding dresses and boys' circumcision outfits. The market is reached by walking north from the Hotel Theranda along Rr Adem Jashari past the *hammam* and the Emin Paša Mosque until you reach it.

Sadly, all of Prizren's Serbian Orthodox churches are now in a ruinous state, wrecked and burnt out like the houses of the town's Serbian community, who have now fled. The **Kaljaja Fortress** high above the town has now been cleared of mines and can be visited. To reach it, follow the road that leads uphill from the river to the left of the Sinan Paša Mosque. This leads up steep, cobbled streets, past ruined houses up to a German KFOR checkpoint beside the razor-wire that surrounds a burnt-out Orthodox church. The soldiers should allow you to continue up the path through woods to the fortress. There is nothing to see at the fortress itself other than the wonderful views west across the town and the Bistrica River, and south to the high valleys of the Šara Planina range that lead into Macedonia. It is a marvellous view but it is depressing to be reminded just how very beautiful Prizren must have been at one time, and how natural splendour does nothing to alleviate hatred and the extremes of human folly.

Dečani

The **Monastery of Visoki Dečani** is located up a wooded valley 2km west of the village of the same name, 10km south of Peć on the Prizren road. The monastery now a UNESCO heritage site, was built by Stefan, son of King Milutin, between 1327 and 1335. Stefan went on to take his name from the project to become later known as King Stefan Uroš Dečanski.

The monastery complex lies behind an imposing wall and is entered through a fortified gate. Few of the monastic buildings survive but the centrepiece is the church of **Christ Pantokrator**, the work of a Franciscan monk from Kotor named Vid. The church, which combines an interesting mixture of Western and Byzantine traditions, is of pink, white and grey marble with a garbled façade and ornate carving around the Romanesque doors and windows. The central door has twin columns supported by lions, and in the tympanum above, the figure of Christ is flanked by two angels beneath an arch that has the 12 signs of the zodiac. The south door has a relief showing the *Baptism of Christ* and an inscription by the architect in Cyrillic. More lions bear columns at the mullioned window on the central apse and similar zoomorphic and anthropomorphic themes are repeated around the church.

The church's interior is rich with frescos, all executed at the command of Dušan, Stefan's son, between 1335 and 1350. Many of these are considered to be masterpieces of medieval religious art. In the narthex are portraits of Dušan, his wife Jelena and their son Uroš, together with a family tree of the Nemanjić dynasty. The naos is entered through a Romanesque doorway that is also flanked by columns supported by lions. Here, there are paintings of saints, scenes from the life of Christ and the *Acts of the Apostles*. On the west wall, are stories from the Book of Genesis and the legend of Solomon; in the centre, the *Last Judgement* and the *Dormition of the Virgin*.

The tomb of Stefan Dečanski, which lies near the iconostasis, has long been considered to have magical healing properties by both Christians and Muslims alike. Dečani has held great sway with the Muslim community since the time, under the Turks, when it was planned to turn it into a mosque. An *imam* visiting the church was killed by a piece of falling masonry as he prayed outside the west door. This was taken as a sign that it was the will of Allah that it should not be altered and it was left well alone from then on.

PEĆ (Albanian: PEJA)
Telephone code: 039
The market town of Peć is very much a mixture of old and new, with modern offices and high-rises contrasting with an old bazaar area where a few Turkish mosques, fountains and artisans' houses still survive. The most important historical treasures, however, lie just outside the town at the Orthodox Patriarchate on the road to Podgorica in Montenegro.

The town, which might seem unremarkable in its present circumstances, was of great importance in medieval times when it was the seat of the Serbian Orthodox Church. In 1253, Archbishop Arsenije I, worried by the activities of both the Bulgarians to the east and the Magyars to the north, moved the seat of the Church from vulnerable Žiča in central Serbia to the Rugova Gorge just west of Peć, a hard-to-reach location that offered far more security. In 1346, the emperor Dušan granted the patriarchy complete autonomy. As a result of this the town became the centre of a Patriarchate that reached all the way west to the Adriatic coast and as far north as Budapest. After the Turkish invasion in the 15th century this importance declined dramatically as it became eclipsed by that of the Archbishopric in Ohrid but Peć reasserted its influence in 1557 when, once again, it became the centre of the Serbian Church until it was abolished by the Turks in 1766. The Patriarchate was moved to Belgrade in 1920 after Turkish rule finally came to an end in the whole of the Balkan region.

Where to stay and eat
The only place to stay in the town centre is the **Hotel Gold** near to the bazaar and the main square (Rr 122/D2 N-106; tel: 34 571, 34 572; fax: 34 571; email: hotel_gold@hotmail.com) that has rooms for €30 single occupancy, €50 double. For eating, there are *qebabtöre* (*čevapčči* places) and *caffe*s everywhere, especially around the central square and the street by the Hotel Korzo.

What to see
The **bus station** in Peć is a ten-minute walk from the town centre. The bazaar area is reached by turning left out of the bus station and walking along the main road for five minutes before bearing left. This leads into an old **bazaar area** full of shoppers:

young women in headscarves linked arm in arm looking at the displays of gold in the jewellery shops; bow-legged old men with gold teeth and white 'egg man' skullcaps; groups of tough-looking young men with sharp haircuts taking a break from the endless round of coffee drinking and cigarette smoking. The bazaar area still retains a number of Turkish buildings, and the endearing Turkish habit of diverting water to run through towns is still evident, with small footbridges leading across streams in several places in the town centre. The **Čaršija Mosque**, badly damaged by fire and in need of repair, is the oldest mosque in the bazaar area and dates from 1471. The portico has three arches with a lead-covered dome over each one.

Walking through and emerging from the bazaar at its west side you come to the town's main square. To the left is a road that runs parallel to a park. This leads to another square that is overlooked by two old-style hotels, the **Metohia** and the **Korzo**, both of which are currently closed, one requisitioned by KFOR and the other in dire need of renovation. Turning right here you will see a strange modernist building on the left, the local UNMIK headquarters, and then the Restaurant California with a small enclosed garden. A bridge crosses the stream by the restaurant. Cross it and turn left along the road. Soon, you should see the small whitewashed 19th-century **Gyl Fatim Mosque** with its stubby minaret to your right on a street corner. Further along this street are the headquarters of the Islamic Relief Organisation of Saudi Arabia in a very attractive Ottoman *konak*. Continuing along the main road, you soon pass a modern Catholic church with an attractive and peaceful garden that has a statue of the Virgin. After another 500m or so, the Italian KFOR checkpoint is reached where the road splits. The right-hand fork, busy with traffic, continues to the Montenegrin frontier, the lower road leads to the Patriarchate. The Italian soldiers should be willing to let you through after a thorough passport check and telephoning ahead.

The **Patriarchate of Peć** (Pećka Patrijaršija) stands enclosed behind high stone walls close to the river in gorgeous mountain scenery. Entrance to the monastery is through a tall gate in the walls. The immediate impression is one of peaceful isolation: the cars thundering towards Montenegro on the road above are just out of earshot and the predominant sound is that of bees buzzing around collecting nectar from the flowers of the monastery gardens (beekeeping is an important activity both here and in other Serbian monasteries; it would seem that the collection and processing of honey has a strong spiritual dimension). To the left are the monastic living quarters – a wooden-framed *konak* – where a few nuns remain to pursue the contemplative life. In the far-right corner are the churches, the only remaining original buildings of the complex.

The three churches of the Patriarchate sit side by side linked by a common 14th-century narthex. The oldest of the three, Archbishop Arsenije's **Church of the Holy Apostles** (*Crkva Sveta Apostola*) is the central one of the group and contains frescos modelled on the Church of Sion in Jerusalem, considered to be the true location of the Last Supper. The church was built in the 13th century and incorporates part of an earlier 12th-century building. The painting style of the frescos inside is that of the Raška School – austere and monumental in scale. On the ceiling of the narthex are scenes from *The Passion* and portraits of Nemanjić kings. On either side of the west door are frescos of *St Nicholas* and *The Virgin and Child*. The figure of Christ looks down from *The Ascension* in the cupola above, with the *Descent of the Holy Ghost*, *Doubting of Thomas*, *Mission of the Apostles*, *Last Supper* and *Raising of Lazarus* adorning the arches beneath. All of these date from the mid 13th century, the work of an artist or artists of the same school that painted Studenica and Mileševa.

The other two churches are later additions from the first half of the 14th century. The **Church of St Demetrius** (*Sv Dimitrije*) is slightly older and has a well-preserved fresco of *The Birth of the Virgin*, alongside frescos showing scenes from the *Legend of St Demetrius* and a *Procession of Saints*. All of the frescos here were painted at the time of building but were extensively retouched in the 17th century. The **Church of Our Lady of Odigtrea** (*Sv Bogorodica*), completed around 1330, is lighter and has less atmosphere than the other two churches. It contains a large number of portraits of the Nemanjić dynasty in the narthex, all 14th-century, alongside a later *Last Judgement*. In the naos are more 14th-century works: a portrait of founder Archbishop Arsenije I offering his plan to the Prophet Daniel, above which is a *Dormition of the Virgin*.

It is when you walk back from the Patriarchate towards the Italian KFOR checkpoint, turning around for a last glance at the monastery, that you really appreciate the magical combination of graceful buildings in a gorgeous natural setting. It seems a pity to have to leave such serenity so soon.

Outside the Patriarchate there may be a few old women in black busying themselves in the monastery's allotment garden, and along the road, a couple of others leading contented cows on ropes, encouraging them to graze on the rich sweet grass of the verge. One of these women stopped me as I was walking back up the road after visiting the church. She had been deep in concentration, studying a Bible that she held in one hand while she tethered her cow with the other. She pointed at the Patriarchate and then at me, asking '*Katolika?*' inquisitively. '*Ne. Protestant.*' I replied, greatly simplifying my true religious affiliations. She shook her head and smiled sadly, pointing up to the heavens. '*Katolika*,' she reiterated, '*Katolika*.' She seemed to have forgotten: in Kosovo, religious conviction does not count for much; it is language and culture, and who your father is, that guarantee your place in heaven.

Crane

Appendix 1

LANGUAGE
Pronunciation and transliteration

In Serbian, almost every word is pronounced exactly as it is written. There are 30 letters in the Serbian alphabet, which is written in both Cyrillic and Latin forms.

Roman		Cyrillic		Pronunciation
A	a	А	а	'a' as in ask
B	b	Б	б	'b' as in boy
C	c	Ц	ц	'c' as 'ts' in flotsam
Č	č	Ч	ч	'ch' as in church
Ć	ć	Щ	щ	'tch' like the 't' in future
D	d	Д	д	'd' as in dog
Dž	dž	Џ	џ	'j' as in just
Đ	đ	Ђ	ђ	'dj' as in endure
E	e	Е	е	'e' as in egg
F	f	Ф	ф	'f' as in father
G	g	Г	г	'g' as in girl
H	h	Х	х	'h' as in hot; as the 'ch' in loch before another consonant
I	i	И	и	'i' as in machine
J	j	Ј	ј	'y' as in young
K	k	К	к	'k' as in king
L	l	Л	л	'l' as in like
Lj	lj	Љ	љ	'ly' like the 'lli' in million
M	m	М	м	'm' as in man
N	n	Н	н	'n' as in nest
Nj	nj	Њ	њ	'nj' like the 'ny' in canyon
O	o	О	о	'o' between the 'o' in bone and the 'aw' in shawl
P	p	П	п	'p' as in perfect
R	r	Р	р	'r' as in rough
S	s	С	с	's' as in Serbia
Š	š	Ш	ш	'sh' as in lush
T	t	Т	т	't' as in test
U	u	У	у	'oo' as in boot
V	v	В	в	'v' as in victory
Z	z	З	з	'z' as in zebra
Ž	ž	Ж	ж	'zh' like the 's' in pleasure

Words and phrases

There is no definite article in Serbian. Nouns may be masculine, feminine or neuter and are declined according to their function in a sentence. In their singular form, masculine nouns end

293

with a consonant and generally end with an 'i' in the plural. Most feminine nouns end in '-a' in the singular and '-e' in the plural. Neuter nouns end in either '-e' or '-o' in the singular; generally, the plural form ends in '-a'.

Stress is usually on the first syllable but in some cases, as in words that have a prefix, stress is on the middle syllable. Stress never falls on the last syllable of a word.

Basics

Yes	*Da*	Sorry	*Pardon*
No	*Ne*	No problem	*Nema problema*
Maybe	*Možda*	Excuse me	*Izvinite*
Hello	*Zdravo*	May I?	*Da li mogu?*
Goodbye	*Do viđenja/čiao*	Please give me...	*Dajte mi...*
Good morning	*Dobro jutro*	That's fine	*U redu je*
Good day/afternoon	*Dobar dan*	Good	*dobro*
Good evening	*Dobro veče*	Bad	*loš*
Good night	*Laku no?*	Little	*malo*
How are you?	*Kako ste?*	Today	*danas*
Well, thank you	*Dobro, hvala*	Yesterday	*juče*
Please	*Molim*	Tomorrow	*sutra*
Thank you	*Hvala*	Mr	*Gospodin*
I don't understand	*Ne razumem*	Mrs	*Gospođa*
I don't speak Serbian	*Ne znam srpski*	Miss	*Gospođica*

Asking questions

Where is ...?	*Gde je ...?*	Do you speak English?	*Govorite li engleski?*
How?	*Kako?*	How much is it?	*Koliko košta?*
When?	*Kada?*	What time is it?	*Koliko je sati?*
Which?	*Koji?*	What's your name?	*Kako se zovete?*
Who?	*Ko?*	Where are you from?	*Odakle ste?*
Why?	*Zašto?*		

Introductions

My name is....	*Ja se zovem...*
I am from... England/America	*Ja sam... Engleske/Amerike*
...Scotland/Wales/Ireland	*...škotske/Velsa/Irske*
I am a foreigner	*Ja sam stranac*
Pleased to meet you	*Drago mi je*

Signs

Entrance/exit	*ulaz/izlaz*	УЛАЗ/ИЗЛАЗ
Open/closed	*otvoreno/zatvoreno*	ОТВОРЕНО/ЗАТВОРЕНО
Information	*informacije*	ИНФОРМАЦИЈЕ
Prohibited	*zabranjeno*	ЗАБРАЊЕНО
Toilets	*toaleti*	ТОАЛЕТИ
Men	*muški*	МУШКИ
Women	*ženski*	ЖЕНСКИ
Danger	*opasnost*	ОПАСНОСТ
Arrival	*dolazak*	ДОЛАЗАК
Departure	*polazak*	ПОЛАЗАК
No smoking	*zabranjeno pušenje*	ЗАБРАЊЕНО ПУШЕЊЕ
No entry	*ulaz zabranjen*	УЛАЗ ЗАБРАЊЕН

Getting around

Where's the...		Gde ye ...	
bus station?		autobuska stanica?	
railway station?		železnička stanica?	
airport?		aerodrom?	
How far is it to...?		Koliko daleko do...?	
What time's the next bus?		Kada polazi sledeđi autobus?	
What time does the ... leave/arrive?		Kada ... polazi/dolazi?	
I want to go to....		Želim da odem u ...	
I would like a...		Želim...	
I want to get off!		Želim da sidem!	
How do I get to...?		Kako mogu da dodgem do...?	
Is it near/far?		To je blizu/dalek?	

bus	autobus	straight on	pravo
train	voz	ahead/behind	napred/iza
tram	tramvaj	up/down	gore/dole
aeroplane	avion	under/over	ispod/iznad
boat	brod	north/south	sever/jug
car/taxi	auto/taxi	east/west	istok/zapad
one-way ticket	kartu u jednom pravcu	here/there	ovde/tamo
return ticket	povratnu kartu	garage	garaža
two tickets	dva karte	petrol (gas) station	benzinska stanica
1st class	prvu klasu	road/street	put/ulica
2nd class	drugu klasu	bridge/river/waterfall	most/reka/vodopad
left	levo	hill/mountain/peak	brdo/planina/vrh
right	desno	village/town	selo/grad

Shopping

bank	banka	newspaper	novine
bookshop	knjižjara	post office	pošta
chemist (pharmacy)	apoteka	postage stamp	poštanska marka
discount	popust	postcard	dospisnica
exchange office	menjačnica	shop	radnja
market	pijaca	souvenir	uspomena
money	novac		

Health

accident	nesređa	eye	oko
allergy	alergija	fever	groznica
ambulance	ambulanta	head	glava
anaemia	anemija	headache	glavobolja
back	leda	heart	srce
chest	grudi	hospital	bolnica
cold	nazeb	indigestion	loše varenje
cough	kašalj	infection	infekcija
dentist	zubar	medicine	lek
doctor	lekar	pain	bol
ear	uvo	stomach ache	bolovi u stomaku
emergency	nužda		

Food and drink

apple	*jabuka*	lunch	*ručak*
baked	*pečeno*	meat	*meso*
bean	*pasulja*	milk	*mleko*
beef	*govedina*	mushrooms	*pečurke*
beefsteak	*biftek*	onion	*luk*
beer	*pivo*	orange	*pomoranđa*
bill	*račun*	pancake	*palačinka*
brandy	*rakija*	pasta	*testenine*
bread	*hleb*	peach	*breskva*
breakfast	*doručak*	pear	*kruška*
butter	*puter*	pepper	*biber*
cabbage	*kupus*	plate	*tanjir*
cake	*kolač, torta*	plum	*šljiva*
carrot	*šargarepa*	plum brandy	*šljivovica*
cheese	*sir*	pork	*svinjetina*
chicken	*piletina*	potato	*krompir*
chicken soup	*pileđa supa*	restaurant	*restoran*
chips	*pomfrit*	rice	*pirinač*
coffee	*kafa*	roasted meat	*pečeno meso*
(Turkish coffee)	*Turskva kafa*	roast chicken	*pečena piletina*
(black/white)	*crna/bela*	roast pork	*svinjsko pečenje*
(cappuccino)	*kapučino*	salad	*salata*
cognac	*konjak*	salt	*so*
cup	*šoljica*	sausage	*kobasica*
dinner	*večera*	soup	*supa, čorba*
drink (noun)	*piđe*	spoon	*kašika*
eggs	*jaja*	strawberry	*jagoda*
fish	*riba*	sugar	*šeđer*
fish soup	*riblja čorba*	tavern	*konak, konoba*
fork	*viljuška*	tea	*čaj*
garlic	*beli luk*	tomato	*paradajz*
glass	*staklo*	veal	*teletina*
grilled	*sa roštilj*	veal soup	*teleca čorba*
ham	*šunka*	vegetables	*povrđe*
home-made	*domađe*	water	*voda*
honey	*med*	(mineral water)	*mineralna voda*
ice-cream	*sladoled*	wine	*vino*
juice	*sok*	(white/red)	*belo/crno*
knife	*nož*	yoghurt	*yogurt*
lamb	*jagne*		

Numbers

0	*nula*	9	*devet*
1	*jedan*	10	*deset*
2	*dva*	11	*jedanaest*
3	*tri*	12	*dvanaest*
4	*četiri*	13	*trinaest*
5	*pet*	14	*četrnaest*
6	*šest*	15	*petnaest*
7	*sedam*	16	*šesnaest*
8	*osam*	17	*sedamnaest*

18	osamnaest	100	sto
19	devetnaest	200	dvesta or dve stotine
20	dvadeset	1,000	hiljada
21	dvadeset i jedan	one million	million

Time

afternoon	popodine	now	sada
autumn	jesen	spring	proleđe
day	dan	summer	leto
evening	veče	today	danas
hour	sat	tomorrow	sutra
minute	minut	week	nedelje
month	mesec	winter	zima
morning	jutro	year	godina
night	nođ	yesterday	juče

Monday	ponedeljak	Friday	petak
Tuesday	utorak	Saturday	subota
Wednesday	sreda	Sunday	nedelja
Thursday	četvrtak		

January	januar	July	juli
February	februar	August	avgust
March	mart	September	septembar
April	april	October	oktobar
May	maj	November	novembar
June	juni	December	decembar

Appendix 2

GLOSSARY OF SERBIAN TERMS

Četnik	Chetnik: member of royalist resistance, now more widely used to describe an extreme nationalist
čoček	fast dance popular with brass bands
dahi	Janissary commander
Đurđevan	St George's Day celebrated on May 6
frula	small, recorder-like instrument
grad	town
gusle	stringed instrument used in performance of epic poems
hajduk	brigand or outlaw who fought against the Turkish occupation
Janissaries	elite Ottoman troops recruited from Christian subject families
jezero	lake
kafana	traditional tavern or café
kajmak	Serbian cream cheese-like product
knez	originally a Serbian local leader; later, a prince
koljivo	ground, cooked wheat used in a *slava* celebration
kolo	circle dance
konak	house in Serbian-Turkish style
konoba	traditional tavern
košava	dry wind from the southeast that sometimes blows in autumn
kula	tower
openac	traditional shoes with turned-up toes
Partisans	World War II Nazi resistance movement led by Tito
paša	Turkish commander in Ottoman period
pašalik	division of Ottoman Serbia
pećina	cave
planina	mountain range
polje	field
put	road
rakija	alcoholic drink, usually made from grapes
rayah	Serbian serfs under Ottoman control
reka	river
sanđak	administrative district of the Ottoman Empire, now a term used to describe the predominantly Muslim region of southwest Serbia
slava	ceremony devoted to commemorating the patron saint of a family, town or village
sloboda	freedom
Spaji	Turkish cavalry unit
sveti	saint
šajkača	traditional Serbian cap
Šumadija	the 'wooded country', a term used to describe central Serbia

šlivovica	alcoholic drink made from plums
trg	square
turbo-folk	modern musical genre that is a fusion of traditional folk tunes, sentimental lyrics and electronic dance rhythms
ulica	street
Ustaša	Croatian Nazi movement in World War II
Vidovdan	St Vitus' Day on June 28, which commemorates defeat at Battle of Kosovo on this date in 1389
vrh	mountain peak
zadruge	loose family groups living together as clans in medieval Serbia
župan	patriarch from around time of first Serbian colonisation

Architectural and religious terms

apse	projected semicircular part of a church by the altar
baroque	style of architecture with elaborate ornamentation
basilica	a Roman-style aisled church with a nave, apse but no transepts
exo-narthex	porch before the narthex of a church
fresco	painting on freshly spread moist lime plaster
Gothic	style characterised by slender vertical piers, pointed arches and vaults
hammam	public bath in a Turkish/Muslim town
icon	religious image painted onto a small wooden panel
iconostasis	screen or partition with icons that separate the nave from the sanctuary of an Orthodox church
kula	tower
mihrab	niche showing the direction of prayer in a mosque
minaret	slender pointed tower attached to a mosque from which the summon to prayer is made
minbar	pulpit of a mosque
naos	innermost part of an Orthodox church beneath the central cupola
narthex	entrance hall of an Orthodox church, often decorated with frescos
nave	main part of the interior of a church, especially the narrow central hall in a cruciform church that rises higher than the aisles
patriarchate	seat of Orthodox bishop or patriarch
pietà	group of the Virgin mourning the dead Christ
Renaissance	neoclassical style in western Europe from 14th–17th century
Romanesque	style between Roman and Gothic characterised by the use of round arches and vaults and decorative arcades
transept	the part of a church that crosses the nave at right angles
turbe	small Turkish mausoleum

Appendix

FURTHER INFORMATION
History and culture
Collin, Matthew *This is Serbia Calling: Rock 'n' Roll Radio and Belgrade's Underground Resistance* Serpent's Tail, 2001

Glenny, Misha *The Balkans, Nationalism, War and the Great Powers* Granta, 1999

Glenny, Misha *The Fall of Yugoslavia* Penguin, 1996

Javarek V and Sudjić M *Teach Yourself Serbo-Croat* Hodder and Stoughton, 1986

Lazić, Mladen (editor) *Protest in Belgrade: Winter of Discontent* Central European University Press, 1999

Lebor, Adam *Milošević: A Biography* Bloomsbury, 2003

Lomas, Robert *The Man Who Invented the Twentieth Century: Nikola Tesla, Forgotten Genius of Electricity* Headline, 2000

Maclean, Fitzroy, *Eastern Approaches* Penguin Press, 1991

Malcolm, Noel *Kosovo: A Short History* Harper Perennial, 1999

Judah, Tim *Kosovo: War and Revenge* Yale Nota Bene, 2002

Judah, Tim *The Serbs: History, Myth and the Destruction of Yugoslavia* Yale Nota Bene, 2000

Little, Allan and Silber, Laura *The Death of Yugoslavia* Penguin, 1996

Newman, Bernard *Tito's Yugoslavia* Travel Book Club, London (out of print)

Pavlowitch, Stevan *Tito: Yugoslavia's Great Dictator – A Reassessment* C Hurst & Co, 1993

Rice, David Talbot *Art of Byzantine Era* Thames and Hudson, 1986

Stephen, Chris *Judgement Day: The Trial of Slobodan Milošević* Atlantic Books, 2004

Tesanović, Jasmina *The Diary of a Political Idiot* Midnight Editions, 2002

Thomas, Robert *Serbia Under Milošević: Politics in the 1990s* C Hurst & Co, 1999

Guidebooks
Pettifer, James *The Blue Guide to Albania and Kosovo* A & C Black, 2001

Ćorović, Ljubica *Belgrade Tourist Guide* Kreativni centar, Belgrade, 2003

Cuddon, J A *The Companion Guide to Jugoslavia* Prentice-Hall, 1984 (out of print)

Travel writing
Aldiss, Brian W *Cities and Stones* Faber, 1966 (out of print)

Kindersley, Anne *The Mountains of Serbia, Travels through Inland Yugoslavia* Readers Union Book Club, 1977 (out of print)

Murphy, Dervla *Through the Embers of Chaos, Balkan Journeys* John Murray, 2003

West, Rebecca *Black Lamb and Grey Falcon: A Journey through Yugoslavia* Canongate, 2001

White, Tony *Another Fool in the Balkans: In the Footsteps of Rebecca West* Cadogan Guides, 2004

Natural history
Heinzel, H, Fitter, R and Parslow, J *The Birds of Britain and Europe* Collins, 1977

Raine, Pete *Mediterranean Wildlife, the Rough Guide* Harrap Columbus, 1990

Polunin, Oleg *Flowers of Greece and the Balkans: A Field Guide* Oxford University Press, 1980

Serbian literature

Andrić, Ivo *Bridge over the Drina* Harvill Press, 1995
Pavić, Milorad *Dictionary of the Khazars* Penguin, 1998
Selenić, Slobodan *Fathers and Forefathers* Harvill Press, 2003
Selenić, Slobodan *Premeditated Murder* Harvill Press, 1996
Tišma, Aleksandar *The Book of Blam* Harcourt Brace and Company, Orlando 1998

Websites

Below are just a few of the many websites devoted to Serbia. This selection gives a fairly good cross-section of cultural and historical information, together with a variety of news sources.

www.focus.co.yu Photo gallery of Serbian photojournalist Andrija Ilić
www.b92.net/english Daily news in English
www.serbianunity.net A Serbian-American website with news and culture
www.serbianna.com Serbian news and culture
www.beograd.org.yu/english Information on Belgrade
www.mfa.gov.yu The website of the Ministry of Foreign Affairs for the Government of Serbia and Montenegro
www.serbia-tourism.org National Tourist office of Serbia website
www.serbia.sr.gov.yu Official Serbian Government website
www.diacritica.com/sobaka A radical web magazine with many articles on politics of Balkan region
www.belgradetourism.org.yu The website of the Tourist Organisation of Belgrade
www.visitvojvodina.com Information on Vojvodina province
www.yubusiness.co.yu/nmuzej.htm National Museum website

Bradt Travel Guides

Africa by Road	£13.95	Kabul Mini Guide	£9.95
Albania	£13.95	Kenya	£14.95
Amazon	£14.95	Kiev City Guide	£7.95
Antarctica: A Guide to the Wildlife	£14.95	Latvia	£12.95
The Arctic: A Guide to Coastal		Lille City Guide	£5.95
Wildlife	£14.95	Lithuania	£12.95
Armenia with Nagorno Karabagh	£13.95	Ljubljana City Guide	£6.95
Azores	£12.95	London: In the Footsteps of	
Baghdad City Guide	£9.95	the Famous	£10.95
Baltic Capitals: Tallinn, Riga,		Macedonia	£13.95
Vilnius, Kaliningrad	£11.95	Madagascar	£14.95
Bosnia & Herzegovina	£13.95	Madagascar Wildlife	£14.95
Botswana: Okavango Delta,		Malawi	£12.95
Chobe, Northern Kalahari	£14.95	Maldives	£12.95
British Isles: Wildlife of Coastal		Mali	£13.95
Waters	£14.95	Mauritius	£12.95
Budapest City Guide	£7.95	Mongolia	£14.95
Cambodia	£11.95	Montenegro	£12.95
Cameroon	£13.95	Mozambique	£12.95
Canada: North – Yukon, Northwest		Namibia	£14.95
Territories	£13.95	Nigeria	£14.95
Canary Islands	£13.95	North Cyprus	£12.95
Cape Verde Islands	£12.95	North Korea	£13.95
Cayman Islands	£12.95	Palestine with Jerusalem	£12.95
Chile	£16.95	Panama	£13.95
Chile & Argentina: Trekking		Paris, Lille & Brussels: Eurostar Cities	£11.95
Guide	£12.95	Peru & Bolivia: Backpacking &	
China: Yunnan Province	£13.95	Trekking	£12.95
Cork City Guide	£6.95	Riga City Guide	£6.95
Costa Rica	£13.99	River Thames: In the	
Croatia	£12.95	Footsteps of the Famous	£10.95
Dubrovnik City Guide	£6.95	Rwanda	£13.95
East & Southern Africa:		St Helena, Ascension,	
Backpacker's Manual	£14.95	Tristan da Cunha	£14.95
Eccentric America	£13.95	Serbia	£13.95
Eccentric Britain	£11.95	Seychelles	£12.95
Eccentric California	£13.99	Singapore	£11.95
Eccentric Edinburgh	£5.95	Slovenia	£13.95
Eccentric France	£12.95	South Africa: Budget Travel Guide	£11.95
Eccentric London	£12.95	Southern African Wildlife	£18.95
Eccentric Oxford	£5.95	Sri Lanka	£12.95
Ecuador, Peru & Bolivia:		Sudan	£13.95
Backpacker's Manual	£13.95	Svalbard	£13.95
Ecuador: Climbing & Hiking	£13.95	Switzerland: Rail, Road, Lake	£12.95
Eritrea	£12.95	Tallinn City Guide	£6.95
Estonia	£12.95	Tanzania	£14.95
Ethiopia	£13.95	Tasmania	£12.95
Falkland Islands	£13.95	Tibet	£12.95
Faroe Islands	£13.95	Uganda	£13.95
Gabon, São Tomé & Príncipe	£13.95	Ukraine	£14.95
Galápagos Wildlife	£14.95	USA by Rail	£12.95
Gambia, The	£12.95	Venezuela	£14.95
Georgia with Armenia	£13.95	Your Child Abroad: A Travel	
Ghana	£13.95	Health Guide	£9.95
Iran	£12.95	Zambia	£15.95
Iraq	£14.95	Zanzibar	£12.95

WIN £100 CASH!
READER QUESTIONNAIRE

**Send in your completed questionnaire for the chance to win
£100 cash in our regular draw**

All respondents may order a Bradt guide at half the UK retail price – please
complete the order form overleaf.

(Entries may be posted or faxed to us, or scanned and emailed.)

We are interested in getting feedback from our readers to help us plan future Bradt
guides. Please complete this quick questionnaire and return it to us to enter into
our draw.

Have you used any other Bradt guides? If so, which titles? . . . .
. . . .
What other publishers' travel guides do you use regularly? . . . .
. . . .
Where did you buy this guidebook? . . . .
What was the main purpose of your trip to Serbia (or for what other reason did you
read our guide)? eg: holiday/business/charity etc. . . . .
. . . .
What other destinations would you like to see covered by a Bradt guide?
. . . .
Would you like to receive our catalogue/newsletters?

YES / NO (If yes, please complete details on reverse)

If yes – by post or email? . . . .

Age (circle relevant category) 16–25   26–45   46–60   60+

Male/Female (delete as appropriate)

Home country . . . .

Please send us any comments about our guide to Serbia or other Bradt Travel
Guides. . . . .
. . . .
. . . .
. . . .

Bradt Travel Guides
19 High Street, Chalfont St Peter, Bucks SL9 9QE, UK
Telephone: +44 (0)1753 893444 Fax: +44 (0)1753 892333
Email: info@bradtguides.com
www.bradtguides.com

CLAIM YOUR HALF-PRICE BRADT GUIDE!

Order Form

To order your half-price copy of a Bradt guide, and to enter our prize draw to win £100 (see overleaf), please fill in the order form below, complete the questionnaire overleaf, and send it to Bradt Travel Guides by post, fax or email. Post and packing is free to UK addresses.

Please send me one copy of the following guide at half the UK retail price

Title	*Retail price*	*Half price*
. . . .	. . . . . .	. . . . . .

Please send the following additional guides at full UK retail price

No	*Title*	*Retail price*	*Total*
. . .	. . . .	. . . . . .	. . . . . .
. . .	. . . .	. . . . . .	. . . . . .
. . .	. . . .	. . . . . .	. . . . . .

Sub total . . . . . .

Post & packing outside UK . . . . . .

(£2 per book Europe; £3 per book rest of world)

Total . . . . . .

Name . . . .

Address . . . .

Tel. . . . .   Email . . . .

☐ I enclose a cheque for £. . . . . . . made payable to Bradt Travel Guides Ltd

☐ I would like to pay by VISA or MasterCard

Number . . . .   Expiry date . . . .

☐ Please add my name to your catalogue mailing list.

Send your order on this form, with the completed questionnaire, to:

Bradt Travel Guides/SER
19 High Street, Chalfont St Peter, Bucks SL9 9QE
Tel: +44 (0)1753 893444 Fax: +44 (0)1753 892333
Email: info@bradtguides.com
www.bradtguides.com

Index

Page numbers in bold indicate major entries;
those in italic indicate maps